D1165801

Bread and the Ballot

Dennis Merrill

Bread and the Ballot

The United States and India's Economic Development, 1947–1963

The University of North Carolina Press

Chapel Hill and London

Manufactured in the United States of America

The paper in this book meets the guidelines for permanence and durability of the Committee on Production Guidelines for Book Longevity of the Council on Library Resources.

94 93 92 91 90 5 4 3 2 1

Library of Congress Cataloging-in-Publication Data

Merrill, Dennis.

Bread and the ballot : the United States and India's economic development, 1947–1963 / by Dennis Merrill.

p. cm.

Includes bibliographical references (p.

ISBN 0-8078-1920-4 (alk. paper)

1. Economic assistance, American—India. 2. United States—Foreign economic relations—India. 3. India—Foreign economic relations—United States. I. Title.

HC435.2.M47 1990

338.9'173054—dc20 90-50012

CIP

Chapter 2 appeared previously, in somewhat different form, as "Indo-American Relations, 1947–50: A Missed Opportunity in Asia," *Diplomatic History* 11 (Summer 1987): 203–26, and is reproduced here by permission of Scholarly Resources.

The table in chapter 1 is taken from Robert C. Johansen, *The National Interest and the Human Interest* (Princeton, N.J., 1980), pp. 128–29, and is reproduced by permission of Princeton University Press.

To the memory of my parents,
Robert and Cathalene Tucker Merrill

Contents

Illustrations

Preface

During the early 1970s, as the Vietnam War wound down and I enrolled in college, it became common in academic and political circles to speak of "development" as one of the key issues in "North-South" relations. The developing nations of the south, as they were referred to at the time, pressed the wealthy nations of the north to offer foreign assistance and loans at low rates, reduce tariff barriers, pay more for imported raw materials through commodity price agreements, and compromise with needy nations that nationalized certain foreign-owned industries. In the United Nations the group of seventy-seven—a coalition of developing nations numbering more than one hundred—articulated Third World discontent in their call for the establishment of a "New International Economic Order." Inspired by the call to international justice, moved by the urgency of the problem, and sensitive to the growing interdependence of nations, I became interested in development. That interest and concern eventually led me to write this book.

Development can be studied from a vast array of perspectives. Since the end of World War II the term has been bantered about by social scientists, philosophers, political leaders, and bureaucrats. This book explores the many meanings of the word, but focuses upon the development process within the context of United States diplomatic history. It traces the evolution of United States economic aid to India during the darkest days of the Cold War when development for American policymakers became synonymous with the foreign policy of containment. India ranked as one of the largest and most populous of the emerging nations and had declared its intention to remain neutral in the great power rivalry. It ultimately became a major prize in the Soviet-American competition and a recipient of large amounts of aid from both sides.

The book derives its title in part from the fact that India has, for the past forty years, maintained the "world's largest democracy." Although the phrase is misleading and not to be interpreted literally, India has struggled over the years to achieve development through democratic means—an uncommon experience in the non-Western world. The title is also drawn from a speech delivered by President Dwight D. Eisenhower in early 1959, at a time when development diplomacy was coming into its own. Speaking out in favor of an enlarged foreign aid budget, the president declared that it was the policy of the United States "to convince a billion people in the less developed areas that there is a way of life by which they can have bread and the ballot, a better livelihood and the right to choose the means of their livelihood, social change and social justice—in short progress and liberty."[1] "Bread and the ballot" was more than just a catchy phrase. The words embodied the very finest American principles and traditions. Assisting India in its plans for democratic, economic development offered American leaders a major opportunity to act upon their stated ideals. The study of United States economic aid to India during the early postwar era offers the historian a special opportunity to measure the degree to which America kept its promise to a significant portion of the world's poor.

This study is the first historical analysis of Indo-American relations based largely on recently declassified, United States government documents. I made extensive use of State Department records for the years 1947 through 1957, housed in the National Archives in Washington, D.C. A great deal of the documentation was drawn from the inner records of the Truman and Eisenhower administrations, available at the Harry S. Truman and Dwight D. Eisenhower presidential libraries. Many records—such as the President's Secretary's File, the White House Central File, minutes of National Security Council Meetings, and National Security Policy Papers—became available only in the late 1970s and 1980s. By using mandatory review procedures, I was able to gain access to hundreds of documents that had previously been closed to researchers. In addition to these sources, the invaluable papers of former Ambassador Chester Bowles at Yale University, and several other private manuscript collections, provided a wealth of information. Research at the British Public Record Office in Kew Gardens, England brought to light the perspectives and insights of that former colonial power on a number of key issues in Indo-American relations.

Although the available historical record is rich, historians of the recent past do face some serious limitations. At this time, State Department records for the period after 1957 remain closed to researchers. Consequently, chapters 6 and 7 of this work, which cover the post-1957 period, unfortunately cannot provide a day-to-day account of policy making. Through enterprising research in presidential and private manuscript collections, I have pieced together an informative story that I think nonetheless sheds considerable light on Indo-American relations during the Eisenhower and Kennedy years. In the course of my adventures with the mandatory review process—whereby documents that are twenty years of age or older are reviewed for declassification—I was grateful to learn that government agencies were more likely to release documents that related to economic rather than political affairs. This was most fortunate in the case of Indo-American relations, in which many of the most interesting issues revolved around the matter of economic development.

Although the focus for this study is on United States policy, I have tried to add depth and clarity to the narrative by paying close attention to the Indian context and presenting Indian views on relevant economic and political issues. In this regard, I was most fortunate to spend the academic year 1983–84 in India as a research scholar under the Fulbright Program for Graduate Study Abroad. Indian government restrictions limited access to official files and manuscript collections for the years after 1946, but published government reports were made readily available. I also used English-language newspapers and periodicals, and interviewed a number of former officials. Most important, I had an opportunity to exchange ideas with Indian scholars, journalists, and government personnel. Living in India acquainted me with that nation's rich cultural traditions, its diverse social landscape, and the intricacies of Indian politics. I observed, first-hand, the heart-wrenching reality of Indian poverty—and the hope of a nation for a better tomorrow.

My completion of this work was made possible through the generous assistance of others. Travel for research in the United States, Canada, and Great Britain was facilitated by grants from the University of Connecticut Research Foundation, the Rockefeller Foundation Archives Center, and the Harry S. Truman, John F. Kennedy, and Lyndon B. Johnson libraries. My work in India would not have been possible without a Fulbright fellowship, administered through the United States Information Agency. A grant from the Institute for the Study of World Politics in New York City enabled me to write my first draft. Generous grant assistance from the research council of the University of Missouri-Kansas City allowed me to devote one last summer to the revision process.

I am very grateful to the staffs of the Harry S. Truman, Dwight D. Eisenhower, John F. Kennedy, and Lyndon B. Johnson libraries and the National Archives who guided me through the search for sources and helped with the declassification of many important documents. Archivists at the Sterling Library of Yale University and at the Rockefeller Foundation Archives Center were similarly indispensable to the research effort. In India, I was fortunate to work at the library of the Indian Council of World Affairs (Sapru House) and the Jawaharlal Nehru Memorial Library (Teen Murti House), both in New Delhi. Their staffs patiently responded to my inquiries and helped open up many fruitful avenues for research. I also wish to thank Jawaharlal Nehru University in New Delhi for the privilege of being affiliated with it during my stay in India. I am especially eager to express my gratitude to the many good people at the United States Educational Foundation in India who helped me make living and travel arrangements in India and establish a network of important research contacts.

My work has also benefited from the ideas and advice of numerous individuals. First, I owe a special debt of gratitude to Professor Thomas G. Paterson of the University of Connecticut for his willingness to share his experience and wisdom with his students. I also wish to thank Professors Gary R. Hess of Bowling Green State University and Robert J. McMahon of the University of Florida, who read various drafts, provided constructive criticism, and offered many helpful suggestions for improvement. Professors J. Garry Clifford, A. William Hoglund, and Edmund S. Wehrle of the University of Connecticut also provided extensive assistance. My friend and colleague Richard D. McKinzie of the University of Missouri-Kansas City read portions of the manuscript and always seemed to be available for engaging conversation and debate on the meaning of American foreign policy. Pranab Basu generously shared his knowledge of Indian culture and politics and helped to make my stay in India an invaluable learning experience. My editor, Lewis Bateman, has been more than patient in nursing this project along, and I deeply appreciate his understanding and encouragement. For their assistance and courtesies, I also thank Mark Addesso, Douglas Brinkley, Julia Cook, Lekshman Dewani, David Diaz, Michael Hogan, Richard Immerman, Mi Kim, Larry Larsen, Douglas Little, Regina Markey, Jane McClain, Karen Toombs Parsons, Stanley B. Parsons, Patrick Peebles, Rhonda Southerland, M. S. Venkataramani, and Thomas Zoumaras. I am grateful to Rhonda Roosa for preparing the maps.

Final thanks go to my special friend, Barbara Shaw, who provided encouragement, support, and her wonderful sense of humor—all of which helped me through crucial stages of this project.

Bread and the Ballot

One

Introduction: American Developmentalism and India

The crumbling of the European colonial system in Asia, the Middle East, and Africa posed one of the most significant challenges faced by United States foreign policymakers in the post–World War II era. Between 1946 and 1960 thirty-seven new nations emerged into what is known today as the Third World. These countries varied widely in culture, ethnic composition, geography, colonial experience, and political orientation. But they shared a common characteristic: all were deeply impoverished. Equally important, the leaders of these new nations shared the belief that national independence would open the door to economic advancement. Lacking the capital and technical expertise to spur rapid economic development, most of these countries looked to the United States to help them fulfill their aspirations.

During the early postwar years, American policymakers formulated an economic aid policy that ultimately encompassed most of the emerging areas. Indeed, at the outset of the 1960s, President John F. Kennedy confidently declared the launching of the "development decade," and scores of diplomats and social scientists predicted the rapid modernization of much of the Third World. Of all the recently decolonized countries that received American assistance during this period, India emerged as America's economic aid priority. Although the level of assistance grew slowly, United States annual grant and loan commitments to India reached over $400 million by 1963, supplemented by nearly an equal dollar value in foodgrain assistance. By the early 1960s, when aid to India reached its peak level, that nation ranked as the world's leading recipient of American economic aid.[1]

India became a major beneficiary of United States aid for a variety of reasons. With a population of 350 million at independence, India stood as the largest and most populous of the recently decolonized nations. Fully one-quarter to one-third of the world's poor resided there. Thus, India's struggle against poverty won a great deal of sympathy from Americans. An impressive list of individuals—including the scientist Albert Einstein, the author Pearl Buck, the socialist Norman Thomas, and civil rights activist Roy Wilkins—tapped the conscience of the nation by calling for aid to India solely on humanitarian grounds.

India also won notoriety because of its international stature. Led by the widely admired Mohandas K. Gandhi, India became in 1947 one of the first former colonies to achieve independence, and during the post–World War II years it often assumed a leadership role among Afro-Asian states. Maintaining a parliamentary form of government, India received special acclaim as the "world's largest democracy." In the United States, popular weekly magazines like *Time* and *Newsweek* periodically featured articles dramatizing India's efforts to develop its economy by democratic means. Chester Bowles, ambassador to India during both the Truman and the Kennedy/Johnson administrations, and a leading figure in Democratic party politics at home, helped popularize in liberal circles the cause of assisting India. Another Kennedy appointee to the New Delhi post, renowned economist John Kenneth Galbraith, lent further support to the undertaking. American liberals such as Walter Lippmann, Walter Reuther, Adlai Stevenson, and Martin Luther King actually made pilgrimages to democratic India. The list of visiting officials included both liberals and conservatives: United Nations representative and former first lady Eleanor Roosevelt, Supreme Court Justice William O. Douglas, Secretaries of State John Foster Dulles and Dean Rusk, Vice Presidents Richard Nixon and Lyndon Johnson, and even President Dwight D. Eisenhower. Everybody who made the journey, Republican and Democrat alike, showered praise on India's democratic experiment.

Yet the impetus for American economic aid programs derived only in part from altruism. It is a long way from the mud huts of rural India and the teeming streets of Calcutta to the hallowed halls of the State Department. Whereas the average Indian citizen thought of life in terms of the endless quest for food, shelter, and personal security; the top leaders of a global power such as the United States viewed the world in terms of the balance of power, balance of trade, and national security. They strove to preserve and augment the power and strategic posture of their already wealthy nation, and to find ways to thwart the ambitions of potential rivals. Administered in timely and well-proportioned dosages, economic aid often contributed to the achievement of their goals. This is not to say that American policymakers were never moved by the plight of the Indian masses, or that they were never inspired by India's democratic aspirations. The basic point is that such considerations never dominated the formulation of policy. Economic assistance to India was more a matter of national security than national sentiment.

American leaders based much of their postwar foreign policy upon the assumption that the Soviet Union intended to engineer a global expansion of the Communist system. The United States sought to contain Soviet influence in areas where it already existed and preserve as much of the world as possible for the expansion of capitalist trade and expansion. Economic aid was used to help stabilize or win the friendship of other countries, to gain access to strategic bases and resources, to foil Soviet designs in particular countries, or to contribute to the making of an international order conducive to private enterprise.

In India, the evolution of American aid policy neatly coincided with shifting tides in the history of the Soviet-American confrontation. From 1947 through early 1950, India received no direct, bilateral assistance from the United States. During this period the escalating Cold War in Europe preoccupied American policymakers and prompted the extension of billions of dollars in economic aid to Western European nations under the Marshall Plan. In 1950, a shift in United States policy occurred in the aftermath of the Communist victory in the Chinese civil war and the outbreak of the Korean War. Emphasizing India's strategic significance, American diplomats signed a $4.5 million Indo-American Technical Agreement in December 1950. This was followed in 1951 by American wheat aid for Indian famine relief. Beginning in 1952, the United States launched a more far-reaching development program for India that involved average, annual expenditures of approximately $65.5 million through 1957. United States assistance to India reached substantial proportions in the late 1950s and early 1960s as Cold War lines hardened in Europe and Washington increasingly turned its attention to the Third World. Aid to India during the latter half of the Eisenhower administration grew from $89.8 million in 1958 to $194.6 million in 1960. During the Kennedy years, aid to India rose further until it peaked in 1962 at $465.5 million. In addition, between 1956 and 1963 the United States agreed to send over $2 billion in American surplus agricultural commodities to India under the Agricultural Trade and Assistance Act of 1954 (PL 480) (see table).

As the geographical focus of the Cold War shifted from Europe toward the Third World, India's efforts to achieve economic development along

Total Grant and Loan Commitments[a] to India for Economic Development from U.S. Agency for International Development and Predecessor Agencies[b]

Fiscal Year	*Total grants and loans in millions of U.S. dollars*	*Total grants and loans per U.S. capita, in dollars*	*Total grants and loans per Indian capita, in dollars*
1950	0.0	0.00	0.00
1951	4.5	0.03	0.01
1952	52.8	0.34	0.14
1953	44.3	0.28	0.12
1954	87.2	0.53	0.23
1955	85.7	0.52	0.22
1956	60.0	0.36	0.15
1957	65.3	0.38	0.16
1958	89.8	0.51	0.22
1959	137.0	0.77	0.33
1960	194.6	1.08	0.45
1961	200.8	1.09	0.46
1962	465.5	2.49	1.04
1963	397.2	2.10	0.86
1964	336.5	1.75	0.71
1965	264.6	1.36	0.55
1966	308.8	1.57	0.62
1967	202.5	1.02	0.40
1968	241.5	1.20	0.47
1969	167.2	0.82	0.32
1970	159.0	0.78	0.29
1971	202.1	0.97	0.37
1972	2.5	0.01	0.00
1973	12.0	−.06	−.02
1974	13.6	.06	.02
1975	19.7	.09	.03
1976	−1.5	−.01	.00
Total net obligations	3,789.2		

Sources: Up to 1971, U.S. Agency for International Development, Office of Statistics and Reports, *U.S. Economic Assistance Programs Administered by the Agency for International Development and Predecessor Agencies, April 3, 1948 to June 30, 1971*. After 1971, U.S. Agency for International Development, Statistics and Reports Division,

democratic lines assumed special, international significance. To United States officials the Third World seemed a dangerous place. Political instability and conditions of economic malaise raised the specter of Soviet-backed revolution or Moscow's exploitation of turmoil. India, where social and economic change took place in a non-Communist and relatively peaceful context, seemed conspicuous as a stable, Third World nation. India's commitment to democratic values also contrasted sharply with authoritarian tendencies in some Communist countries. Citing India as the world's largest democracy, United States officials hoped to establish that nation as a showcase for American-backed development in the Third World—and as an Asian counterweight to the Communist model in the People's Republic of China. As the National Security Council concluded in 1959: "The extent of India's development will have international ramifications. . . . Asia and Africa will be watching and comparing what the Indian and Chinese regimes are achieving for their peoples, in terms of rapid industrialization, as well as in terms of the impact on human freedoms and living standards."[2]

Office of Financial Management, *U.S. Overseas Loans and Grants and Assistance from International Organizations, July 1, 1945–June 30, 1973,* and subsequent years. Population figures for computing per capita amounts were taken from United Nations, *Demographic Yearbook.*

[a] Commitments may be defined as development loans authorized and obligations of other AID funds. Annual commitment data are on a "net" basis, that is, new obligations from funds appropriated for that fiscal year, plus reobligations and minus deobligations of prior years' funds. Negative figures represent deobligations in excess of new commitments during one fiscal year.

[b] Predecessor agencies dealing with economic assistance programs during the Marshall Plan period and the Mutual Security Act period were, successively: The Economic Cooperation Administration (1948–1951); the Mutual Security Agency (1951–1953); the Foreign Operations Administration (1953–1955); the International Cooperation Administration (1955–1971); and the Development Loan Fund (1957–1961).

Note: Table reproduced from Robert C. Johansen, *The National Interest and the Human Interest* (Princeton, N.J., 1980), pp. 128–29, by permission of Princeton University Press.

Thus, United States national security interests and India's development needs momentarily overlapped and brought about a major American economic aid program for India. United States relations with India from 1947 through 1963, however, evolved slowly and were marked as much by stress and strain as by efforts at mutual understanding and collaboration. Washington proved reluctant to accept the need for large-scale aid to India, and many officials remained skeptical of the linkages between India's economic development and United States security. Other regions of the world, especially strategic Western Europe and crisis-ridden East Asia, often assumed priority status in the dispersal of aid, and many policymakers emphasized the importance of military aid at the expense of overseas economic assistance. Bureaucratic politics within the executive branch, and budget battles in Congress, also continuously disrupted Indo-American relations.

Most important, American and Indian officials often held conflicting views on the meaning of the term "development." Development is, after all, a relative term. It implies a process of change that generates economic growth, but no consensus exists on the methods of achieving growth. Nor is there agreement on what the basic goals of growth should be. How fast should it take place? For whose benefit? What doctrines should guide it? What political and economic institutions are appropriate?[3]

Going well beyond issues of Cold War politics, the aid process joined together two very dissimilar nations, each of which addressed these questions from different perspectives. Indeed, while the United States and India shared a commitment to representative government, it is difficult to imagine two more different countries. The United States in 1947 was a "have" as opposed to a "have not" nation. It was a highly industrialized, mass production/mass consumption society, whose wealth and status made possible its role as a global benefactor. As European colonialism in India and the rest of the Third World melted away after World War II, the United States increasingly assumed the mantle of world leadership and sought to maintain order and stability in developing areas. India's status, on the other hand, was that of a "have not" nation. Newly independent of colonial rule, India was largely an agrarian society with little economic or military power. As a leader in the Afro-Asian world, it often championed causes such as revolutionary nationalism, anticolonialism, and the restructuring of international economic relations, which brought it into conflict with the United States. In short, the Indo-American aid relationship involved a complex interaction of divergent economic needs, diplomatic interests, historical vantage points, and ideologies.

As the United States and India grappled with the challenges of development, they naturally drew upon different historical experiences and perspectives. Before the end of World War II, American relations with most of the non-Western world, and its involvement in Third World development, had been restricted in scope. During the first century of its history, the United States had been preoccupied with internal problems such as continental expansion, slavery, and industrialization, and it lacked the economic and military power to extend its influence abroad. By the turn of the twentieth century, the United States possessed a mature industrial economy, an enlarged and modern navy, and a growing conviction that national greatness hinged upon foreign expansion. Still, American interests in the Third World remained confined mainly to nearby Latin America and to a lesser extent certain areas of the Pacific and the Far East. Most of Asia, the Indian subcontinent, the Middle East, and Africa fell under European colonial rule. Thus, Washington simply lacked the opportunity to participate in the development process in most of the non-Western world.

Even in areas where the United States did wield significant power, American policymakers hoped to limit the government's role in promoting economic development. America's long-held suspicion of big government and its equally strong commitment to capitalist free enterprise helped shape notions of legitimate economic and political development abroad. Liberal doctrine called for limited government intervention in the development process and stressed the tenets of private enterprise, open access for foreign investment and trade, democratic self-determination, and the free flow of information and ideas. In order to modernize, a nation needed extensive private capital generated by foreign investments and exports, construction of transportation and other infrastructures, and the introduction of Western technology. All of this would enable others to emulate the American experience and lay the foundation for the making of prosperous, democratic societies.[4]

The clearest statement of United States foreign policy principles at the turn of the century came with the enunciation of the Open Door doctrine toward China. But Washington's call for free trade and its denunciation of European and Japanese spheres of influence in China never opened the door to America's participation in that nation's economic and political development. American leaders waxed eloquent over the potential of the vast China market and America's civilizing mission in Asia, but the United States lacked the power to enforce its liberal vision. American contributions to China's development remained largely confined to the activities of a small number of private philanthropic organizations such as the YMCA, the Rockefeller Foundation, and a community of Protestant missionaries that numbered about 25,000 by 1925. Although these groups disseminated Western ideas and values and engaged in a variety of uplift work, they had only a small impact on China's long-term development.[5]

Given the difficulties inherent in implementing liberal development, American private interests during the early twentieth century usually put the open door to one side and consistently turned to Washington for governmental assistance in the marketplace. Government, in turn, responded by implementing tariff, monetary, diplomatic, and military policies that helped to promote and regulate overseas development and to protect United States business interests. The ideology of liberal development underwent its most substantive modifications as United States influence penetrated Third World areas in the Western Hemisphere and the Pacific. In these traditional societies, United States policymakers found widespread poverty, inequality of wealth, and the absence of democratic political traditions. Fearful that unsettled conditions might foment political instability, revolution, and European intervention, United States officials employed a number of statist policies, such as the imposition of colonial rule and military intervention. Reflecting the Progressive Era's penchant for order and efficiency, United States leaders placed a premium on the establishment and maintenance of political stability. Entrepreneurial savvy and imported technology would unleash forces of social change, and effective political controls would help accommodate the process of change to United States economic and security interests. This did not mean that Americans completely abandoned their liberal principles. It did indicate that as the United States arose as a major actor in international affairs, its leaders faced the challenge of reconciling ideals with the pursuit of self-interest and power.[6]

The Philippines, where the United States established direct colonial rule, offers one of the best examples of how American foreign policymakers worked to merge notions of legitimate social change with their own nation's economic and strategic interests. To impose its control over this steppingstone to China, the United States used armed force to crush an indigenous, nationalist movement and then complemented its military policies with a series of development measures. Working closely with elite Filipino collaborators, United States military and civilian authorities inaugurated programs to extend public education, build roads and other infrastructures, and secure access to the American market for Philippine agricultural products. These initiatives were accompanied by a process of gradual political devolution that granted voting and office-holding rights to privileged Filipino groups, and after the Jones Act of 1916, promised eventual independence. Yet American-backed development in the Philippines never included programs such as land reform that might have redistributed wealth and power and promoted more balanced growth. Behind the appearance of liberal devolution and developmental progress, American policies actually sanctioned elite rule and nurtured dependence upon the United States.[7]

In most of Latin America, where the United States exercised enormous influence over economic development, Washington sought to avoid formal colonization but still pursued the closed door through a policy frequently referred to as "dollar diplomacy." Under the Roosevelt Corollary to the Monroe Doctrine, the United States during the first one-third of the twentieth century frequently resorted to military intervention in Caribbean and Central American nations such as Cuba, the Dominican Republic, Haiti, and Nicaragua. In most cases, American officials assumed direction over customs houses, managed national treasuries, enforced health and sanitary standards, and recruited and trained national militia. Seeking to impose stability and protect United States interests in this revolution-prone region, they tried to instill respect for law and order and the sanctity of private property. In a limited sense, Washington may have remained true to the American mission of guiding others toward liberal development. The heavy-handed use of force and economic controls nonetheless confirmed the existence of a conservative United States sphere of influence in much of northern Latin America.[8]

American private capital did play a large role in promoting social and economic change in Latin America. By 1929, the United States had emerged as the dominant foreign economic power in the region with private investments valued at approximately $5 billion and exports and imports between the United States and its southern neighbors totalling nearly $1.8 billion. But this immense flow of trade and investment benefited Latin America only marginally. Extensive trade with the United States relegated most South and Central American countries, which were largely agrarian, to a disadvantaged status as suppliers of raw materials and foodstuffs, and restricted opportunities for industrialization. Dependence on primary product exports, moreover, disproportionately served the interests of foreign investors and local elites who usually controlled productive facilities. Combined with American military interventions, this mode of capitalist development often embittered Latin American opinion against the "colossus of the north," and failed to establish a liberal hemispheric order.[9]

During the 1930s, the administration of President Franklin D. Roosevelt proclaimed a "Good Neighbor" policy toward Latin America and pledged nonintervention in the internal affairs of neighboring republics. As part of the Good Neighbor dictum, the United States also created the Export-Import Bank (Ex-Im) to supply financial aid to spur industrialization, and the State Department's Office of Inter-American Affairs (OIAA) to provide technical assistance to help modernize agriculture. Although these New Deal–style reforms foreshadowed some of the large foreign aid efforts of the post–World War II period, they did not substantially alter the nature of inter-American relations. The Roosevelt administration preserved much of the United States' influence in Latin America by cultivating warm relations with military strongmen such as Fulgencio Batista in Cuba, Rafael Trujillo in the Dominican Republic, and Anastacio Somoza in Nicaragua. In addition, Ex-Im loans involved only small amounts of capital and were usually directed toward the region's traditional export sectors. Similarly, the OIAA received only meager budgetary support for its development activities.[10]

Although these development policies had, in some ways, served United States economic and strategic interests in the early twentieth century, American policymakers after 1945 faced a series of new international realities that forced a rethinking of attitudes toward developing societies. America's drive for global hegemony after World War II, and the decolonization of Asia, the Middle East, and Africa that followed, greatly expanded the United States' role in the Third World. The coming of the Cold War between the United States and the Soviet Union also heightened Washington's interest in non-Western areas. The stakes were high. While the Afro-Asian states were poor in terms of standards of living, they were rich in terms of raw materials essential to the industrial nations, potential markets for manufactured products, and strategic sites for air and naval bases.

United States officials continued to hope that American leadership might one day usher in the creation of a liberal, capitalist world order. American experiences prior to 1945, however, offered only limited guidance as to how to engage independent, Third World nations in the endeavor. Given volatile conditions in emerging areas and the perceived Soviet threat, Washington could not merely resuscitate the Open Door policy and rely solely on private capital to spearhead the effort. At the same time, Third World nationalism and America's limited resources precluded the adoption of controls such as those imposed earlier on United States colonial possessions and Latin America. In this context, Washington constructed a new policy of using large government funds, or foreign aid, to stimulate Third World development.

Just as the economic depression of the 1930s had given rise to New Deal reforms on the homefront; World War II, the Cold War, and America's growing international responsibilities transformed liberal America into a global welfare state. At the Bretton Woods Conference in 1944 the United States oversaw the creation of the International Bank for Reconstruction and Development (IBRD, or the World Bank) to help rebuild postwar economies and the International Monetary Fund (IMF) to promote currency stabilization and balanced world trade. During the war, the United States provided two-thirds of the $4 billion spent by the United Nations Relief and Rehabilitation Administration (UNRRA) to help meet the immediate needs of war-torn areas. In addition, between V-E day and early 1947 the United States provided $9 billion in bilateral grants and loans to Europe. The United States' most significant experience with foreign aid in the early postwar period came with the Marshall Plan in Western Europe when American policymakers concluded that the mere imposition of liberal capitalism in the industrial non-Communist world would not ensure its long-term recovery. The economic revival of Western Europe and the containment of Soviet power required a massive infusion of American capital.[11] As United States officials extended the line of containment across Asia, the Middle East, and Africa in the following years, American aid dollars followed.

In order to administer the aid, American policymakers drew upon a body of economic thought that had emerged during the Great Depression of the 1930s and the Second World War. Both of those events demonstrated the weakness of the market economy in dealing with economic crisis or in restructuring the direction of an entire economic system. Inspired by the unorthodox ideas of Britain's John Maynard Keynes, Western economists during the 1930s and 1940s called for an enlarged role for government in the planning of capitalist enterprise. Although Keynes himself wrote little on the problems of the Third World, his theories identified certain key variables that governments could manipulate in order to induce economic growth and plan economic performance. During the 1950s and 1960s, a wide array of renowned social scientists—including John Kenneth Galbraith, Walt W. Rostow, David Bell, and Paul Rosenstein-Rodan, among others—applied Keynesian macro-theory to non-Western economies. Most of these analysts counseled that investments in capital, technology, and education were most central to increased output, employment, and growth. While private enterprise could be relied upon to supply much of what was needed, native governments would be required to regulate trade and investment, build local institutions, and oversee currency. The governments of developed nations, principally the United States, would provide crucial transfers of technology and capital through foreign assistance programs.[12]

Economic development theory, as it evolved after World War II, was naturally based on what Western economists knew of modern European and, to a lesser extent, Japanese history. It hypothesized the existence of a lineal line of global economic development that placed the nations of Asia, Africa, and Latin America several centuries behind the developed areas in economic maturity. Value-laden and paternalistic, these ideas predicted that developing areas would repeat the Western experience as long as they implemented the key policy variables recommended by their mentors. At the same time, Western economists and policymakers assumed that economic growth would provide a foundation for political democracy and an antidote to authoritarian communism in the developing countries. Thus, the aid process promised to simultaneously nurture liberal development and make the Third World secure from the Soviet threat.[13]

The success of the Marshall Plan during the late 1940s suggested that Keynesian economic planning could achieve speedy results in a foreign setting. As the aid process incorporated the non-Western world, however, United States officials encountered far more difficulties than they had in Europe. Rural economies, more deeply impoverished than those in the developed nations, seemed less responsive to aid. Whereas the European nations sought to reconstruct what had once been industrialized economies, Third World nations faced the imposing task of developing entirely new economic and social structures. In addition, ambiguous and often intractable political conflicts tended to disrupt stable economic development in recently decolonized nations, and proud, nationalistic leaders frequently resisted American prescriptions for economic and political change. Thus, while United States aid usually served as an effective tool of diplomacy and economic recovery in Western Europe, it brought few immediate benefits to the Third World. This certainly proved to be the case in India, the nation which eventually became an experimental laboratory for American-backed development.

United States influence in India never reached hegemonic proportions. In spite of the large influx of aid during the late 1950s and the early 1960s, Washington never established firm, controlling authority over India's decision-making processes, and the American presence in India remained limited. Yet United States leaders can be said to have harbored hegemonic ambitions relating to India's development. In this sense, the American effort to make India a model for capitalistic economic growth and non-Communist political evolution can be understood to have constituted an effort to implement indirect control over that nation's future. The crucial problem that arose in India, and which endlessly frustrated Washington, was that of reconciling American developmental policies with the economic and political realities in the recipient nation.

Just as the United States lacked experience in using aid as a foreign policy tool, it also lacked extensive knowledge of India. Prior to 1947, British imperial rule inhibited the development of both economic and political relations with India, and the Indian subcontinent fell well outside of the geographic parameters of American foreign policy concerns. American missionaries, both Protestant and Roman Catholic, forged the most extensive links between the two countries, but these contacts failed to stimulate a broader interest in India.[14] As late as the interwar years only eight American universities—Harvard, Yale, Princeton, Columbia, the University of Pennsylvania, John Hopkins, the University of Chicago, and the University of California—maintained chairs of Sanskrit or Indic Studies devoted to scholarship in classical Indian languages, literature, and philosophy. Social scientists evidenced little interest in India.[15] As a consequence, American policymakers had little chance of understanding India's unique developmental needs.

The establishment of India's formal independence from Great Britain on 15 August 1947 evoked elation throughout the country. The new nation, nevertheless, faced a myriad of extraordinarily complicated problems. The government of India first had to contend with the basic question of how to weld a nation out of the diverse regions and communities within the country. The decision to partition the subcontinent along communal, or religious, lines and to create the Islamic state of Pakistan ignited a spiral of violence in 1947 that ultimately left one-half million dead, and approximately fifteen million displaced. The partition also left a legacy of hatred and distrust between India and Pakistan. Beyond this, Indian leaders confronted a nation consisting of fourteen regionally based linguistic groups, not counting the hundreds of local dialects, each of which feared an overly intrusive federal state. In addition, India's centuries-old, Hindu-based caste system divided the new nation. Hereditary caste groups, each placed in a position of ritual superiority and inferiority to others, had traditionally provided the foundation for Indian social organization. But in a modernizing India, the possibility existed that the caste system might also generate class antagonisms and disrupt efforts at national consolidation.[16]

India's widespread poverty lay at the heart of the country's economic problems. At independence, India was very much an agrarian nation. British colonial rulers had sanctioned only limited industrialization on the subcontinent. Eighty-five percent of India's population lived in rural areas, and industries employed only one-tenth of the labor force, mostly in cottage and small-scale processing activities. Equally important, India's agrarian sector was abysmally poor. The use of fertilizers, irrigation facilities, and modern agricultural methods had not been widely adopted.[17] Even with the import of two to three million tons of foodgrains annually, daily grain consumption averaged a meager nine ounces per person. And in a nation of inequalities, where 22 percent of the rural population owned no land and another 25 percent owned fragments of less than 2.5 acres, food consumption for many fell well below the national average. In this setting, illiteracy reached 84 percent; mass communicable diseases such as malaria, smallpox, and cholera ran rampant; and mortality rates of 27 per 1,000 ranked among the world's highest.[18]

Given these conditions, it is not surprising that the Indian government sometimes adopted economic and political policies that conflicted with America's liberal, Cold War agenda. First, Indian leaders refused to give wholehearted endorsement to the tenets of liberal capitalism. During the 1920s and 1930s, as India's movement for independence gained momentum, many members of the Congress party—including future Prime Minister Jawaharlal Nehru—had been attracted to the Soviet model of economic planning. Determined to make rapid economic growth a vehicle for national unity, they had feared that private development in India would mean development engineered and controlled by foreign interests. The responsibilities of power and the influence of industrialists and landed interests in the Congress organization dictated a more pragmatic approach once freedom had been attained; and radical theories on redistribution gave way to a new emphasis on production. "If nationalization would increase our production we will have it," Nehru explained at one press conference. "If it does not, we shall not have it."[19] Still, Nehru and other leaders continued to talk of India's "tendency toward socialism," and India's shortage of private capital dictated nationalistic plans for the maintenance of government ownership over basic industries such as iron, steel, transportation, communications, and electricity.[20]

Indian nationalism at times also brought India into conflict with United States foreign policy goals. Prime Minister Nehru advanced the concept of nonalignment in the Cold War. "We propose," he explained as early as September 1946, "as far as possible to keep away from the power politics of groups, aligned against one another, which have led in the past to world wars and which may again lead to disaster on a wider scale."[21] India's nonalignment derived from pragmatic considerations: its location near Soviet borders; its need for aid from both the West and the Eastern bloc; and its position of political, military, and economic weakness. It also reflected India's natural emphasis on Asian and colonial affairs rather than East-West relations. In early 1947, for example, India hosted the region's first Asian relations conference. Above all else, however, nonalignment grew out of Indian history, particularly its long history as a British colony.[22] "For too long we of Asia have been petitioners in Western courts and chancellories," Nehru declared in March 1947. "That story must now belong to the past. We propose to stand on our own legs. . . . We do not intend to be the plaything of others."[23]

For New Delhi, the Soviet-American confrontation was a great power rivalry—pure and simple; and India was determined to act independently on Cold War issues and to assume a leadership position among the emerging, new nations. As ardent champions of decolonization, Indian officials spoke out against a number of American foreign policy initiatives in Asia, especially the inclination to support Cold War allies in colonial disputes. The Nehru government first did so in the case of the Indonesian revolution of the 1940s when it took a strong stand against Dutch militarism, which was underwritten in part by the United States. An even more serious point of contention arose over United States military aid to India's regional rival Pakistan after 1954. American policymakers conceived of the arrangement as part of its worldwide collective security system against communism. India perceived the shipment of American military equipment to Pakistan as a direct threat to its own national security.

India's national pride also found expression in the enormously complex personality of Jawaharlal Nehru. The precise impact of personality on relations between states is difficult to gauge, but in the case of Indo-American relations it certainly left a mark. Nehru devoted most of his adult life to the service of his country, first as Gandhi's young lieutenant in the

Indian Congress party and the independence movement, and later as prime minister of the new nation. For Nehru, nationalism represented more than a political concept, it was a heartfelt emotion that defined modern India's soul. At the same time, however, the Indian patriot never fully divorced himself of all British trappings. A privileged member of the Indian elite, Nehru had been sent to England as a young man and schooled at Harrow and Cambridge. Later, as a law student in London, he had imbibed English constitutional principles and procedures. In short, British manners and morals had helped mold his character. As Nehru himself acknowledged in looking back upon his youth: "I was perhaps more an Englishman than an Indian. I looked upon the world from an Englishman's standpoint."[24] Part Indian patriot, part Indian Brahmin, and part English gentleman, Nehru's fervent nationalism combined both populist and aristocratic strains—and defied easy definition.

Nehru's attitude toward America was as complicated and, at times, as contradictory as the man himself. Without a doubt, the youthful Nehru had acquired a degree of Victorian England's disdain for "boorish" and "materialistic" Americans. As a Third World nationalist, he also familiarized himself with the history of United States intervention in Latin America and the Far East. At the International Congress for Oppressed Nationalities in Brussels in 1927, for example, Nehru denounced American as well as European expansionism.[25] As prime minister, Nehru's criticisms of Washington's Cold War policies often assumed a shrill and self-righteous tone.

Yet America also held a certain attraction for him. In British prisons during the 1930s, Nehru devoured American literature and history and even copied the full text of Lincoln's Gettysburg Address into his notebook.[26] During the war years, Nehru and most politically conscious Indians came to admire President Franklin D. Roosevelt for his espousal of the principle of self-determination in the Atlantic Charter, and for his intercessions with British Prime Minister Winston Churchill on behalf of Indian self-rule.[27] Nehru remained convinced, moreover, that the United States would continue to reach out to India and other newly emerged nations during the postwar period. As was the case with many other Indian officials, Nehru believed that America's liberal form of capitalism mitigated against overt imperialism. The soon-to-be prime minister speculated in his 1946 synthetic work, *The Discovery of India*: "The British colonial outlook does not fit in with American policy and expansionistic tendencies. The United States want open markets for their exports and do not look with favor on attempts to control or limit them. They want industrialization of

Asia's millions and higher standards everywhere, not for sentimental reasons but to dispose of their surplus goods."[28]

Nehru's paradoxical view of the United States is essential to an understanding of the Indo-American aid relationship. Nehru's India sought American economic aid after 1947 because it concluded that the absence of assistance would prove disastrous to its well-being and because its leaders assumed that the United States could be counted upon, for economic and diplomatic reasons of its own, to provide much needed help. Indian officials, nonetheless, remained ever vigilant lest their nation become dependent on the United States. With needs that were very great, and having little to offer in return, they feared that the United States might use economic assistance as leverage to make India adopt policies, both foreign and domestic, that more nearly conformed to the wishes and dictates of its benefactor. In accepting American assistance, they constantly worked to minimize the disadvantages arising from the aid relationship. In so doing, they contributed to tensions in Indo-American relations and often derailed America's hegemonic designs.

India approached the United States on the matter of economic aid even before the arrival of independence. On 9 July 1947, Nehru met with the new United States ambassador in New Delhi, Henry F. Grady. In a month's time, the proud Indian leader would stand before an evening session of the Indian Constituent Assembly and speak of freedom from British colonial rule as the "redemption of a tryst with destiny."[29] But as Nehru conversed with the American ambassador, he focused his attention not on India's coming political triumphs but on the economic challenges that still lay ahead. As he outlined his country's predicament, Nehru minced no words. He noted that while some in India feared possible "economic penetration" by the United States, India "would want U.S. exports—particularly capital goods. . . . In fact," Nehru observed, "[the] U.S. was [the] only country from which [the] quantities needed could be obtained." The prime minister further informed Grady that India would probably approach the American-backed World Bank for loan assistance.[30]

The prospects for Indo-American economic cooperation seemed good. Indeed, the Truman administration had already sent encouraging signals to India. Shortly after the British announced their intention to transfer power on the subcontinent in early 1947, President Harry S. Truman told a press conference: "Officials of the [United States] Government have on various occasions made it clear that we stood ready to assist India in its commendable plans for economic development in all appropriate ways which would prove of benefit to our two countries and the world."[31] A message of congratulations followed on 14 August in which Truman expressed unbounded optimism for future relations. "In the years to come," the president declared, "this great nation will find in the United States a constant friend."[32]

In spite of Indian hopes and American assurances, United States economic aid would not be immediately forthcoming. Instead, the Indo-American aid relationship evolved slowly and with a great deal of uncertainty. As had been the case historically, American policymakers would attempt to channel the development process along lines that were in keeping with their own notions of acceptable social change and United States security interests. For its part, India would prove extremely sensitive to matters relating to its own national prerogatives. Sometimes the goals of the two nations clashed, and understanding and collaboration proved difficult to achieve. Truman's February 1947 pronouncement on aid to India contained an important qualifier that bears repeating. The United States would assist India, the president noted, "in all appropriate ways which would prove of benefit to our two countries and the world."

Two

A Missed Opportunity, 1947–1950

When President Truman declared in early 1947 America's willingness to assist India economically, he most likely thought of expanding trade with that nation rather than providing aid. American policymakers placed immense faith in the redemptive qualities of capitalism and free trade. In part, this belief derived from America's long-standing attachment to liberal ideology. In part, it sprang from the experiences of the 1920s and 1930s when restrictive trading practices, unfair economic competition, and excessive nationalism helped to induce economic depression and war.[1] It also grew out of self-interest. In 1932, at the depth of the Great Depression, United States exports had totaled only $1.6 billion, but by 1945 they grew to $10 billion, and in 1947 they reached $14 billion—accounting for one-third of the world's total.[2] In the post–World War II era, American leaders hoped to use this immense economic power to maintain an "open world" conducive to international trade and investment. "A large volume of soundly based international trade," President Truman declared in 1946, "is essential if we are to build a durable world economy, and attain our goal of peace and prosperity."[3]

United States officials soon realized that trade alone would not bring about a peaceful, capitalist world order. Given wartime destruction and the emerging Soviet threat, policymakers concluded that if the world were to be kept prosperous and politically stable, the United States would have to promote economic development through aid as well as trade. By the time India achieved its independence in 1947 and made known its need for economic assistance, foreign aid had already been established as a major tool of American diplomacy. Yet from 1947 to 1950 India's frequent requests for bilateral economic assistance either went unanswered or were turned down. One 1947 State Department document that listed nations in need of aid did not even mention the Indian subcontinent.[4] The specific reasons for rejecting Indian requests varied according to the occasion, but one generalization best explains American policy during these years. United States officials declined to make aid available to India and many other needy nations because they did not believe that assistance to such nations would significantly advance United States foreign policy interests.

President Truman enunciated the guiding principle behind aid on 12 March 1947, when he appeared before Congress to request $400 million in economic and military assistance for Greece and Turkey. In the preceding weeks the British government had informed the United States that it could no longer bear responsibility for those strategically placed countries. Washington viewed Britain's abdication with particular concern because Greece was at that moment torn by a civil war that pitted a weak, pro-Western regime against a popular, Communist-backed insurgency. The Truman administration eschewed details—such as the lack of evidence linking Greek Communists to the Soviet Union and the corrupt and undemocratic nature of the Greek government—in presenting its alarmist case for intervention. In his speech to Congress, Truman asserted that the United States faced a choice between supporting the forces of freedom or watching additional nations fall to Communist totalitarianism. "I believe," the president posited, "that it must be the policy of the United States to support free peoples who are resisting subjugation by armed minorities or outside pressure."[5] Congress obliged the president and approved the request for funds.

The open-ended Truman Doctrine called for an American effort to contain communism on a global scale and suggested that aid would be an important weapon in the struggle.[6] United States officials initially focused most of their attention on Europe, first with aid to Greece and Turkey, and later with the multibillion dollar Marshall Plan for Western Europe.[7] Then, from 1948 through early 1950, developments on the continent of Asia increasingly captured Washington's attention. From British India to French Indochina nationalist movements, some with a Marxist orientation, pressed their colonial rulers for freedom.[8] In China, Asia's largest and most populous country, Communist forces emerged triumphant in late 1949 after years of bloody civil war.[9] In this context, the Truman administration began to put together plans for a comprehensive aid program in Asia.

For a brief time in 1949, American policymakers considered making close United States ties to India central to its plans for Asia. The talk at that point was of buttressing India—the area's largest and most populous country after China, and a nation committed to representative government—with economic aid. Some prominent officials even entertained hopes that United States interests throughout Asia could best be pursued through economic measures. In late 1949 and early 1950, however, such a strategy was discarded. Following a visit to Washington by Prime Minister Jawaharlal Nehru in October, just weeks before the Communists seized power in China, the Truman administration decided to downplay India's role in the region and go forward with a containment policy that emphasized military aid, not economic assistance. Specifically, policymakers decided to strengthen American defense capabilities in Japan and the Pacific and to extend military aid to anti-Communist regimes in Taiwan, the Philippines, Thailand, Indonesia, Burma, and French Indochina. An examination of these decisions suggests that the administration, by rejecting the Indian option, may have missed a major opportunity to set United States relations with India, and Asia as a whole, on a more peaceful and constructive path.[10]

When American policymakers during the early Cold War years spoke of the South Asian region, which included Pakistan, Afghanistan, Ceylon, and Nepal as well as India, they did so in terms of the area's potential value to United States economic and security interests. In line with their global objectives, they hoped that India and the other nations of the subcontinent would remain politically stable, open to foreign trade and investment, and generally oriented toward the West. Reports generated in the State Department and the Central Intelligence Agency made note of India's importance as a future market for American goods and its massive reserves of strategic raw materials.[11] Policymakers were particularly impressed that India possessed one of the world's most extensive deposits of manganese, a metallic element used in the production of steel alloys, which before the beginning of the Cold War had been provided to the United States chiefly by the Soviet Union.[12] As early as 1946, the Defense Department and the Joint Chiefs of Staff emphasized the area's geographic proximity to both the Soviet Union and the oil-rich Middle East. They speculated that the Indian subcontinent, especially the Karachi-Lahore regions of what would become Pakistan, might provide suitable locations for American air bases, naval ports, and listening posts.[13] Several policy papers noted that in the event of war India could provide the West with a virtually inexhaustible source of manpower.[14]

Despite its vast potential, United States officials saw no immediate need to launch an aid program for India. With their attention in 1947 and early 1948 focused upon Europe, the oil-bearing states of the Middle East,

Japan, and China, high-ranking policymakers gave minimal attention to India. An array of postwar issues, both domestic and foreign, preoccupied President Truman. No evidence exists that this practical Missouri politician ever reserved time for penetrating thought on India. Nor did Secretary of State George C. Marshall take a deep interest in India or the South Asian region. Consequently, responsibility for policy tended to fall upon lower-echelon officials, such as regional experts in the Department of State and officials in the American embassy in New Delhi headed by Ambassador Henry F. Grady. The Truman administration, of course, had a policy toward the subcontinent. For the most part, it continued to see India as falling within the British sphere of responsibility. One State Department document made the point: "Bearing in mind the commitments which the United States has made elsewhere, it would appear to be in our interest that the British continue to have, from the global point of view, the paramount responsibility for the maintenance of international peace and security in South Asia."[15]

Perhaps the most striking feature of American policy at this time was the relative lack of interest in India at the very time the Nehru government evolved policies contrary to United States goals. By early 1948, Prime Minister Nehru had already introduced India's nonaligned foreign policy to the rest of the world, and India had emerged as a strong advocate of decolonization in the United Nations. In domestic affairs, the Indian government had adopted the Industrial Resolution of 1948, which mandated state ownership of key industries including munitions, atomic energy, and railways, and reserved to the state the right to start new enterprises in coal, iron, steel, ship and aircraft manufactures, communications, and minerals. In the field of foreign investment, foreign capital was allowed a maximum of 30 percent ownership in joint ventures.[16]

Although Indian policies largely grew out of pragmatic and nationalistic considerations, they would eventually arouse deep distrust in Washington. Nonalignment came to be seen as running counter to America's Cold War aims, and Nehru's "tendency toward socialism" was deemed to be inimical to American plans for a capitalist world order. But in 1947 and early 1948 the president and the highest ranking State Department officials evidenced minimal concern. Lesser officials, who followed India more closely, sometimes expressed annoyance with Nehru. When India voted with the Soviet Union on various colonial issues during the 1946 session of the United Nations General Assembly, for example, United States delegate John Foster Dulles boldly claimed to newsmen that in India "Soviet Communism exercises a strong influence through the interim government."[17] When Dulles's remarks evoked an uproar of protest in India, Secretary Marshall sent instructions to New Delhi to "inform Nehru that we have followed with deep interest his various expressions of Indian foreign policy . . . and have been favorably impressed by India's avowed intention to pursue an independent but cooperative policy based on [the] U.N. Charter."[18] In another case, Ambassador Henry Grady wrote to Truman in the summer of 1947 to decry India's "growing sense of nationalism," which manifested itself in criticisms of the United States and Great Britain.[19] Truman answered with a single line that reflected his detachment: "Your reference to the attitude of Asia toward the United States and Great Britain is one that is to be expected and all we can do is to try to live it down."[20]

The one issue in South Asia that did win Washington's attention was the Indo-Pakistani dispute over the still independent, princely state of Kashmir. Soon after partition this Muslim majority, border territory in northern India—ruled by a Hindu Maharaja—became a serious object of controversy on the already tense subcontinent. On 24 October 1947, Pakistan-backed Pathan tribesmen brazenly invaded the state, established a provisional "Azad," or free, Muslim government, and quickly made their way toward the capital city of Srinagar. Two days later the Maharaja appealed to the Indian government to send troops—a favor that Nehru granted in exchange for Kashmir's accession to the dominion of India. Indian troops were dispatched and soon the Azad forces, now fighting with the open assistance of Pakistani troops, were pushed to the northwest section of the state. Charging Pakistani aggression in December 1947, Nehru referred the matter to the United Nations.[21]

American interests in either India or Pakistan were not considered to be of enough consequence to warrant siding with either party, but the United States did seek to promote South Asian stability. American policymakers feared that war on the subcontinent might increase Soviet influence in the region. As Under Secretary of State Robert Lovett explained to British officials in January 1948: "We could not be sure of Russia taking a quiescent attitude in this matter . . . it could adopt an obstructionist role merely in order to keep the pot boiling."[22] To avoid charges of bias and to help effect a cease-fire, the Truman administration banned arm sales to both nations in March 1948. At the urging of Great Britain, the United States lent its support to United Nations efforts to bring about a plebiscite in Kashmir to determine the state's future status. In May, American representatives were named to the United Nations Commission for India and

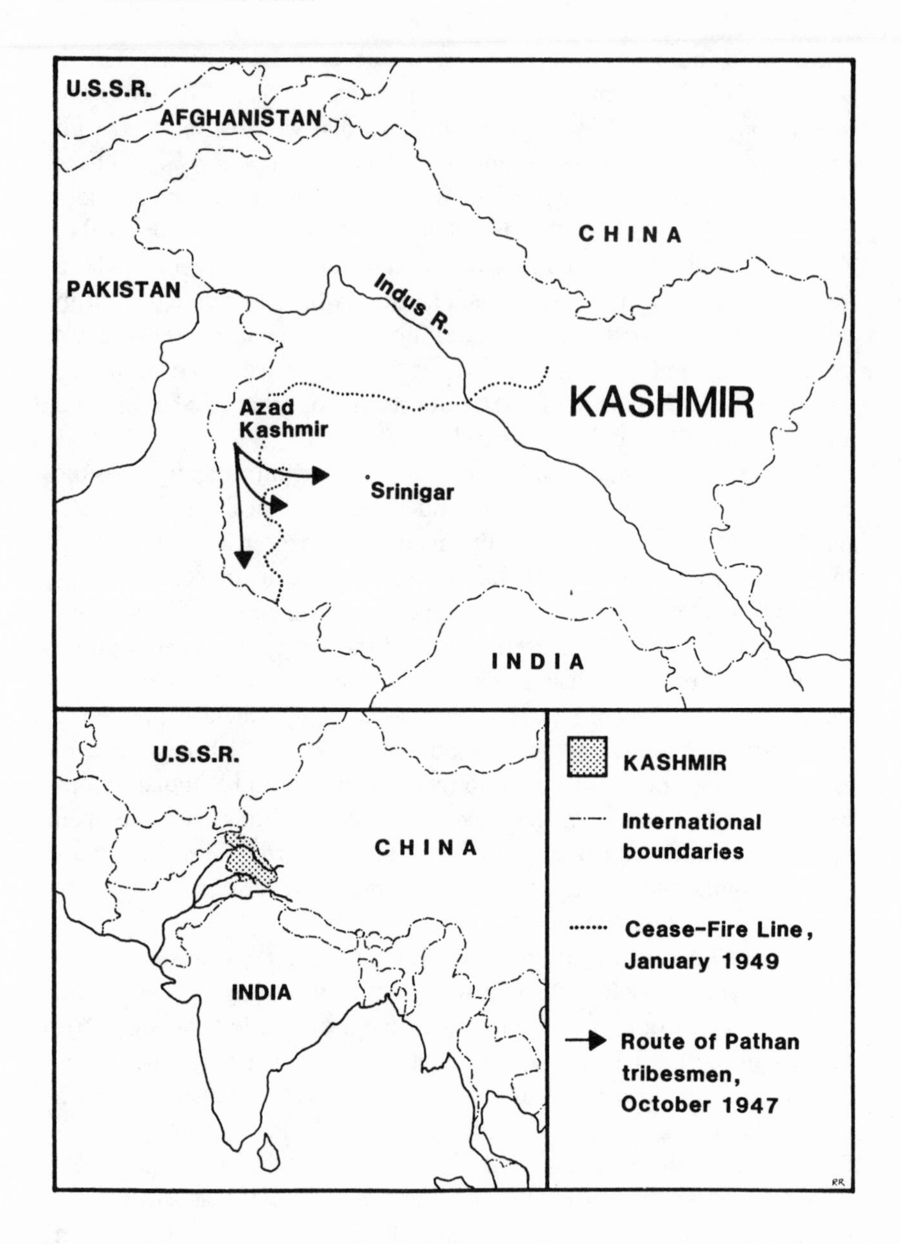

Map. 1. *Indo-Pakistani Dispute over Kashmir*

Pakistan, and Secretary Marshall agreed to the appointment of Fleet Admiral Chester Nimitz as plebiscite administrator. A cease fire was finally implemented in January 1949, and talks to determine a truce and plebiscite followed.[23] Final settlement, however, proved elusive. India, in particular, adopted an intransigent position, refused to relinquish its occupied territory in Kashmir, and resented Washington's relatively evenhanded approach, especially its support for a plebiscite.

Despite United States interest in Kashmir, India remained a low priority in American foreign aid lists. Unlike Western Europe, where American trade and investments were substantial, United States trade with India was valued at only $473 million in 1950, and America's $212 million in exports to that nation accounted for less than 1 percent of the national total. The value of direct investment in India came to a mere $38 million in 1950 out of total American private foreign investments of approximately $11.8 billion. Moreover, the Communist movement in India, in contrast to nations such as Italy and France, was a fledgling one with little chance of toppling the existing government. Regarding India, a State-War-Navy Coordinating Committee document concluded in June 1947: "The situation in India is not now, nor is likely to be within the next five years, so critical as to necessitate special appropriations of American public funds in order to safeguard United States security by extraordinary measures of financial aid to India."[24]

At least one major United States official, however, showed a great deal of interest in India—Ambassador Henry F. Grady. Grady was a noncareer appointee who had served both the Roosevelt and Truman administrations in a variety of capacities. In 1942, he headed a United States Technical Mission to India that prepared an unused blueprint for developing war-related industries on the subcontinent. If the United States had wished to involve itself in India's postwar development, no one would have been better prepared to spearhead the effort than Grady. In addition to having had experience in India, he carried impressive credentials as a former banker, dean of the University of California's College of Commerce, and a member of the Department of Commerce's Business Advisory Board.[25]

Henry Grady was not only a man of vast experience but also a person with deep convictions. In his youth he abandoned preparation for the Roman Catholic priesthood to seek a career in business. Yet he maintained a missionary-like zeal as an advocate of liberal, capitalist development and the containment doctrine. Nehru's nonaligned policy struck him as being morally obtuse, and India's economic policies seemed socialistic. "Speaking for the capitalists of my own country," Grady admonished one Indian audience, "I can say that while under proper terms and conditions they are willing to lend money to this country and to other countries, they are not prepared to beg that their capital be received."[26] Grady nonetheless believed that India could be redeemed, and unlike President Truman, he was not willing to wait and "live down" Indian attitudes.

In late 1947 and early 1948, Grady became the administration's leading advocate of aid for India. Although the Indian government had not made any specific requests for aid, Grady surveyed the Indian economy during the fall of 1947 and quickly pinpointed the area where the United States might effectively apply foreign assistance. Of all of India's economic problems, none seemed more urgent than that of food production. Both Grady and Indian officials considered an increase in India's food supply, then dependent upon the import of two to three million tons of foodgrains annually, to be essential to economic and political stability. The Nehru government approached the matter in pragmatic fashion. It launched three multipurpose, river valley schemes in 1947, modeled after the American Tennessee Valley Authority.[27] Downplaying India's dire need for land reform at this time, Nehru decided that the river projects provided the key to increased food output. While they would eventually provide electricity and flood control, the primary consideration was that, taken together, the three projects would irrigate 16.5 million acres of farmland—a phenomenal feat in a country where only 48 million acres were currently irrigated. Productivity, scale, and technology—the prospects dazzled Indian planners and thrilled Henry Grady.[28]

Grady lost no time in offering American assistance. In October 1947, he initiated talks with several Indian cabinet ministers, and raised the idea of contracting with an American engineering firm to carry out at least one of the projects. He also suggested that low-interest financing might be made available through the United States Export-Import Bank.[29] At the same time, Grady contacted an old friend, Stephen Bechtel of the world famous Bechtel International Corporation, and asked him to come to India to discuss his company's possible participation in dam construction. He explained his plans in a breezy uninhibited style. "As you know," he told Bechtel, "one of the reasons I came here, in fact, the principal reason, was to endeavor to keep India in our camp." "We can demonstrate that our system is better," he went on, "by helping India in an unselfish way to develop her own resources. . . . I would like to strike while the iron is hot."[30]

Bechtel shared Grady's enthusiasm, and although his firm was not interested in doing business in India, he did arrange for a friendly competitor, the Morrison-Knudsen Corporation, to work with the ambassador. Bechtel even accompanied Morrison-Knudsen officials to New Delhi and took part in negotiations with the Indian government. In one meeting with Nehru, Grady and Bechtel waxed exuberant over the proposed project. Just hand over one project to Morrison-Knudsen, Grady told Nehru, and you will be surprised "at how fast the dirt will fly."[31] The prime minister had reservations. There would have to be training programs for Indian engineers, provisions to limit the use of machinery so as to ensure jobs for unskilled workers, and Indian government supervision over Morrison-Knudsen. Grady grew impatient. "They seem to prefer to build [the dams] with workers carrying dirt in baskets on their heads and to take ten years to do it," he complained to Bechtel.[32] Despite the complaints, negotiations continued, and the ambassador remained hopeful.

In mid-December 1947, Grady returned to Washington for a briefing at the State Department where he presented an exposition of his views on aid for India. On the morning of 16 December he participated in broad-ranging discussions with officers of the Department's South Asian and Near Eastern Division; of course, they took a much greater interest in India than their superiors. When the conversation turned to Nehru, Grady informed the group that he was disturbed by Indian policies. With regard to nonalignment, he recalled that he had once told the prime minister: "This is a question that cannot be straddled and that India should get on the democratic side immediately." The ambassador also observed that Nehru might yet prove useful to American interests. When pressed as to how this might come about, Grady did not go into specifics on the Indian river valley projects, but allowed that "American influence should increase greatly through economic help." "It is our most effective channel," he argued, "for keeping India on our side and under our influence."[33]

It does not appear that Indian aid was discussed with the president or the secretary of state at that time. But Grady's hopes soared in early 1948 as political events in India pushed Nehru in the desired direction. The drama began when the Communist party of India (CPI) launched a series of labor strikes and protest marches in opposition to the Congress party's mixed economic policies. Various state governments, with Nehru's tacit approval, outlawed the CPI, seized its presses, and jailed its leaders.[34] The prime minister became convinced that the Soviet Union had given the CPI moral and financial support. At the same time, a stream of Soviet propaganda denouncing nonalignment flowed from Moscow. And in meetings with

Madame Vijayalakshmi Pandit, Nehru's sister and India's ambassador to the Soviet Union, Russian diplomats demanded that India declare its true allegiance.[35] An indignant Nehru went before Parliament on 8 March to issue a clear warning to the Soviet Union. He insisted that India would always remain nonaligned in principle, but emphasized that circumstances might require that the policy be modified. "I can quite conceive of our siding with an imperialist Power," Nehru declared, "I do not mind saying that in a certain set of circumstances that may be the lesser of two evils."[36]

Grady excitedly reported these developments to Washington and predicted that Nehru would soon alter his nonaligned posture.[37] In fact, Nehru sent his secretary general for External Affairs, Sir Girja Bajpai, to Washington in late March for consultations with United States leaders. Bajpai knew the American setting well, having worked in the United States as British India's agent general during the Second World War. During a series of high-level meetings Bajpai made known his government's dismay over Soviet policy. Following his prime minister's instructions, Sir Girja noted that fear of Soviet reprisal and domestic, political considerations prevented India's public alignment with the United States. But he assured senior State Department officials: "Should the world once again become involved in conflict, India could only associate itself with those nations holding the same ideals of freedom and democracy."[38]

The secretary general also took advantage of the occasion to present Acting Secretary of State Lovett with India's first, formal request for economic assistance. Noting that "the U.S. is the only country which is in a position to aid India," Bajpai specifically raised the issue of the river valley projects. The Indian diplomat also queried Lovett on the possibility of acquiring United States military assistance. Bajpai framed the request for military aid in Cold War terms with references to Soviet support for the CPI.[39] It seems likely, however, that the Nehru government's foremost worry related to Pakistan and Kashmir. Indeed, the Pakistani's had already approached the United States with similar anti-Communist professions in an effort to attain American arms.[40]

The State Department wisely dismissed the Indian request for military assistance, as they had done with Pakistani entreaties. Unfortunately, the idea of providing economic aid was also rejected. Although Bajpai's overture was exactly what Grady had worked for, it did not impress Washington. In a cable to Grady, Lovett observed that the United States had "no doubt [that] India will support efforts [to] uphold freedom and democracy in [the] present critical phase [of] world affairs," but added that the department was "reluctant" to endorse India's continued, public policy of "overt neutrality."[41] It is doubtful that apprehension over Nehru's nonalignment had been the major determinant of the matter. Very little high-level discussion of Bajpai's overture had actually taken place. There appears to be no record of the secretary general's remarks having been brought to the attention of the president. Nor is there any evidence of discussions of the Indian request having taken place among assistant secretaries of state or regional bureau chiefs.[42] Sir Girja must have sensed the American mood when he remarked to Loy Henderson, Director of the Office of Near Eastern Affairs, that there was "something of an impression in India that the United States had very little interest in that country." Henderson responded with the truth. "Unfortunately," he explained, "the United States found it necessary to concentrate its efforts and resources on resisting aggression in certain other parts of the world."[43]

Yet events were already under way that would widen the theater of the Cold War beyond Europe and cause Washington to take a closer look at India. By 1948 much of Asia seethed with discontent. Colonial regimes were crumbling, new aspirations were being awakened, and social and political revolution was engulfing much of the region. In French Indochina, in Dutch Indonesia, and in British Malaya nationalist groups demanded freedom, colonial rulers resisted, and armed insurgencies grew in influence and strength. In such independent nations as the Philippines, Thailand, and Burma, breakdowns in governmental authority and widespread poverty spawned similar movements. The most striking revolutionary event of all took place in China. Nurtured by years of great-power exploitation, grinding poverty, and the corrupt authoritarianism of Jiang Jieshi (Chiang Kai-shek), the Communist challenge of Mao Zedong (Mao Tse-tung) stood poised for victory in the Chinese civil war.

United States policymakers viewed the Asian drama within the context of their Cold War objectives. Deeply engaged in Europe, and with growing commitments in the Middle East and Japan, they tried to limit American involvement on mainland Asia. On colonial issues United States officials generally believed that decolonization was, as one State Department study asserted, "the wave of the future."[44] But the Cold War often inhibited support for independence in the rest of Asia. The United States granted independence to the Philippines in 1946 and gave limited diplomatic support to non-Communist nationalists in Indonesia after 1945.[45] But in certain, crucial cases—such as French Indochina—United States leaders assumed that the source of revolution could be traced to Moscow, and they were disinclined to see, as Secretary of State Marshall put it, "colonial empires and administrations supplanted by philosophies and political organizations emanating from the Kremlin."[46] In addition, they feared that by interfering in colonial disputes the United States might lose the friendship of important, European allies. Thus, the United States initially adopted a policy of only limited engagement in Asian affairs.

Even in China, which Franklin Roosevelt had granted a somewhat illusory status as one of his four world policemen, the Truman administration sought to avoid direct intervention. The United States had sent over $2 billion in economic and military aid to Jiang since V-J day only to see most of the aid squandered or pocketed by corrupt and incompetent officials. As Jiang suffered one military setback after another in 1948, the Joint Chiefs of Staff (JCS) estimated that only massive, armed intervention by the United States could prevent a Communist takeover. The JCS agreed with others in the administration that such costly action was unlikely to bear fruitful results. Under pressure from Congress, the Truman White House maintained a small aid program for Jiang, but most foreign policy analysts agreed that a Communist victory in China was inevitable.[47]

The Indian government viewed events in Asia differently. At least since the Asian Relations Conference of 1947, Nehru had considered the region a vaguely defined sphere of Indian interest and influence. During most of 1947 and 1948 the prime minister had been too caught up in domestic affairs and Kashmir to act upon this view. Those problems appeared manageable by late 1948, however, and Nehru began to wrap his foreign policy in the garment of Asianism, or regionalism. "When we talk of Asia," he told Parliament in early 1949, "remember that India, not because of any ambition of hers, but because of the force of circumstance, because of geography, because of history, and because of so many other things, inevitably has a very important part in Asia."[48] Ever wary of the CPI, Nehru anxiously watched the growth of communism in neighboring areas. But, in contrast to American policymakers, he also worried about the specter of a resurgent colonialism and believed that colonial oppression and the nationalist urge, rather than Soviet intrigue or Communist ideology, had supplied the major impetus for Asia's discontent.[49]

Nehru and Secretary Bajpai advanced Indian views to American officials, but they did not receive a sympathetic hearing. The prime minister met with Secretary Marshall on 16 October 1948 during a Paris meeting of the

United Nations General Assembly. According to Marshall's notes of the conversation, the Indian leader recognized "the interaction of Soviet policy and world Communism." But the secretary complained that in discussing Asia, Nehru "glossed over" the Communist threat and overemphasized the evils of colonial rule. Yet Nehru did signal a willingness to cooperate with the United States. While he did not make an outright request for economic assistance, he steered the conversation to the subject of economic development and asserted that "in working for itself India was working for all of Asia, especially in view of the tragic course in China." Nehru, moreover, hinted that India would play an important, stabilizing role in the region and dwelt on the "close and friendly relations" that his government enjoyed with Burma, Ceylon, and Indonesia "and [the] way in which these countries sometimes solicited and accepted Indian advice." The implication seemed to be that American aid could help India to become a major force for stability in Asia. Marshall did not respond to Nehru's remarks, however, nor did he seem to understand the prime minister's references to India's neighbors. On the contrary, he interpreted Nehru's pleas as implying an effort to "counter Pakistan charges [that] India was [an] aggressive neighbor," the secretary noted.[50]

In December, Bajpai met twice with the new American ambassador in New Delhi, Loy Henderson, and elaborated upon India's regional perspective. At both meetings Bajpai traced the origins of Asian communism to nationalist fervor. In the case of China, he argued, any new Communist regime that might come to power would prove to be ardently nationalistic, and not necessarily a Soviet puppet. Bajpai also took the opportunity to restate India's desire to work with the United States in Asia. He reaffirmed that India's "logical place" in world affairs lay with the "Democratic Powers," and further noted that "following the collapse of China, India is now the chief stabilizing factor in Asia." Warning that "India will not be able to maintain her internal stability unless she is able to meet her economic problems," Bajpai specifically pointed to his country's need for United States economic assistance. Henderson—a career diplomat, former Director of the Office of Near Eastern and African Affairs, and a seasoned Cold Warrior—was not convinced. He did not reply to the aid overture, and in reporting the conversation to Washington, he discounted the argument that nationalism was an effective counterweight to communism. "In general," he observed, "I find a certain smugness in Indian Government circles regarding China."[51]

In late 1948 and early 1949, India and the United States clashed in the public arena. The immediate problem centered upon Dutch action in Indonesia where, over the previous months, the United Nations Security Council had ironed out a truce between warring Dutch and nationalist forces. In mid-December 1948, Dutch troops swooped across the cease-fire line and arrested many of the leaders of the Indonesian Republican Army. The military operation enraged Asian opinion, and Nehru took the lead in denouncing the aggression. On 31 December, the prime minister invited all states in the Indian Ocean region to come to New Delhi to confer on the crisis. In a speech the following day, he accused the Netherlands of attempting to "revive a dying imperialism and colonialism" by using "armed force to suppress a people and government." He also criticized the United States for failing to restrain its European ally, noting his "sorrow that the attitude of some powers has been one of tacit approval and acceptance of this aggression."[52]

United States officials were not pleased with their Dutch allies. Ironically, Indonesia, where the anticolonial movement was decidedly anti-Communist, had been one case where the United States had been quietly negotiating behind the scenes to bring about decolonization.[53] But American policymakers were taken aback by Nehru's confrontational stance on the issue. They suspected that the Indian leader intended to forge an anti-Western "Asiatic Association." Loy Henderson reported to Washington on Nehru's "lack of stability" and his "animosity" toward the United States.[54] For the first time leading State Department officials examined India's policies in depth. George F. Kennan, head of the Policy Planning Staff, expressed worry over a "possible polarization between the Atlantic Community and Asia." "This would not be such a serious trend for us were we only an Atlantic power," Kennan told Henderson, "but as we are [a] world power with vital interests and therefore responsibilities on all the globe we must regard recent developments in southern Asia with deep concern."[55]

Yet, predictably enough, Nehru's rhetoric proved far more radical than his actions. Even before the New Delhi Conference convened, the prime minister had met privately with Ambassador Henderson and explained that he had acted in response to colonial aggression and not in a spirit of hostility toward the United States. Emphasizing his own distaste for communism, he told Henderson that "if India should fail to take leadership in the removal of the last vestiges of European imperialism in Asia, [the] Soviet Union would do so in a manner which would strengthen Communist influence in the various movements."[56] When the New Delhi Conference met from 22 to 24 January the proceedings took on a distinctly moderate tone. The most far-reaching resolutions simply called for the reestablishment of the Indonesian Republic. Nehru did not seek sanctions against the Netherlands, made no public criticisms of the United States, and did not try to organize a formal Asian bloc. The participants also reaffirmed their commitment to the United Nations and their support for Security Council negotiations.[57]

The outcome of the New Delhi Conference pleased American policymakers. Although United States representatives had not been invited to take part in the proceedings, Ambassador Henderson had met secretly with delegates from pro-Western states such as Egypt and Thailand and encouraged them to urge caution upon the conference.[58] Henderson and Secretary of State Dean Acheson believed that these activities, along with the ambassador's personal intercession with Nehru, had weakened India's anticolonial resolve. In a cable sent to American embassies throughout Asia, Acheson observed that the New Delhi Conference had adopted a position not unfriendly to the United States "due partly [to] Department representation designed [to] encourage [that] the Conference remain within the framework [of the] UN, [and] avoid precipitous action such as [the] establishment [of an] anti-Western bloc."[59] In actuality, Nehru probably never intended to promote Asian animosity toward the West. He had, after all, repeatedly sought United States backing for his regional policies over the previous several months. More than anything else, the New Delhi Conference demonstrated that while both India and the United States desired a peaceful and stable Asia, they held widely different perspectives on how to bring that goal to fruition.

By early 1949, contradictions wracked United States policy toward Asia. The New Delhi Conference spoke moderately, but the message was clear. Nationalists throughout the region urged the United States to declare its support for the principle of self-determination. At the same time, however, beleaguered European allies beseeched Washington to come to their assistance in the struggle against communism and against the disintegration of their empires. On the homefront, a vocal China lobby in Congress, led by a cadre of conservative Republicans but carrying the support of moderates in both parties, tried to prevent the "loss" of that important nation. In February 1949, fifty senators introduced a bill to provide $1.5 billion in aid to Jiang Jieshi. The Truman administration managed to reduce the package to $50 million, but was still left in a quandary over how to proceed in Asia.[60]

Truman seemed to speak to the problem in his January 1949 inaugural address. Taking his audience by surprise, the president called for a "bold new program" of financial and technical assistance for underdeveloped areas—including Asia. In outlining the famous fourth point of his foreign policy, Truman argued that economic aid to needy nations would counter the Communist threat, help create a base for capitalist development, and signal America's support for newly independent peoples. One week later, Secretary Acheson told a news conference that India would be covered by Point Four. Unfortunately, the Point Four concept had been drawn up more with an eye toward enhancing the president's political stature than as a well-planned component of United States diplomacy. Inserted at the suggestion of White House assistants George Elsey and Clark Clifford, its primary purpose was to add drama to an otherwise uneventful ceremony. Point Four had not been discussed with senior State Department officials, and little thought had been given as to exactly where, how, or when to implement it. The administration did not submit the measure to Congress until June. As low-priority legislation, Congress did not act on it in 1949.[61]

The force of events, nonetheless, compelled the Truman administration to take a more penetrating look at Asia. In early June 1949, W. Walton Butterworth, director of Far Eastern Affairs at the State Department, observed that Mao's southward progress toward an Indochina in colonial rebellion "introduced a new element that transforms an already serious situation into an emergency."[62] A few days later Defense Secretary Louis Johnson wrote to the Executive Secretary of the National Security Council (NSC) recommending a study of United States policy in Asia. "I am becoming increasingly concerned at the course of events in Asia," Johnson noted. "The advance of communism in large areas of the world and particularly the success of communism in China seriously affect the future security of the United States," he warned.[63]

In this setting influential voices began to raise the idea of working with India to contain communism. The first such voice to be heard in 1949 advocating aid for India came from outside the administration. Writing in the aftermath of the New Delhi Conference, the popular journalist Walter Lippmann praised Jawaharlal Nehru as "the greatest figure in Asia." Observing that the Indian leader wielded prestige and influence throughout the area, Lippmann recommended that the United States consult with Nehru on China, Indochina, and other regional issues.[64] At the same time such widely read magazines as *Life*, *Time*, and *U.S. News and World Report* carried feature articles on Nehru and speculated over India's growing stature in Asia.[65] In Congress, meanwhile, a number of liberals were drawing attention to India's democratic orientation and issued the first call for economic aid. Senator Hubert Humphrey, the most prominent member of this group, summed up the attitudes of his colleagues: "Our foreign policy in Asia is so messed up right now that we simply have to look for a new start. . . . From every point of view—economically, politically, and for purposes of defense—India is the logical choice."[66]

The Indian government also recognized the possibilities. Nehru wished to assume a leading role in Asian affairs, but he knew that India's position of economic and military weakness inhibited too ambitious a policy. He had already deduced that if India was to realize its regional goals it would need the active assistance of a more powerful friend, and he did not shy away from the possibility of cooperating with the United States. As he explained in early 1949 to his foremost foreign policy adviser and confidant, V. K. Krishna Menon: "Why not align somewhat with the United States and build up our economic and military strength?"[67] Of course, the New Delhi Conference had demonstrated that aligning "somewhat" did not mean marching in lockstep with Washington. But it might mean searching for common ground, playing a constructive and moderate role in Asia, and perhaps most important, gaining economic support from the Americans.

Both Nehru and Bajpai had already approached United States officials in late 1948, along vague lines, on the subjects of economic development and assistance. The Indian government was then developing a series of economic projects that made external help desirable. Having failed to obtain United States support for any of the large, river valley schemes during Henry Grady's tenure as ambassador, India faced the prospect of increasing food deficits through the late 1950s when those projects were scheduled for completion. Therefore, in early 1949 the government implemented a new, less expensive "Grow More Food" (GMF) campaign to raise production over the short run. The GMF campaign included land reclamation projects to increase cultivated areas, technical advice for peasant farmers, and government loans for the purchase of fertilizers, improved seed, and small-scale irrigation. The goal was to raise foodgrain output by 4.8 million tons and achieve self-sufficiency by 1951.[68]

In April 1949, discussions took place at the American embassy in New Delhi on the possibility of United States assistance for the GMF program, and Indian officials made a formal request for aid. At the same time, the Indian government also floated a proposal to obtain one million tons of American wheat on concessional or easy terms—most likely as a low-interest loan. Part of the wheat would be held in storage, and part would be used to augment the government's rationing system. The anticipated effect would be an increase in the food supply, a decline in food prices, and the release of foodgrains held by speculators.[69]

A series of cordial diplomatic gestures accompanied the requests for aid. In February, Nehru indicated a desire to visit the United States sometime during the coming year to confer directly with the Truman administration and to undertake an extended, educational tour of the country. In March, the two governments agreed that the trip would be scheduled for the following fall. In April, Nehru announced the appointment of his sister, Madame Pandit, as India's new ambassador to the United States.[70] Also in April, the government of India announced more liberal policies toward foreign capital and its intention to join the British Commonwealth. Membership in the Commonwealth entitled India to certain economic advantages, protected the status of some 2.5 million to 3 million people of Indian origin living in other Commonwealth countries, and prevented Pakistan—an early Commonwealth member—from reaping undue diplomatic advantages. But more than this, it also demonstrated Nehru's marked leaning toward the Western powers.[71]

Friendly overtures and pragmatic shifts in policy combined with Cold War considerations to guarantee that India's requests for aid would be given a more thorough hearing. The British took the lead. The British had been concerned for some time over what one official described as the tendency of American policymakers to "decrease rather than increase their commitments in Asia."[72] Although the British were rapidly losing their colonies in the region—in 1948 Burma and Ceylon had joined India and Pakistan as independent states—they still hoped to maintain access to Asia's raw materials and to exercise a degree of political influence. To do so, they concluded that it would be necessary to convince their wealthy American allies to take the initiative. Specifically, the Foreign Office envisioned a Western-backed, Asian regional association. "The immediate object of such an association," a 1949 Foreign Office report explained, "would be to contain Communist and Russian expansion, while its long-term object would be the creation of friendly partnership between East and West."[73] From their extensive experience in Asia and reading of the events of the previous year, the British concluded that intraregional rivalries and national pride precluded the establishment of an anti-Communist political or military union.

United Kingdom officials believed that the West could best achieve its goals by providing help of a "technical, financial, and economic nature" to Asian nations. Because Great Britain suffered extensive financial difficulties of its own and relied itself on American foreign aid, it logically turned to the United States to fund the bulk of the program.[74]

The British attached special significance to India. Possessing Asia's largest industrial base—in terms of raw materials, railroad networks, and infant industries—India could serve as the hub of a regional economic association. Carrying enormous political stature, India might also take the lead in promoting Asian diplomatic and military cooperation with the West in later years. As the permanent under secretary's report on Asian regional cooperation put it: "India is the key to Southeast Asia."[75] The British had their differences with Nehru. Like the Americans, they had been wary of the New Delhi Conference and suspicious of India's nonaligned posture in world affairs. But when India accepted membership in the Commonwealth, and as Nehru increasingly showed himself to be a "practical statesman," British misgivings diminished. Indeed, officials in London seemed quite at ease with the notion of making their former colony, whose leaders maintained a certain cultural affinity for England, a leader in Asia. The chief problem, British policymakers came to realize, would lie in persuading the United States to undertake an expensive economic program in Asia and in making India—a nation which openly criticized American policies—a major beneficiary of such a program.[76]

Foreign Secretary Ernest Bevin first broached the subject during a meeting with Secretary of State Dean Acheson in Washington in April 1949. Acheson, a deeply conservative man whom Madame Pandit once described as "more British than the British in the heyday of the Empire," did not offer encouragement.[77] Although Acheson showed a degree of enthusiasm for some kind of economic program in the oil-rich Middle East, he proved evasive on plans for Asia. When Bevin raised the idea of helping India "reduce famine," Acheson acknowledged that nation's low-priority status by admitting that American thinking on India had only been "along vague lines." In an obvious reference to Nehru's independent policies, he also told Bevin that the United States was "doubtful about India."[78]

In May, perhaps due to British pressure, the United States gave support to World Bank plans to lend between $75 million and $100 million to India.[79] Not thoroughly satisfied with these arrangements, British officials continued to lobby for a more substantial aid program.[80] On 20 July, Bevin invited United States Ambassador Lewis Douglas to his office to confer on the subject. He called India the pivotal nation in the region and suggested that while Nehru undoubtedly opposed military association, he might be persuaded to assume leadership of a Western-backed, Asian economic conference. The foreign secretary noted that the Indian leader had shown some promise as of late, and tried to downplay the role that India might play in Asian affairs. "Nehru [was] increasingly concerned [by the] spread of Communist influence [in India]," Bevin said, "and consequently could be counted upon to pay progressively less attention to foreign affairs."[81]

The Bevin-Douglas meeting was followed by similar discussions between British and American officials in New Delhi and Washington. In New Delhi, Britain's high commissioner, Sir Archibald Nye, conferred with Loy Henderson on 12 September and stated his government's position on India's need for economic aid. Since the United Kingdom "will be unable in view of its own precarious financial position to give any substantial additional assistance," Nye observed, it would be necessary for the United States "to give greater assistance . . . in stemming the rising tide [of] Communism in Asia."[82] That same day M. E. Dening, head of the Foreign Office's Far Eastern Division, led a British delegation in discussions with State Department officials in Washington. Dening delivered an oral presentation delineating the British perspective and left behind a printed proposal for an Asian economic conference.[83]

American responses varied. W. Walton Butterworth, who headed the State Department delegation, on 12 September expressed skepticism that economic development could serve as a "general panacea" for Asia. He also had reservations regarding India's role in regional affairs. "India should recognize the character of the Communist menace," he told Dening, "not only to her but to the other states of Southeast Asia." It "should be moved to impress upon her neighbors the fact that the great enemy to their independence and political and economic welfare was not colonialism but Communism."[84]

From India, Loy Henderson took a more positive tack. He told Nye that India's significance was such that the West could not "content itself with platitudinous expressions of interest in India's welfare." "Something more concrete should be done than hitherto," he added. Several days later the ambassador cabled Washington: "We believe that the UK initiative represents [a] genuine modification, possibly of far-reaching economic and political importance, in [the] traditional attitude [of the] UK regarding this area as [a] private British economic preserve." He observed that "although not so drastic, it recalls [the] UK shift regarding Greece in 1947."[85]

The mixed reviews given to the British proposals reflected the Truman administration's uncertainty regarding both Asia and India in late 1949. Most officials were still "doubtful" about nonaligned India. But with Asian policy in a state of transition and support for India building outside of the administration, there was also an inclination to consider all options. Nehru's fast approaching visit to the United States gave American policymakers occasion to review their stance on India. Originally intended as nothing more than a goodwill gesture, the invitation to Nehru assumed greater significance as the event drew near. In mid-August, Secretary Acheson wrote to Truman regarding preparations for the visit: "Mr. Nehru is today and probably will be for some time the dominant political force in Asia."[86] Secretary of Defense Louis Johnson, who had served as President Roosevelt's personal envoy to India during the Second World War and had worked closely with Nehru in an abortive effort to negotiate home rule from the British, even called for a comprehensive study of India. "Pandit Nehru is not only a personal friend of mine," he wrote in a letter to Acheson, "but I believe he is one of the best and potentially one of the strongest friends of the United States in the whole of Asia."[87]

More cautious State Department officials did their best to contain rising expectations. Responding to Johnson's letter, Under Secretary of State James Webb warned that the United States should "not attempt to obtain too much from Nehru in the way of a public and definite commitment to align India with the United States." Webb stressed that this was to be a good will visit and that policy goals for India were still vague at best.[88] Others echoed this view. As the director of the Office of South Asian Affairs explained in one interdepartmental note: "There should be no great expectation of Nehru's visit. . . . there is little hope that Nehru will dramatically announce that he has seen the light."[89]

Despite these warnings, hopes for improved ties to India continued to grow. On 2 September, Phillip Jessup, a close adviser to Acheson and head of a special consultative committee on Asia, issued a preliminary report on the region that emphasized India's importance. The immediate goal in Asia, Jessup observed, should be "to check and roll back . . . the threat of Soviet Communism." Beyond this, Jessup also argued that the United States should seek to maintain in the area "independent governments which are progressing toward stability through a gradual process of satisfying the needs and aspirations of their peoples." This line of reasoning led him to conclude that policy should not be narrowly focused on specific crisis areas such as China or Indochina, but should attack the fundamental problems of "the region as a whole." Thus, Jessup drew attention to problems such as colonialism and economic development as well as communism. Agreeing with both British and congressional advocates of aid to India, Jessup concluded: "It is believed that India and particularly Nehru represents the most solid element with which the United States can associate itself for the promotion of its general policy in the area."[90]

It was left to Ambassador Loy Henderson to recommend aid for India. One week before Nehru's arrival, Henderson came to Washington to help prepare for the visit. In a memorandum to Under Secretary Webb, he adopted the British view almost in total. His striking presentation said:

> India with its expanding population already numbering 340,000,000 will be one of the factors determining the direction which the energies of an awakened Asia are to take. With the active friendship and effective aid of the Western world, India might possibly develop into a stalwart and worthy champion in Asia of collaboration with the West. Without such friendship and aid it might degenerate into a vast political and economic swamp, the unclean exhalations of which would pollute the international atmosphere for an indefinite period of time. It might without such friendship and aid, be transformed into a totalitarian state which would cooperate with similar states against the free West.

Accordingly, Henderson proposed a five-year, $500 million economic aid program for India. The money was to be made available in the form of interest-free loans and used to help India increase food production. Henderson also endorsed India's request for one million tons of wheat.[91]

Although Henderson's recommendations did not win immediate approval, administration officials decided that they would take advantage of Nehru's visit to explore the India option. Originally, only one high-level Indo-American meeting had been planned. But on 10 October, just one day before Nehru's arrival, Acheson and Assistant Secretary of State for Near Eastern and African Affairs George McGhee agreed that additional opportunities should be provided for "a frank and sincere exchange of views" with Nehru. Issues to be covered included China, colonialism, and Asian regional cooperation. The forums for discussion would be dinner at Acheson's home on 12 October and a meeting the following morning with Kennan, Jessup, and McGhee.[92] Certainly these discussions, along with Nehru's three weeks of travel, would give ample opportunity for American officials to appraise Nehru.

Nehru arrived in Washington on 11 October. Coming after weeks of speculation and rising expectations, the Nehru visit proved to be a great disappointment for nearly all concerned. The prime minister's three-week, whirlwind tour of the United States was, in and of itself, a fiasco. The itinerary—which included receptions with the mayors of New York and Chicago, a stopover in California, a visit to the Tennessee Valley Authority, a quick run to Hyde Park to meet Eleanor Roosevelt, and the inevitable pilgrimage to Niagara Falls—was probably more exhausting than educational. In addition, awkward incidences and gaffes plagued the tour. The occasional flaunting of American wealth particularly offended a status-conscious Nehru. At one luncheon with businessmen in New York, Nehru took particular offense as the man seated next to him pointed around the table and boasted that the combined party represented a net worth of over $20 billion.[93] To Americans, on the other hand, Nehru seemed formal and aloof. Henderson reported that American businessmen had perceived the Indian leader to be "wooley and evasive" on questions relating to trade and investment.[94] Acheson complained that Nehru would not relax, and that he conversed "as Queen Victoria said of Gladstone, as though I were a public meeting."[95]

The private discussions held between Indian and American officials proved especially disappointing. In accordance with the prearranged schedule, Nehru met first with Acheson at the secretary's home on the evening of 12 October. Although the conversation lasted 2.5 hours, the two found very little room for agreement. Whereas Nehru described the upheaval in China as an "agrarian revolution" and hinted that India would soon grant diplomatic recognition to the Communist government, Acheson denounced the evils of "Communist control" and counseled that recognition should be postponed. When the prime minister predicted that the French-backed "Bao-Dai experiment" in Indochina was "doomed to failure," Acheson responded with praise for French Premier Robert Schumann. And while Nehru emotionally sketched the chronology of events in Kashmir, Acheson listened politely, but noted in his memorandum of the conversation that "at this point either due to the lateness of the hour or the complexity of the subject, I found myself becoming confused and suggested that we adjourn the discussion."[96]

The next day's meetings did not prove any more fruitful. Nehru's parley with State Department officers lasted less than one hour. While George Kennan outlined the fundamentals of United States foreign policy and America's "responsibilities as a major power," the Indians present made almost no contribution.[97] Later in the afternoon Nehru met briefly with President Truman, and the conversation was confined mainly to generalities. When Nehru tried to impress upon the president the importance of the anticolonial cause in Asia, Truman responded with references to what he believed to be the relevant lessons from American history. "We had found that the solution of the colonial problem was not the end," Truman lectured. "It had taken a great civil war to teach us that we must live peacefully together and it had taken involvement in two world wars to bring home to us that we could not be independent of peoples beyond our shores." The parallels to Kashmir and India's neutrality were, no doubt, meant to impress Nehru.[98]

Truman, Acheson, and Nehru hardly touched upon the subjects of economic development and aid. Although the Indian leader specifically mentioned India's request for one million tons of wheat, he did not elaborate on India's many economic needs. In his memoirs, India's finance minister C. D. Deshmukh, who accompanied Nehru to Washington, has noted that Nehru ignored his suggestions for more extended talks with American leaders on this question. Proudly nationalistic, the prime minister apparently thought it beneath India's dignity to appear to be too eager a supplicant. Truman and Acheson did not raise the issue, most likely because they had yet to determine if India warranted American aid. Each told Nehru that the United States would "like to be of assistance" with regard to the request for wheat, but extended no guarantees.[99]

In the last analysis, both sides came away from the episode with a sense of frustration. "I was convinced that Nehru and I were not destined to have a pleasant personal relationship," Acheson later recalled. "He was so important to India and India's survival so important to all of us, that if he did not exist—as Voltaire said of God—he would have to be invented. Nevertheless, he was one of the most difficult men with whom I have ever had to deal."[100] For Nehru, who truly desired closer relations with the United States, the encounter had been equally unsettling. The Americans "had gone all out to welcome me and I am grateful to them for it and expressed myself so," he explained in a letter to his chief ministers shortly after returning to India. "But they expected more than gratitude and goodwill and that more I could not supply them."[101]

Having met Nehru and realized the depth of his independence, American officials hastily rejected the notion of providing India with economic assistance. Indeed, there does not appear to have been any significant administration discussion or debate on the matter. In early November, barely a week after Nehru's departure, Acheson cabled Henderson to inform him that the State Department had decided against the ambassador's proposed, five-year, $500 million program. Between its own resources and those of the World Bank, Acheson told him, India could adequately carry out its economic plans.[102]

The request for wheat was more difficult to resolve. In late 1949, an oversupply of wheat glutted the international market and commodity prices plummeted. The United States government might have eased the impact on American farmers by making some of the troublesome surplus available to India. American policymakers, however, hoped to win strategic advantages from the transfer of wheat as well. They did not demand a shift in India's foreign policy, but they proposed to barter the grain for Indian raw materials, especially manganese. In late 1948, the Soviet Union, the world's largest source of manganese, had placed a limit on exports of this strategic mineral. Within one year India reached a point where it supplied the West with 20 percent of its manganese imports.[103] The benefits of an Indo-American barter arrangement were clearly greater for the United States than for India. In exchange for a surplus commodity, the United States would receive materials upon which India depended for real, export earnings.[104] Whether or not the deal can be considered a form of aid is questionable.

United States officials first proposed the exchange to Finance Minister Deshmukh on 13 October. Despite misgivings, the Indian government seriously considered the barter arrangement. It became impractical only after India, in coordination with Great Britain and other Commonwealth countries, devalued its currency in early November. On 16 November, Deshmukh informed the State Department that due to India's adverse balance of payments position, made more difficult by devaluation, his country could ill-afford to forego dollar earnings from the normal export of manganese. American officials tried to keep the negotiations alive, but their Indian counterparts had little room in which to maneuver. There was thus no direct United States assistance for India in 1949.[105]

United States policy toward India, and Asia as a whole, crystallized in December 1949. At the end of the month, after much deliberation, the National Security Council staff completed a draft paper, "The Position of the United States with Respect to Asia" (NSC 48). Downplaying the regional sources of instability, NSC 48 traced the roots of Asian instability to the spread of communism in the area and assumed that local Communist movements in the region were little more than an extension of a broader, global threat. Noting Soviet ties to Communist groups in China, North Korea, and Southeast Asia, the NSC proclaimed: "The U.S.S.R. is now an Asiatic power of the first magnitude with expanding influence and interests throughout continental Asia and the Pacific."[106]

Operating from global assumptions, it is hardly surprising that NSC 48 categorically dismissed the possibility of making support for India the keystone for American policy. India, the report noted, refused "to align itself with any power bloc," seemed eager "to form and lead a regional bloc or third force," and did not adequately appreciate the Communist menace. The NSC staff concluded that "it would be unwise for us to regard South Asia, more particularly India, as the bulwark against the extension of Communist control in Asia." NSC 48 acknowledged that economic assistance might help strengthen India as a non-Communist state, but it maintained that the "external financial aid required is of such a limited character that it can be adequately provided by the International Bank and the Export-Import Bank."[107] Thus, aid to India in the near future would be limited to loan assistance rather than grants such as had been extended to European nations under the Marshall Plan. Once more, while the World Bank had already indicated a willingness to provide India with small-scale loans, the Export-Import Bank had made no such plans.

Although the Truman administration determined not to extend significant aid to India, it decided that the time had come to intervene more forcefully in Asia. NSC 48 called for a series of military measures to contain the spread of communism. The document established that American bases offshore of mainland Asia in Japan, the Ryukyus, and the Philippines would constitute the "first line of defense." These crucial facilities were to be defended directly by United States forces. Countries facing "the most immediate threat from Communist aggression, internal or external," would constitute the second line of defense and should be provided with United States military assistance and modest levels of economic aid.[108]

Not long after the completion of NSC 48 American policymakers decided exactly where to concentrate their military aid. On 18 January 1950, the People's Republic of China recognized Ho Chi Minh as the legitimate leader of Vietnam. The Soviet Union followed suit on 30 January. For United States officials, these developments confirmed suspicions that the Kremlin planned to establish a Communist axis in Southeast Asia. The Truman administration responded by granting recognition to the French-backed governments of Vietnam, Laos, and Cambodia. Then, on 9 March 1950, Truman received a memorandum signed by both Acheson and Johnson recommending that $15 million in emergency military supplies be rushed to French Indochina.[109] A few weeks later the JCS completed their own study of Asia and advised that military assistance be provided to Thailand, Indonesia, the Philippines, and Burma, as well as Indochina. Summing up the dominant attitude in Washington, the Joint Chiefs of Staff posited that Southeast Asia had become the "vital segment in the line of containment of communism stretching from Japan southward and around the Indian peninsula."[110] The United States would attempt to bring stability to mainland Asia by forcefully confronting communism in the continent's southeast corner.

United States reluctance to advance economic aid to India from 1947 to early 1950 stemmed from many factors. First, American policymakers placed far greater emphasis on Western Europe than they did on India or the rest of Asia. While billions of aid dollars made their way to strategically and economically important European nations, India was largely overlooked. Second, Truman administration officials demonstrated little understanding of, or respect for, India's nonaligned foreign policy or its mixed economy. Sometimes they confused nationalism with communism; and at other times they simply viewed nationalism as endangering United States interests. Unlike Indian leaders, they clearly did not see nationalism as a reliable bulwark against communism. Even personal relations between leading American officials and Prime Minister Nehru generated antagonism, partly due to Nehru's arrogant and sometimes overbearing manner, but mostly because he refused to assume the role of a compliant Third World leader. Third, guided by a global perspective, the Truman administration never came to terms with the regional origins of Asia's unrest. Nehru's advocacy of anticolonialism and economic development seemed naive to American policymakers, who were more deeply alarmed by their reading of Soviet intentions.

When American officials concluded that India counted for little in terms of United States foreign policy, they denied that nation's requests for economic aid. The irony of all of this is that a practical case was made for assisting India at the time. By providing assistance, the United States would have signaled a willingness to help an important, Third World country overcome a part of its colonial legacy—economic underdevelopment. Extending aid in spite of India's independent policies would also have demonstrated American tolerance for the nationalistic perspective in India and throughout a newly awakened Asia. Finally, by making economic support for India, rather than military aid to Southeast Asia, a focal point for American policy in Asia, the United States might have averted what proved to be a tragic course after 1950.

British Foreign Office diplomats, far more familiar with the Asian context than American policymakers, recognized the useful role that Jawaharlal Nehru and India might play in bringing peace and stability to the area. Carrying enormous prestige as an Asian critic of colonialism, the Indian leader nonetheless advocated gradual change and opposed communism. And while he personally deplored revolutionary violence, Nehru nonetheless understood the regional and local roots of insurgency movements. Far better than American officials, he understood the futility of responding with counterviolence. Most important, while he clung tenaciously to a nonaligned position, Nehru repeatedly conveyed his desire to cooperate with the West. In short, economic aid to India might not have guaranteed a non-Communist Asia, but it may have laid the foundation for a more peaceful, stable Asia.

Three

War and Aid, 1950–1951

Although NSC 48 and the policy decisions of early 1950 de-emphasized India's strategic significance, American policymakers did not neglect the South Asian nation. Due to its nonaligned policy and the immediate need to bolster countries plagued by insurgency movements such as in Indochina, Thailand, and the Philippines, NSC 48 counseled against making India "the sole bulwark" against communism in Asia. Nonetheless, pointing to its size, its strategic location, its vast resources, and its non-Communist orientation, the National Security Council noted that India, along with the other nations of South Asia, might still contribute to the containment of communism in the region. For the time being, economic assistance was to be restricted to World Bank loans. But NSC 48 did advise that the United States should "exploit every opportunity to increase the present Western orientation of South Asia and to assist, within our capabilities, its non-Communist governments in their efforts to meet the minimum needs of their people."[1]

In early 1950, the National Security Council completed work on one of the most significant policy papers of the early post–World War II era, NSC 68, "United States Objectives and Programs for National Security." NSC 68 both recommended a course for American global policy and set the context for future relations with South Asia. Written in the aftermath of the Communist victory in China and the Soviet Union's successful detonation of an atomic weapon in late 1949, NSC 68 proposed a most ambitious containment strategy. It called for a massive increase in ground, air, and naval forces and the atomic capabilities of the United States. NSC 68 also urged the continuation and expansion of programs—such as foreign aid—that would contribute toward the development of "a healthy international community." The document further counseled that a "consensus" would have to be molded in the public arena to support the unprecedented, peacetime buildup of military power.[2]

One overriding problem remained: how to "sell" the expensive under taking to American taxpayers? An answer to this question was soon at hand.[3] On 25 June 1950, North Korean forces dashed across the thirty-eighth parallel, the boundary line in Korea drawn after World War II by the

United States and the Soviet Union. Hours later the United Nations passed a resolution calling for a cessation of North Korean aggression and the withdrawal of North Korean troops from South Korean territory. In the absence of the Soviet Union, which was protesting the organization's refusal to seat the People's Republic of China, the United Nations proved an effective vehicle for confronting the Korean crisis. A few days later President Truman ordered American soldiers into combat. Despite the lack of evidence, no one in the decision-making establishment doubted that the Soviet Union had masterminded the attack. The relationship between Russia and North Korea, one State Department official quipped, was "the same as between Walt Disney and Donald Duck."[4]

Korea instantly became a testing ground for American policymakers—the place where they sought to demonstrate their determination to resist communism in Asia. In the Oval Office, Harry Truman pointed to Korea on the globe and remarked: "This is the Greece of the Far East. If we are tough enough now there won't be any next step."[5] The North Korean attack also provided United States officials with an opportunity to begin acting upon the directives set forth in NSC 68. Immediately following the North Korean attack the president asked Congress for a special $16.8 billion defense appropriation, started negotiations for West German rearmament, and increased foreign military assistance. In Asia, the United States expanded its program of support for French Indochina and the Philippines and intervened again in the Chinese civil war by placing the seventh fleet in the Formosan Straits.[6]

In this setting, the United States first extended economic aid to India. In the summer of 1950, shortly after the outbreak of the Korean War, Truman approved plans to help finance Indian efforts to increase food production. Then, in the spring of 1951, after excruciating delay, the United States made an emergency loan of two million tons of wheat to India to help alleviate famine conditions. These initiatives marked the beginning of the Indo-American aid relationship. Yet taken in response to a major Cold War crisis, they did not represent a fundamental shift in America's approach to India. The Truman administration continued to view India from a global rather than a regional perspective, and economic aid became inextricably linked to broader Cold War aims. It was a strategy that was bound to create new difficulties in relations with India.

In the months immediately preceding the outbreak of war in Korea, Nehru's nonaligned policy increasingly took on a shrill and indignant tone. Perhaps it had been the disappointing trip to Washington in the previous fall. Or it may have been the emergence of a new China that seemed to threaten India's radical credentials and its claim to regional influence. But no matter what the cause, Nehru's rhetoric took on a sharper anti-Western edge. His nonaligned posture, originally grounded in practical and historical considerations, assumed a stronger moral dimension. Indeed, Nehru's pronouncements probably equaled those of some staunch American Cold Warriors in terms of their self-righteous resonance. This is not to say that the Indian leader's words no longer provided insight into world affairs. They usually did. Nehru simply failed to communicate his perspective in a manner that was likely to persuade skeptics and nonbelievers.

When Nehru journeyed to Colombo, Ceylon, in January 1950, for a conference of Commonwealth prime ministers, he presented a stinging, public critique of United States policies toward Asia. The Colombo Conference had been called by the British to set into motion their long-delayed plans for a regional economic program. Although Whitehall urged American participation, United States representatives were conspicuous in their absence. Nehru took advantage of the meeting to castigate American leaders for their preoccupation with communism in Asia, their confrontational stance toward China, and their support for French colonialism in Indochina. He drove home his fundamental point concerning the region: "Any policy which was to have a reasonable chance for success," he lectured, "would necessarily have to encourage and satisfy the nationalist urge." Taking note of increased militarization in Asia, Nehru argued that Soviet influence could most effectively be met by Western economic aid, offered "without strings."[7]

At the same time, Nehru also grew increasingly critical of United States policy toward Kashmir. In actuality, the United States continued to adhere to a neutral position on the issue. Distrustful of United States intentions in Asia, Nehru often assumed the worst with regard to Kashmir. When the United States and England supported United Nations efforts to force arbitration of the dispute in late 1949 and early 1950, Nehru fumed. "I am sick and tired of the attitude that the British and American Governments have been taking on this matter," he confided to India's representative at the United Nations, B. N. Rau.[8] Nehru's anger deepened in May 1950, when Pakistani Prime Minister Liaquat Ali Khan visited the United States. Prior to

Liaquat's visit, the Truman administration had shown even less interest in Pakistan than in India. The general American consensus was that, of the two South Asian nations, India was by far the greater prize. Yet to soothe Pakistani anxieties over the Nehru visit, the State Department had issued a formal invitation to Liaquat in late 1949.[9] Liaquat's visit did not produce any major agreements between the United States and Pakistan, but everywhere he traveled the prime minister was accorded the same red carpet treatment given to Nehru. "I must say that the Americans are either very naive or singularly lacking in intelligence," the prime minister wrote sardonically to Madame Pandit. "They go through the identical routine whether it is Nehru, or the Shah of Iran, or Liaquat Ali. . . . All this lessens the value of their fervent protestations and the superlatives they use. . . . Having been trained in a school of more restrained language and action, I am afraid I do not appreciate this kind of thing."[10]

United States officials did not take kindly to Indian criticisms and often adopted an equally belligerent stance toward New Delhi. Reporting from India in early 1950, Ambassador Henderson sketched India's dissatisfaction with American policies. "Indian leaders, particularly Nehru," he complained, "have been cajoled and treated as spoiled children so long by members of the Commonwealth that they have tendencies to become outraged when they encounter opposition on the part of western countries to any of their cherished schemes."[11] In April, Henderson cabled Washington again, observing that Kashmir and economic aid seemed to be the two issues that most rankled Indians. Secretary Acheson dismissed Indian apprehensions over Kashmir as a "possible tactic designed [to] influence [the] US to cease following a strictly impartial line." Regarding aid, he simply informed Henderson: "As in [the] past, so in the future, economic assistance to India and other countries can only be forthcoming when there is coincident Indian receptivity and our own ability, and constructive purpose to be served."[12]

Given American foreign policy goals, little probability existed in early 1950 of India's becoming a major aid recipient. Congress raised a small measure of hope when it took up Truman's Point Four proposals. But as passed in May 1950, the president's "bold new program" to assist underdeveloped economies provided a mere $35 million for the entire Third World. India's allocation came to only $4.5 million. The funds were appropriated primarily to send a handful of American agricultural experts to India to serve as advisers to the Indian government's Grow More Food program. The meager budget precluded any United States help for the purchase of badly needed equipment and machinery.[13]

Despite the general lack of concern, one leading official of the Truman administration did take a deep and abiding interest in the Indian subcontinent—Assistant Secretary of State for Near Eastern, South Asian, and African Affairs George McGhee. A Rhodes scholar with a Ph.D. from Oxford University, the thirty-nine-year-old McGhee had already acquired a reputation at the State Department as being a "brilliant young man." Questioning the relative lack of emphasis placed upon South Asia and the Near East, this ambitious career officer put his staff to work in early 1950 formulating a more vigorous policy for the region. After several months of deliberation, McGhee forwarded the main recommendations to Secretary Acheson in a 7 June memorandum, "Economic Aid to South Asia and the Near East."[14]

McGhee crafted his pre–Korean War proposal wisely. He did not base his argument for aid upon the regional perspective advanced by Nehru and to some extent by the British. Instead, he set forth the view that providing economic assistance to South Asia would be an integral part of the global effort to contain communism. The assistant secretary drew attention to the fact that India, along with Pakistan and Afghanistan, were the only countries bordering the Soviet Union and its satellites that did not have American aid programs. "Experience has shown," he wrote, "that countries in such close proximity to the USSR orbit need the stiffening and strengthening provided by United States economic assistance." "Economic aid," he continued, "is necessary if we are to assure [the] increased stability of the non-Communist governments of this region and [the] maintenance of and increase in their western orientation." Asserting that Point Four funds were "not adequate to make an impact on the needs of the area," McGhee concluded, "I believe we should begin to plan a program to enable the countries of South Asia—India, Pakistan, Ceylon, Afghanistan—beginning in FY [fiscal year] 1952, to carry out developmental projects which would provide the basis for long-term progress in the economic sphere, particularly in agriculture." McGhee's Office of Near Eastern Affairs estimated, on the basis of rough figures, that a maximum of $200 million annually would be required to carry out the program.[15]

McGhee's proposal was surprisingly well received in the State Department. Although Acheson did not immediately endorse aid to South Asia, Under Secretary of State James Webb and the Policy Planning staff agreed that the possibility should be explored by an interdepartmental working group. A policy initiative like McGhee's, however, could not come to fruition solely through the efforts of one bright and energetic bureaucrat. It had to appeal to the thinking of higher officials, and its aims had to conform to the general goals of United States foreign policy, which McGhee's proposal did. Perhaps most of all, it had to be well timed, and McGhee's timing was absolutely uncanny. The outbreak of the Korean War just two weeks later lent an almost irresistible persuasion to McGhee's arguments.

The Korean War initially placed new obstacles in the path of Indo-American cooperation. On 25 June, India's B. N. Rau, having had no time to consult with his government, voted for the Security Council resolution condemning North Korean aggression. While Delhi belatedly approved of Rau's action, it instructed him to avoid any further commitments without prior consultation. Thus, on 27 June, India abstained from voting on a second United Nations resolution that directed member states to furnish assistance to South Korea. At this point, Ambassador Henderson paid a personal call on Nehru and beseeched the prime minister to reconsider India's position. Nehru was also lobbied by Indian officials, such as his conservative deputy prime minister, Sardar Patel, who sympathized with American goals in Korea. After two cabinet meetings, the Indian government issued a statement supporting the second United Nations resolution.[16]

While Nehru accepted the two resolutions with less than total enthusiasm, he nonetheless believed that India had pursued the proper course. "I think that logically and practically there was no other course open to us," he wrote to his chief ministers.[17] Yet Nehru never accepted the American thesis that North Korean aggression signaled the opening round of a new Soviet offensive. In fact, he thought that the Truman administration had responded in hysterical fashion. Most of all, the Indian leader feared that this latest Cold War crisis would encourage the United States to redouble its militaristic efforts in Asia and stiffen its support for the relics of colonial rule. "They may win a war," Nehru wrote Rau, "but how can they possibly deal with any part of Asia afterwards."[18]

Nehru subsequently launched an ill-fated attempt to defuse the crisis. On 11 July he sent identical letters to Marshall Joseph Stalin, Prime Minister Clement Atlee, and President Truman, proposing to localize the conflict and bring a restoration of peace to Asia. The plan included provisions for seating the People's Republic of China in the United Nations, the return of the Soviet Union to the Security Council, and a concerted effort by those powers and the United States to seek a negotiated solution to the Korean issue. While the proposal won a sympathetic hearing from the Russians and the Chinese, Washington treated it with outright contempt. Acheson reasoned that Communist China's admission to the United Nations would "divide and break up" that body, and in a closed session of the Senate Committee on Foreign Relations he derisively referred to Nehru's diplomacy as "a terrible headache."[19] In his formal reply to Nehru, the secretary of state simply asserted: "We do not believe that the termination of the aggression from northern Korea can be made contingent in any way upon the determination of other questions currently before the United Nations."[20]

Irritations notwithstanding, when American policymakers took stock of India's response to aggression in Korea, they were not entirely dissatisfied. India's support for the two United Nations resolutions and Nehru's condemnation of North Korea impressed them. Even Acheson reported to Truman in July 1950 that Nehru's views seemed to be developing "in the right direction." No one was more pleased with India's performance than George McGhee. In early July, the Office of Near Eastern Affairs (NEA) submitted a review of United States policy toward South Asia that observed: "The countries of South Asia now realized more clearly the intentions of Communist-dominated governments; they recognize that the Korean incident may expand into another world conflict."[21]

In this setting, McGhee's proposals for economic aid to South Asia won White House approval. On 2 August Under Secretary Webb sent McGhee's recommendations to Acheson with an enthusiastic endorsement. Acheson, in turn, took them to the president on 28 August. As presented to Truman, the plan called for economic assistance of approximately $300 million a year, over a five-year period, for the nations of South Asia, the Arab states, and Iran. A two-page memorandum, written by McGhee, summarized the case for aid in the following terms: "The viability of a non-Communist Asia hinges upon the chance of maintaining, in this area, free institutions, stable governments, and the right orientation of men's minds. These cannot be maintained—indeed they are gravely threatened now—if these countries in question are unable to grapple effectively with hunger and a general deterioration of economic conditions."[22]

Truman, it appears, did not ponder the matter deeply. At Acheson's urging, he approved the broad outline of the program, but the two men agreed that it would be impossible to prepare a proposal for presentation to Congress during the upcoming year. Instead, they decided to include a request for South Asia and the Near East in the 1951 Mutual Security

Program.[23] The Department of State consequently abandoned efforts to secure a major economic aid program for the region in 1950. In cooperation with the Bureau of Public Affairs, George McGhee went to work drafting plans for an informational policy to stimulate congressional and public interest for the 1951 initiative and began meeting with legislative leaders on the matter.[24]

The economic program for South Asia would not be formally introduced to Congress until June 1951. During the ensuing months, however, United States interest in the region continued to grow. As the Truman administration increasingly focused upon the need to strengthen the military capabilities of the United States and its allies after the outbreak of war in Korea, McGhee began to consider the prospects for defense collaboration in South Asia. He specifically thought in terms of bringing nonaligned India into the Western fold, along with its regional rival, Pakistan. Together, these two archenemies—one of whom was an outspoken critic of the Cold War—would help defend their part of the world from Soviet aggression.

As early as July 1950, McGhee recommended that nongrant, military aid be made available to India and Pakistan.[25] Then, in September, the assistant secretary traveled to London and raised the possibility of South Asian military cooperation with officials of the British Foreign Office. Any revision of United States strategic policy in the region required the approval of the British, who heretofore had assumed primary responsibility for the security of the subcontinent. In a 18 September meeting, McGhee informed his British counterparts that he had conceived that India and Pakistan "might collaborate on some territorial guarantee of the non-Communist countries of South and Southeast Asia." As the conversation unfolded, both sides agreed that India could be most useful as a protector of Nepal and Burma and as a stabilizing force in general for Southeast Asia. Pakistan's geographic location and Islamic culture made it a potential key player in the Persian Gulf area. The British stressed, and McGhee acknowledged, that considerable problems stood in the way of such a plan. Kashmir and the poor state of Indo-Pakistani relations prevented immediate military collaboration, and Nehru's nonalignment further complicated the question. But McGhee hoped that as Communist intentions became more transparent, these difficulties would diminish and India and Pakistan would join with the West in opposing a common enemy.[26]

Shortly after McGhee's return from London another policy paper, this time prepared in the Office of South Asian Affairs (SOA), elaborated upon American plans for the subcontinent. The report dismissed the immediate prospect for a regional defense association. Nonetheless, in keeping with McGhee's views, SOA speculated that if the Cold War continued over the next five years, "the international posture of South Asia offers the possibility of bringing about a gradual strengthening of the association between the region and the Western democracies." Among other objectives, the report stated the desirability of developing "an attitude in South Asia which would assist the United States and its allies to obtain the facilities required in time of peace or in the event of war, and which would prevent the USSR from obtaining military support from these nations."[27]

How could the United States go about developing such an attitude? SOA suggested working toward the settlement of regional disputes, developing closer consultations with South Asian nations on world affairs, and supporting non-Communist, prodemocratic elements in the region. Yet one additional way remained to achieve United States aims. The United States should endeavor "as a matter of urgency," SOA noted, "to obtain congressional authorization and appropriations for a program of economic grant aid to the countries of the region, particularly India and Pakistan." Special attention should be given, the report continued, "to projects which have a popular appeal in the region and which promise early and obvious results."[28] The economic aid program for India that was already in the planning stages would be integrally related to long-term plans for military cooperation in South Asia.

So long as the United States enjoyed success in Korea, American policymakers could afford to take a patient approach to India and South Asia. By early fall 1950 the war effort was, indeed, going well. Initially pushed to the Korean peninsula's southern extremity during the summer, American fortunes reversed following General Douglas MacArthur's brilliant, amphibious assault at Inchon on 15 September. The Truman administration sensed victory as United States troops advanced to Seoul, and then north toward the thirty-eighth parallel. On 27 September, the president ordered MacArthur to proceed above the parallel, and within a few weeks the general's army stormed toward the Yalu River.

As the Korean War progressed, India grew colder toward the American effort, especially United States plans to unite the two Koreas by force. One week after the Inchon landing, Nehru's ambassador in Beijing (Peking) relayed the first of two warnings issued by Chinese Foreign Minister Zhou Enlai (Chou En-lai) stating that "if America extends her aggression China will have to resist."[29] The meaning could not be misunderstood: do not advance above the thirty-eighth parallel toward China's border. Aware that China was using India as its intermediary with the West, Nehru immediately passed the ominous message to British and American officials. Still, the American advance continued. On 26 October, the Chinese struck back by sending "volunteers" into North Korea. This action may have constituted another Chinese warning, for after a brief period of intense combat the Chinese retreated.

Fearing that a war of Asian origin might escalate into a great power conflict, Nehru now publicly suggested that military methods need not be pursued "to the utmost and last" in Korea. The United States ignored his counsel, and on 3 November a confident United States government steered the "Uniting for Peace" resolution through the United Nations General Assembly. Introduced in anticipation of the return of the veto-wielding Soviets to the Security Council, the resolution gave the General Assembly the right to recommend collective security measures, including the use of force, in Korea. An embittered Nehru resolved to stand with Argentina in abstaining from the "Uniting for Peace" resolution. The measure, he complained, "seemed like converting the U.N. into a larger edition of the Atlantic Pact."[30]

Nehru's actions perplexed American policymakers. Unable to determine a rational basis for Nehru's policies, they turned to the mysterious realm of the psyche for an explanation. In November 1950, NEA officials completed work on a paper, "Nehru's Attitude toward the United States," that won effusive praise from Secretary Acheson, and that provides a great deal of insight into American thinking on Nehru.

This unusual document began by describing Nehru as a "hypersensitive egoist . . . quick to take offense at our slights, real or imagined, and reluctant to appear subject to our influence." Acknowledging that India's colonial past and strong nationalist sentiments partially explained Nehru's attitudes, NEA placed far greater emphasis on two peculiar aspects of the Indian leader's personality. First, Nehru was a "frustrated revolutionary" whose plans for socialist transformation had been thwarted by Gandhi's denunciation of violence and by Great Britain's decision to withdraw "graciously and gracefully" from the subcontinent. Consequently, Nehru was "full of spleen," the report asserted, and naturally prone to denouncing American wealth and power. Second, a Brahmin by birth and an English gentleman by training, Nehru was described as "an aristocrat in circumstances which required that he profess democracy." His approach to the

Indian masses was "Brahmanic." "He is their leader," the report continued, "their teacher, their guide, their critic; they look to him for guidance, not he to them." From this, State Department officials concluded that Nehru was "fundamentally unable to have full confidence in a government based on the franchise of self-reliant people," and therefore was disinclined to cooperate with the more truly democratic United States.[31]

While there is no denying that Jawaharlal Nehru could be arrogant and that his diplomatic style was often abrasive, NEA's analysis suffered from ethnocentrism and bias. Based on a misreading of Indian history and distorted views of India's political culture, the report, more than anything else, reflected the power of wartime emotion in Washington and the administration's own self-righteous attitude toward the trying Korean conflict. Commenting upon the American approach to matters in the Far East at the time, the British High Commissioner in Washington, Oliver Franks, mockingly observed that "there are too many Puritan avenging angels about, who feel at last a straight moral issue of real principle has been raised and there is a clear call to get on with punishing the guilty. To people in such a mood the longer processes of history and the unfailing regularity with which all diplomatic checkers one day come home to roost, appear tiresome irrelevancies in the light of divine call."[32]

Interestingly, the British Foreign Office, which maintained somewhat similar policies to those of India on issues relating to China recognition and the broadening of the Korean War, interceded to soothe Indo-American relations. When a group of British and American officials met in Washington on 22 July to discuss Far Eastern affairs, an incredulous Dean Rusk asked if Nehru really believed that the United States had imperialistic ambitions in Asia. M. E. Dening of the Foreign Office replied in the manner of a gracious tutor. He explained that while India did not suspect that America entertained territorial ambitions, Nehru and others did fear that America's Cold War policies might lead to a war that could easily involve India. Regarding China recognition, the British officials pointed to India's own geographic proximity to China and its vulnerability to attack as a motivating force for seeking normal relations.[33]

Perhaps influenced by British views, the Truman administration did not give up on Nehru. "I should like to emphasize that Nehru's present attitude toward the United States presents a challenge, not an excuse for defeatism," McGhee explained to Acheson in a cover memorandum accompanying NEA's character study. "India is too important to us and Nehru too important to India for us," he emphasized, "to take the easy road of concluding that we cannot work with him." Thus, McGhee counseled that the administration should "redouble" its efforts to find ways and means of strengthening the ties of mutual interest between the United States and India.[34] To this end, Secretary Acheson instructed lower-level officials to refrain from making public remarks that might be considered to be critical of Nehru or India. McGhee and Acheson took special precautions to limit the circulation of materials relating to India and to safeguard against departmental leaks.[35] George McGhee also arranged for high-ranking officials to meet regularly with the Indian ambassador, Madame Pandit, so that she might feel she was, in McGhee's words, being kept "au courant" on United States policy and world affairs.[36]

Most important, plans for providing India with economic assistance went forward. After consultation with McGhee, Senator Claude Pepper and Representative Harold Cooley visited India and discussed with Nehru the prospects for aid in fiscal year 1952. The prime minister seemed more intent on airing his views on Korea than discussing aid, but several weeks later Madame Pandit assured McGhee that, as had been the case for over two years, India stood ready to accept assistance "as long as there were not political strings attached."[37]

In New Delhi, Loy Henderson tried to smooth over differences with Nehru. On 3 November the American ambassador shared dinner with the prime minister and happily reported afterward that Nehru reacted by being "more frank and friendly than he had been in any of our previous conversations." Wrote Henderson, "I concentrated on endeavoring to disarm him; to extirpate so far as I could during the course of one evening some of the deep-rooted prejudices against [the] US and [the] American people which for so many years have been eating at him."[38] When China occupied Tibet in late October and early November 1950, Henderson and others hoped that India, which shared a common border with Tibet, might modify its policy toward the People's Republic. But when Nehru continued to emphasize the importance of friendly ties with China, United States officials refrained from criticism.[39] It had already been determined that the winning of India would be a long-term process.

The changing course of the Korean War soon brought about a shift in policy toward India. On 26 November China made good on its threats, conveyed to the West through Nehru, and sent thousands of troops across the Yalu River into North Korea. American forces, assured only days earlier by MacArthur that they would be home by Christmas, reeled back across the thirty-eighth parallel. President Truman's immediate response was restrained. He countermanded MacArthur's order to bomb Chinese troops and supplies in Manchuria. At a news conference on 30 November, however, Truman declared that the United States would use all the power it possessed to contain the Chinese and explicitly did not rule out using atomic bombs. In December and January, Truman requested emergency powers to speed war mobilization, and revised his defense budget upward from $13.5 billion to $50 billion. As part of the mobilization, he doubled the number of air groups to ninety-five and increased army personnel by 50 percent.[40] In short, by late 1950 and early 1951, the administration was well on its way to having implemented the recommendations set forth in NSC 68.

In this context, the National Security Council began work on its first study of United States policy toward the subcontinent, "The Position of the United States with Respect to South Asia." The draft statement, numbered NSC 98/1, was completed in early January 1951 and fully reflected the wartime mood. "The loss of China, the immediate threat to Indochina and the balance of Southeast Asia, the invasion of Tibet, and reverses in Korea," the authors declared in the introduction of the paper, "have greatly increased the significance to the United States of the political, strategic, and resource potential of the countries of South Asia."[41]

NSC 98/1 reiterated all of the arguments previously advanced by George McGhee and NEA on the need for improved relations with the nations of the region. In light of the Korean fiasco, it placed particular significance on the military potential of the area—especially that of India and Pakistan. India's "existing and potential industrial development," NSC 98/1 observed, along with its "raw material, manpower, and other resources" constituted "a basic war potential of major importance." On Pakistan, the report noted that "air bases at such places as Karachi, Rawalpindi, and Lahore [would be] nearer a larger portion of Soviet territory including the industrialized area east of the Urals, than bases in any other location in Asia or the Near East." With these factors in mind, NSC 98/1 set forth two major policy objectives. First, the United States should seek to promote "a regional association of non-Communist countries in South Asia." Second, it should attempt to secure "such military rights in South Asia as the U.S. Government may determine to be essential." It was important, the NSC staff stressed, that the "political, strategic, manpower, and resource potential" of South Asia be "marshalled on the side of the United States."[42]

Although NSC 98/1 outlined the importance of both India and Pakistan, it seemed to attach greater significance to India. The NSC went so far as to assert: "The loss of India to the Communist orbit would mean that for all practical purposes all of Asia will have been lost; this would constitute a most serious and threatening blow to the security of the United States." The problem, as defined by the National Security Council, was that in spite of its acceptance of earlier United Nations resolutions on Korea, India seemed to be veering back toward "a policy of neutrality." As a remedy, NSC 98/1 supported the implementation of economic aid programs in India and other countries in the area, noting "the political urgency of reversing the trend towards economic deterioration and of improving the western orientation of India, in particular."[43]

American policymakers feared that time was quickly running out. Whereas they had been willing to be patient with India prior to Chinese involvement in Korea, NSC 98/1 advised that the United States should seek to achieve its goals in India and the rest of South Asia with greater speed and forcefulness. As the draft statement declared: "The time has come to pursue our objectives in South Asia with more vigor. We are now in a position to assess the attitudes and policies of the area governments, as well as the possibilities and the limitations of our influence. We must henceforth more frequently accept calculated risks in attacking the problems of South Asia."[44]

At this stage, the Truman White House had already begun to plan the implementation of McGhee's aid proposals of June 1950 for South Asia and the Near East. But, as previously noted, Truman and Acheson had decided to put off any formal presentation to Congress until they advanced their foreign aid requests as a whole in the spring or summer of 1951. Thus, the program would not actually go into effect until fiscal year 1952. What United States officials needed in late 1950 was an opportunity to hasten American activities in South Asia—a way in which to pursue their objectives "with more vigor" in the immediate future. In India, just such an opportunity was well in the making.

As American policymakers decided that the Cold War crisis necessitated the taking of "calculated risks" in South Asia, India experienced a crisis of its own. By late 1950, that nation was caught in the grips of its most serious food shortage since independence. The difficulties began as early as the winter and spring of 1950, when the monsoon rains failed in the southern state of Madras. Later that year, drought—preceded by floods—spread to several northern states as well. Reports arrived from Bengal and Assam documenting hundreds of deaths due to malnutrition and starvation.[45] According to the blueprint for the Grow More Food campaign, 1951 was to be the year by which India would achieve self-sufficiency in foodgrains. "We should live on the food we produced after two years, or die in the attempt," Jawaharlal Nehru had declared in March 1949.[46] Two years later the prophetic Nehru visited ravaged districts in northern India. "Why do you shout slogans in my praise," he was quoted as asking the inhabitants of one village, "when I cannot feed you to keep you strong?"[47]

Even before the food shortage had reached the crisis stage, Indian government officials approached the United States for help. In July 1950, India urgently requested that the United States provide 500,000 tons of sorghum milling offal, or milo, used primarily in the United States as poultry feed, on concessional terms. Noting that "humanitarian" assistance could contribute to American political aims in India, George McGhee recommended a positive response. It does not appear that any high-ranking official in the United States government dwelled upon the possibility that if Nehru's 1949 request for one million tons of wheat had been met, some of the suffering might have been avoided. In September, Secretary Acheson approved the sale of 500,000 tons of milo to India. The Indian government agreed to pay for the bulk of the grain, with the United States providing $4.5 million out of a special Asian contingency fund to cover the difference.[48]

By the time the agreement on milo was struck, conditions in India had seriously deteriorated. As drought widened, food production plummeted and pressures on supply intensified. Black marketing and corrupt handling of the government's procurement and rationing efforts only exacerbated the disaster. In late 1950, the government of India revised its import quotas upward—first from 2.5 million tons to 4 million tons, and then to an astronomical 6 million tons. By reducing daily rations to nine ounces per person, stretching foreign exchange resources to the limit, and arranging for purchases from abroad, India was able to reduce the deficit to two million tons.[49] On 6 November a beleaguered K. M. Munshi, India's increasingly unpopular food minister, approached Henderson on an informal basis to discuss the possibility of further assistance.[50] A formal request for food aid came on 16 December when Madame Pandit met with Acheson at the State Department. The Indian ambassador outlined the magnitude of the problem and asked for United States assistance in making up the two million ton deficit. Acheson noted that such a large request would require congressional approval and that he could make no promises. But he reassured Madame Pandit that the United States "desired to be helpful" and would "explore the situation urgently and thoroughly."[51]

By the time the Indian government had approached the United States for help, the State Department had already gathered considerable data on the food crisis. The American embassy in New Delhi had monitored the problem for well over a month. In addition to sending statistical material back to Washington, the embassy graphically depicted the severe human suffering in drought-plagued areas. Touring Madras in November 1950, American Social Welfare Attaché Evelyn Hersey witnessed villagers pounding and grinding bits of wood to sawdust, which they consumed in lieu of grain.[52] For domestic political reasons, the Indian government defined the crisis as an "impending famine." Yet with hundreds of deaths due to starvation already documented, American officials generally acknowledged that India was experiencing the first stage of a very real famine. If the United States did not provide assistance, Indian officials estimated that ten to thirteen million of their countrymen would perish.[53] The Truman administration was also aware that the United States Commodity Credit Corporation held approximately 319 million bushels of surplus wheat in reserve and that a 2-million-ton shipment to India would require only 75 million bushels.[54] In short, India's need was well known, the crisis was extraordinarily urgent, and the United States was in a strong position to help.

By late 1950, a litany of policy papers on the subject of aid had repeatedly emphasized the political importance of assisting India economically. NSC 98/1, stressing India's heightened strategic significance, had especially underscored the need to provide that nation with economic aid. Consequently, the Indian request for two million tons of wheat received immediate attention. Division nevertheless arose within the Truman administration over the question of providing the assistance. On the one hand, George McGhee's NEA eyed the political benefits to be reaped by a prompt and positive response and almost immediately endorsed the idea of advancing the wheat to India. "Failure to respond to India's emergency request for foodgrains would seriously endanger the Nehru Government," one NEA report argued, "and any other government which might follow would be decidedly worse from our point of view."[55] On the other hand, the Department of the Treasury and the Bureau of the Budget voiced reservations over the cost of assisting India.[56]

More important, doubts arose within the State Department over how to proceed. On 22 December high-ranking officials discussed the issue at a meeting chaired by Under Secretary Webb. Assistant Secretary of State Willard Thorp found NEA's analysis of the political benefits to be derived from an act of generosity to be lacking. He advised that Congress would not be swayed by humanitarian considerations and that a more persuasive rationale should be developed. "What that is and how we get it are the key questions," Thorp added.[57] One week later on 29 December Acheson and McGhee met with Madame Pandit to discuss India's request for wheat. Examined in view of the directives set forth in NSC 98/1, especially the NSC's desire to promote military collaboration in South Asia, these conversations suggest that the Truman administration had developed a very convincing political rationale for advancing the food aid.

Two conversations on 29 December had an important bearing on the fate of Indian food aid. The first meeting took place between Acheson, McGhee, and Madame Pandit in the secretary of state's office. At this time, Acheson informed the Indian ambassador that the administration was "very sympathetic towards the request." In fact, while the government of India had not specified what terms it might seek in attaining the wheat, Acheson said that he was inclined to ask Congress for a grant-in-aid. Knowing that a grant, as opposed to a loan, would be more difficult to guide through Congress, Acheson immediately warned the Indian ambassador that "it would be unwise to approach Congress without a reasonable assurance that Congress would act favorably." Then the secretary unmistakably drew a connection between India's need for food and American foreign policy interests. He mentioned that "India's attitudes" on two foreign policy matters would be of particular significance in dealing with Congress. First, Acheson referred to "differences between India and Pakistan," noting the desirability of a settlement of the Kashmir dispute. "If this were done," he posited, "the people on the Hill would be favorably impressed." Second, Acheson turned to Korea and told Madame Pandit "that members of Congress would ask whether India understands the depth of the danger we now face."[58]

Having come to Foggy Bottom to discuss food aid, the Indian ambassador found herself defending India's foreign policy. When she replied that India continued to oppose communism, but would also stand by its nonaligned policy, Acheson did not press further. Instead, McGhee concluded the discussion by injecting that "the question of an all-out alignment did not necessarily arise." The assistant secretary then escorted Madame Pandit to his office for more frank discussions.[59]

"Not necessarily" were diplomatic code words employed to suggest that a deal might be in the offing. Sitting in his own office, McGhee reviewed Indo-American differences on China and Korea with Madame Pandit, but took an upbeat approach. Foreign policy differences between India and the United States, he observed, were "not so much a question of substance as of public relations." The assistant secretary further stated that he was convinced that India shared America's concern over Communist expansion and "appeared to recognize at least the possibility of Chinese aggression." This led him closer to the major point of the conversation. "A responsible government," he continued, "should, of course, take reasonable precautionary measures against all events of this grave nature which are possible, even though they may be accorded a low degree of probability." McGhee then raised the "general question of collective security in South and Southeast Asia," pointing out that "if the Chinese Communists did turn out to be aggressive there was no apparent defense for Southeast Asia except on the basis of collective security including India and Pakistan."[60]

At this point in the conversation each participant became somewhat evasive and tried to determine what sort of commitment the other might be willing to make. Madame Pandit reiterated that her government opposed the idea of power blocs, but that she felt "some sort of grouping was desirable and should be possible." When McGhee queried about the "nature" of such a grouping and whether it would involve "mutual defense arrangements," she coyly answered that "it could probably not as a first step," but "that this might come later." She then inquired where the necessary arms would come from in the event of a pact. The astute McGhee opined that the United States might supply "small amounts of arms," but added that "our case was made more difficult by the neutralization of the military dispute between India and Pakistan." "However," McGhee noted, "if one could see effective military potential in the subcontinent, particularly in connection with a pact that would make it available for the defense of South and Southeast Asia generally, arms requests would be much easier to grant." In this regard, he told the Indian ambassador that the United States would eagerly await the outcome of the upcoming Commonwealth conference in London, scheduled to take place in early January, where the topic of collective security should be broached.[61]

As to the question of food aid, Madame Pandit expressed concern that Congress might attach conditions to the aid, noting that "statements might be demanded which India could not make." McGhee answered once more that he did not feel this was "necessarily so." What was needed, he continued, "was a feeling of confidence in India's underlying objectives in the present world situation." He did not specify what India might do to win American confidence, but hinted "that in time of world crisis there was a tendency of people with common objectives to assess their interdependence and to draw together."[62]

While Acheson and McGhee had not categorically made food aid contingent upon a reorientation of Indian policy, the linkages were obvious. Citing congressional pressure, despite the fact that Congress had not even yet been consulted, the two diplomats had clearly indicated that food aid would easily be forthcoming if India reached an accommodation with Pakistan, and initiated plans for a regional defense pact—a major United States goal. McGhee had even dangled the possibility of military assistance before the Indian ambassador.

It is particularly important to note that Acheson offered to make grain available to India on a grant basis even though the Indian government had never indicated a preference for a grant. In doing so he had rejected, from a congressional relations perspective, the less complicated option of extending the wheat as a loan. The secretary told Madame Pandit that he had opted for a grant because of his longstanding opposition to intergovernmental loans, and he accurately noted that he had once resigned from government because of his views on the liquidation of World War I debts.[63] His statement belied the fact that the United States had extended billions of dollars in foreign loans since the end of World War II.

Why did Acheson now insist on a grant-in-aid for India? While a grant would certainly have been advantageous for financially strapped India, Acheson did not tell Madame Pandit that a food grant also carried certain tactical advantages for the United States. First, since a grant would be more difficult to steer through Congress than a loan, it enabled Acheson and McGhee to apply increased pressure on the Indian government to modify its policies and enabled them to do so without facing charges of direct administration interference in Indian affairs. Second, as the United States broached the sensitive topics of Kashmir and collective security, the grant-in-aid could serve as a sweetener to make the idea of military collaboration more palatable for India. It bears repeating that NSC 98/1 had called for the taking of "calculated risks" in South Asia in the wake of the growing Communist threat. Tying India's urgent need for food to America's need for strategic cooperation constituted the first such risk.

The gamble did not pay off. In early January 1951, before the Truman White House had even gone to Congress with the request for wheat, the Commonwealth prime ministers met in London. This was where George

McGhee had hoped that Madame Pandit would relay United States views to Nehru and arrangements for collective security might begin. Instead, Nehru took advantage of the conference to argue once more in favor of China's admission to the United Nations and to press for the convening of a four-power conference—to include the United States, China, Britain, and the Soviet Union—to negotiate a peaceful solution to Korea and other Asian problems. Despite British reservations, the Commonwealth leaders agreed to work together in the General Assembly to bring about such a conference. No agreements for collective security were struck, and the Kashmir dispute and Indo-Pakistani tensions received only scant consideration. Again, the regional rivals could not reach accommodation. Nothing had turned out as the United States had hoped.[64]

To make matters worse, upon his return from London, Nehru addressed the Indian people by radio on 24 January and publicly criticized American policy in Asia. "Let no man think," the prime minister declared, "that any good to him or his country will come of war. A war will convulse the whole world, bringing not only infinite destruction in its train but also corrupting the souls of those who remain."[65] These were not the words of a leader warm to a military alliance with the United States. At about the same time, Madame Pandit returned to Washington bearing a confidential message from Nehru that acknowledged Indo-American differences over Korea and China, but nonetheless conveyed India's fundamental sympathy with the Western democracies. United States officials were not satisfied. George McGhee told Acheson that Nehru's public actions "invalidate any reassurances which may be conveyed in his personal message."[66] Acheson merely dismissed India's call for a four-power conference.[67]

The Truman administration's failure to reach a defense accord with India did not doom that country's request for foodgrains. After allowing sufficient time for India to respond to America's bid for military partnership, George McGhee submitted a report on 24 January 1951, "India's Request for Foodgrains: Political Considerations." Although the report made no specific mention of Nehru's refusal to align militarily with the United States, it did stress that "considerable annoyance and concern" had been created in Washington by India's independent policies. McGhee, nevertheless, warned that the threat of famine in India promised to "create conditions ideally suited to the subversive activities of the Communist Party of India." Indeed, while the CPI was still a weak national force, it did maintain regional strongholds in southern and eastern India—precisely where the impact of food shortages had been most severe. If India and the rest of South Asia were to fall under Communist control, the report continued, a strategic area containing nearly half a billion people, extensive resources, and potential bases would "be denied to us." McGhee concluded: "A quick response to the Indian Government request for food grains is the most effective means, immediately available to our Government, of countering Communist subversion in India."[68]

India's request for food was still far from being granted. It had to win congressional approval, a task which McGhee and Acheson knew would be difficult—even in a Congress dominated by Democrats. McGhee first took the matter to a subcommittee of the Senate Foreign Relations Committee that met in executive session on 26 January, but he did not receive an encouraging reception. The senators raised questions about India's nonaligned policies and challenged the advisability of reducing American wheat stocks during wartime. Unaware of the administration's attempt to fashion a military accord with India, some asked what India would be willing to do for the United States in return for the wheat. But the point that generated the most criticism was that the grain would be made available in the form of a grant. Even Senator J. William Fulbright commented: "I think it should be strictly on a business basis. . . . It does not appeal to me to give it to them." Democratic Chairman Tom Connally, a staunch critic of nonalignment, complained that "Nehru is out giving us hell at this time," and then asked, "is this a proposition to buy him?"[69]

Having been turned down by Nehru on the issue of defense collaboration, the Truman White House now faced the prospect of failing to gain approval for a measure it considered necessary to prevent the spread of communism. To alter course at this point, however, and ask Congress for a loan rather than a grant, might cause misunderstanding with India.

The Truman administration decided to undertake what would prove to be a nearly disastrous course of action. On 30 January, McGhee sent his final recommendations to Acheson, in which he counseled that the effort to win a grant-in-aid should go forward. "If we do not assist India in its present crisis," he ominously warned, "elements inimical to the United States and the Western world generally will be strengthened." To this he added that food aid would help strengthen "our friends" in India and help counter "much of the anti-Western bitterness which enables Nehru to maintain his present posture in foreign affairs."[70] At his general staff meeting later that day, Acheson gave his renewed support for the food grant and emphasized that the administration would have to take the offensive in pushing the proposal, "rather than just backing into it." The president, he observed, "should make a big play of it."[71]

Support had already been building for an Indian aid bill among certain legislators. As early as 8 January, New York Representative Jacob Javits offered a concurrent resolution before Congress calling for immediate food aid to help arrest famine conditions. On 30 January, a bipartisan coalition of senators and representatives—including Senators Hubert Humphrey, H. Alexander Smith, and Leverett Saltonstall and Representatives John McCormack, Mike Mansfield, and Walter Judd—sent a letter to the president urging prompt action on India's behalf. Meeting with representatives of this group on 6 February, Truman and Acheson voiced support for an emergency aid measure but asked that congressional leaders take the lead in introducing the legislation. A presidential message on Indian food aid would be forthcoming shortly, they promised.[72]

Having begun talks in Congress, Truman met with former President Herbert Hoover on 8 February and won a public endorsement from that influential Republican leader. "This doesn't fall into the category of politics," Hoover said of Indian food aid, "it falls into the category of Christianity."[73] It is doubtful that Hoover had any knowledge of the administration's previous discussion of defense matters with the Indian government.

On 12 February 1951, President Truman sent messages to both houses of Congress in support of legislation to provide India with a grant of $190 million for the purchase of two million tons of surplus American wheat. Truman's carefully crafted message contained something for everyone. For hardheaded realists, he stressed the need to counter the Communist threat in India. For democratic idealists, he referred to India's emerging, parliamentary institutions. For humanitarians, he spoke eloquently on the American "tradition of friendly aid to alleviate suffering."[74]

In response to Truman's message, supporters of Indian food relief introduced identical bills for a grant-in-aid in the Senate and the House. Even forceful Republican critics of Truman's foreign policy—such as Senators Robert Taft, William Knowland, and Joseph McCarthy—lent their support to the proposed aid. By 1 March, the House bill had won the speedy endorsement of the Foreign Affairs Committee. The bill authorized the immediate shipment of one million tons of the badly needed wheat and delivery of the remainder after further review of Indian food conditions had been made.[75]

The Indian Wheat Bill also garnered substantial support from the American press and public. The *Washington Post* editorialized that "our own self-interest is directly involved, for the consequences of Indian famine could adversely affect the security of the United States." The New Delhi correspondent of the *New York Times* wrote that if the Indian request should be denied "friends of the United States in the Government [of India] . . . will suffer a great loss of influence in the wave of anti-American feeling that is likely to arise." The *Christian Science Monitor* also enthusiastically backed the bill as an effective, anti-Communist measure. At the grassroots level the bill won support from numerous church groups, the National Association for the Advancement of Colored People, the Congress of Industrial Organizations, and the National Farmers Union. A Gallup poll taken in March showed 59 percent of those questioned in favor of providing India with the needed wheat, and only 31 percent opposed.[76] The Truman strategy seemed to be working superbly.

Yet all did not go according to plan. Although the House Foreign Affairs Committee gave quick approval to the Indian Wheat Bill, the Senate Foreign Relations Committee, engaged in hearings on the assignment of ground troops to Europe, delayed consideration. Chairman Tom Connally, who had already voiced strong disapproval of the proposal, gave no sign of a willingness to reschedule the committee's busy agenda. In the meantime, strong opposition to the bill began to emerge in the House. While most members of the Foreign Affairs Committee continued to support the concept of helping India avoid famine, a few openly criticized Nehru's nonalignment. But the most often expressed and damaging criticism of the proposal once again centered upon the terms upon which the aid would be made available. Again and again, critics asked why the grain could not be provided in the form of a loan, rather than a grant. Led by Republican Representative John M. Vorys of Massachusetts, a group within the Foreign Affairs Committee submitted a minority report calling for a loan of wheat to India repayable with three strategic materials: manganese, beryl, and monazite sands (rare earths containing elements of radioactive thorium).[77]

The matter was forwarded to the House Rules Committee for a resolution. There a group of conservative Republicans and southern Democrats managed to keep the bill bottled up for nearly two months as the debate over loan versus grant continued. In the Senate, Connally's Foreign Relations Committee still refused to begin hearings. By early April 1951, five months had passed since the Indian government had first asked for assistance. No reliable statistics exist on how many additional, famine-related deaths occurred during this period but the Indian press, initially buoyed by Truman's support, became increasingly critical of the delay. The *Hindustan Times* questioned whether the food would reach India in time to avert widespread starvation. "To delay aid under the circumstances is to deny it," one editorial commented.[78] *The Hindu*, southern India's leading daily, declared that "while America may not win India with wheat, America will lose India without wheat."[79] Numerous Indian officials expressed concern over the holdup and lamented undiplomatic slurs voiced against Indian policies in Congress. Nehru told a visiting American journalist in New Delhi: "The way in which you are handling our request for grain is insulting and outrageous. If we go through centuries of poverty and millions of people die of hunger, we shall never submit to outside pressure."[80]

The Truman administration responded by redoubling its efforts. In late March, Acheson met with Connally and implored the powerful senator to initiate hearings on the wheat bill, and Truman opened a news conference on 29 March with a statement calling for quick action on the bill.[81] Soon the Indian government came to Truman's assistance. In early April, Nehru sent word to Washington that the Indian government was dismayed by provisions in the original House bill, which according to standard practice required United States supervision of the distribution of the food aid. Complaining that the draft bill "practically" converted India "into some kind of a semi-colonial country," Nehru issued instructions to Sir Girja Bajpai to seek the food aid on terms of deferred payment, rather than as a grant.[82] The prime minister hoped that under such circumstances the United States would dispense with supervisory procedures.

While the Truman White House could not revise Economic Cooperation Agency guidelines that mandated American oversight of all economic aid, it could now go to Congress with a new willingness to compromise on the grant-loan controversy. The logjam rapidly broke. On 16 April, the Senate Foreign Relations Committee finally began to deliberate on the Indian food crisis, and four days later reported out a bill that provided India with one million tons of wheat on a grant basis, and one million tons in the form of a loan. On 24 April, the House Rules Committee ended its long deadlock and approved a bill that provided all of the wheat in the form of a loan, partially repayable in unspecified raw materials. The House Foreign Affairs Committee promptly gave its assent.[83]

Before India could be assured of an adequate food supply, one more obstacle arose. After meeting with Ambassador Henderson, Nehru consigned himself to the inevitability of American supervision of grain distribution efforts. After all, European recipients of United States assistance had accepted similar requirements without any loss of sovereignty.[84] But the question of repayment of the loan in raw materials made Nehru bristle. India already supplied the United States with 500,000 tons of manganese annually, and under the terms of a secret agreement, it had also guaranteed a steady supply of beryl.[85] The snag arose over monazite sands. Hoping to use this thorium-producing substance for its own future atomic development, India had placed an embargo on the export of monazite sands in 1946. Suspecting that Congress might demand this particular material in exchange for food, Nehru stood firm. In a broadcast to the nation on 1 May, he categorically rejected making major concessions in exchange for aid:

> While we welcome all help we can get from foreign countries, we have made it clear that such help must not have political strings attached to it, any conditions which are unbecoming for a self-respecting nation to accept, any pressure to change our domestic or international policy. We would be unworthy of the high responsibilities with which we have been charged if we bartered away in the slightest degree our country's self-respect or freedom of action, even for something which we need so badly.[86]

Congress was in essence demanding the same conditions for food aid that the administration had set forth during its 1949 negotiations with the Indian government. Now State Department officials found themselves arguing against such measures. Throughout the 1951 congressional hearings the White House counseled that India would resent the attachment of strings to the food aid, and gave assurances that India had been cooperative in supplying United States needs. In regard to monazite sands, Acheson testified that the Atomic Energy Commission used only small amounts solely for experimental purposes. The United States had only a "preclusive interest" in the material, he told the Senate Foreign Relations Committee—that is, ensuring that fissionable thorium not fall into Communist hands. Since India had placed an embargo on monazite exports, Acheson observed, American interests had been satisfied.[87] Nehru's public criticisms of Congress, nonetheless, temporarily derailed the Indian Wheat Bill. As one legislator told the *New York Times*, the bill had been put into a "deep freeze." On 2 May, the day after the prime minister's radio broadcast, both houses of Congress postponed further consideration of the bill.[88]

State Department officials now turned their attention toward Nehru.

Acting upon instructions from Washington, Ambassador Henderson met with the Indian leader to urge conciliation.[89] Ever mindful of India's need for food, Nehru went before Parliament again on 10 May and clarified his position. Of the two bills before Congress, the prime minister stated a preference for the House bill that called for a loan of wheat to India, as opposed to the half loan / half grant proposal in the Senate. While there would be no objection to partial repayment in raw materials that India could spare, Nehru refused to compromise on the issue of monazite sands: "It is a fundamental part of our policy that such material as is particularly related to the production of atomic or like weapons should not be supplied by us to foreign countries."[90]

With that gesture, Congress quickly moved to resolve the issue. On 16 May, the Senate passed an Indian Wheat Bill that in accord with Nehru's statement made two million tons of wheat available to India on a loan basis. The Senate bill called for repayment in raw materials and included a specific reference to monazite sands. The House proved more conciliatory. The following week it authorized the required loan, partially repayable in raw materials, but made no mention of monazite sands. A House-Senate conference subsequently worked out a compromise formula that essentially conformed to the House bill. The House overwhelmingly approved the conference bill on 6 June by a vote of 256 to 82. The bill easily passed by voice vote in the Senate on 11 June, and President Truman signed the Emergency Indian Wheat Bill on 15 June 1951.[91]

The troubled odyssey of the Indian Wheat Bill would seem to demonstrate how a recalcitrant Congress could obstruct a president's foreign aid priorities. Yet upon closer examination, the question of whether or not India would receive food assistance need never have been placed in doubt. Even the seasoned professional and Speaker of the House, Sam Rayburn, described the difficult passage of the bill as "one of the most amazing things I have ever witnessed."[92] Once the Truman administration determined that providing India with wheat served the foreign policy interests of the United States, it had very little difficulty in rallying support to its side. Both the media and the American public quickly fell into line, and a number of longtime administration foes in Congress backed the measure as well. Most opponents of the proposal never took an irreconcilable stand against helping India during its food crisis. A movement never developed in Congress to force India to join with the United States and Pakistan in a military alliance. The sticking point developed over the issue of the terms by which assistance would be made available. The administration's decision to offer a

At the end of a long, difficult fight in Congress, President Harry S. Truman signs the Emergency Indian Wheat Bill, 15 June 1951. Indian ambassador Madame Vijayalakshmi Pandit (seated) and Secretary of State Dean Acheson (to the ambassador's right) look on. (U.S. Department of State, courtesy Harry S. Truman Library)

grant-in-aid enabled American officials to pressure the Indian government on issues such as Korea, Kashmir, and collective security. But when India refused to bend, and the proposal made its way to Capitol Hill, the grant provision nearly destroyed the bill's chances for passage.

During 1950 and 1951, as millions of Indians struggled each day to survive on as little as nine ounces of foodgrains, American policymakers sought to work India's distress to America's advantage. The Korean War, which the Truman administration viewed as a direct Soviet challenge to American interests in Asia, provided the backdrop. It was in response to that Cold War catastrophe that United States policymakers first planned in 1950 to make economic assistance available to India. The war also significantly affected India's request in 1951 for famine relief. In each case, India's dire need for help became bound up with the United States' drive for military allies, bases, strategic materials, and political influence.

In the end, American aid made its way to India, but not until precious months, made more precious by the haunting threat of famine, had ticked away. And not until a great deal of ill will had been generated between the United States and India. From its very inception, the Indo-American aid relationship demonstrated many of the difficulties inherent to relations between two, divergent cultures. Because Indian and American leaders espoused different views on the Cold War, Korea, and a host of other foreign policy issues, the aid process bred mutual distrust as well as mutual cooperation. Indian officials resented American high-handedness and were extremely sensitive, given their very recent experience under colonialism, to any implied recriminations against their sovereignty. United States officials compared Indian policymakers to "spoiled children," viewed nonalignment—in some measure—as a reflection of psychosis, and often ran roughshod over Indian sensitivities. These attitudes cast a dark shadow over the prospects for collaboration in economic development, in the fight against poverty, and in world politics.

Four

A Matter of Priorities, 1951–1953

The Indian Emergency Assistance Act of 1951 was the first American aid program to be implemented directly in India, but as its title implied, it was a onetime, stopgap measure. From 1951 through 1953, American policymakers worked out a long-term program of economic assistance for India. Although they did not entertain hopes that Nehru would abandon nonalignment and dramatically announce his country's allegiance to the West, United States officials believed that economic assistance to India still served United States interests. India was, after all, the world's second most populous nation, and the mere existence of a non-Communist government there was deemed to be a foreign policy asset. Economic aid would not win a military ally or rights to base facilities, but it might help assure the political stability of the Asian giant and thus reduce opportunities for Communist-inspired, revolutionary forces. As one NSC report put it in early 1951, India was "the keystone of stability" in South Asia, "and every effort must be made to stabilize conditions" in that country. Economic assistance would "contribute to the stability of the area, strengthen the Western orientation of the region, and facilitate the transfer to the United States of [strategic raw] materials related to national defense."[1]

As American policymakers formulated plans for India between 1951 and 1953, they had to determine the scope of the program. Two competing, yet interrelated, philosophies emerged. Most senior officials in Washington primarily viewed aid from a short-term, national security perspective. In light of the Korean War, these policymakers placed more emphasis on the extension of military assistance to strategically placed allies than on economic aid to peripheral, emerging areas. Although they accepted the need for economic assistance to India and other developing nations, they envisioned the establishment of only small-scale programs designed to meet the minimal needs of the recipients. At the same time, the American embassy in New Delhi and some lesser officials at the State Department strongly advocated a longer-term commitment to promote liberal development. Led by Ambassador Chester Bowles, this liberal contingent argued that a large, multiyear infusion of aid provided the surest route to non-Communist stability in India and other new nations.

Bowles and his supporters articulated a strong case for development diplomacy and may have laid the foundation for future economic aid programs. But they only marginally affected policy during the period under consideration. Simply put, military strategy and concern over the possibility of direct Soviet aggression weighed most heavily in the rationales and objectives of American foreign aid during the Korean War years. In 1949, the ratio of economic to military aid was about four to one, by the end of 1950 that ratio had been reversed—and for the next several years the emphasis on military aid characterized nearly all United States aid programs. In Europe, even Marshall Plan expenditures shifted from capital goods to defense items. And in developing areas, aid flowed overwhelmingly to areas of military crisis, especially to Korea, Taiwan, and French Indochina.[2] Given these policy factors, it is not surprising that economic aid to India and other newly emerged nations received only minimal funding and involved mainly assistance to pilot, agricultural projects. In short, India's economic development did not yet register as a foreign policy priority.

At its inception, the United States economic assistance program for India was intended to be small. Plans were based upon George McGhee's proposals of early June 1950, which President Truman had approved shortly after the outbreak of the Korean War. McGhee's original recommendation of $200 million to $300 million annually for South Asia and the Near East paled in significance when compared to the billions of dollars poured into Europe under the Marshall Plan. In addition, whereas the Marshall Plan initially provided funds to help rebuild Europe's industrial base, the South Asian program focused almost wholly upon less expensive agricultural programs. In presenting the case for aid to India, McGhee had concentrated on the political rationale, but in his August 1950 memorandum to the president he did note in passing that the "first emphasis" of the South Asia program would be toward achieving a "prompt and substantial improvement in the indigenous food supply." McGhee argued that the development of an adequate food supply was a prerequisite for social and political stability in the region.[3]

During the summer of 1950 the State Department determined that economic assistance to India and the other nations of the region would be implemented by the Technical Cooperation Administration (TCA)—the administrative arm of President Truman's much-celebrated Point Four program. Wrapped in the prevailing ideology of liberal development, Point Four aid promised to foster capitalistic growth and trade and counter the Communist threat in underdeveloped areas. "Greater production is the key to prosperity and peace," Truman had declared in his 1949 inaugural address.[4] As noted earlier, the Point Four legislation passed by Congress in 1950 provided only $35 million in technical assistance for fiscal year 1951 to finance the cost of technical and economic advisers for all the Third World. But as planning for fiscal year 1952 got under way, administration officials came to envision what one State Department report referred to as a "Point Four Plus" program for the Near East and South Asia. According to this blueprint, the United States would not only supply advisers but a degree of capital and commodity assistance as well. In India, American policymakers planned to concentrate their efforts on helping to carry out the Grow More Food campaign, mainly by providing increased supplies of improved seed, fertilizer, hand implements, mechanical farm equipment, and small-scale irrigation equipment.[5]

The case for development assistance to emerging areas was reinforced in late 1950 and early 1951 when presidential commissions headed by Gordon Gray and Nelson Rockefeller submitted their respective reports on foreign aid. Although the Gray report was firm in advocating the primacy of European rearmament in the wake of Korea, both Gray and Rockefeller reflected a growing awareness of America's strategic stake in the economic and political stability of emerging areas and called for increased economic and technical aid to the Third World. Each report estimated that programs for technical and capital assistance would require funds of up to $500 million annually for several years. The Rockefeller report further recommended that the United States subscribe $200 million to an international development authority empowered to make overseas grants and another $150 million to an international finance corporation to encourage private investment in developing nations.[6]

The first official estimate of expenditures for South Asia came in late 1950 after McGhee met with British officials in London. By that time the South Asian states had, in accordance with directives set forth at the Commonwealth's Colombo Conference of January 1950, submitted a series of six-year, economic development plans. The collation of these plans provided the foundation for Britain's long delayed, regional economic initiative. The "Colombo Plan," as it came to be known, envisioned about $900 million in expenditures, and while Pakistan, Ceylon, and Burma also participated, the plan slated approximately $700 million for India alone. The South Asian governments would finance $350 million of the total outlay themselves—leaving a gap of about $550 million. After reviewing the proposal, McGhee reported to the State Department that England could, through sterling balance arrangements, provide about $200 million in assistance.[7] Shortly after the assistant secretary's return to Washington, the NSC staff completed work on NSC 68/3, an update of basic national security policy that recommended that the United States make $154 million, or about one-half of the Colombo Plan deficit, available to the nations of South Asia.[8]

Although McGhee had presented what was, in many ways, a meager budget for South Asia, the region's allocation of aid never reached the $154 million mark. When the Truman administration submitted its foreign assistance program, or Mutual Security Program as it was now called, to Congress in May 1951, the proposals included only $78 million for South Asia—consisting of $65 million for India, $12.5 million for Pakistan, and $700,000 for Ceylon, Nepal, and Afghanistan.[9] The reduced level of funding simply reflected the strategic priorities of the Korean War era. Out of the recommended $8.5 billion, Truman asked for $7 billion for nations in Western Europe and about $930 million for Asia and the Pacific. Of those totals, $5.5 billion of the European allocation and $555 million of the Asia program were designated as military aid. The administration earmarked most of the Asian military aid for Korea, Formosa, and French Indochina.[10] Highlighting the obvious linkage between foreign aid and America's wartime needs, one State Department report summarized: "[The] New foreign aid program reflects a marked shift in emphasis from economic aims to support of military build-up."[11]

The Indian program experienced a further setback when a budget-conscious Congress authorized only $7.3 billion of Truman's request. While cuts came across the board, legislators made a disproportionate reduction in economic aid in general, and funding for Asia and the Pacific, the broader heading under which the India program fell, particularly suffered. With little debate, Congress subtracted a total of $150 million from the administration's allocation of $375 million in economic aid for that region, and India's share fell from $65 million to $54 million. Congress, however, did not alter the basic orientation of Truman's program. The ratio of military aid to economic aid was about 2.5 to 1, and the needs of

United States allies were substantially met.[12] Nor does the evidence suggest that congressional actions on Asia and the Pacific caused deep concern in the administration. As NSC 114, the official policy paper on Mutual Security, summarized the issue shortly after Congress completed its work: "Our aid programs in Asia and the Pacific are essentially ameliorative in character, designed in the first instance to arrest the progressive deterioration in conditions and therefore to establish a solid basis for sustained and prolonged improvement. . . . The amount, form, and timing of our aid programs approach the minimum needed to maintain the situation in our favor."[13]

Yet just as the United States decided to launch an aid program in India demonstrating only a limited commitment to that nation, the Truman administration named a new ambassador to New Delhi who attached great significance to India—former Connecticut Governor Chester Bowles. Born in Springfield, Massachusetts, Bowles had already pursued a successful business career in the famous Manhattan advertising firm of Benton and Bowles. During the 1940s he fulfilled a lifelong ambition by entering government service, first as director of the wartime Office of Price Administration, and later as United States delegate to the United Nations Educational and Science Organization. An ardent New Dealer and a confirmed internationalist, Bowles held a very deep interest in the emerging Third World. India, the world's largest democracy, particularly fascinated this liberal idealist. "I had never been to India," Bowles recalled in his memoirs, but "I had read a great deal about its problems and prospects and had come to see India as the key to a free and stable Asia." "It was not only a matter of India's size and geographical position," he emphasized, "the struggle by Gandhi and Nehru for freedom from British rule through non-violent means had established India as a testing ground for democratic government in a period of rapidly receding colonial dominance."[14]

Truman did not appoint Bowles because the president shared the latter's enthusiasm for India. Rather, the nomination sprang from practical politics. In 1948, Chester Bowles had been elected governor of Connecticut and during his term he played an instrumental role in persuading Connecticut Republican Raymond Baldwin to retire from the United States Senate. Baldwin apparently wished to step down for personal reasons, but Bowles's offer of a position on the State Supreme Court clinched the matter. This was no small accomplishment, for Bowles's appointment of his former business partner, William Benton, to the vacant Senate seat assured the Democratic party of a one-vote majority in that chamber. After Governor

Bowles narrowly lost his bid for reelection in 1950, Truman decided to reward him with an ambassadorial post. When the president asked Bowles what one country he would most like to be assigned, the latter said that India would be his top choice. "Why on earth would you want to go to India?" Truman characteristically replied.[15]

Bowles's unusual request coincided with the conclusion of Loy Henderson's scheduled tour of duty. So, despite Acheson's misgivings over the governor's lack of diplomatic experience, Truman nominated Bowles. The nomination faced strong opposition in the Senate where conservative, Republican leader Robert A. Taft led a major effort to stop the appointment, and Bowles's own enthusiasm nearly undermined his cause. At one executive session of the Senate Foreign Relations Committee, Bowles's assertion that he would like to see economic aid to South Asia increased to $250 million annually brought shudders to certain committee members. It also brought forth a less than honest denial from George McGhee that the State Department had ever considered such a figure. In spite of an intense lobbying effort, Taft and his allies only mustered thirty-eight votes against the nomination, and in the fall of 1951, Bowles departed for India.[16] The context for the Indo-American aid relationship had been set. In Washington, a security-minded policymaking establishment had initiated a limited program of assistance for India, and in New Delhi an ambitious American ambassador was preparing to go to work to expand the level of United States support for India.

Ambassador Bowles brought nearly boundless energy to his new job. Over the course of 1.5 years he immersed himself in Indian political and economic affairs. Like an American politician on the hustings, he logged thousands of miles traveling across the subcontinent. He visited isolated rural villages, inspected prominent construction sites, and paid flattering visits to a wide array of national, state, and local political leaders. Along the way, he delivered over one hundred speeches and held twenty-five press conferences. There was also the special Bowles touch: informal parties at the family home; the Bowles children enrolled in Indian schools; and even parking the embassy automobile and taking to the streets of New Delhi on bicycle. All of this helped to make Bowles enormously popular in India, and he quickly won the confidence of many government officials. Even Nehru gradually came to view the ambassador as being a genuine friend of India. The *Times of India* summed up the prevailing attitude following

Bowles's first press conference, in which he openly expressed his hopes for increased financial assistance for India without political or economic strings: "The new U.S. Ambassador to this country has the right approach."[17]

The most pressing task, of course, was development of a program to assist India's economy. The government of India had just completed the *Draft Outline* of its first, five-year economic plan in July 1951. Although the term "economic planning" conjures up thoughts of radical, redistributive policies and government ownership of the means of production, the Indian Planning Commission, the government agency charged with formulating the economic agenda, took a distinctly conservative approach. Industrial and landed interests within Nehru's Congress party, who staunchly defended the rights of private property, served to moderate any inclination toward bold, reformist initiatives. But these interest groups were not alone in opposing radical measures. Even Prime Minister Nehru advocated cautious policies. "We have to consider things as they are," he explained in one speech, "we cannot lay down any slogan or watchword and try to force it through to its logical conclusion." "Whether it is in India or anywhere else," he declared, "only those policies can succeed which promise to deliver the goods."[18] Thus, as Nehru had consistently done since independence, the *Draft Outline* placed primary emphasis on the goal of increasing the production of goods rather than their equitable distribution. The authors of the plan sounded the guiding principle when they warned: "A hasty implementation of measures intended to bring about economic equality, may in the shortrun, affect savings and the level of production adversely."[19]

In keeping with previous policy, the *Draft Outline* assigned highest priority to agricultural production, rural development, and electric power. Together, outlays for these headings accounted for Rs 641 crores (one crore equals ten million rupees), or 43 percent of a total plan expenditure of Rs 1493 crores (about $7 billion). Outlays for industry amounted to only Rs 101 crores, or 6.7 percent of the total.[20] The Planning Commission's agricultural policy was in line with its overall developmental strategy. It proposed to continue efforts begun under the Grow More Food campaign to bring about an increase in India's food supply by providing modern, productive inputs—seed, fertilizer, farm tools, and irrigation facilities—to Indian farmers. The stated goal was to raise output of foodgrains and achieve self-sufficiency in this important area by the end of the plan period in 1955–56. Planners specifically rejected any notion of substantial land reform: "Any large scale attempt to break up existing holdings may give rise to such organized forces of disruption as may make it extremely difficult to bring about the very transformation in the organization of agriculture which is needed."[21]

The Indian strategy for economic development complemented the capitalistic aims of United States aid policy. In accordance with the Indian Policy Resolution of 1948, certain key industries such as transportation, communications, munitions, and electric power were to be wholly government owned. But the accent on production assured the evolution of a mixed economy in which private enterprise in numerous other industries would thrive. The focus on agriculture also fit well with the modest goals set forth in the Point Four assistance program. From an economic perspective, the prospects for successful Indo-American cooperation seemed bright.

The *Draft Outline*, however, also contained serious shortcomings. Most Indian observers applauded the planner's emphasis on agriculture, an obvious need in a nation where approximately two-thirds of the population depended upon farming for their livelihoods.[22] But a vocal group of critics—including Gandhians, Socialists, and Communists—pointed to the need for a more comprehensive approach to rural development. They especially advocated support for village-based industries, programs to improve health and sanitation, literacy programs, and land reform to benefit landless peasants—nearly one-quarter of the rural population. The most basic point advanced was that the introduction of modern tools and production methods alone would not be enough to bring about the social regeneration of rural India.[23] Reacting to these points, an Indian government commission on agriculture joined in recommending a more broad-ranging effort at rural reform.[24]

At this critical juncture, Ambassador Chester Bowles arrived and became involved in the Indian planning process. With $54 million in aid, the ambassador immediately set out in search of a way to put the money to work. He received important assistance in this effort from an old friend, Paul Hoffman, the former Marshall Plan administrator who had recently become director of the Ford Foundation. The Ford Foundation had decided during the previous year to establish an office in New Delhi and to launch development assistance programs of its own in India and Pakistan. Aware of State Department planning for economic aid to South Asia, Hoffman hoped to establish these two influential nations, which sat on the rim of China, as laboratories for non-Communist development. After a brief visit to India in August 1951, he wrote to Bowles concerning the prospects for rural uplift on the subcontinent. Drawing on the China example, Hoffman noted that if village assistance programs had been implemented there immediately following the Second World War, "the end result would have been a China completely immunized against the appeal of the Communists." "India," he warned, "is today what China was in 1945."[25] Sympathetic to Bowles's humanitarianism, he encouraged the ambassador to visit Indian government project sites in the districts of Etawah and Faridabad, where reformist approaches to rural development had recently been undertaken.

First, Bowles traveled to the Etawah District in the state of Uttar Pradesh in northern India where the state government had contracted with two Americans, a Chicago-based, community planner named Albert Meyer and an agricultural extension expert named Horace Holmes, to launch a pilot project in rural uplift. Like the central government's GMF campaign, the Etawah project placed priority emphasis upon making modern, agricultural equipment and technical advice available to farmers. But programs were also undertaken in each of the district's ninety-seven villages to improve health and sanitation, promote literacy, and stimulate a sense of grassroots enthusiasm for modernization. This integrated approach to community planning impressed Bowles, and the ambassador took special note that in just three years Meyer, Holmes, and the Uttar Pradesh government had engineered a 50 percent increase in food production. On the way back to New Delhi, after spending three days in Etawah, Bowles began to calculate how all of rural India might be revitalized along similar lines.[26]

Bowles followed up the trip to Etawah with a visit to a government of India settlement for postpartition refugees at the city of Faridabad, just fourteen miles south of New Delhi. In this new community of 30,000 people, each family had been provided with a house and running water; and a hospital, three public health centers, a number of schools, and several factories had been built. The urban center was linked to 300 villages in the surrounding countryside to which the Faridabad Development Board (FDB)—the administrative agency in charge of the project—extended agricultural, health, and educational assistance. Again, Bowles approved of the integrated approach that combined an emphasis on economic productivity with social welfare measures. The ambassador befriended Sudhir Ghosh, the director of the FDB, and began to refer to Faridabad along with Etawah as a model for an American-backed program in India.[27]

By mid-November Bowles had formulated a plan for utilizing American aid funds that he outlined in a letter to George McGhee. Envisioning a program of "community development" based upon the Etawah-Faridabad examples, the ambassador divided India into a series of "development areas." Each area comprised a population of 150,000 to 300,000 people and would eventually revolve around a newly established central town of perhaps 5,000 to 10,000 inhabitants. The town, as in the case of the Faridabad experiment, would house administrative offices, small industries, a hospital, and serve as the headquarters for agricultural, health, and educational services; and a system of newly constructed roads would radiate outward to serve as vital connecting links to the countryside. Along the same lines as the Etawah project, farmers would be supplied with improved seed, tools, irrigation facilities, and fertilizer. Village-level workers, one for every five or so villages, would help distribute these items and teach peasant cultivators how to use them.[28]

Bowles lost no time in taking his ideas to the Indian government. On Thanksgiving day, 1951, he presented to Nehru a two-page, rough draft of the proposal. It called for the creation of an All-India "Development Authority" to implement a wide-ranging Community Development Program (CDP) to raise health and literacy standards, expand agricultural extension, and generally improve rural living conditions. He explained to the prime minister that the proposal was "entirely personal and unofficial," and "represents simply my own views on how the experience already gained at Faridabad, Etawah, and other projects may be expanded into a dynamic, cooperative effort to raise living, health, and literacy standards in all parts of India."[29] The two discussed the problems and promises of India's future for two hours, and Nehru gave his assent to the scheme.[30] Several weeks later, on 5 January 1952, an Indo-American Technical Agreement was signed. It formally established a joint fund that consisted of $54 million in American dollars for the purchase of supplies and hiring of technicians not available in India, and an equal amount in Indian rupees to pay for the local costs of the program. At the same time, the Ford Foundation agreed to provide $2.9 million to establish regional training centers for the soon-to-be recruited village-level workers.[31]

Chester Bowles attached great significance to the Community Development Program, but he viewed it as only the first step toward India's modernization. If India could become self-sufficient in food by the end of the First Five-Year Plan, a goal that he believed community development would make possible, it could then turn its attention to the task of industrialization. Bowles estimated that by discontinuing food imports India would free up between $600 million and $800 million annually in foreign exchange. This capital base, along with India's extensive natural resources, large internal market, and bountiful labor supply, could be used to develop the nation's industrial infrastructure—especially vital areas such as transportation, mining, steel, electric motors, and chemicals. In five years' time, he optimistically predicted, India would be poised for rapid economic growth.[32]

Bowles believed it essential that the United States help steer India's development along a proper path, and he expressed strong reservations over Nehru's commitment to a mixed economy. Viewing India's five-year plan as "a fuzzy compromise among many conflicting ideas,"[33] he hoped that the Community Development Program would provide a foundation for liberal, capitalist development in India. The ambassador calculated that over the next several years food production would increase "in the average Indian village by fifty percent," but he wondered if Indian cultivators, after having achieved a degree of security, would continue to increase production or whether they would be content to simply seek "more leisure time?" Bowles concluded that if the productive effort were to become self-sustaining, incentives would have to be provided. The solution seemed to lie in making privately produced, consumer goods—radios, bicycles, sewing machines, and apparel—available to rural dwellers. The desire to acquire these goods would drive villagers to expand food production and at the same time help fuel a new, dynamic, and capitalistic durable goods industry. "How I would love to see Sears and Roebuck come out here and really tackle the problem of inexpensive distribution of consumer goods, keyed to the Indian market," Bowles told one State Department official. "Such an undertaking could open immense possibilities for village industries, which in turn could provide the goods which would give the cultivators the incentives we are going to need three or four years from today if we are going to maintain the maximum production which our technical efforts make theoretically possible."[34]

Chester Bowles promoted liberal development in other ways as well. He frequently met with Indian officials and tried to impress upon them the need to loosen restrictions on private investment so as "to pull this country up by its bootstraps."[35] He took particular pride in helping to negotiate, in late 1951, contracts for two American-owned oil refineries in India that included twenty-five-year guarantees against nationalization and liberal provisions for the repatriation of profits.[36] Bowles did not, however, endorse laissez-faire capitalism. In the tradition of twentieth-century American reform, he readily accepted the need for some economic planning. He patterned the administrative structure of the Community Development Program after that great model in New Deal experimentation—the Tennessee Valley Authority. He fashioned the project's extension services after the American county agent system. He even commissioned several studies on India's land tenure system and complained about Nehru's cautious attitude on land reform.[37] Observing that India's only exposure to capitalism had been to the British "cartel" variety, Bowles was eager to demonstrate "that our own [American] private enterprise system is a very different kind of capitalism which can be socially conscious and yet efficient and dynamic."[38]

If Bowles was enthusiastic about the prospects for capitalism in India, he was equally devoted to the task of defeating communism in that nation. Indeed, much of the impetus behind the Community Development Program can be ascribed to Bowles's Cold War convictions. Immediately after his arrival in India, the new ambassador took his cue from Paul Hoffman and began to draw comparisons between economic conditions in India and Communist China. Chester Bowles became the first high-ranking, American official to articulate what would later become accepted wisdom when he wrote to Assistant Secretary of State George McGhee: "Communist China and an India striving to remain democratic would inevitably be placed in economic competition."[39] If India's democratic experiment faltered while China advanced, he reasoned, the consequences would be catastrophic. Not only might India succumb to the false promises of communism, the scenario ran, but all of South Asia and the Near East might follow. On the brighter side, Bowles told President Truman: "If India . . . under democratic government grows stronger, all of the free nations of South Asia and the Middle East will be buttressed."[40] The required antidote, according to Bowles, was American economic aid, and the effort would have to begin at the village level with community development. As he explained to George McGhee: "This is where the communists won in China. This is where the battle for India will be decided."[41]

Yet Bowles proved to be a cautious Cold Warrior. He recognized that regional factors, such as a strong opposition to colonialism and fear of a great power rivalry over Asia, often lay behind Nehru's policy statements. "Nehru is no more of a Communist than Robert Taft," he told one friend, "and in my opinion has a much better grasp of the Soviet threat."[42] India's nonaligned posture, Bowles also observed, had geographical, political, and historical roots, and he advised the State Department to be patient with India. In one letter to Acheson he explained that the United States would make more "progress" with Nehru "if we let India know that as much as we disagree with her, we respect her desire to remain aloof for the present."[43] At the same time, Bowles expressed skepticism toward United States programs to shore up Asia militarily. The key to defeating communism in the region, he insisted, lay in successful economic rather than defense planning.[44]

Bowles's analysis harbored flaws. Faithful to his views on the power of incentives, Bowles assumed that America's style of welfare capitalism could be grafted easily onto the Indian setting. He clearly underestimated the historically rooted obstacles to the creation of a modern, consumer society: India's caste structure, underdeveloped industrial capacity, antiquated system of land tenure, and ever-growing population—to list just a few. In addition, there was the question of whether the Nehru government possessed the political will to enact reforms and break down some of the barriers. Bowles's go-getter style and natural optimism, or what George F. Kennan has termed "the great American capacity for enthusiasm and self-hypnosis," simply led him to misjudge the seriousness of certain harsh realities.[45]

The ambassador's political projections were sometimes equally facile. Economic growth in India might very well lead to an improved standard of living, political stability, and a strengthening of democracy. But it could also create rising expectations, awakening frustrations, and the temptation to promote change through authoritarian measures. Even if the democratic alternative came to fruition in India, no guarantee existed that the experience would be duplicated in other Asian and Near Eastern nations, each of which possessed a unique history, culture, and social structure. With an eye toward the Soviet-American contest, Bowles had adopted the notion that underdeveloped countries could, without much difficulty, evolve into nation-states that were politically, socially, and economically like his own.[46]

Despite its shortcomings, the Bowles agenda had positive attributes. The ambassador was, after all, one of the first United States officials to grapple with the complexities of Indian development. While he did not dismiss India's need for industrialization, as some State Department officials had done, he joined Indian policymakers in making food production a priority—a requirement for successful development in a largely agrarian nation. In addition, during his short stay in India he had already discerned that some degree of social reform, as well as increased productivity, should be made a part of the development process. In the political sphere, he did not allow his Cold War assumptions to shield him completely from the regional point of view, and he demonstrated sensitivity to the ideological and geopolitical roots of nonalignment. In short, the Bowles approach contained elements for the making of a constructive policy toward India. It remained to be seen if Bowles could persuade the Truman administration to reorder its priorities and to make development aid for India a primary policy objective.

Given his grandiose hopes for liberal development in India, it is hardly surprising that Bowles soon determined that the level of aid would have to be substantially increased. The outcome of India's first general elections in January 1952 reinforced this inclination. Although the Congress party won the largest single bloc of votes, it had garnered only 45 percent of the total in parliamentary contests. A total of seventy-seven opposition parties shared the remaining vote. While none of those parties seemed strong enough to pose an immediate threat to Congress predominance, Bowles took special note of the growing popularity of the Communist party of India. The CPI had won only 5 percent of the vote nationwide, but it had proved itself a powerful force in a number of local strongholds, mainly in southern India, and had emerged from the elections as the largest opposition group in the Indian Parliament.[47] Immediately after the elections, Bowles returned to Washington to publicize the growing Communist danger in India and argue his case for a four-year United States commitment to India totaling $1 billion.

Presented to officials in Washington in mid-January 1952, Bowles's proposal consisted of two major components. First, it called for $125 million annually in direct, financial assistance to help India pay the foreign exchange costs of imported supplies such as fertilizer, steel for the manufacture of farm implements, tube wells, small pumps for irrigation, and DDT to kill mosquitoes for malaria control. Second, it proposed another $125 million per year in surplus agricultural commodities—mainly wheat and cotton—that would ease India's need for imports and that would be sold by the government on the domestic market to raise rupees for financing the internal costs of community development. While Bowles realized that such a program far exceeded the Truman administration's plans for India, he tried to put the matter in perspective for the president. The "total four year cost for 360 million Indian people," he told Truman, will be "no more than [the] amount spent [on] economic aid [for] Greece and annual economic and military aid to Formosa, an island of 8 million which symbolizes [the] Communist victory in China, a nation of 400,000,000."[48]

Bowles lobbied for his $1 billion program with all the zeal characteristic of a Manhattan advertising executive. During his brief visit to Washington he held meetings with the president, the secretary of state, and NSC officials, and after returning to India he issued a constant stream of letters to various policymakers, including periodic Indian "progress reports" to members of Congress.[49] Bowles also established lines of communication with a number of the nation's top newspapers and journalists. He even went so far as to requisition the services of an old business acquaintance, Edward Bernays, to design a public relations campaign on India's behalf in the United States.[50]

Bowles achieved only limited success. The ambassador's program did win support among lower-echelon officials within the State Department's Office of South Asian Affairs and the Office of Near Eastern Affairs.[51] He could also count on backing from a circle of liberal legislators—including Senators Hubert Humphrey of Minnesota and Herbert Lehman of New York; and Representatives Jacob Javits and Emanuel Celler of New York and John F. Kennedy of Massachusetts—who had consistently called for increased economic aid for developing nations.[52] The Bureau of the Budget and the Mutual Security Administration, however, doubted India's ability to utilize large-scale aid efficiently and questioned the rate at which the Ford Foundation and the government of India could provide trained leadership for the program. Some State Department officials expressed concern over the impact of increased aid for India on relations with Pakistan. And nearly everyone in the administration assumed that it would be difficult to win wide congressional support for a large aid program in an election year.[53]

At the higher levels of decision making, Truman, Acheson, and other senior officials certainly approved of their ambassador's goal of promoting capitalistic development in India and creating stable economic and political conditions. The chief problem was that the magnitude of the plans far exceeded the narrow scope of the Point Four program for South Asia. In late January, the State Department's South Asian Affairs division persuaded Acheson to raise Point Four's projected outlays for India for fiscal year 1953 from $90 million to $115 million, nearly meeting Bowles's request for financial assistance. Communist party successes in the 1952 elections seem to have been the decisive factor in winning over the secretary of state. But the administration resisted entreaties for $125 million in commodity assistance. Most policymakers agreed that whereas an incremental adjustment in aid for the purchase of foreign supplies and equipment could be justified as falling within the parameters of the Point Four Plus approach, support for the domestic, rupee costs of Indian development could not. As one State Department official told Bowles: "The kind of program that you are talking about for India simply does not fit within the structure of present T.C.A. plans."[54]

As had been the case with the previous year's Mutual Security Program, United States commitments elsewhere took priority over South Asia. Of the $7.9 billion foreign aid budget submitted to Congress in March 1952, the White House earmarked over $5 billion as military aid for Europe. The administration increased allocations for Asia and the Pacific to slightly over $1 billion, but $610 million of that amount was slated as military assistance. Most of the remaining economic aid for Asia was directed toward political hot spots in East Asia, with nearly one-quarter of the total going to Formosa.[55] Acheson and W. Averell Harriman, director for Mutual Security, explained policy in a letter to Truman: "With the global requirements and United States availabilities in mind . . . the Administration requested only $115 million for India rather than the amount of $200 million to $250 million . . . suggested by Bowles."[56]

The aid program for India experienced further reversals as it made its way through Congress. Despite Bowles's intensive efforts, many legislators remained unconvinced of India's importance to the United States. In fact, the flow of letters and progress reports from New Delhi baffled many senators and representatives. Even Bowles's closest political ally, Connecticut Senator William Benton, advised the ambassador to let up on the pressure. "It is hard for you to realize how remote India is to people in Congress," Benton wrote, "Chet, it is never mentioned; it is never talked about; it's as remote as Antarctica. Thus it seems strange to have 'progress reports' coming in from this far off and remote and forgotten land. I know this isn't the way it ought to be. I'm merely reporting to you the way it is."[57] With fall elections just around the corner, Congress looked for crowd-pleasing ways to reduce the federal budget. Lacking a strong domestic constituency, economic aid for Third World nations became an irresistible target.

When the House of Representatives debate opened on an amendment to reduce overall funding for Point Four technical assistance, Indian aid became a particularly controversial item. Some critics raised questions concerning India's nonaligned foreign policy, especially its less than total commitment to the Korean War effort. "They talk about the fact that this is to make friends," Democratic Representative Howard Smith of Virginia complained, but if "there is anybody in the House who has ever seen or heard that Nehru has ever made a statement favorable to the United States, I would like to hear him say so now."[58] Others drew attention to Point Four's originally limited goals of providing low-cost technical services to needy nations and found fault with the more expensive Point Four Plus approach to India, which included funds for the purchase of capital goods. "If this thing is not brought to a halt," Democrat James Davis of Virginia warned, "there is no telling how many billions of dollars do-gooders and world spenders are going to take from the pockets of American taxpayers."[59] Javits, Celler, Kennedy, and others rallied to India's defense and argued that liberal development provided the best means by which to make non-Communist India secure and to eventually persuade Nehru to modify his neutralism. As young John Kennedy put it: "The Communists are now the second largest party in India. . . . The most effective weapon to stop them is technical assistance."[60] Yet when the Mutual Security Act of 1952 passed in June, Truman's overall request had been reduced from $7.9 billion to $6.5 billion. India's allocation fell from $115 million to $45 million—less than 20 percent of what Bowles had initially recommended.[61]

During the months of June and July, Bowles pressed Truman, Acheson, and Harriman to approach Capitol Hill with a special appropriation for India, but the White House demurred.[62] Acheson and Harriman counseled that such a strategy might try the patience of key legislators and undermine the administration's credibility on foreign aid altogether. Most important, India simply did not warrant such a gamble. As they concluded in a memorandum to Truman on the Bowles proposal: "It seems clear that our decision must rest on a determination as to how vital to United States objectives in India immediate action on his additional program is. In the absence of a critical emergency, it is extremely difficult to see how separate legislation could be justified."[63] The Truman White House had decided that while India carried enough stature to merit the continuation of a modest aid program, it still remained a secondary consideration among other foreign policy objectives.

Yet in the face of Bowles's continuous pressure and State Department concern over the growing popularity of the Communist party of India, both

Acheson and Truman finally conceded in June that they would try to increase India's allocation the following January when the administration submitted its foreign aid proposals for fiscal year 1954.[64] At one point the president even promised to direct a reassessment of the India program.[65] Charged with enthusiasm, Bowles initiated another lobbying effort, presumably to insure that Washington kept its promise. In alarmist letters to Truman, Acheson, and Harriman he warned of India's possible "disappearance behind the Iron Curtain" and argued that the "continued existence of India as a free and friendly nation is second only in importance to the survival of Western Europe." In a more carefully reasoned communication he pointed out that the dollar cost of "helping France and Vietnam to stop Communist aggression in a shooting war in Indochina approaches $500 million annually," nearly double the preventative costs of economic aid for India.[66]

As the prospects for Indian aid improved in Washington, events in India also took a positive turn. The government of India officially launched the Community Development Program on 2 October—the eighty-fourth anniversary of Mahatma Gandhi's birth. At the village of Alipore, eleven miles outside of New Delhi, Prime Minister Nehru symbolically dug and hauled a basketful of earth and declared that the CDP marked the beginning of a "peaceful revolution" that would "change the whole face of rural India."[67] Standing next to Bowles, he further remarked that India was "grateful indeed to America for the aid that we are receiving in futherance of our objectives."[68]

While the CDP initially established only fifty-five community projects, incorporating about 17,000 villages, planners aimed to bring all of the nation's 500,000 villages under the fold within ten years. Indeed, the final version of the *First Five Year Plan*, published in December, announced that the community development projects constituted the "focal centers" of India's agricultural policy. The revised plan even called upon Parliament to enact legal ceilings on land ownership and redistribute the surplus to the poor. Service cooperatives were to be formed to help farmers purchase agricultural equipment and supplies. Democratically elected village councils, called *panchayats*, would be organized to draw up local development plans.[69] On the surface of things, at least, India seemed to be alive with a grassroots fervor for social and economic change.

At the same time, the United States and India came together on the diplomatic front, at least momentarily, to work toward a settlement of the Korean War. By the spring of 1952 the war had stalemated and peace talks

Shirt-sleeves diplomacy. On an inspection trip visiting development projects in southern India in 1952, Ambassador Chester Bowles stops to help fishermen on the Malabar coast pull in a net. (Courtesy Chester Bowles Papers, Manuscripts and Archives, Yale University Library)

at Panmunjom had stalled over United States insistence on the voluntary repatriation of prisoners of war (POWs)—a demand that went against usual international practice. Urged on by Bowles, Nehru directed his representative at the United Nations, V. K. Krishna Menon, to undertake one last effort to exploit India's open lines of communication to Beijing, Moscow, and Washington and mold a compromise.[70] Menon was well known in international circles for his spirited nationalism, his role in helping to frame India's nonaligned foreign policy, and his frequent verbal attacks against United States Cold War policies. Indeed, Menon's acid tongue and his vain personal demeanor deeply annoyed most American policymakers who mistakenly viewed the diplomat as a Communist sympathizer.[71]

In spite of his abrasive style, Menon demonstrated real political savvy in his Korean War diplomacy. In November 1952, he formally introduced a resolution to the United Nations that included provisions for a cease-fire, an exchange of willing prisoners, and the creation of a four-member Neutral Nations Repatriation Commission to supervise POWs who resisted exchange. Once armistice arrangements had been made, prisoners resisting repatriation would be turned over to a postwar Korean Political Conference. Deeply suspicious of India's intentions and viewing Menon's proposals as deceitful and inadequate, Secretary of State Acheson initially opposed the Indian resolution. Ironically, the Soviet Union, which suspected that Menon secretly favored the Anglo-American cause, issued the first formal rejection of the plan, and Beijing quickly followed Moscow's lead. In the face of Soviet and Chinese opposition and strong allied support for the Indian measure, Acheson decided to back the Menon resolution after winning several amendments, the most important of which assured that the political conference would release all remaining prisoners within four months of an armistice. Although the fighting dragged on until July 1953, the revised resolution, which now guaranteed voluntary repatriation, provided a foundation for the ultimate POW settlement that helped end the war.[72]

While the launching of the CDP and limited collaboration at the United Nations did not necessarily mark the beginning of a close Indo-American friendship, these developments reinforced the Truman administration's inclination to go forward with Bowles's economic aid proposals. After months of waiting, Bowles received official word from Acheson in early January 1953 that the president's 1953 Mutual Security Program included $7.6 billion in foreign aid, and that India's allocation would "approach $200 million." Acheson even seemed to adopt at least part of Bowles's rationale for extending aid to India. The secretary wrote:

> In the best interests of the United States, India must be encouraged to remain in the democratic free world. Such encouragement can best be given by an acceleration in the rate of Indian economic development, with the consequent rise in the standard of living of the Indian people; to help accomplish this, substantial funds must be made available in the next few years from the United States for technical and economic assistance. . . . India's success not only will be significant in terms of benefits to India and the United States, but also will hearten and stimulate other underdeveloped countries of the world which are striving to overcome economic difficulties similar in many ways to those of India.[73]

Still, the future of the Indian program remained in doubt. After all, Truman's was a lame-duck presidency by January 1953, a factor which must be kept in mind in analyzing Washington's willingness to give in to Bowles in the first place. More important, by early 1953, United States policy toward South Asia had undergone another significant reassessment that did not bode well for Indo-American relations.

The Truman administration's decision to increase economic aid to India coincided with its renewed determination to pursue military defense and aid arrangements with a number of Middle Eastern nations, including India's regional rival, Pakistan. On their very last day in office in January 1953, Secretary Acheson, Secretary of Defense Robert A. Lovett, and Harriman submitted a report to the National Security Council, "Re-examination of United States Programs for National Security." The report expressed remorse over the failure to strengthen defenses in the Middle East and South Asia, and noted that the United States might suffer "substantial cold war losses" in the coming years if new policies were not forthcoming. Specifically, it called for the establishment of a Middle East Defense Organization (MEDO), to include—perhaps—Egypt, Greece, Turkey, Iran, and Pakistan. Regarding the subcontinent, the authors observed: "It is believed that Pakistan's active cooperation in defense of the Middle East might be obtained without involving unmanagable problems with India. . . . The first installment of substantial military aid to Pakistan should be supplied at an early date."[74]

The origins of a strong United States interest in Pakistan as an element of Middle East defense can be traced back to the months immediately following the outbreak of the Korean War, when administration officials came to view the Soviet Union as having become a more dangerous aggressor.

Washington had originally viewed India and Pakistan as a strategic unit, but after India spurned American overtures for defense collaboration in January 1951, the administration took up bilateral discussions with Pakistan.[75] Unlike Nehru, Pakistani leaders cultivated United States friendship by wholeheartedly endorsing American policies in Korea, China, and elsewhere in Asia. Equally important, while most administration officials had demonstrated little interest in Pakistan prior to the Korean War, American military planners had long perceived that nation as potentially a major strategic asset. As early as 1948, one CIA report had emphasized that Pakistan's near-contiguous border with the Soviet Union and its proximity to the Persian Gulf made it an ideal location for air bases and listening posts.[76] A Joint Chiefs of Staff study in March 1949 emphasized that the Karachi-Lahore area, in particular, "might be required as a base for air operations against [the] central USSR and as a staging area for forces engaged in the defense or recapture of Middle East oil areas."[77] By early 1951, a large number of policymakers had come to agree with the JCS that Pakistan's participation was essential to the defense of the Middle East. "With Pakistan, the Middle East could be defended," Assistant Secretary of State George McGhee declared during a high-level meeting at the Pentagon on 2 May, "without Pakistan, I don't see any way to defend the Middle East."[78]

Throughout 1951 and 1952, the Truman administration searched for a way to bring about a Western-backed Middle East defense system but ran into an endless series of obstacles. Initially Washington supported a British-inspired Middle East Command (MEC) with Egypt, whose important Suez Canal made it the key nation in the region, at the hub. In 1952, however, a military coup in Egypt led by Major General Mohammad Naguib and his colonels established a highly nationalistic government that rocked the nation and precluded military arrangements with the West.[79] In addition, elements within the British government also doubted the wisdom of pursuing the alliance system with Pakistani membership. While the British favored a regional defense system, they generally feared that Pakistan's immediate inclusion would alienate India, heighten tensions over Kashmir, and not significantly contribute to Middle East security.[80] One Foreign Office memorandum explained to High Commissioner Oliver Franks in Washington: "We are anxious lest United States impatience with India should lead them to discount risks involved with India." [81]

In mid-1952, British and American planners abandoned MEC in order to organize the less formal Middle East Defense Organization that carried the advantage of not requiring member states to contribute permanent forces. The British proved more amenable to these arrangements and more hopeful that Pakistan might participate without provoking India's wrath.[82] In late 1952, however, rumors of MEDO, spawned by articles in the *Washington Post* and *New York Times*, circulated in New Delhi. Street demonstrations broke out and Nehru called Ambassador Bowles to his office to complain that arms shipped to Pakistan would more likely be used against India than against the Soviet Union. Bowles immediately wrote to Presidential Assistant Charles Murphy that military cooperation with Pakistan would "destroy the effort we are making to create a solid basis of understanding and friendship" with India.[83]

On 13 January 1953 the Indian ambassador in Washington, G. L. Mehta, met with Acheson. Mehta observed that while India held no objections to United States economic assistance to Pakistan, "military aid and the development of air bases was another matter." Mehta warned that if a Pakistani-American military accord came to fruition, "the work of Ambassador Bowles and of himself and his predecessors in Washington, which had been directed toward cementing Indo-American friendship, would be to a large measure, destroyed." Acheson responded by pointing to difficulties in Egypt that mitigated against early implementation of MEDO and reassured the ambassador that the United States remained sensitive to India's apprehensions. Although the secretary of state admitted that some future approach to the Pakistanis had been contemplated, he stated that no formal discussions had yet taken place and that the United States hoped it "could go forward with our planning without further increasing complications now existing in the Middle East."[84]

For the time being, regional difficulties in the Near East and South Asia prevented the establishment of MEDO. Bowles, moreover, could take solace in the fact that he had won the administration's endorsement of a $200 million aid package for India. Serious obstacles still stood in the path of successful economic development in India. It remained to be seen if Nehru and his Congress party would actually enact and enforce reform legislation, and it would, of course, take years, perhaps decades, before the fruits of modern rural development could really be assessed. Of more immediate concern in early 1953 was the question of United States aid priorities. Bowles knew that the decision to increase economic aid to India and to drop military plans for Pakistan had been reached only after Truman had removed himself from presidential politics. The fate of Bowles's program, and MEDO, would rest with the new Eisenhower administration.

The inauguration of Dwight D. Eisenhower as the thirty-third president of the United States did not bring any immediate shift in American foreign policy. Before reaching the White House, the popular World War II hero had supported all of Truman's major decisions: the containment policy, North Atlantic Treaty Organization, and intervention in Korea. During the 1952 campaign the Republicans had often attacked containment as a weak-kneed response to communism and had talked of liberating the "captive peoples" of Eastern Europe. But President Eisenhower never translated these slogans into policy. His secretary of state, John Foster Dulles, lent a particularly strident rhetoric to United States diplomacy. Words like "immoral" and "enslavement" were among the secretary's favorites when the topic of discussion turned to communism. But Dulles, too, had been an active supporter of the previous administration, and the responsibilities of power sobered even this harsh critic of the Kremlin. Thus, when Eisenhower and Dulles spoke of the evil nature of communism, they did so as true believers. Yet their formula for dealing with the "menace" was still containment.[85]

Eisenhower and Dulles made no radical departures in foreign economic policy. In the 1952 campaign, candidate Eisenhower promised to reduce foreign aid as part of a broader effort to balance the ever-growing federal budget and espoused the view that by increasing channels for international trade, most forms of economic aid could be eliminated.[86] As president, Eisenhower quickly concluded that United States security interests precluded any radical revision of the foreign aid program. At one National Security Council meeting in early 1953, Dulles described Mutual Security as a major factor "in preventing global war" and advocated "a firm policy to hold the vital outpost positions around the periphery of the Soviet bloc." He cited the North Atlantic Treaty Organization nations, Japan, Indochina, Iran, India, and Pakistan as being especially worthy of United States aid. Eisenhower spoke out in agreement, remarking that while a balanced budget might be desirable, "we can't suddenly cut off our developing policies and programs for national security." His own belief, the president continued, was that "we should now show our determination to move in the direction of a balanced budget rather than making a sudden cut to achieve that objective now."[87] In short, Cold War internationalism won out over fiscal conservatism.

While the new administration decided that foreign aid should not be drastically cut back, it did not envision any significant expansion of United States commitments—particularly in India. Although Secretary Dulles acknowledged India's importance as a vital outpost on the periphery of the Soviet bloc, he had long entertained doubts about that nation's nonaligned policy. Distrust between the two went back as far as 1946 when Dulles had voiced dismay over Communist influence in India's interim government. Then, in 1951, differences arose between Dulles and Nehru over the long-delayed United States peace treaty with Japan that Dulles had negotiated. When the treaty was signed in September, India specifically criticized provisions allowing for the continued presence of American troops and military bases and the maintenance of an American trusteeship over the Ryukyu and Bonin islands. To Nehru, these stipulations seemed tantamount to making Japan a quasi colony of the United States. Dulles, on the other hand, complained that India had adopted the Communist Chinese slogan of "Asia for Asians."[88] So when Dulles assumed the helm at Foggy Bottom in January 1953, he was not predisposed toward substantially increasing aid for India.

No sooner had the new team settled into work when Chester Bowles's letters and memorandums began to pour in. In correspondence to Eisenhower, Dulles, and other officials the ambassador restated his views that the United States should adopt a policy of tolerance toward nonalignment, and that India's "survival," so vital to the United States, could only be secured through the implementation of his $250 million a year program.[89] Although the Office of Near Eastern Affairs stood by earlier plans for $200 million in aid for India, Eisenhower voiced skepticism toward these recommendations and he ordered Dulles to review the India program. When the State Department's Mutual Security recommendations came to Dulles at the beginning of March he sent them back noting: "I do not wish to sign this as long as it carries the sum of $200 million for India. I doubt that this amount is justified by the facts or could be justified to Congress."[90] The department finally sent a recommendation of $140 million for India to the Bureau of the Budget. In the meantime, Dulles and Eisenhower began to scout replacements for Bowles, and they soon settled upon career officer George V. Allen for the job.[91]

While the Eisenhower administration rejected Bowles's ambitious agenda, the 1953 Indian aid program did not signal a major change in United States policy. After the Bureau of the Budget reviewed Mutual Security as a whole, the president went to Congress with a $5.8 billion request that included $110 million for India. Although $90 million less than the amount planned by the lame-duck Truman administration, this amount was only $5 million less that what had been asked for in the last active year of Truman's presidency. More important, the Eisenhower White House succeeded in winning congressional authorization of $89.1 million, nearly double what had been authorized the previous year.[92] In addition, the primary motive behind American generosity remained constant—Cold War politics. Dulles struck a familiar chord while defending the India program before the Senate Foreign Relations Committee by warning that "present economic conditions in the area [South Asia] provide a happy hunting ground for the Communists." But in accord with precedent, he also stressed that the American effort in the region would be limited to small-scale projects mainly in the agricultural field.[93]

Except for the overall reduction in the Mutual Security budget that resulted from the winding down of hostilities in Korea, Eisenhower's priorities resembled those of his predecessor. In keeping with policies set down at the onset of the Korean War, the major portion of aid funds for fiscal year 1954 continued to be allocated for military assistance to United States allies. The Eisenhower administration budgeted two-thirds, or $4 billion, of its total 1953 request for "mutual defense training." Allocations for this form of aid rose slightly for the Far East and Near East regions, but $2.53 billion was still reserved for Western Europe.[94] Under Dwight D. Eisenhower's leadership, then, American policymakers continued to place a premium upon bolstering Europe and other strategically placed nations militarily and to give short shrift to the economic needs of nations like India.

From 1951 through 1953, the United States evolved and implemented its first economic development program for India and embarked on a new era of development diplomacy. Under the energetic leadership of Ambassador Chester Bowles, the American embassy in New Delhi helped the government of India devise a potentially far-reaching Community Development Program. The principal economic and social aims of the effort were to increase food production, to improve the quality of life for the hundreds of millions of people who inhabited India's rural heartland, and to lay the groundwork for India's capitalistic development. Politically, the American ambassador hoped to make non-Communist India a stable and reliable friend of the United States. Although the Bowles approach bore shortcomings, it also showed real potential. Initiated just five years after the coming of political independence, the promise of community development seemed to rekindle a zeal for reform among Indian leaders that was reminiscent of the earlier freedom struggle. Equally important, Indo-American relations showed signs of improvement as both nations backed away somewhat from their confrontational stances on Korea and the Cold War.

As Bowles pushed ahead with his plans for liberal development, however, senior officials in Washington implemented a global foreign aid strategy that derived from a much narrower conception of national security. Primarily concerned over the threat of direct Soviet aggression, the Truman and Eisenhower administrations determined that military aid rather than economic aid ranked as a foreign assistance priority. From a regional perspective, the strategic nations of Western Europe and insurgency-plagued areas in Southeast Asia assumed far greater significance than India and South Asia. In addition, a coalition of budget-minded opponents of economic aid and critics of India's nonalignment formed in Congress and brought about further reductions in aid for India. Even when the Truman administration belatedly gave its support to the Bowles program in late 1952 and early 1953, the prospects for its passage on Capitol Hill were bleak.

Yet once the linkage between Third World development assistance and United States national security had been established, it would be difficult to completely derail the aid process. By 1953, policymakers no longer debated whether or not to extend economic aid to India. They pondered, instead, the magnitude of the aid and the terms on which it would be made available. This is not to downplay the importance of obstacles that remained in the way of Indo-American economic cooperation. Bureaucratic infighting in Washington, legislative battles on Capitol Hill, and India's strong nationalist policies all created problems for the aid program. Still, the concept of development assistance for India had been endorsed by two administrations and had gathered a core of support in Congress. As the Korean War wound down, moreover, the need to extend large-scale military aid abroad abated. American policymakers seemed increasingly likely to turn their attention to a new constellation of problems in the developing nations of the Third World.

Five

A Changing Cold War, 1953–1956

In spite of the less than promising beginning, the outlook for aid to India improved somewhat during Dwight D. Eisenhower's first term in office. The most important catalysts for new policy initiatives arose from the changing nature of the international setting. The process started as early as March 1953, when Premier Josef Stalin passed from the world scene and new Soviet leaders adopted a more conciliatory stance toward the West. Peace soon came in Korea, Soviet trade with the West opened, Russian controls over Eastern Europe loosened, a treaty guaranteed Austria's neutrality, and in 1955, a Soviet-American summit met in Geneva. John Foster Dulles went to Geneva wearing a grimace, and the concrete accomplishments of Soviet-American diplomacy were few, but both sides seemed to welcome a thaw in the Cold War. And both sides seemed to acknowledge that geopolitical lines had hardened in Europe.

At the same time, a series of revolutionary events shook the Third World. In Asia, a defeated French army withdrew from Vietnam in 1954, but fighting between Communist and non-Communist forces continued. In Latin America, also in 1954, a reformist regime—with some Communist support—came to power in Guatemala. In the Middle East, Gamal Abdel Nasser consolidated control over Egypt, and by 1956 his brand of anticolonial nationalism had gained popularity throughout the region. The widespread instability and American fears of Soviet exploitation of unrest caused Washington to increasingly turn its attention to non-Western areas and strengthened arguments for providing increased economic assistance to the newly emerged nations—including India.

The Eisenhower administration, however, proved reluctant to adjust to change. As their Mutual Security Program for 1953 demonstrated, the Eisenhower/Dulles team initially remained wedded to Cold War policies that placed a premium on bolstering the military capacities of America's overseas friends and allies. The trend continued after 1953 and carried immense ramifications for India when it resulted in the consummation of a United States military pact in 1954 with India's foremost rival, Pakistan.

The prospects for Indo-American relations reached an all-time low following the United States–Pakistan alliance, as New Delhi issued forth a stream of protest that severely tested Washington's patience.

Yet from 1954 through 1956, the Eisenhower administration also began to slowly reconsider American policy toward the Third World in general, and India in particular. As Cold War tensions receded in Europe, United States policymakers awakened to the growing tumult in non-Western regions and gradually became more sensitive to the force of nationalism and the urge for economic development. Most important, Eisenhower, Dulles, and other officials showed special concern when a new Soviet leadership reached out to India and other neutral Third World nations with a series of highly publicized economic aid programs. Faced with a changing Cold War, the administration struggled with itself and with Congress to devise an appropriate economic aid strategy.

The drive to garner and strengthen military allies was intensified at the beginning of the Eisenhower years. Indeed, the term "pactomania" has been used to describe Eisenhower's policies in the Third World that led to the creation of the Southeast Asia Treaty Organization (SEATO) in 1954 and the Baghdad Pact in the Near East the following year. But in many ways the Eisenhower/Dulles team merely picked up on the legacy and policy planning bequeathed to them by their predecessors. The new president and his secretary of state found themselves in agreement with the thinking of the Truman administration on the special need to build up American defenses in the Middle East, including the creation of a Middle East Defense Organization and the establishment of a military relationship with Pakistan. Unlike their predecessors, the Eisenhower/Dulles team found a way to work through the maze of regional complications in order to put a plan into operation. The process began in May 1953, when Secretary Dulles traveled to eleven Middle Eastern and South Asian nations, including Egypt, Iraq, Turkey, Pakistan, and India.

It is doubtful that Dulles stopped off in New Delhi to sound out Nehru on MEDO. The secretary's memorandum of his conversation with the Indian leader indicates that India and the United States were far apart on the usual issues of colonialism, defense, and the Cold War. But the two nations did hold a common concern in regard to Korea—probably the principal reason for Dulles's visit. In preceding months, as the fighting stalemated at the 38th parallel, armistice talks had continued to bog down over United States insistence on the voluntary repatriation of prisoners of war. Knowing that the Indians maintained lines of communication with China on the issue, Dulles took the opportunity to announce publicly in New Delhi that if the Communist side did not accept United States demands, hostilities in Korea might become "more intense." This threat coincided with soundings from the White House on the possible use of atomic weapons in Korea. It has long been speculated that Dulles directly threatened the use of nuclear weapons in his private talks with Nehru. In fact, the secretary's declassified notes of his conversations with Nehru, and the testimony of former Indian officials, do not substantiate the rumors. No such threat was necessary, moreover, for Nehru had clearly been impressed by Dulles's public utterances, news of which was sure to make its way to Beijing. Dulles reported to Eisenhower:

> Nehru brought up [the] Korean armistice, referring particularly to my statement of [the] preceding day, that if no (repeat no) armistice occurred hostilities might become more intense. He said if this happened it [was] difficult to know what [the] end might be. He urged the withdrawal of our armistice proposals as inconsistent with the Indian resolutions. He made no (repeat no) alternate proposal. He brought up again my reference to intensified operations, but I made no (repeat no) comment and allowed the topic to drop.[1]

Apparently MEDO was the major topic of conversation in the other countries that Dulles visited. In a meeting of the National Security Council on 1 June 1953, the secretary of state gave a country-by-country summary of his trip and commented upon the potential value of each in terms of American military aims. He emphasized that Egypt, "the key country" in the region, was unlikely to prove an immediate asset, due to its internal political climate and its tendency to underestimate the Soviet Union. Therefore, the MEDO initiative seemed to be impractical. At the same time, however, Dulles showered praise upon countries such as Turkey, Iraq, Syria, and Pakistan whose leaders realized the Communist danger. Comprising the "northern tier" of the region, Dulles explained that these nations together could form a more effective defensive ring to encircle the Soviet bloc. In discussing the Indian subcontinent, he told his colleagues that he had found Nehru to be "an utterly impractical statesman," but that he had been "immensely impressed by the martial and religious characteristics of the Pakistanis."[2]

The National Security Council adopted the northern tier strategy in early July 1953, but it took over a year and one-half to bring about the creation of the Baghdad Pact between Turkey, Pakistan, Iraq, Iran, and Great Britain.[3] The reasons for the delay were numerous. The administration still held out hopes for coming to terms with Egypt. In addition, the State and Defense Departments proceeded with customary, bureaucratic caution. But the most important impediment continued to be concern over India's reaction. As rumors of a United States–Pakistan Pact floated in New Delhi during the fall of 1953, Nehru declared that such a turn of events would "have far-reaching consequences on the whole structure of things in South Asia."[4] Meanwhile, the British continued to voice doubts about a Pakistan alliance, especially the haste with which the Americans proceeded. As one Foreign Office report noted in December 1953: "The Americans have on more than one occasion shown a tendency to rush matters."[5]

Ironically, these entreaties ultimately reinforced America's inclination to go forward with the Pakistan pact. Now, it seemed as though a decision not to go ahead with the arrangements would be viewed as an American effort to appease Nehru's neutralism. Dulles suggested in one memorandum to Eisenhower that failure to conclude a pact "would do a great deal to establish Nehru as the leader of all South and Southeast Asia and nations in that area would henceforth be reluctant to proceed on matters with the West without Nehru's support."[6] Although Eisenhower shared some of the British government's misgivings, he gave his assent to Pakistan military aid on 5 January at a White House meeting with Dulles, Director of Mutual Security Harold Stassen, and Secretary of Defense Charles Wilson.[7]

The first step in implementation came in early February 1954, when, after extensive consultation with Washington, Turkey and Pakistan announced plans for military cooperation. On 22 February, Pakistan's Prime Minister Mohammed Ali Bogra told a press conference: "The Government of Pakistan has made a request to the Government of the United States for military assistance within the scope of the United States Mutual Security legislation." Three days later President Eisenhower announced that the United States intended to meet Pakistan's request.[8] Before the year was out Pakistan had joined yet another American-inspired military alliance, SEATO. Incorporating the United States, Britain, France, Australia, New Zealand, Thailand, the Philippines, and Pakistan, this treaty system aimed to stabilize the troubled Southeast Asian region in the aftermath of the French defeat at Dien Bien Phu in Vietnam.

The Indian government reacted angrily to these developments. Dulles had assured Nehru during their meeting in New Delhi that the United States had "no present plans that would bring it into [a] military relationship with Pakistan which could reasonably be looked upon as unneutral as regards India."[9] The prime minister feared that the move would embolden Pakistan to act aggressively in Kashmir, and that it would needlessly bring the Cold War to the subcontinent. Worst of all, Nehru believed that the United States had aimed its military power against India as much as it had against the Soviet Union. In a private letter he drew somewhat exaggerated conclusions: "In effect Pakistan becomes practically a colony of the United States. . . . The United States imagine that by this policy they have completely outflanked India's so-called neutralism and will thus bring India to her knees."[10]

President Eisenhower had, to some extent, expected the adverse reaction. On 24 February, he instructed Ambassador George Allen to hand deliver a personal letter to Nehru, explaining that the United States had acted in the name of international security and not in a manner of hostility toward India. The president also offered to make military equipment available to India upon request. In the following months Indo-American relations nevertheless deteriorated badly. Nehru scorned the offer of the military aid and remained convinced that the pact threatened India's wellbeing. "That is one area of the world," Eisenhower told Dulles in a reference to South Asia, "where, even more than most cases, emotion rather than reason seems to dictate policy."[11]

Nehru's spirited condemnation of United States policy no doubt exaggerated the detrimental effects of the alliance, but numerous critics at home, including Chester Bowles, Senator J. William Fulbright, the *Christian Science Monitor*, and the *Washington Post* offered more carefully reasoned arguments. Taken together, they pointed out that among other consequences, the pact would result in an escalation of Indo-Pakistani tensions, encourage each nation to divert resources from economic to defense programs, and increase Indian—and Afghan—ties to the Soviet Union.[12] In short, they accurately predicted that the negative impact would be felt for decades to come.

While the United States–Pakistani arms agreement proved to be a serious setback to Indo-American relations, it did not preclude future cooperation. Indeed, when the Eisenhower administration assembled its 1954 foreign aid programs it chose neither to reduce nor eliminate economic assistance for India. The administration set forth its first comprehensive policy statement on the Indian subcontinent in early 1954 in NSC 5409, "United States Policy toward South Asia." Covering the usual ground to outline American interests in the region, NSC 5409 referred to the subcontinent's strategic location, its vast mineral wealth, and its manpower resources. The major difference between NSC 5409 and similar, previous documents was the emphasis placed upon the importance of military ties with Pakistan. Yet NSC 5409 recognized that India remained the largest and most populous nation in South Asia. India's "loss" to communism, the document observed, "would constitute a major reversal to the free world." While the authors of the NSC document acknowledged that a Soviet invasion of India was not likely, they did fear that India's fragile economic and political stability offered opportunities for Communist subversion. They therefore restated the familiar argument that economic aid to India and other South Asian nations might "be a strong factor in determining whether they develop into more stable and viable components of the free world or lapse into a state of international weakness inviting Communist domination."[13]

The decision to continue the economic program in India cannot be fully understood without examining the Eisenhower administration's response to an escalating Cold War crisis in Indochina. By early 1954, America's North Atlantic Treaty Organization (NATO) ally, France, seemed to be losing its war against the Communist-led Vietminh. In January, the National Security Council staff completed work on another important document, NSC 5405, "Statement of Policy by the National Security Council on United States Objectives and Courses of Action with Respect to Southeast Asia." It began with the assumption—popularly known as the "domino theory"—that a Communist takeover in Indochina would "lead to submission or alignment with communism" by other countries in the region. If all of Southeast Asia were to fall, policymakers reasoned, "an alignment with communism in India, and in the longer term of the Middle East (with the possible exception of at least Pakistan and Turkey)" would follow. To prevent such a scenario, NSC 5405 emphasized the usefulness of a regional defense mechanism, but also recommended that the United States undertake "limited economic and technical assistance programs" to convince non-Communist Asian governments that their security and independence would be best preserved through "cooperation and stronger affiliations with the rest of the free world."[14]

Just as NSC 5409 and NSC 5405 reiterated the importance of economic aid to United States security interests, a White House appointed Commission on Foreign Economic Policy completed a special study that recommended sharp reductions in foreign aid. Headed by the president of Inland Steel, Clarence Randall, the commission harkened back to the theme articulated by Eisenhower during the 1952 campaign that the United States should, in time, eliminate most forms of aid and promote worldwide economic growth through the liberalization of international trade and investment. The Randall Commission specifically called for an early end to grant aid and its replacement with low interest, dollar loans repayable in local currencies (called "soft" loans); the continuation of small-scale technical assistance programs; revisions in the revenue code to encourage private investment abroad; and tariff reductions.[15]

Although the "trade not aid" philosophy embodied in the report appealed to Eisenhower's fiscal conservatism, the ideas advanced by the Randall Commission were not translated into policy. First, protectionist forces in Congress prevented any drastic revisions in United States trade policy. Second, and perhaps more decisive, United States security interests precluded abandonment of the foreign economic aid program. In 1954, Eisenhower reduced, but showed no inclination to eliminate, funding proposals for the Mutual Security Program. For fiscal year 1955, the president requested about $3.5 billion, a reduction of $2.3 billion from his fiscal year 1954 request.[16]

In keeping with trends established during the Korean War, Eisenhower's 1954 Mutual Security Program emphasized a defense buildup. Over 80 percent of the funds requested were for military aid or had a military purpose, such as strengthening the economies of countries receiving military assistance. The Mutual Security Program of 1954 did signal a departure in terms of regional focus. Although the administration scheduled the majority of the aid for Western Europe, a larger percentage was slated for Third World countries than in previous years, with nearly $1 billion in military aid for Southeast Asia and the Pacific.[17]

A less emphasized although important part of Eisenhower's 1954 Mutual Security request was the $256 million it recommended as economic assistance for underdeveloped nations. The largest authorization in this category was the $104 million allocation for India. While Eisenhower and Dulles viewed Nehru as a "nuisance" and discounted the Indian leader's usefulness as a military ally, they believed that conditions in Asia required United States efforts to strengthen Nehru's non-Communist government.[18] In discussing aid to India before Congress, Dulles took note of Indo-American differences but stressed Nehru's staunch opposition to the Communist party of India, his nation's adherence to democratic principles, and the need to counter destabilizing forces in India. He even resurrected Bowles's argument that the "comparison of the economic progress made under the democratic system of India and the Communist dictatorship in China" would influence all of Asia.[19]

One piece of legislation passed in 1954 that widened the scope for future economic development assistance was the Agricultural Trade Development and Assistance Act, or Public Law 480 (PL 480). This bill, which provided for increased United States food aid abroad, had its roots in the emergence of large agricultural surpluses in the United States. By 1954, the Department of Agriculture's Commodity Credit Corporation, charged with purchasing farm surpluses in order to prevent excess supplies from deflating prices, spent over $1 million daily to store surplus commodities. With little hope of curbing overproduction in the near future, the White House and Congress, pushed by farm state legislators, farm organizations, and agribusiness lobbyists, concluded that there seemed to be no alternative to, as one administration official put it, "exporting our problem."[20]

As passed in July 1954, the $700 million PL 480 consisted of three major titles. Title I authorized the sale of surplus, agricultural commodities to "friendly" governments for local currencies, an arrangement that allowed purchasers to conserve valuable dollars. Sales agreements were not to disrupt the "usual marketings" of the United States and not to "unduly disturb" world prices. Title II provided for donations of surplus food for famine relief and other emergencies. Title III authorized food grants for emergencies within the United States and to nonprofit organizations abroad and established a barter program that allowed the United States and foreign governments to exchange surplus agricultural goods for strategic materials. Although PL 480 would eventually become a much used form of economic aid to Third World nations, as introduced in 1954 it was primarily a surplus disposal program.[21]

When all was said and done, the Eisenhower administration's approach to foreign assistance in 1954 included no major departures in policy toward India or other Third World nations. United States officials still viewed economic programs as being secondary in importance to military priorities. Congress once again reduced funding for economic assistance in underdeveloped areas, but at the end of the legislative process India was awarded $85.7 million, about the same amount authorized in 1953.[22] The one innovation incorporated into the Mutual Security Act was the White House's request that, in conformity with the Randall Commission report, some economic aid should be made available in the form of soft loans rather than grants. About $45 million of the aid set aside for India for fiscal year 1955, or one-half of the total, consisted of loans.[23] In later years the Eisenhower administration would use the soft loan strategy to make increased assistance to India and other developing countries more palatable to budget-conscious opponents of foreign aid. But in 1954 the proposal simply reflected the administration's own desire to cut back on the cost of economic programs that it considered to be of less consequence to Cold War objectives than military assistance.[24]

Despite the disinclination to undertake major initiatives in regard to Indian economic aid, the Eisenhower administration began to consider in 1954 a few innovative proposals in the area of foreign economic policy. None of the proposals advanced brought about an immediate revision in policy, and none specifically centered on India. But they did represent a subtle shift in orientation that would deeply affect United States economic relations with India and the Third World later during the Eisenhower years.

The earliest and most forceful advocate of increased financial assistance was C. D. Jackson. Jackson had served as a speech writer and special adviser on psychological warfare and Cold War affairs during the first year of Eisenhower's presidency. By early 1954, he had left the White House staff to resume his position as vice-president of Time-Life Incorporated. But his close ties to the administration, especially his personal friendship with Secretary of State Dulles, assured him of easy access to the circles of power. In the spring of 1954, Jackson adopted the cause of Third World economic aid as his own and began a major lobbying effort to revise United States foreign economic policy.[25]

The brainstorming started, according to Jackson, over lunch with Dulles one day in April 1954 when the two discussed a wide range of topics. The conversation turned toward Indochina and Asia, and Jackson took the opportunity to suggest the creation of a multibillion dollar, soft loan agency for developing nations.[26] As the concept evolved over the next few months, the Time-Life executive came to envision a five-year, $10 billion, "World Economic Policy" (WEP). Jackson argued to administration officials, including President Eisenhower, that whereas the United States had begun to implement a long-term military strategy to contain communism, it had failed to formulate a long-term economic program. The WEP would fill the gap and serve as a "peaceful weapon" in Asian, Near Eastern, and Latin

American nations.[27] "It is the kind of big, bold approach that is typically American, and that the American people want," he told Eisenhower.[28]

Jackson won a sympathetic hearing from Dulles, who had become increasingly worried by events in Indochina and Southeast Asia. It faced stiff opposition, however, from a number of administration officials due to its cost. Joseph Dodge, head of the Council on Foreign Economic Policy that was formed in the aftermath of the Randall Commission study, Secretary of Treasury George Humphrey, and Under Secretary of State Herbert Hoover, Jr.—all staunch fiscal conservatives—criticized the "budget busting" aspects of the plan.[29] And when Jackson urged Eisenhower to push ahead and propose the WEP in a presidential address, the chief executive declined, noting that "a new and bold approach" to foreign aid would be viewed by cynics as "bigger and better give-aways."[30] Even Dulles, who told Jackson that "I am 100% behind your type of investment program," did not give his wholehearted support. As he explained, "the task of fighting these things out within Treasury, Budget, World Bank, Ex-Im, not to mention Congress," would be a long and arduous task.[31]

A second advocate of increased economic aid, Harold Stassen, director of the Foreign Operations Administration (the successor agency to the Mutual Security Administration), achieved only slightly greater success. Stassen, a representative of the Republican party's liberal wing, presented his economic program in the summer of 1954.[32] Somewhat more refined than the global WEP, the Stassen proposal called for a loan program geared specifically to the crucial Asian region. His timing was excellent, for in May 1954, the French finally conceded defeat at the battle of Dien Bien Phu in Vietnam, and the Eisenhower administration launched efforts to build the SEATO military alliance. An Asian economic initiative would nicely complement the defensive program, Stassen emphasized in one memorandum to Dulles, and help to strengthen the region against communism.[33]

Stassen went public with the idea in October, when he spoke at a meeting of the Colombo Plan nations in Ottawa, Canada. Even though he carefully avoided any precise mention of dollar amounts, the speech created controversy within the administration. Secretary George Humphrey, perhaps the most conservative cabinet member, raised the old specter of rising budget deficits and decried Stassen's promise of still more expenditures in Asia. But Eisenhower apparently had already given Stassen some measure of backing. Talking the matter over with Humphrey, the president questioned Treasury's view toward spending. "I hope I am not one of your spendthrift people," he told Humphrey, "but in advancing [the] budget, even cutting back $100 thousand for Defense bothers me." Eisenhower noted that with regard to foreign aid he was "frightened most about Asia." "I want to put out something hopeful," he expounded, "to show that the world has hope of going up in its standards. I'm talking about [being] really ready to meet this challenge head on. . . . Asia to my mind has gotten very critical. . . . We must have courage to do some tough figuring here."[34] At a December news conference, Eisenhower announced that during the coming year he would recommend the establishment of an Asian Development Fund in addition to regular Mutual Security appropriations.[35]

Meanwhile, a hopeful Stassen had set out to prepare a far-reaching, $10 billion, five-year program for Asia. His guiding principle was that Asian communism could only be contained through a long-term effort to promote not only agricultural, but industrial development.[36] "It will be a long-term struggle," he counseled Eisenhower, but "acceleration of industrialization is an indispensable part of a successful program."[37] Despite the heightened interest in the region, however, the administration did not plan a very ambitious scheme. Meeting with congressional leaders in late 1954, Dulles discussed the Communist threat in Asia and hinted that "we may come to you for an authorization" of special aid funds. But the secretary quickly added that the planned request was "certainly not on the scale of the Marshall Plan."[38] To determine the actual level of spending, the National Security Council appointed a committee headed by the conservative Herbert Hoover, Jr., and when the committee finished its work in January 1955, it recommended the establishment of an Asian Development Fund with a capitalization of only $205 million.[39]

Although the Eisenhower administration had decided against dramatically increasing economic aid to Third World nations, a significant change in thinking had begun to take shape. C. D. Jackson and Harold Stassen led the way with their ambitious proposals, but Eisenhower and Dulles also demonstrated at least some measure of awareness of the Third World's economic needs. Once again, a Cold War crisis, this time in Southeast Asia, provided the impetus. While the limited resources allocated to the Asian Development Fund proposal in early 1955 reflected only a minor commitment to change, American policymakers were becoming increasingly cognizant of the Third World and seemed to be groping for a new foreign economic policy to meet the challenge.

Neither Jackson nor Stassen addressed their proposals particularly to India's economic needs, but both men had India in mind as a possible beneficiary of United States aid. Jackson talked in broad, sweeping terms while campaigning for WEP, but in one letter to Dulles he noted the special importance of reaching out to Asian nations that had not joined in military alliance with the United States. He even referred to the WEP's "special hooker for India, Burma, [and] Indonesia."[40] Since Stassen zeroed in upon Asia, he analyzed the topic with a bit more precision, and his reports on the Asian Development Fund consistently took note of India's significance as a democratic model for development.[41] If the United States launched a substantive economic program for underdeveloped nations in the future, India was sure to become a major recipient.

By 1954 and early 1955, however, Indo-American relations had become badly strained. Shaken by the Pakistani-American partnership and the increasing militarization of Asia, Nehru set out to meet with other Afro-Asian leaders who shared his perspective. First, he exchanged visits with Foreign Minister Zhou Enlai of the People's Republic of China. Contrasting Indian and American approaches to communism, Nehru succeeded in winning Zhou's approval of his famous "five principles," or *Panchsheel* in Hindi. The two leaders pledged: (1) mutual respect for each others territorial integrity; (2) mutual nonaggression; (3) noninterference in the internal affairs of other nations; (4) relations based upon equality and mutual benefit; and (5) peaceful coexistence. For Nehru, the five principles were more than a guidepost for Sino-Indian relations. They represented an Asian alternative to Cold War diplomacy. After China, similar exchanges followed with the leaders of Burma, Ceylon, Egypt, Indonesia, North Vietnam, and Yugoslavia—all nations that criticized United States collective security arrangements. In each instance the Indian leader conspicuously paraded his five principles.[42]

The flurry of meetings culminated in April 1955 at a formal conference of twenty-nine Afro-Asian nations at Bandung, Indonesia. Indonesian President Sukarno opened the meeting on 15 April with a keynote address that eloquently recalled the anniversary of the "shot heard round the world" and America's inspiring, anticolonial revolution, but it was America's Cold War policies that dominated subsequent debate. Nehru directed his aim against the United States by proposing that conference participants pledge not to enter foreign military alliances that, he maintained, assumed the face of colonialism. Delegates from pro-Western nations took issue and pointed to Soviet expansionism in Eastern Europe as a more ominous expression of imperialism. While Nehru argued that such matters were not the proper concern of an Afro-Asian meeting, he was forced to compromise. In the end, the Bandung Conference adopted a resolution that condemned colonialism in all forms and expanded India's highly prized five principles to a list of ten—which included the right to collective self-defense.[43] Still, Nehru, Sukarno, and other nonaligned leaders had succeeded in using the Bandung Conference as a forum for airing their views.

The Eisenhower administration showed increased interest in India as the prime minister traveled to meetings with foreign leaders. Expanded economic aid was not immediately in the offing, but beginning in the summer of 1954 attempts were made to improve the climate of Indo-American relations. Eisenhower and Dulles took the first step by looking for a new ambassador to replace George Allen, the unfortunate career officer who had borne the task of keeping Nehru abreast of American dealings with Pakistan. Eisenhower's first choice was Paul Hoffman, former Marshall Plan administrator and president of the Ford Foundation. After considering the ambassadorial post, Hoffman turned it down, citing the personal difficulties of moving his family abroad.[44] Through the summer and fall Eisenhower continued the search. At one point he even considered bringing Chester Bowles back into his former position, an idea that Dulles quickly vetoed for fear of runaway foreign aid requests.[45] The president and his secretary of state finally agreed upon John Sherman Cooper, a recently defeated Republican senator from Kentucky. Cooper, who had come to know Dulles as a member of the United States delegation at the United Nations in 1949, was a confirmed internationalist. Eisenhower expressed doubts about the senator's lack of familiarity with India, but after meeting with Cooper he came away impressed by the latter's warm, personable style—a key asset, Eisenhower thought, in dealing with a difficult Nehru. The nomination sailed through the Senate, and the new ambassador departed for New Delhi in February 1955.[46]

Despite the appointment of a new ambassador, impediments continued to stand in the way of Indo-American relations. Nehru remained at odds with the United States on issues such as Indochina, China, and collective security. Eisenhower, on the other hand, still struggled to understand the wellsprings of Indian nationalism and nonalignment. Reacting to the rhetoric of Bandung, the president observed to journalist Malcolm Muir in May 1955 that "underneath everything about Nehru was this terrible resentment . . . to domination by the white, he doesn't differentiate, he doesn't admit any changed relationship." "The fellow is a strange mixture," Eisenhower concluded, "intellectually arrogant and of course at the same time suffering an inferiority complex—schizophrenia."[47]

If Nehru evoked puzzlement, Krishna Menon could induce outright anger. Eisenhower and Dulles had worked with the abrasive Indian diplomat during the closing stages of the Korean War and had come to view him as being pro-Communist. During the spring and summer of 1955, Menon shuttled between Beijing, London, and Washington in an attempt to produce direct talks between the People's Republic of China and the United States. The United States eventually began talks with China on its own accord in early August 1955, but at one point during the negotiations both Eisenhower and Dulles concluded that Menon was not only needlessly interfering in the matter but that he was also tilting toward the Chinese in his sympathies.[48] An infuriated Eisenhower confided to his diary on July 14: "Krishna Menon is a menace and a boor. He is a boor because he conceives himself to be intellectually superior and rather coyly presents to cover this, a cloak of excessive humility and modesty. He is a menace because he is a master at twisting words and meanings of others and is governed by an ambition to prove himself the master international manipulator and politician of the age."[49]

Given the limited opportunities for diplomatic success, the Eisenhower administration might have resorted to increasing economic aid to help improve ties with India. But the 1955 economic aid request for India reflected the ambiguities inherent in Indo-American relations. For fiscal year 1956, Eisenhower requested about $70 million in aid for India. This amounted to $34 million less than the previous year's request, but the Asian Development Fund, from which India was tentatively scheduled to receive $20 million, largely offset the difference.[50] Presenting the India program to Congress, White House officials put their own misgivings about Nehru to one side and fended off critics of aid for neutral nations. In a June 1955 meeting with congressional leaders, Senator William Knowland of California—a particularly rabid anti-Communist and staunch opponent of nonalignment—complained that "it would be bad if the impression got around the world that we reward neutralism." Dulles summoned all of his persuasive abilities: "We are not awarding gifts for policies we dislike," he responded, "we are simply trying to prevent India from moving towards Communism."[51] Eisenhower echoed these views in another exchange. Taking note that "Nehru personifies the spirit of neutralism," the president nonetheless argued that "neutralism is better than hostility, and we need to try to improve the climate there. We shouldn't neglect an area simply because it is neutralist."[52]

President Dwight D. Eisenhower (left) receives Secretary of State John Foster Dulles (second from left), Indian diplomat V. K. Krishna Menon (third from left), and Indian ambassador G. L. Mehta at the White House, 14 June 1955. Menon came to report on his recent peacemaking mission to the People's Republic of China. (National Park Service, courtesy Dwight D. Eisenhower Library)

Yet India remained a low priority for American foreign aid. The projected $90 million for India made up less than 3 percent of a $3.5 billion Mutual Security request. Once again, about 80 percent of the total aid consisted of defense-oriented items that would benefit America's allies. The administration also directed most of the economic funds to those nations, who unlike India, had shown themselves to be steadfast friends of the United States. As Dulles explained while defending aid to India: "We give much more assistance to the other nations who are willing to stand up and be counted."[53] The White House even downplayed the innovative Asian Development Loan Fund. "This fund," Dulles told congressional leaders, "is a pump priming allocation. [It] is not a grant operation—[it] is a matter of getting certain things underway."[54] In keeping with usual practice, Congress pared the request by over $560 million. Appropriations for India for fiscal year 1956 fell to $60 million, and the Asian Development Fund was established with only $100 million, instead of the requested $200 million.[55]

Although the 1955 Mutual Security Program did not reflect any basic change in attitude, the Eisenhower administration had begun to wrestle with Third World economic issues and to seek accommodation with India. The process of reevaluation quickened in the second half of 1955 and early 1956, spurred on by new, Soviet policies toward India and other developing nations.

Bandung was not the last expression of Nehru's discontent with the United States. During the summer of 1955, the prime minister traveled to the Soviet Union for his first visit there as a head of state. In addition to conferring with the new Soviet leadership, Nikita Khrushchev and Nikolai Bulganin, he toured the Russian countryside, visited Soviet factories, and inspected several atomic power plants. Russian leaders seemed particularly eager to soften traditional, Soviet antagonism toward nonalignment. The final joint statement endorsed India's five principles, the Bandung declaration, and committed the Soviet Union to seeking complete, nuclear disarmament.[56]

More spectacular than Nehru's journey to Russia was the Bulganin-Khrushchev tour of India in November and December 1955. Large, tumultuous crowds greeted the Soviets wherever they went, and the two leaders responded with equal enthusiasm. At Agra, Khrushchev skillfully praised the beauty of the Taj Mahal while paying tribute to the suffering of those who had built it. Over the course of their three-week sojourn, both Khrushchev and Bulganin repeatedly denounced colonialism, military pacts, and the nuclear arms race. They also took the opportunity to announce the Soviet Union's support for India's position on the Kashmir dispute. For his part, Nehru showed a degree of reserve. While he expressed gratitude to the Russian visitors, he also raised critical points such as alleged Soviet support for the Communist party of India and Russia's veto of the admission of eighteen recently decolonized nations to the United Nations. Still, Nehru was impressed by what he called "this feast of friendliness between Soviet leaders and the Indian people."[57]

The exchange of visits was certainly momentous, but a February 1955, Soviet agreement to help build a government-owned, one-million ton capacity steel mill at Bhilai in the Indian state of Madhya Pradesh was of equal significance. The arrangement called for a loan of $112 million in capital equipment to be repaid over a twelve-year period with a low, 2.5 percent interest rate. A Soviet offer to expand trade with India, including exchange of industrial equipment for raw materials and local currency, accompanied the steel mill agreement. Not only were the Russians willing to step up aid and trade in India, but their program centered upon the economic sector that the United States had largely overlooked—India's industrial sector. Indeed, just prior to negotiations with the Russians, the government of India had approached the World Bank for the financing of the Bhilai plant only to be rebuffed on the grounds that the bank did not extend loans for government-owned projects.[58]

The American embassy in New Delhi followed these developments with great interest. In one particularly alarmist cable, Ambassador Cooper reported: "Along with their current drive into the Middle East and relentless pressure in Southeast Asia, Communist powers may well regard [the] total conquest of Asia, which would set [the] stage for continuing their advance in Europe."[59] The administration responded by redoubling its own diplomatic efforts. The president sent Prime Minister Nehru a warm, personal letter in July 1955, thanking the Indian government for helping to establish lines of communication with the People's Republic of China. Later that month, the two leaders exchanged letters on the Soviet-American summit at Geneva. Nehru reacted positively to these gestures and even invited Eisenhower to visit India—no doubt to balance the upcoming Khrushchev-Bulganin visit. It was at about this time that Eisenhower reported to Dulles: "In the Indian situation I am struck by the amount of evidence we have that Nehru seems to be more often swayed by personality than by logical argument. He seems to be intensely personal in his whole approach."[60]

Discussing the possibility of a trip to India, Eisenhower told Dulles that he looked upon India as a country having a "special status," and that he was inclined to give the invitation serious consideration. But when Dulles cautioned that a goodwill tour of India would probably have to be duplicated in numerous other countries, the president readily abandoned the idea. Instead, the White House decided to resurrect a months-old option of bringing the Indian leader to Washington sometime during the following year. In early August, just after Nehru's return from Moscow, Ambassador Cooper extended a formal invitation, and the Indian government immediately accepted.[61]

Obstacles, nevertheless, continued to stand in the way of Indo-American friendship. In December 1955, the Eisenhower administration wounded Indian pride when it became embroiled in the Indo-Portuguese dispute over Goa—today, a small, Indian state located on India's southwest coast. First seized in the sixteenth century, Goa had remained under Portuguese colonial rule after 1947, and by 1955 was a hotbed of anticolonial unrest. In this setting, Secretary Dulles met with Portugal's foreign minister in Washington in December. At the conclusion of their meeting, the two diplomats issued a joint statement that dealt mainly with NATO matters, but that also contained a reference to Goa as a province of Portugal. The use of the word "province" created an uproar of protest in India. It was made all the more embarrassing for the United States by the fact that Khrushchev, then visiting India, had just announced Russia's support of the Indian claim to Goa. Ambassador Cooper cabled the State Department and advised that an official apology would be in order, but Dulles obstinately refused. He explained to Cooper that the statement had not been an endorsement of Portugal's position in the dispute, but a response to "the campaign to promote hatred which was being waged by the Soviet rulers in India."[62]

The narrow scope of United States economic aid programs presented the most serious impediment to improved Indo-American relations. The Soviet visit and the Bhilai agreement did nurture American concern, but the administration's limited budget for aid to India left policymakers with little room in which to maneuver. C. D. Jackson, who still advocated the implementation of a World Economic Policy, wrote to White House assistant Nelson Rockefeller in early November 1955 that "the Soviets are holding the pistol at our heads in India."[63] Rockefeller, in turn, wrote Eisenhower that "the visit of Mssrs. Bulganin and Khrushchev to India on the eighteenth or twentieth of this month could mark a turning point for India. The danger in the Middle East and Asia may be as critical for the free world today as that which Europe faced in 1948." Citing Soviet support for the Bhilai steel mill, Rockefeller urged the president to send a personal message to Nehru pledging cooperation with India in its long-term development goals.[64] Following State Department counsel, however, Eisenhower reacted with restraint. A departmental memorandum on Rockefeller's proposal pointed out that a presidential message would "encourage Nehru to believe that substantial amounts of aid would be forthcoming" at a time when such assistance could not be delivered. It noted, moreover, that Nehru might easily construe such a message to be a shallow propaganda device to counter the Khrushchev-Bulganin visit.[65]

A proposal for assisting India's steel industry won more careful consideration before being rejected. Despite their preference for government-owned mills, Indian officials had granted permission in late 1954 to India's largest, private producer of steel, the Tata Iron and Steel Corporation, to expand its productive capacity. Tata executives approached the United States Export-Import Bank in May 1955 for a $62.5 million loan to help finance the expansion.[66] The request stood dormant until late October when Nelson Rockefeller learned of the proposed transaction and wrote directly to the president in the hope of expediting the proceedings. "India's strategic importance to the United States in Southeast Asia," he advised, made it desirable to get "a new U.S.-built steel mill in operation before the Soviet-built mill is completed for the Indian government." Emphasizing the private enterprise aspect of the loan, Rockefeller observed: "This will provide a very interesting and important comparison in many aspects of U.S. versus USSR enterprise and achievement."[67]

Eisenhower's private secretary, Ann Whitman, recorded in her diary that the president showed an unusual degree of interest in the project. He directed White House Chief of Staff Sherman Adams to call George Humphrey, whose Treasury Department oversaw Ex-Im, to encourage the loan. "It seems important to him," Whitman noted of Eisenhower, "to keep one free enterprise operation of this kind going."[68] Yet the proposal soon ran into insurmountable difficulties. Goaded by the Indian government, the Tata Corporation had simultaneously approached the World Bank for assistance. Although the World Bank had refused to lend support to the public project at Bhilai, it had conveyed to the Indians an interest in aiding a private mill. While Tata executives preferred a United States government, dollar loan that mandated the purchase of high-grade American equipment, the government preferred that the loan be taken from the World Bank, which allowed the purchase of less expensive equipment from countries such as Germany or England, payable in less scarce, foreign exchange. Tata, therefore, came to the conclusion that an Ex-Im loan would be acceptable to the Indian government only if it were offered at an interest rate of 4 to 4.5 percent, as opposed to the standard 5 percent rate. Such an arrangement would offset the increased cost of American equipment.[69]

As the details of the steel loan negotiations became known to high-level administration officials in mid-November, enthusiasm for the Ex-Im loan waned. Rockefeller continued to push for it by arguing that a project "with a clear label of U.S. accommodation for a private enterprise, American equipped steel mill" would be preferable to an internationally financed mill.[70] Even Eisenhower observed at one meeting that Ex-Im had, in the past, "made a number of so-called political loans on which no return was anticipated."[71] The State and Treasury Departments, nonetheless, adopted a narrower financial perspective. They opposed the Ex-Im loan on the grounds that a special interest rate for Tata would "encourage other borrowers to threaten not to buy American equipment unless they received special rates on loans . . . and impair the efficacy of the Bank as an instrument of government policy."[72] Tata subsequently negotiated the required financing from the World Bank.

As policymakers in Washington held the line on interest rates and expenditures, the aid program in India maintained its basic orientation toward agriculture and rural improvement. The Technical Cooperation Mission (TCM), established in 1952 by Chester Bowles as a division within the American embassy in New Delhi, continued to serve as the primary administrative arm of United States aid and employed a staff of over two hundred personnel by 1956. About 37 percent of the technicians worked in the area of agriculture and natural resources; 29 percent focused on industry; and most of the remainder concentrated on health, education, and social welfare.[73] The Community Development Program continued to rank as TCM's priority project, with United States aid helping to pay for fertilizer, seed, jeeps, wireless radios, crop sprayers, well-drilling and irrigation equipment, and other basic supplies.[74]

In terms of itemized expenditures, the bulk of American aid dollars helped India to import finished capital goods and raw materials needed for rural development. The largest allocation consisted of $20 million for imported iron and steel to be used for the manufacture of farm implements. TCM also poured a large component of the aid into malaria eradication in rural areas, mainly for the purchase of the chemical, DDT. The one nonagricultural project to receive a substantial amount of American support was railroad rehabilitation. Nearly 20 percent of the approximately $330 million in development and technical assistance received by India during the period 1951 to 1956 contributed to the modernization and expansion of surface transport facilities.[75]

The United States government effort received assistance at times from the Ford and Rockefeller Foundations. Having helped in 1952 to launch the Community Development Program, the Ford Foundation continued to play a supplementary role in implementing it. During the 1950s approximately 35,000 community development, village-level workers underwent training in foundation-run training centers. In addition, a Ford Foundation representative in India, Douglas Ensminger (a former official of the Department of Agriculture's Office of Foreign Agricultural Relations), forged a strong working relationship with the Indian government and became closely associated with India's planning process. The Rockefeller Foundation, which had first established roots in India during the 1920s, also remained active on the Indian scene during the postindependence period. In 1956, it helped to establish a modern postgraduate school at the Indian Agricultural Research Institute in New Delhi (IARI). IARI engaged in research on high-yield maize, sorghum, and millet—and helped to provide an institutional foundation for India's "green revolution" two decades later.[76]

In spite of these impressive programs, the fact remained that the American undertaking in India continued to be an extremely limited one. Low-level funding prevented the expansion of American activities beyond the agricultural sector. And with the exception of railroad rehabilitation, American aid was widely scattered among a great many small-scale, short-term rural projects. All of this, of course, contrasted sharply with the Soviet aid strategy, which concentrated resources in well-defined long-term industrial projects, especially the well-publicized Bhilai steel mill. United States private trade and investment in India, moreover, did not register a major impact on that nation's development. Although Bowles and other American officials had hoped that economic assistance would provide a foundation for capitalist development, United States private investment in India had only increased slightly from $38 million to $68 million between 1950 and 1953. And the value of Indo-American trade during the same period actually fell from $473 million to $379 million.[77] Taken together with the unstable nature of Indo-American diplomatic relations, the American approach to development assistance in late 1955 did not speak well of America's ability to compete in a changing Cold War.

If the Indo-Soviet aid and trade agreements of 1955 had been isolated phenomena, United States policymakers might have been content to maintain the status quo in its relations with India. By late 1955 and throughout 1956, however, the Russians negotiated similar accords with other Asian, Near Eastern, and Latin American countries. Between 1953 and 1956 the Soviet bloc more than doubled its trade with the Third World until it reached a value of $900 million. By April 1956, Sino-Soviet aid technicians were stationed in fourteen developing nations, and long-term credits to such countries totaled $820 million, with another $180 million under consideration. The terms of trade and aid, in most cases, resembled those in the Indo-Soviet agreements.[78]

The "Sino-Soviet Bloc Economic Offensive" came to preoccupy United States officials in late 1955 and 1956. The National Security Council, the State Department, and the Council of Foreign Economic Policy undertook regular studies on its magnitude and goals. Even biweekly "Economic Intelligence Reports" were prepared by the Central Intelligence Agency. The myriad of reports recognized that an industrialized Russian economy would benefit from the importation of Third World raw materials, but all of the studies agreed that the ultimate Soviet aim was political.[79] Soviet strategy, American policymakers concluded, was now adding the tactics of economic cooperation and the rhetoric of peaceful coexistence to military power. President Eisenhower summarized these views when he told former ambassador to the United Kingdom Lewis Douglas that it was "idle to suppose that Russia has any friendly interests in the countries that she professes to help; her purpose is, of course, to damage our relationships with those countries and use economic penetration to accomplish political domination."[80]

United States officials took special note that the Soviets were being highly selective in their choice of aid recipients and trading partners by focusing upon nonaligned developing countries. In August 1956, the Central Intelligence Agency reported that over 90 percent of all Soviet bloc credits had been advanced to four such nations: Yugoslavia, Egypt, India, and Afghanistan. Policymakers further observed that the Soviets administered their program with considerable skill, particularly in their support for popular public sector projects.[81] Surveying the field of Soviet economic activity, one State Department report warned that "the USSR, like Dr. Johnson's lady preacher, has been able to do it all. We need always reflect that for the less developed countries of Asia, the USSR's economic achievement is a highly relevant one. That the USSR was able to industrialize rapidly, and as they see it from scratch is, despite any misgivings about the Communist system, an encouraging fact to these nations."[82]

The problems posed by the Soviet economic offensive perplexed American policymakers. Dulles confided to C. D. Jackson in early 1956 that the outward Soviet "appearance, mood, and behavior" had changed. He observed: "Frowns have given way to smiles. . . . Guns have given way to offers of economic aid."[83] Soviet policies also worried Eisenhower. "So long as they used force and the threat of force," the president wrote Dulles, "we had the world's natural reaction of fear to aid us in building consolidations of strength in order to resist Soviet advances." Suddenly that edge had been lost. Eisenhower further lamented that the Soviets had attained an advantage by taking the offensive. Under a dictatorial regime they could move "secretly and selectively" in implementing their plan. The "defensive," on the other hand, suffered the disadvantage of "trying to secure an entire area. . . . Thus, while we are busy rescuing Guatemala or assisting Korea and Indochina, they make great gains in Burma, Afghanistan, and Egypt." Eisenhower concluded that if the United States was to meet the threat it would have to "plan and organize properly" and conduct policy "over the long-term."[84]

Dulles, Humphrey, and Defense Secretary Charles Wilson met with the president at Camp David on 8 December 1955. The group examined a number of matters, but the Soviet economic offensive and American aid policies dominated the discussions. Dulles took the lead by noting that United States economic aid programs generally lacked "flexibility and continuity," and that current foreign loan policies were "too restrictive and the interest rates too high." Obviously drawing upon C. D. Jackson's earlier ideas for a World Economic Policy, he suggested the organization of an institution with substantial capital to make soft loans to underdeveloped countries. Humphrey, by this time a well-established foe of increased aid, objected that the administration would never be able to depend on Congress to provide the long-term funding needed for specific development projects. But Dulles countered that he envisioned the creation of an independent financial institution to which Congress would grant general authority to make loans to projects that "had several years to run." Alluding to the success of the Soviet economic offensive, he noted: "Only thus could we dependably support major projects which were of a character to catch the popular imagination and produce the psychological results we sought."[85] The secretary recorded that "the idea then developed" that the administration "might ask Congress for authority to use not more than one-hundred million dollars a year for ten years for soft, local currency loans." As had been the case with the Marshall Plan, actual appropriations would be made on an annual basis. The net result would enable the United States to support "long-term projects," aggregating one billion dollars in value. Dulles also noted that "the President thought this was an interesting idea to be explored."[86]

As United States officials deliberated the question of foreign aid, the government of India completed work on its own, second, five-year plan. Plan formulation took place from late 1954 through early 1956 in an atmosphere that can only be described as euphoric. At that time it seemed as though the American-backed Community Development Program had worked a miracle in Indian agriculture. During the first planning period, irrigation had been introduced to over 16 million acres of cropland, and the total area under foodcrop cultivation increased from 257 million to 272 million acres. Use of ammonium sulfate fertilizer rose from 275,000 tons to 610,000 tons. Most important, the output of foodgrains climbed steadily upward from 50 million tons in 1950–51, to 51.2 million tons in 1951–52, to 58.3 million tons in 1952–53, and to 68.7 million tons in 1953–54.[87] All of this progress had taken place without implementing any major land reform or other redistributive policies.

As Indian planners drew up a second plan, they operated under the assumption that the food problem had been largely overcome. Thus, whereas the first plan had concentrated resources in the agricultural sector, the next phase of development would focus on rapid industrialization. In addition, the planners stated their preference for launching new industries in India's "socialistic" public sector, as had been the case with the Bhilai steel mill. As early as December 1954, the Indian Parliament decreed that "the objective of our economic policy should be a socialistic pattern of society."[88] This did not imply complete government ownership of the means of production, but merely that "the basic criteria for determining the line of advance" was not private profit, "but social advance."[89] Indian planners took this to mean that the economy should continue to evolve along mixed lines with a special emphasis on breaking the nation's dependence upon foreign sources of basic capital goods such as steel, heavy machinery, and electrical supplies, and helping to prepare India for future capital formation.[90]

When *The Second Five Year Plan* was completed in February 1956, the most significant innovations were the overall size of the plan and its emphasis on the industrial sector. The ambitious plan called for total outlays of Rs 7200 crores, or about $14.7 billion, more than double the spending incurred under the first plan. Whereas expenditures for industry and mining had made up only 7.6 percent of the first plan's budget, they now comprised 18.5 percent of the total outlay. The proportion of funds allocated for agriculture and irrigation fell from 34.6 percent to 17.5 percent. Due to the increase in total spending, actual expenditures for agriculture rose slightly, but the priority was absolutely clear—rapid industrialization.[91]

While the *Second Five Year Plan* envisioned a very brisk rate of industrial growth, from the start it contained two major shortcomings. First, the Planning Commission calculated that because of population growth, the need to improve per capita consumption, and a rising demand due to increased purchasing power, India's requirements for foodgrain production would double over a ten-year period. Yet according to the planner's own estimates, the capital outlay for agriculture in the second plan would yield only a 15 percent increase in production from 65 million tons in 1955–56 to 75 million tons in 1960–61.[92] Indeed, while productivity had improved considerably since the early 1950s, shortages of certain commodities had already sprung up in urban areas. Agricultural prices, which had declined from 1953 to early 1955, began to rise in late 1955 and early 1956 and threatened to produce general price instability throughout the economy. In addition, if the government was forced to increase imports of food, foreign exchange would be drained from industrial projects.[93]

A large gap in financial resources constituted the second glaring deficiency. This involved a $2.5 billion deficit in rupees needed for the internal costs of development. Perhaps even more crucial, the plan contained a shortfall of nearly $1.7 billion in foreign exchange required to pay for imported capital equipment. After accounting for anticipated foreign assistance from the World Bank, the International Monetary Fund, the United States, the Soviet Union, and Britain, India would still desperately need over $1 billion dollars.[94]

These problems provided American policymakers with an opportunity to come to India's assistance, counter Soviet economic diplomacy, and cement closer ties with India. Just a few weeks after the completion of the plan, Ambassador Cooper put together a three-pronged aid program. First, Cooper recommended that the United States pledge $500 million in development loans to be distributed over the five-year duration of the plan to help India overcome its foreign exchange shortage. This aspect of the program would not require a substantial increase in annual assistance, but Cooper stressed the importance of adopting a "long-term," multiyear approach to Indian aid. Second, the ambassador suggested a long-term moratorium on India's repayment of $120 million in Lend-Lease silver loaned during World War II. Third, he urged that the United States make available $300 million in surplus agricultural commodities under the PL 480 program.[95] PL 480 aid would allow the government of India to reduce inflation and save valuable foreign exchange. Under the terms of Title I, commodities would be paid for in rupees, but the Indian currency generated by the sale would be loaned back to India for use in mutually agreed upon projects.[96]

Cooper presented his proposals to Dulles when the latter visited India on 10 March at the conclusion of a SEATO conference in Karachi, Pakistan.[97] The secretary promised to consider the program after he returned to Washington, but before doing so he sounded out Nehru on rumors that the Soviets had approached India on the subject of arms sales. When Nehru told Dulles in confidence that the government of India was thinking of buying Soviet IL 28 aircraft, the secretary grew livid with anger. "I told him as a first reaction," Dulles reported to Eisenhower, "that I could only tell him frankly that I felt it would greatly vex our relations." At a dinner meeting the following night, the visiting dignitary elaborated on his feelings. He firmly linked United States economic aid, only vaguely discussed during their talks, to India's rejection of the Russian offer. "Why do you do this?" Dulles queried, "I cannot see why you should buy planes from the Russians knowing that it would make it almost impossible for [the] US to carry on its efforts to assist you materially in your second five year plan. . . . I do think that you ought to know what are the probable consequences and then you yourself can judge what is the best course for India."[98]

In late March, Nehru declined the Soviet offer, probably as a result of both Dulles's pressure and British warnings that if India concluded a Soviet arms deal, Great Britain would reconsider its arms sales to India.[99] Several weeks later, at the end of April, Dulles created a special study group within the State Department to study the Cooper program. While the group issued a report that failed to endorse most of the ambassador's specific proposals, it nonetheless put into place a new, multiyear aid package for India. According to the State Department blueprint, the Eisenhower administration would request $75 million in development assistance for India annually over a five-year period. In addition, the report recommended that the administration negotiate a $300 million PL 480 agreement with India.[100]

The State Department report was especially noteworthy for its emphasis on India's status as a leading Afro-Asian nation and a recipient of Soviet economic assistance. "Even though India does not agree with the United States on all major aspects of foreign policy (and for that matter on all aspects of internal economic policy)," the authors noted, "India is a democratic country and is the largest free country in Asia." The Soviet economic offensive in India, they reasoned, was "an attempt to undermine the West in

Asia." Agreeing with Ambassador Cooper's central point, the State Department urged that the India program "should be a long-term program . . . for the purpose of planning of optimum use of the country's own resources as well as for political impact." Equally important, the policymakers advised that a portion of the aid money should be set aside for large-scale, industrial projects that "would bear the U.S. label" and generate "popular appeal" in India—an obvious counter to Soviet projects such as the Bhilai plant.[101]

The administration's 1956 Mutual Security recommendations to Congress contained provisions that would allow the United States to meet the goals laid down by the State Department's report on India. The request for India included $70 million in development assistance loans and $10 million for technical assistance.[102] Thus, the development assistance portion came very close to the $75 million recommended by the State Department. No provisions authorized funding over a five-year period, but in his overall program the president did ask for the creation of a "flexible" loan agency, capitalized at $100 million annually, to make "long-term," ten-year commitments. This was the soft loan agency that Dulles had advocated the previous December at Camp David. Eisenhower also asked Congress to restore the $100 million cut made in the Asian Development Fund in 1955, sought $100 million for a "President's Emergency Fund," and requested a special $100 million fund for the Middle East and Africa. The total Mutual Security Program submitted by the president came to $4.67 billion and was almost $1.4 billion greater than that authorized the previous year.[103] Although about 80 percent of the funding request still consisted of military assistance, the proposed special loan programs reflected an increased interest in Third World economic development.

As the Eisenhower administration began to rethink foreign aid priorities in 1956, it faced the task of selling its economic programs for the Third World to Congress—an especially difficult undertaking in an election year. The president took the lead. On 21 April, he sounded the dominant themes in an address delivered to the American Society of Newspaper Editors. Opening his speech with a commemoration of the 181st anniversary of "a revolution that still goes on," Eisenhower turned from Concord to Bandung and addressed the "spirit of freedom" that had swept the Afro-Asian world. The heart of the speech dealt with the matter of economic issues. Many of the new nations, Eisenhower remarked, were steeped in "abject poverty . . . lacking in trained men for management, production, education, and the professions." He warned: "The Communists . . . falsely pretend that they can rapidly solve the problems of economic development and industrialization." To meet the challenge, he called for a departure from the Point Four policy of short-term, small-scale, aid programs, and stressed that United States assistance to developing countries could no longer be a "transitory policy." "The problems of economic progress," he declared, "are not to be solved in a single spurt. Our efforts must be sustained over a number of years."[104]

Numerous opponents arose in Congress. Longtime critics of foreign aid spending, such as Republican Senator William Knowland of California, were joined by Democratic internationalists, such as Senators Walter George and Richard Russell of Georgia and Mike Mansfield of Montana, in questioning the affordability of the program. Some of those who spoke out viewed the Soviet economic offensive as a reason to reduce, not expand, foreign aid. As one House member from Wisconsin commented: "If we are so foolish as to enter into a competitive economic race with the Communists, we will come out second best. We know they can offer a sales program that promises the moon or everything that the people of Asia desire." In House and Senate hearings, administration officials countered these arguments by reiterating again and again that, as Dulles put it, "new Communist tactics [made] it more than ever imperative that the U.S. should continue the economic phase of [the] Mutual Security Program with greater flexibility and . . . greater assurance of continuity than ever before."[105]

In the end, the White House secured most of the economic aid that it had requested. Congress appropriated only $3.8 billion for fiscal year 1957—$1 billion less than the president had asked for—but only $73 million of the cuts came from nonmilitary assistance. While the provision allowing up to $100 million in loans annually for a ten-year period was dropped, legislators did authorize $100 million for the President's Emergency Fund. The Asian Development Fund and the special outlay for the Middle East and Africa each failed to win approval, but the appropriation for them was merged into the regular, development assistance program.[106] India received $65 million of the $70 million that Eisenhower had requested for development assistance and an additional $10 million for technical assistance.[107] This figure approximated the recommendations of the State Department report on India.

In August 1956, the White House supplemented the Indian aid package by successfully negotiating a $360 million, PL 480 agreement. The terms of the accord provided for the shipment of 3.5 million metric tons of wheat, 200,000 tons of rice, and 500,000 bales of cotton to India over a three-year period. Although the negotiations had been delayed by the Department of Agriculture's efforts to include 6 million tons of surplus tobacco, a commodity for which India had little use and whose officials refused to accept, the final transaction was the largest in PL 480 history to that date. That the arrangements would be carried out over a three-year period also reflected the Eisenhower administration's growing commitment to long-term aid policies.[108]

With the exception of the PL 480 agreement, the total amount of aid to India for fiscal year 1957 had not been substantially raised over the previous year's appropriation. Nor had the administration won congressional authority to make long-term commitments to Third World nations. Still, the Eisenhower White House had demonstrated increased awareness of Afro-Asian economic priorities and introduced new ideas to the foreign aid debate. Indeed, as the debate continued and as the White House began to win converts to its side, one of the most frequently heard complaints was that the 1956 Mutual Security Program had not gone far enough in addressing the economic needs of the Third World and still placed far too much emphasis on foreign military assistance. "It is a militaristic request," Senator J. William Fulbright complained. "It does not conform to what you say [about the need for economic programs]."[109] Similarly, House Republican Lawrence Smith of Wisconsin termed the military orientation of the proposal "fatal to the establishment of a sound relationship with other nations in the world." Senator Theodore Green, a Democrat on the Senate Foreign Relations Committee, couched his criticisms in the administration's own language. While the Soviet Union had adopted new tactics in its dealings with underdeveloped nations, Green observed, "there is little evidence that the Administration has shown the flexibility to meet these challenges."[110]

The vigorous discussion over foreign aid in 1956 led to a growing feeling, shared by both supporters and opponents of increased economic assistance, that the issue had to be examined more closely. During the summer of 1956, the Senate, the House of Representatives, and the White House each decided to establish special commissions to study economic aid. In so doing, each took note of the Soviet economic offensive, the rising importance of the Third World to United States interests, and the need to formulate a long-term approach to economic assistance. In August, Eisenhower appointed Benjamin F. Fairless of the United States Steel Corporation to head up the administration's study team.[111]

Although the foundation for expanded economic cooperation with India had been laid by late 1956, one matter remained problematical—Indo-American political relations. Just as Eisenhower's foreign economic policy was caught in transition from 1954 to 1956, so was the administration's attitude toward nonaligned India. While Eisenhower and Dulles had already made a concerted effort to improve relations through the appointment of a new ambassador and by regular correspondence with Nehru, they had also shown insensitivity to India's foreign policy perspectives, particularly in the cases of the Goa matter and Dulles's direct pressure on Nehru over Soviet arms. But as the Soviet Union adopted a more tolerant attitude toward nonalignment in 1955 and 1956, Eisenhower and Dulles tried to do likewise. They were often awkward and uncomfortable, but they continued to seek an understanding with Nehru just the same. The alternative, as they saw it, was to lose India to communism.

The Eisenhower White House had already demonstrated a degree of tolerance toward Indian policies in defending aid to India before Congress. The process continued in 1956 as a number of congressional critics, led by William Knowland, vociferously attacked the idea of assisting nonaligned, or neutral, nations. The California senator antagonized Eisenhower so much that the president once remarked to General Alfred Gruenther, his successor as head of NATO, that "Knowland has no foreign policy except to get high blood pressure whenever he mentions the words Red China."[112] In a June 1956 legislative leadership meeting with the president, Knowland once again raised the issue, observing that Nehru was out "traveling around trying to get other countries to desert our security alliances." Eisenhower took on Knowland's argument by commenting that "the cold war was just as serious as a hot one." "What would be gained by turning our backs on a situation and walking away from it?" he asked.[113]

The president was at his analytical best in an early 1956 letter to his archconservative brother Edgar that dealt exclusively with the issue of nonalignment. He began by arguing that there was no such thing as a "neutral position between honesty and falsehood" or between "moral value and its opposite." "However," he noted, "the concept of neutrality for a nation does not necessarily mean that a nation is trying to occupy a position between right and wrong." Eisenhower posited that in many cases neutrality in international relations simply meant that a nation had an aversion to military alliances. He drew upon American history and pointed out that the United States had, during the first 150 years of its existence, followed a neutral course in world affairs. Turning to more practical considerations, the president observed that if a neutral country such as India were to side openly with the United States and was subsequently attacked, "many in the world would view the attack as a logical consequence" of alignment. To the contrary, "if the Soviets were to attack an avowed neutral, world opinion would be outraged." In other words, neutrality could provide the United States with a moral line of defense against communism.[114]

Dulles, who had often defended India before hostile congressional committees, had a harder time convincing himself of the validity of his arguments. As late as June 1956, the secretary of state publicly declared that neutrality had "increasingly become an obsolete conception and, except under very exceptional circumstances, it is an immoral and shortsighted conception."[115] Yet even the rigid Dulles edged away from traditional Cold War dogma. When asked at a news conference several days later precisely which nations he would define as being neutral, he replied that his remarks applied to "very few neutrals, if any." Only a nation that was indifferent to others and believed in "security through isolationism" could be termed neutral, the secretary explained. A nation could absolve itself from immorality, he implied, simply by being a member of the United Nations, whose charter obligated all participating states to support collective security.[116] "The official doctrine," quipped Walter Lippmann, "is that neutrality is immoral but that there are no neutrals who are immoral."[117]

Despite the ambiguity of his public statements, Dulles went to great lengths to discuss issues other than Soviet arms and to reach some meeting of the minds with Nehru during his March 1956 visit to New Delhi. Indeed, over a two-day period, Dulles and Nehru spent more than five hours in one-on-one discussions on the ranking international issues of the day. The topics discussed ranged from the nature of the new Soviet leadership, to the decline of European colonialism, to American military aid to Pakistan. While the two men disagreed strongly on many matters, they expressed their views in a frank and open manner. Dulles reported back to the president that he had had a "most interesting" visit with the Indian leader. "He had completely cleared his calendar for the two days of my visit," Dulles observed, "I was amused that toward the end of the conference he was sitting on the back of the sofa with his feet on the seat. We really took our hair down."[118]

Meanwhile, President Eisenhower maintained steady correspondence with the prime minister and was assisted, at times, by the course of world events that improved America's image in India. A flurry of exchanges took place between the two leaders in October and November 1956 when British, French, and Israeli forces invaded Egypt in an attempt to fasten control over the strategic Suez Canal, nationalized by Egypt after the Aswân Dam deal fell through. Eisenhower described action taken by America's allies to Nehru as a relic of a bygone colonial era, and Nehru publicly applauded America's condemnation of the aggression.[119] India's reluctance to denounce the simultaneous Soviet invasion of Hungary initially strained Indo-American relations. But in his private letters to the prime minister, Eisenhower spoke with restraint, and simply stated that he hoped that India would "find it possible to join us in supporting proposed United Nations actions to deal with the situation."[120] The low-key approach brought success. After the Indian government had acquired more information on Hungary, Nehru spoke in Parliament on 19 November and openly criticized Soviet actions in that nation.[121]

Eisenhower made his greatest diplomatic advance when Nehru visited the United States in December 1956. The president carefully prepared for this long-awaited state visit, already postponed once due to Eisenhower's illness during the previous summer. Cooper sent special reports on topics ranging from India's foreign policy to the history of the caste system, and Eisenhower met with journalist Norman Cousins who had established a friendship with Nehru over the years. Cousins advised him to swap stories with the prime minister on the antics of their grandchildren. At Cooper's suggestion, the visit was to last a maximum of five days—as opposed to the three-week extravaganza of 1949. Travel was limited to Washington and New York, with the exception of a two-hour trip by automobile to Eisenhower's farm in Gettysburg. These arrangements were made in the hope of providing a relaxed atmosphere and stimulating, frank discussions between the president and Nehru. Long conversations were fully anticipated. "One can't talk with Nehru as with others," Dulles coached his boss. It is necessary "to start with world philosophy and take the long approach."[122]

At noon on 16 December, the prime minister and his daughter Indira Gandhi were met at Washington's National Airport by Vice-President Richard Nixon and his wife. They rode by limousine to the White House, where a smiling "Ike" rushed down the front steps to take the hand of an equally enthusiastic Jawaharlal Nehru. The warm greeting was immediately followed by a private luncheon at Blair House and dinner that evening hosted by Supreme Court Chief Justice Earl Warren. At 9:00 A.M. sharp the next morning, the president called upon the prime minister, and their party departed for Gettysburg. For the next two days, at both Gettysburg and Washington, Eisenhower and Nehru carried on extensive talks on nearly every world issue. Differences over relations with Russia, the People's

Republic of China, and the relative importance of communism and nationalism separated the two statesmen. Neither Eisenhower nor Nehru, however, resorted to a lecture format, and they searched earnestly for common ground.

Nehru went to great lengths to convey his personal disdain for Soviet aggression in Hungary, and said that "it spelled the death knell of International Communism." Eisenhower condemned the actions of Britain, France, and Israel at Suez as a violation of the United Nations Charter. On nonalignment, Nehru emphasized that he used the word "in its traditional sense as meaning a position of aloofness from power combinations," and not "to distinguish between concepts of government based on the dignity of man and those based on dictatorships." In Asia, he maintained that Western support for nationalism would provide the best defense against communism. For his part, Eisenhower did not debate any of these points. Although he drew attention to the great danger that Soviet Russia and "the Marxist doctrine for world revolution" posed to all nations, the president told Nehru of his desire for peaceful coexistence with the Soviet Union. In regard to Pakistan, Eisenhower once more promised that the United States would never permit the Pakistanis to use American arms against India.[123]

On the issue of economic aid, Eisenhower was very eager to reach an understanding with India. Two days before Nehru's arrival, the president told Under Secretary of State Hoover that he was "inclined to think" that the United States should give a "substantial loan to India." With the deficiencies of India's second five-year plan in mind, he mentioned the figure of $500 million.[124] The offer never materialized because Nehru, probably as a matter of national pride, avoided the topic of aid altogether. The prime minister did, nonetheless, casually leave behind several pamphlets on India's second plan. Even more important, at the conclusion of their last discussion, Eisenhower took the initiative and told Nehru that if India found itself in need, "particularly if there was some kind of investment or money involved—you make the request and I will certainly give it every possible consideration."[125]

Although the Nehru-Eisenhower meeting did not produce an immediate increase in economic aid to India, it did reflect a significant shift in United States attitudes toward India and the Third World. After having concluded military arrangements with Pakistan in early 1954, the Eisenhower administration slowly set out to improve its ties with India. American policymak-

President and Mrs. Eisenhower welcome Prime Minister Jawaharlal Nehru and daughter Indira Gandhi to the White House, 16 December 1956. Vice-President and Mrs. Nixon are on the right. (National Park Service, courtesy Dwight D. Eisenhower Library)

ers continued to emphasize the importance of building military strength in Asia and the Near East. But the growing crisis in Indochina, the voice of Bandung, and the Soviet economic offensive pushed them toward a greater awareness of Afro-Asian political sensitivities and economic needs. The careful preparation for the Nehru visit, and Eisenhower's willingness at least to consider an enlarged, long-term aid program for India, reflected this new orientation.

Behind the carefully orchestrated demonstration of interest in India lay hardheaded, foreign policy motives. Eisenhower and Dulles, it appears, seldom agonized over or even discussed the plight of India's poor outside of a political context. The Eisenhower administration's increased willingness to tolerate Indian nonalignment sprang similarly from foreign policy objectives. Competing with the Soviets for the hearts and minds of Third World peoples required greater tact than American policymakers had previously practiced in their relations with India. In short, after a difficult period of transition, the Eisenhower administration had slowly begun to alter its tactical approach to economic and political relations with India in keeping with the requirements of a changing Cold War.

Six

Take-Off, 1957–1961

President Eisenhower began 1957 and his second term in office with a growing awareness of the importance of the Third World and the issue of economic development. "We must use our skills and knowledge and, at times, our substance," the president declared in his 20 January inaugural address, "to help others rise from misery, however far the scene of suffering may be from our shores. For wherever in the world a people knows desperate want, there must appear at least a spark of hope, the hope of progress—or there will surely rise at last the flames of conflict."[1] Over the next four years, the Eisenhower administration substantially increased United States economic aid to the Third World in general and to India in particular. Indeed, India became for United States leaders a model nation where American-backed development was to be tested and proven efficacious.

The decision to go forward with a major economic program in India came in response to the Soviet economic offensive and the changing nature of the Cold War. Yet, as American policymakers confronted the issues of aid and development, they faced a host of questions and challenges. How could the effort to build up India economically be coordinated with the military effort in Pakistan? What doctrines, or economic ideas, should guide the effort? What type of political and economic development should be fostered in India?

In early 1957, the Senate, the House, and the president's Fairless Commission completed their respective studies of the Mutual Security Program. The International Development Advisory Board, an executive agency established in 1950 by Congress as a public, advisory group on foreign aid, finished a fourth review. Their conclusions varied, especially regarding the overall size of the foreign aid program and the relative importance of trade, aid, and private investment in the development process. Most important, however, was their consensus on the need to modify existing policies. All four studies agreed that the nature and location of the Cold War had shifted as a result of Soviet economic diplomacy. And as Eisenhower and Dulles had already determined, the study groups agreed that economic competition with the Soviet Union in underdeveloped areas required long-range planning and that aid should be extended in the form of soft loans (low-interest loans repayable in local currencies).[2]

As the consensus for revising foreign aid jelled in the public arena, the State Department's Policy Planning Staff in January 1957 completed its own examination of United States foreign assistance. Pointing to the Soviet challenge, the Bandung Conference, and the need to place American aid on a long-term footing, the Policy Planning Staff recommended the creation of a multiyear, $2 billion soft loan fund for underdeveloped areas. The United States had "few other bases for communication" with many less-developed nations, the report noted. Many of these states avoided "military association with the United States," had "no strong cultural ties" with the West, and wished to "remain outside the great power struggle." But they did want economic growth. "To the extent that we set ourselves to the same goal," the report concluded, "we will have a shared interest in a matter of major concern to these countries."[3]

Before the public studies on aid had even been released, Dulles endorsed the Policy Planning Staff's recommendations and sent them to Eisenhower.[4] The president was already inclined favorably toward expanding aid to the Third World, but waited for the strategic moment to introduce legislation. In May, after the public studies on aid had been finished and publicized, Eisenhower included a request for a three-year, $2 billion Development Loan Fund (DLF) in his 1957 Mutual Security Program. In spite of the well-laid groundwork, a Democratic-controlled Congress upset somewhat the administration's plans by changing the proposal for a multiyear authorization and reducing the DLF's first-year appropriation from $500 million to $350 million. In each succeeding year, the Eisenhower White House nonetheless won progressively larger allocations for the fund, and it conducted policy on the assumption that the DLF would continue for a number of years.[5] The establishment of the DLF marked the beginning of a new era in American foreign economic policy in which the non-Western world emerged as the primary focus of economic assistance programs.

A foregone conclusion within the administration was that the new policy on foreign aid would benefit India. The Policy Planning Staff's report on foreign assistance repeatedly referred to India as a nation where American aid could serve a particularly useful purpose. It stressed that India's "moderate" Congress party precariously held power in an impoverished country where nationalist fervor ran deep. Economic failure might unleash the extremes of either Communist forces or bellicose right-wing sentiments for war with Pakistan. United States loans, the Policy Planning Staff hypothesized, would help the Nehru government overcome the serious foreign exchange bottleneck of the second plan and promote political stability. American aid might also counteract growing Soviet influence in India.[6] The fact that by 1961 India had received 40 percent of all DLF funds demonstrates that the reorientation of United States aid policies came about in good measure as a response to relations with India.[7]

As American policymakers laid plans for the DLF in early 1957, the National Security Council staff completed work on NSC 5701, a revised statement of United States policy toward South Asia. NSC 5701, approved by the president on 10 January 1957, reaffirmed the strategic importance of the populous, resource-rich, and politically influential region. In keeping with previous policy papers, it underscored the importance of preventing the area's fall to communism, cultivating a western orientation among South Asian nations, maintaining access to the region's raw materials, and holding Pakistan as a military ally. NSC 5701 differed from earlier policy statements, however, in that it placed far greater emphasis on the importance of India's economic development. Noting that India had "emerged as a foremost representative of the Afro-Asian, or Bandung region," and that "the USSR is engaged in a vigorous and open" diplomatic offensive there, the NSC staff advised that the United States should "provide economic and technical assistance to India, placing emphasis on projects and programs having the maximum potential of support of the goals and aspirations of India's second five-year plan."[8] NSC 5701 went so far as to declare that "the second five-year plan provides at present the best vehicle for action to promote U.S. interest in an independent and stable India."[9]

In addition to bolstering India domestically, NSC 5701 noted that economic development in India carried "international ramifications." As the Cold War increasingly spread to the Third World, it took on a psychological as well as a strategic dimension. By early 1957, American policymakers were not only cognizant of the propaganda value that the Soviets attached to assisting underdeveloped nations, they had also grown worried over reports emanating from the People's Republic of China that detailed surges in agricultural and industrial output under communism. As Chinese leaders prepared to launch their First Five-Year Plan in 1957, it seemed to many in the American decision-making establishment that Asia's largest nation had hit upon a formula for rapid development that might prove attractive throughout Asia, the Near East, and Africa.[10] If the United States expected to capture the imaginations of the world's poor, it would have to demonstrate that non-Communist development provided a better path to improved living standards. India—the world's largest democracy, a prominent representative of Afro-Asian interests, and the most populous nation after China—seemed to be the logical testing ground. While both the Truman and Eisenhower administrations had previously referred to Sino-Indian economic competition to help sell their foreign aid proposals to Congress, the concept first appeared as part of official policy in NSC 5701. "The outcome of the competition between Communist China and India," the National Security staff wrote, "will have a profound effect throughout Asia and Africa."[11]

While numerous foreign policy differences continued to plague Indo-American relations, especially India's nonaligned status, the frequency and intensity of the disagreement had diminished. Still, some high-ranking officials questioned the wisdom of building up nonaligned states such as India. At a meeting of the NSC on 24 January 1957, Assistant Secretary of Defense Reuben Robertson and Admiral William Radford of the Joint Chiefs of Staff argued that increased aid to neutral nations would weaken the resolve of military allies to stand by the United States. It was none other than John Foster Dulles—the administration's staunchest, public critic of neutralism—who countered the Pentagon's perspective.[12]

Dulles accepted the view that nations actually aligned with the United States should usually receive preference in the dispersal of aid. But unlike the military establishment, he believed there should be exceptions to the rule. Radford was appalled when the secretary of state hypothetically observed that it might be expedient one day to extend military assistance as well as increased economic aid to nonaligned India and Burma. He made the point that this would especially be the case in the event that the Soviets offered military aid. When Radford commented that the United States would "never be able to keep our allies in Southeast Asia" if such a policy were adopted, Dulles retorted that "we had better begin getting rid of our allies if having such allies was going to prevent us from doing what is in the best interests of the United States." The exchange reached a crescendo when Dulles remarked that he "would rather see us lose Thailand, an ally, than to lose India, a neutral."[13]

Having carefully defined India's increased strategic and psychological significance, and with the new Development Loan Fund in place, it was only a matter of time before the Eisenhower administration extended large-scale assistance. As early as December 1956, during the course of Nehru's visit to the United States, Eisenhower had assured the Indian leader that if India found itself in need, it should not hesitate to make a request for aid. That request soon came.

Both Indian and United States officials had long observed that India's Second Five-Year Plan suffered serious deficiencies. The Cooper plan of 1956 had been implemented by American policymakers with a view to correcting the shortcomings. But the magnitude of the problem had been underestimated, and by late 1957 India's foreign exchange difficulties reached crisis proportions. While Indian planners had originally predicted a manageable balance of payments deficit of about $550 million for the five-year period, the aggregate deficit reached $400 million during the first two years of the plan alone. State Department officials, who closely monitored India's economic performance, estimated in May 1957 that the dollar gap for the remainder of the planning period would lie somewhere between $700 million and $900 million.[14]

A number of factors contributed to the Indian foreign exchange crisis of 1957. A rising defense budget in the aftermath of the Pakistani-American arms deal, spiraling costs of imported iron and steel needed for industrialization, and the greater cost of capital goods in general all worked havoc on the Indian economy. Lax controls over import licenses and increased imports in a booming private sector also played a role. In response, the Indian government cut all but the most crucial plan projects, drew $200 million from the International Monetary Fund, and placed restrictions on the importation of nonessential items. The Nehru government even talked of increased taxes on higher-income groups in order to raise revenue.[15]

Shortfalls in food production exacerbated the problem. Assuming success for the Community Development Program, Indian planners had estimated that production of foodgrains would rise from 65 million tons to 75 million tons during the second plan with only a minimal increase in government spending.[16] It became clear from the start, however, that the 10 million ton increase would not meet the needs of a burgeoning population and an ever-growing urban demand. Recognizing the pitfall, the Planning Commission revised the target upward to 80 million tons in late 1956, but again without augmenting financial outlays for the agricultural sector.[17] Instead, as American policymakers decided to make India a democratic model for Third World development—and an Asian counterweight to the People's Republic of China—the government of India dispatched two study teams to China in 1956 to study that nation's revolutionary cooperative movement. By imitating the Chinese example of labor-intensive, cooperative agriculture, Indian planners reasoned that their nation could raise production with only limited financial investment.[18]

The call for cooperative agriculture predictably met stiff resistance from Indian landowners, particularly politically influential, large planters. The Congress party organization responded by backing off from the reform agenda. While the final draft of the second plan set ambitious goals for the creation of service and credit cooperatives and the formation of communally owned farms, it made association with such institutions voluntary. Most landowners did not rush to embrace the social experiment.[19] Lacking the political will to reorganize the agrarian sector, the government fell back upon the underfunded Community Development Program. Even by the most optimistic forecasts this strategy would have failed to raise output to 80 million tons. Then, during the summer of 1957, the monsoon rains failed in northern India and the supply of foodgrains plummeted to 62.5 million tons.[20]

By the fall of 1957, India's economy was in shambles. Indian officials approached as early as the spring of 1957 both the American embassy in New Delhi and the State Department in Washington, D.C. on the subject of aid.[21] But Nehru, perhaps reluctant to appear a supplicant, waited until the fall—by which time economic difficulties had reached an emergency stage. In an interview on 6 September with *New York Times* correspondent Henry R. Lieberman, the desperate Indian leader indicated that his government would welcome a $500 million to $600 million American loan. He also took advantage of the opportunity to announce that India's finance minister, T. T. Krishnamachari, would be sent to Washington later in the month to begin aid negotiations.[22]

The fact that India's economic development had come to be perceived as a matter of importance to United States foreign policy interests ensured a thorough and sympathetic hearing. The looming question for administration officials was Congress's willingness to extend substantial aid to India. Economic recession at home in 1957 and 1958 made the issue especially sensitive, and exploratory talks between White House and legislative leaders indicated that Congress would not be generous.[23] Yet the newly restructured foreign aid program, featuring the DLF, as well as the long-established Export-Import Bank, gave the executive branch a degree of flexibility. Funds from these agencies could be distributed according to the president's choosing, without congressional approval. Armed with these resources, the administration deliberated on India's request.

The White House began to lay plans for India as early as spring 1957, when an interdepartmental study group formed to examine that country's foreign exchange crisis. In May, the group issued its report, which forecasted India's needs, and recommended use of DLF and Ex-Im resources to help solve the problem.[24] Although the Treasury Department and the International Cooperation Administration expressed misgivings over the cost of assisting India, Deputy Under Secretary for Economic Affairs C. Douglas Dillon, who led the State Department's lobbying effort, effectively argued that aid could be provided without a special appropriation from Congress and that support for India served United States foreign policy interests.[25] Communist party election victories in India's southern state of Kerala in the summer of 1957 bolstered Dillon's case. One State Department paper at the time noted: "No American wants to see the Communists take over India—if assistance given in time and in the right amount can substantially contribute to forestalling this, it would be a reasonable investment from the point of view of the national security of the United States."[26] In early November, Dulles received the president's approval for plans to provide India with "somewhere around $250 million" annually in assistance over and above previously planned outlays during the last three years of India's Second Five-Year Plan.[27]

Eisenhower met in the Oval Office on 16 November with Dulles, Dillon, Vice-President Nixon, Under Secretary of State Christian Herter, Secretary of the Treasury Robert Anderson, Robert Brundage of the Bureau of the Budget, and Sherman Adams. Anderson, who had only recently replaced the conservative George Humphrey at Treasury, opened the discussion. He reported that it now appeared that India's foreign exchange deficit for the next three years would reach an astronomical $1.4 billion. He warned: "If we were to provide that kind of money we would have to go to Congress for a special loan." At this point, Nixon asked what sort of a program might be assembled without special legislation. Ideas began to fly. Dillon suggested that the administration "might be able to prevail upon the Ex-Im Bank" to advance loans to India. Anderson, whose department oversaw that institution, chimed in that the bank could provide up to $200 million. Germany, he added, could probably be persuaded to grant export credits as well. Dulles called attention to the newly established DLF and estimated that $50 million might be forthcoming from that institution. Before the meeting adjourned, the secretary of state reviewed the outcome. The administration would not go to Congress for a special grant, Dulles concluded. Instead, it would break the problem down into parts: "We will try to get the Germans to cover the Indian trade deficit with them; we will try to cover our deficit through the Ex-Im Bank, perhaps $200 million; we will try to provide $50 million or so from the development fund."[28]

On 16 January 1958, after consultations had taken place with India's finance minister, the Eisenhower administration announced that the United States would immediately lend $225 million to the government of India: $150 million from the Export-Import Bank and $75 million from the DLF. Although the total amount fell short of meeting all of India's financial requirements and certainly did not constitute an Indian Marshall Plan, it did mark a significant departure in United States policy. Never before had such a large sum been made available to India. And when Dulles announced the $225 million package, he intimated that additional assistance might soon be forthcoming.[29]

American interest in India's economic development intensified and the flow of aid rose steadily after the January 1958 announcement. Omitting the 1958 Export-Import Bank loan, total United States grants and loans committed to India grew from $89.8 million in 1958, to $137 million in 1959, and to $194 million in 1960.[30] To maximize the utility of the funds, the United States took a leading role in August 1958, in organizing a five-nation consortium of Indian aid donors—Britain, Canada, Germany, Japan, as well as the United States—under the auspices of the World Bank. After the first meeting of the consortium in Washington, D.C., the *New York Times* reported that the group had devised "the largest multi-nation economic aid plan ever arranged for an underdeveloped country"—together pledging $350 million in immediate emergency assistance and laying plans for another $600 million through 1961.[31] In addition to capital assistance, the United States concluded a series of PL 480 commodity agreements with the government of India. In May 1960, for example, the United States and India signed a four-year, $1,276 million PL 480 accord that supplanted the 1956 Indo-American agreement as the largest in the history of the program.[32]

Increased aid for India came about only as part of an expanded economic program for the Third World as a whole. In 1958, for the first time since the outbreak of the Korean War, the White House asked Congress for less money for military hardware ($1.8 billion) than for economic aid ($2.1 billion). And in 1959 and 1960, Eisenhower's Mutual Security requests continued to hover at $4 billion, with nearly equal allocations for military and economic aid. Although overall outlays for foreign assistance remained consistent with previous years, and a significant portion of economic aid was categorized as "defense support" assistance (aid that strengthens a recipient nation's defense capabilities as well as its economy), a subtle change in emphasis had become apparent. Between 1958 and 1960, the administration won increased funding for the DLF; liberalized the lending practices of the Export-Import Bank; expanded the PL 480 program; supported the creation of an Inter-American Development Bank for Latin America; increased United States contributions to the International Monetary Fund and the World Bank; and endorsed the establishment of a soft loan agency within the World Bank known as the International Development Association.[33] All of these initiatives demonstrated a growing conviction that economic aid served as useful a foreign policy purpose as military aid. "Better with our $700 million of DLF than with the last several billion of defense funds," Eisenhower told legislative leaders in July 1958.[34]

The rationale for stepping up economic activity in the Third World became all the more urgent during these years. Political instability and revolutions in countries such as Iraq, Lebanon, and Cuba and the quickening pace of decolonization in Africa strengthened the case for aid. Testifying on behalf of the Mutual Security Program before the Senate Foreign Relations Committee in 1957, Dulles pointed to the newly emerged nations and warned: "These people are determined to move forward. . . . If they do not succeed there will be increasing discontent which may sweep away their moderate leaders of today and bring to power extremist measures fostered by international Communism."[35] Assistant Secretary Dillon reviewed the counterrevolutionary aims of the foreign aid program in a confidential 1958 report, "Moderating the African-Asian Revolution": "We do not want to prevent change in the less developed areas, but neither can we accept the prospect of its evolving along lines which could throw Asia and Africa open to the unrestrained play of revolutionary enthusiasm and national ambition. We want to help new governments to attain their reasonable goals."[36] The president drew the starkest scenario in early 1960, when he argued for further enlargement of the DLF. One and one-quarter billion people lived in underdeveloped areas outside "Red China," Eisenhower observed to a group of legislators, and America had a simple choice between "aid or chaos."[37]

In this setting, India's role as a democratic, non-Communist model for development acquired added significance. Administration officials harped on India's moderate development policies in presenting aid proposals to Congress, and the comparison to China was accented again and again in State Department reports and NSC policy papers. The Eisenhower administration, of course, continued to provide a great deal of assistance to nondemocratic allies such as Taiwan, South Korea, and South Vietnam. But in India strategic interests coincided with ideals. Here was a nation moving along a relatively peaceful path toward modernization, avoiding revolutionary excess, maintaining a degree of social and political order, and successfully executing democratic elections.

Indeed, aid to India became something of a cause célèbre in the United States at this time. India had always garnered the support of a handful of American liberals. As early as 1949 Senator Hubert Humphrey had referred to that nation as the logical replacement for China as a focal point for United States policy in Asia. In the early 1950s, Ambassador Chester Bowles had helped generate further interest in India by inviting famous personages such as Eleanor Roosevelt and Adlai Stevenson to visit the subcontinent, and by publishing books and articles after his return to the United States.[38] In the late 1950s, this support for India broadened. Leading newspapers and magazines wholeheartedly endorsed the administration's programs. "India is the most populous and most important of the non-Communist nations of southern Asia," the *New York Times* editorialized in October 1957, "and on the success of India's great experiment . . . the growth of democracy in all southern Asia may depend." *Newsweek* declared that India's successful economic development would mark "a great leap forward . . . rivaling that of Red China." *Business Week* described India as "the main test for Western-aided economic development in Asia."[39]

In the United States Senate, an ambitious, young senator named John F. Kennedy joined with former Ambassador John Sherman Cooper, who had become a Republican senator from Kentucky, in proposing a congressional resolution that singled out India for an open-ended commitment of United States funds for completion of its second plan. Kennedy spoke with characteristic vigor of the race between India and China for economic progress and asserted: "A successful Indian program is important at least as much for the example it can set for the economic future of other underdeveloped countries as for its own sake. . . . India, like the United States, is engaged in a struggle of coexistence—in its case with China, which is also pursuing a planning effort being put under consideration all over the world."[40] The 1958 Kennedy-Cooper resolution, attached to the Mutual Security Act, passed the Senate, but stalled in the House where many members questioned the desirability of making reference to a particular nation. Nonetheless, the Senate-House Conference Report noted that "it was the opinion of most of the conferees on both sides that Indian economic development is of the utmost importance and the act should be administered in a manner which recognizes this fact."[41]

Kennedy and Cooper introduced a second resolution the following year, this time calling upon the World Bank to send a team of experts to India. The World Bank mission would make recommendations to the five-nation consortium on aid for the completion of the second plan and on assistance for India's upcoming Third Five-Year Plan (1961–66). Unlike the previous year's resolution, the 1959 version won Eisenhower's endorsement after provisions were made for the study group to consult with all of the countries of South Asia—including Pakistan. It easily passed when Congress voted on Mutual Security in September.[42]

Interest in India ran so high that on 4–5 May 1959 the Committee for International Economic Growth of Washington, D.C. sponsored a conference, "India and the United States—1959." The program featured an impressive array of participants from government, business, and academia. Nearly everyone spoke in glowing terms of India's economic prospects, but the high point of the conference came on 5 May when presidential aspirants John F. Kennedy and Richard M. Nixon each delivered speeches—and vied for recognition as India's best friend. Kennedy reiterated his call for increased aid through the five-nation consortium.[43] In terms almost identical to the senator's, Vice-President Nixon also supported India aid:

> In my own mind what happens in India, insofar as its economic progress is concerned in the next few years, could be as important or could be even more important in the long run, than what happens in the negotiations with regard to Berlin. . . . There are two great peoples in Asia. The peoples who live under the Communist government of China, and the people of India. . . . What happens in India will have a tremendous impact on the decisions made in other countries in Asia, in the Near East, in Africa and even in the Americas.[44]

The Eisenhower administration's 1960 Mutual Security proposals fully reflected the mounting attraction to India's democratic experiment. With the DLF established, the White House no longer submitted specific, capital assistance requests for India. It was simply assumed that a major portion of the $700 million from DLF would flow to that nation. Indeed, in presenting the 1960 program to Congress, administration officials proposed that United States economic assistance be concentrated in certain "islands of development." India, along with certain other Asian states, was defined as being an especially key island nation where the benefits of democratic development could be demonstrated to the rest of the Third World.[45] In private circles, some high-ranking officials, such as Assistant Secretary Dillon, spoke of providing India with $1 billion annually for the next five-year period.[46] In February 1960, speculation arose that the administration was considering a sum of $300 million for fiscal year 1961—a 50 percent increase over fiscal year 1960.[47] Decisions regarding the magnitude of American aid for India in 1961 ultimately fell to the new, Kennedy regime. But it was clear that by the end of the Eisenhower years, the United States had already made economic assistance for India a policy priority.

Originally implemented in response to the Soviet economic offensive and the Bandung movement, increased aid for India had developed into somewhat of an ideological crusade by the late 1950s. As the level of aid to India rose, additional diplomatic factors influenced the aid process. Most important, United States economic aid to India during the last years of the Eisenhower administration became enmeshed in the complicated regional politics of South Asia.

American policymakers understood that increased economic aid to India posed risks to the United States military alliance with Pakistan. Since the consummation of the Mutual Defense Agreement of 1954, Washington and Karachi had disagreed over the level of military assistance that should be provided and over the issue of direct United States access to military bases. A large flow of American aid dollars to India, which would allow New Delhi to allocate greater resources to military spending, promised to further unsettle the Pakistanis and give rise to a counterproductive arms race on the subcontinent. Indeed, as early as fall 1957, when the State Department had first assembled a comprehensive aid program to help India through its foreign exchange crisis, the Eisenhower administration had recognized the dilemma.[48] Large development assistance to India, Dulles observed at the time, "has implications all across the map." While the secretary noted that allies such as Turkey, Iran, and Pakistan might take offense at the policy, he expressed particular concern over the balance of power in South Asia.[49]

Sensitive to the need for a reduction of political tensions in South Asia, and hoping to strike a balance between India and Pakistan, the administration developed a "package plan" in late 1957 and early 1958 to defuse the emerging crisis. The undertaking, however, underestimated the depth of regional animosity. The plan, prepared by the State Department and approved by the president, proposed United States mediation of the three major sources of tension between India and Pakistan: the disposition of the disputed waters of the Indus River, the accelerating arms race, and Kashmir. The strategy was to move from the easiest to the most difficult issue until all had been resolved. In reality, the initiative never moved much beyond the planning stages. When Eisenhower sent out feelers to each government later in the month, he received back an unqualified acceptance from Karachi, and an equally firm rejection from Nehru. The proposal was stillborn.[50]

For the next year, the administration refrained from any direct mediation efforts in South Asia. In the spring of 1959, however, intelligence reports depicting a brewing border dispute between India and the People's Republic of China rekindled hopes in Washington that India might modify its policies. The roots of the border dispute can be traced at least as far back as 1954 when—even as the two governments forged improved diplomatic ties—extensive correspondence and discussion took place on the Himalayan border region. Two major areas were at issue. First, questions developed over the exact demarcation of Indian and Chinese territory along India's northeast frontier, where the People's Republic of China repudiated the McMahon line that had been drawn in 1914 by Britain, Tibet, and China. Second, disagreement arose over the western Sino-Indian border in Aksai Chin, located in the Ladakh section of Kashmir in northwest India. Tensions accelerated in 1958 when Indian intelligence discovered the existence of a recently constructed Chinese roadway through Aksai Chin (see Map 2, chapter 7). Prime Minister Nehru protested to the Chinese government, but in January 1959, Foreign Minister Zhou Enlai answered by claiming sections of Aksai Chin and challenging the validity of the McMahon line in the northeast as well.[51]

Sino-Indian relations deteriorated further in March 1959, when in the aftermath of an unsuccessful Tibetan uprising against China, Nehru granted political asylum to the Dalai Lama, Tibet's spiritual and temporal leader. During the following summer and fall, Indian and Chinese border patrols clashed in both Aksai Chin and the northeast frontier. In August, Nehru rose in Parliament and publicly acknowledged for the first time the existence of the dispute.[52]

American policymakers closely watched the course of the Sino-Indian relations in the hope that they might exploit the rift. In late 1959, President Eisenhower optimistically reported to congressional leaders that in light of the border skirmishes, Nehru was "coming out of the clouds," and that "even Menon is saying that possibly India has misjudged her Chinese friends."[53] At the same time, the administration began to generate plans for India's possible incorporation into America's system of collective security alongside of Pakistan. Resurrecting the previous years' diplomatic initiative, the administration hoped that the mounting Chinese threat might finally stimulate negotiations between India and Pakistan.[54] NSC 5909, a July 1959 revision of "United States Policy toward South Asia," spelled out the ultimate aim: "As friendly relations between the two countries are developed, seek to persuade them to participate in joint defense planning of the subcontinent."[55]

Expectations soared in August and September 1959, when India and Pakistan achieved a breakthrough in World Bank–sponsored negotiations over the Indus River. The tentative agreement, formally signed one year later, settled long-standing differences over the use of the river and its tributaries, which penetrated the borders of both countries. The terms of the settlement specified that $1 billion in external assistance would be divided between India and Pakistan for the construction of an elaborate system of dams and canals to direct the waters along mutually agreed upon routes. The Eisenhower administration demonstrated that United States economic assistance could serve as a tool of regional diplomacy by pledging $515 million in American loans and grants to spur completion of the various projects.[56]

Encouraged by the Indus Waters agreement, the administration began to entertain exaggerated hopes for a rapid solution to the long-standing Kashmir issue and other political problems on the subcontinent. Dulles's death from cancer in May 1959, and Eisenhower's growing tendency to act as his own secretary of state, may have also affected policy at this point. Meeting with members of Congress, Eisenhower naively observed that if the Kashmir problem could be settled he "would not be surprised to see India and Pakistan merge." Noting that the two nations shared common languages and traditions—and demonstrating his ignorance of their deep-rooted religious and political antagonisms—he stated that there was simply "no good sense in their being separated."[57] The president soon decided to intercede directly with the two nations in order to encourage Indo-Pakistani political and military cooperation.

In December 1959, Eisenhower embarked on a three-week trip abroad that included stops in Paris, Madrid, Casablanca, Rome, Tunis, Athens, Ankara, Kabul, Karachi, and New Delhi.[58] Of all of the stops, India seemed uppermost in the president's mind. Before departing on the trip, he confided to the British secretary of Commonwealth Affairs, Lord Plowden, that in all of the other countries he would be "making a bow and expressing American respect," but that he was "doing all of this just to get to India." "Here is a neutral nation," Eisenhower remarked, "of tremendous importance."[59]

The president stayed in India from 10 December through 14 December. The visit proved an enormous public relations success. Large crowds lined the streets of New Delhi the day of his arrival and cheered him enthusiastically. At a civic reception at the Ram Lila grounds in the old, former Mughal section of Delhi, officials estimated the crowd at one-half million, and many more had to be turned away due to lack of space. Looking out over the crowd, Nehru told his guest that India had presented him a priceless gift—"a piece of her heart." In addition to ceremonies in the capital city, Eisenhower was treated to a short jaunt to the Taj Mahal. He also made a brief visit to a nearby village where he made a small, financial contribution toward the purchase of a community radio.[60]

The most important aspect of the visit was the private discussions held between Eisenhower and Nehru. As had been the case with their 1956 meeting, the two leaders talked amiably and touched on a number of topics in world affairs. Diplomatic issues in South Asia, however, dominated the discussions. Eisenhower told Nehru that he had not come to South Asia "in the position of a mediator," but that he "regarded the subcontinent as of such importance to the free world that he would be glad to be helpful in anyway he could." The president voiced his pleasure over the Indus Waters accord and the recent improvement in relations with Pakistan and mentioned that he had just visited with Pakistan's head of state General Ayub Khan in Karachi and had come away impressed by the general's "sincerity of purpose in his desire to live at peace with India." Indeed, he went so far as to describe Ayub, who had only recently come to power through a military coup, as "progressive, forward-looking and deeply concerned with the welfare of his people."[61]

Eisenhower then asked straight-out if it might not be possible for India and Pakistan, their differences notwithstanding, to cooperate militarily in the event of overt Chinese aggression. While Nehru politely explained that such an arrangement would violate India's nonaligned principles, he made a counterproposal that pleased the president. India, he stated, would be willing to issue a joint declaration with Pakistan pledging that "all questions, forever, between them" should be settled by peaceful negotiation "without resort to force or war." Eisenhower's confidential account of the prime minister's presentation continued: "If this were done, Nehru indicated—without being precise about it—that he would then be less opposed to our modernizing the Pakistan army. He said he would talk to his people, but he expected that, if we were to go forward with modernization in those circumstances, they would simply not take note of it or make an issue of it."[62]

Eisenhower left New Delhi extremely optimistic about the prospects for Indo-Pakistani cooperation and the advancement of United States security interests in South Asia. The day after his last meeting with Nehru, he wired instructions to the American ambassador in Karachi, William Rountree, to approach General Ayub Khan "on a secret and personal basis" to obtain his reaction to Nehru's no war proposal. The president specified: "Our purpose would be to make sure that President Ayub understands the great opportunity this could give him in [the] modernization of his army."[63] Shortly after returning to Washington, Eisenhower included a reference to the need for increased aid to India and Pakistan—in part to help finance the Indus River project—in his 1960 State of the Union address. In South Asia, he declared, "in two nations alone are almost five hundred million people, all working and working hard, to raise their standards, and in doing so, to make themselves a bulwark against an ideology that would destroy liberty."[64] In his February 1960 Mutual Security message to Congress, Eisenhower reiterated the importance of assisting India and Pakistan on the Indus River matter, as well as in their broader, development goals.[65]

Through the remainder of 1960, however, Indo-Pakistani rapprochement proved to be an elusive goal. Ayub Khan rejected India's call for a no-war pact and in its place suggested that the two nations immediately begin working out arrangements for joint defense of the subcontinent—a recommendation that was sure to meet with an Indian refusal. In fact, when the issue of joint defense planning came up in Parliament in August 1960, Nehru categorically dismissed the option, noting that India would not abandon the basic tenet of nonalignment.[66] Eisenhower had clearly failed to gauge the depth of regional antagonisms in South Asia. United States policymakers nonetheless remained hopeful, and in September 1960, India and Pakistan formally signed the Indus Waters Treaty. By that time the United States Congress had given its approval to a $550 million appropriation for the DLF with full knowledge that a significant portion of the total would go to India and Pakistan. It had also issued a statement of support for $515 million in loans and grants, over and above the DLF appropriation, for the Indus River project.[67] The Eisenhower administration still held out the hope that as the Chinese threat intensified, India and Pakistan would eventually come to terms.[68]

By the late 1950s, economic aid had become a very active tool of American diplomacy in India. Yet, as had been the case in previous years, very little thought had been given to how aid might advance the standing of the United States in the world economy. At the beginning of the decade, Chester Bowles had explained how aid could be used to promote liberal capitalism in India. But high-level policymakers, who concentrated more narrowly upon Cold War objectives, had given little attention to the Bowles agenda. It was only after India's strategic significance had been redefined in the latter half of the decade—and after the decision had been taken to expand the aid program—that United States officials developed a coherent strategy for pursuing liberal development in India.

The Eisenhower administration had a body of economic development ideas upon which to draw. Beginning in 1954, C. D. Jackson, the earliest and most persistent advocate of economic aid for underdeveloped nations, had circulated among leading administration officials unpublished reports and papers written by two social scientists from the Massachusetts Institute of Technology (MIT), Walt Whitman Rostow and Max Millikan.[69] Rostow and Millikan advocated a liberal "diffusionist" model for Third World development, a strategy based on the assumption that economic growth would come about through the diffusion of capital, technology, and culture from Western, developed nations to the poor nations.[70]

Drawing upon the Western historical experience, Rostow defined five stages of development through which all societies must pass. In the "traditional stage," economic assistance helps a country accumulate sufficient savings and technical know-how to advance to the "preconditions for take-off," then to the "take-off stage," and the "drive for maturity." Finally, "self-sustained economic growth" ensues and a significant portion of the population gain "command over consumption which transcends basic food, shelter, and clothing." According to this blueprint, the process of diffusion takes place through capitalistic investment and trade, supplemented by timely dosages of Western economic and technical assistance. In the end, not only does economic growth take place in the Third World but the developed nations come to enjoy enhanced business opportunities as well.[71]

While Rostow did not publish his theories until 1959 in his classic study *Stages of Economic Growth*, both he and Millikan began writing and lecturing on the need to assist Third World development in the early 1950s. The timing of their work coincided with the escalation of the Cold War crisis in Indochina and Southeast Asia, a political context that greatly influenced their economic analysis. Indeed, Rostow subtitled his famous work on the stages of growth "A Non-Communist Manifesto," and immodestly described his theory as "my alternative to the historical analysis of Karl Marx."[72] Rostow and Millikan maintained that a transfer of capital and technology to underdeveloped regions would not only promote world economic growth but also encourage a peaceful, evolutionary pattern of social transformation. The ingredients of change were capital, technology, and self-help—not class conflict, civil war, and revolution. Difficulties would arise along the way, Rostow and Millikan admitted, but once the preconditions for growth were established and take-off ensued, liberal development would be self-sustaining and automatic. "In the end," Rostow confidently wrote, "the lesson of all this is that the tricks of growth are not all that difficult."[73]

When C. D. Jackson first introduced the ideas of the MIT economists to administration officials in 1954, Eisenhower, Dulles, and other top policymakers did not give the various Rostow-Millikan papers a great deal of attention. Once the decision to expand aid had been made, however, the simplicity of Rostow's formula, and its appealing Cold War logic, proved irresistible. Explaining the need for the Development Loan Fund to the Senate Foreign Relations Committee in 1957, Dulles compared economic development to the task of getting an airplane off the ground: "You have to achieve a certain minimum speed to take-off. It would not be prudent to invest our resources in development programs which are too small to offer any hope of eventually achieving a self-sustaining rate of growth."[74] In July 1959, Jackson sent a Rostow paper, "The Stages of Economic Growth and the Problems of Peaceful Coexistence," to the president. A pleased Eisenhower wrote back: "Your record remains perfect. I quite agree with your verdict on Professor Rostow's talk . . . and I am grateful to you for giving me an opportunity to see it."[75]

Rostow and Millikan, like other advocates of aid, assigned special significance to India. In 1958, the MIT Center for International Studies (CENIS), established by the two economists, launched a special study of India's economy and the following year set up a study center in New Delhi.[76] CENIS also provided Senators John F. Kennedy and John Sherman Cooper with statistical data, reports, and speech drafts for the Kennedy-Cooper resolutions of 1958 and 1959.[77] In a letter to Jackson that outlined the need for increased assistance to Third World nations, Rostow described India as "the big urgent test case for all these principles."[78] In a report to the Draper Committee, a presidential commission organized in 1959 to examine the foreign aid program, Max Millikan optimistically observed that India possessed all the resources needed for "sustained growth." It was one of the few newly emerged nations, Millikan noted, that maintained "a governmental structure; a skilled labor force; a supply of trained administrators; and a network of basic transportation, communications, and power facilities."[79] Rostow and Millikan also highlighted India's political importance. As the world's largest democracy, gradually working its way toward modernization, India seemed the perfect model of stable, non-Communist, diffusionist development.[80]

The Indian government's commitment to a "socialistic pattern of society" posed challenging questions to theorists who expounded the benefits of capitalism, but Rostow and Millikan were not deterred. They observed that India's was a mixed economy and that given its underdeveloped status, Indian planners had reason to continue public sector activity on a large scale. Millikan pointed out to the Draper Committee that without an expansion of public "social overhead"—that is, projects such as railroad rehabilitation, communications, electrical power, and irrigation that provided an economic infrastructure—"the private economy of small scale operators will probably stagnate."[81] Thus, the United States would have to lend assistance to such undertakings—some of which were in India's public sector—so that domestic Indian savings could be channeled into private investment.

Rostow and Millikan took special note of the fact that it had been the buoyancy of private sector growth that had increased India's demand for imports and contributed greatly to the foreign exchange crisis of 1957 and 1958. If the United States and other donors filled the exchange gap, India's private entrepreneurs could continue to expand their operations and lead the nation out of the take-off stage and into self-sustained growth. In 1958, Rostow explained the process to an aid critic, Representative John Vorys and said:

> I am now convinced that the Indians have passed over a great hump and now have private businessmen capable of carrying forward with

> great vigor the process of economic growth. I would hate to see the momentum slowed down because the Indian government must ration foreign exchange in favor of railways and electric power equipment, at just the stage when the private sector can productively absorb increased flows of machine tools and industrial materials from abroad. The issue in India is now the future of both democracy and capitalism, not merely some form of socialist democracy.[82]

During the late 1950s, the Eisenhower administration followed the Rostow-Millikan strategy of supporting large-scale, industrial infrastructure projects in India. After 1957, the DLF and the Export-Import Bank replaced the Technical Cooperation Mission as the primary distributors of aid to India. From Ex-Im came $150 million for the import of capital goods. The DLF provided approximately $105 million for railroad rehabilitation; $73.2 million for various hydroelectric and thermal power projects; and almost $84 million for steel imports. A large portion of the financial aid went to India's public sector. For example, Indian electric power plants—many of which were patterned after the New Deal's Tennessee Valley Authority—were wholly government owned. So were Indian railways. And probably close to one-half of the imported steel went to public projects. In December 1960, the DLF even made a $29.3 million loan to help build a government-owned and managed fertilizer plant located just outside of Bombay.[83]

President Eisenhower himself adopted a tolerant attitude toward India's mixed economy. As early as February 1955, the president happened upon a recent article in *The Economist* (London), "India's Progress and Planning," that delineated the need for government intervention in that nation's underdeveloped economy. Emphasizing India's lack of capital and technical expertise, along with its ever-growing and extremely poor population, the article noted that an enlarged public sector was a matter of practicality rather than dogma. In conversation with Dulles, Eisenhower described the piece as "instructive" and urged the secretary to "pick it up and read it."[84] The president later sent copies to Harold Stassen, Nelson Rockefeller, and Joseph Dodge.[85] He also demonstrated a measure of understanding a few months later during a meeting with Krishna Menon. Although the two men strongly disagreed on international issues, they were not very far apart on questions of economic development. Eisenhower told Menon at one point in the conversation, "I am perfectly certain that if you start an industrial revolution in a country which is heavily and thickly populated, there has got to be more [governmental] management. . . . I can understand differences."[86]

Some administration officials lamented United States support for government-owned enterprise abroad. George Humphrey, a long-time opponent of big budgets and government intervention in the marketplace, was the most vocal critic. Writing in March 1957 to former Marshall Plan administrator and Ford Foundation president Paul Hoffman, Humphrey questioned the need for an enlarged foreign aid program and predicted that American aid would inevitably go to publicly owned industries in less-developed nations, "building big governments and government-owned property and more government control of the daily lives [of the people in those countries]." This process, he warned, would stifle the individual incentive and initiative needed to spur development. Humphrey looked back nostalgically to a simpler time in history: "My mind goes back to just over the short period of my own business life to a cornfield on a bend in the Ohio River which a few men purchased because they were protected in their rights of ownership and the benefits they might create from its better use. . . . Now, a little over thirty years later . . . one of the most modern steel plants in the world provides over 25,000 people with good jobs each day, high annual earnings, and more daily comforts and recreation than millionaires had when the farm was purchased."[87]

But the Treasury chief, who would leave the administration in July 1957, held views that were rapidly falling out of favor. Hoffman forwarded the letter to Eisenhower who, in turn, felt compelled to respond. The president went straight to the point. "Personally I feel that the things argued in your letter to Paul Hoffman," he told Humphrey, "would have had particular application during the first decade and a half of this century and to the period between the two world wars." "Circumstances and conditions," he continued, "that allowed a few men to put up a steel plant in a cornfield . . . are as different from today's conditions in most of the Afro-Asian nations as day is from night." Eisenhower made note of the rate of population growth, the absence of concepts of "personal rights," and "the spirit of nationalism" that precluded a narrow, private enterprise approach to development in these countries. He also stated his "personal conviction" that "almost anyone of the new-born states of the world would rather embrace Communism or any other form of dictatorship than to acknowledge the political domination of another government even though that [government] brought to each citizen a far higher standard of living."[88]

For Eisenhower, the Cold War still provided the most persuasive rationale for assisting mixed economies such as India's. The president pleaded to Humphrey: "A country such as ours could not exist, alone, in freedom were we surrounded by a sea of enemies, which all would be if they were Communist-dominated." To protect "our own interests and our own system," the United States would have to try to understand the "deep hunger" for improved living standards in the Third World. If this required more expenditures and a greater degree of government intervention, so be it—American security was at stake.[89]

In 1959 and 1960, high-ranking administration officials went so far as to consider lending assistance to the construction of a government-owned steel mill in India. The Indian government had already begun building three publicly owned steel plants during the second five-year planning period. The Soviet Union, Britain, and Germany had each extended capital and technical assistance for one of the mills. American policymakers had been particularly dismayed by the publicity attached to the Soviet-backed undertaking. In June 1959, Indian planners approached the American embassy in New Delhi—now under the direction of career diplomat Ellsworth Bunker—and indicated that a fourth public steel mill was being considered. The embassy quickly relayed the information to Washington and urged careful consideration of the matter. India's Third Five-Year Plan would not be finalized until 1961, and no formal, Indian request was immediately forthcoming. But Ambassador Bunker advised that the Indian overture provided an opportunity to "increase [United States] influence on [the] Government of India," affect the "direction we desire to see [the] economy take generally," and to "fill [a] void which [the] Soviets [are] attempting [to] fill."[90]

In Washington, Assistant Secretary Dillon and Clarence Randall of the Council on Foreign Economic Policy shared the embassy's interest in the plant, and both policymakers hoped that Indian planners might be persuaded to permit the mill to be built by American-backed private investors. Accordingly, they contacted a number of United States firms and Indian entrepreneurs, as well as the DLF and the Export-Import Bank, to work out the details of a private, joint venture. Randall and Dillon agreed, however, that due to the limited profit-making potential of such an enterprise, it would be difficult to convince an American company to step in. Therefore, they simultaneously began to lay plans for possible United States assistance for a government-owned plant.[91] On 8 June, Randall sent a short note to Assistant Secretary of Commerce Henry C. Kearns, an opponent of aid to public sector projects abroad, and explained the dilemma. "You and I would be in complete agreement that the efforts of our Government should be devoted vigorously to the promotion of private enterprise," he told Kearns, but "that is not quite the question involved in the [embassy] cable from New Delhi. . . . In light of that despatch, the problem becomes that of whether when private capital fails to enter the field, it is the lesser of two evils for us to finance Government projects rather than permit the Soviets to do so."[92]

The issue of aid for India's fourth public sector steel mill would not be resolved until Eisenhower's departure from office. It awaited the actual completion of India's third plan and the presentation of a formal Indian request. It seems clear, nonetheless, that the Eisenhower administration, or at least some of its influential members, was preparing the path for such a project in 1959 and 1960. During the Kennedy years, the White House would carry these plans a step further by submitting a request for the undertaking to Congress.[93]

All of this did not mean that the Eisenhower administration meant to promote socialism in India. United States support for public sector projects made up only part of a broader push for development. Significant amounts of assistance went directly to the private sector as well. In December 1959, for instance, Randall reported that $80 million of $110 million in Ex-Im Bank credits committed to India had been loaned to private firms.[94] In 1957, the chairman of the House Committee on Agriculture, Harold D. Cooley, introduced and won passage of an amendment to an agricultural surplus disposal bill mandating that up to 25 percent of counterpart funds generated as a result of the PL 480 program be made available to United States companies operating overseas.[95] Shortly afterward, the government of India agreed to use $55 million in counterpart funds to help establish the Industrial Credit and Investment Corporation of India—modeled after the American Reconstruction Finance Corporation—to channel loans to medium-sized, private industries.[96] The DLF also advanced considerable amounts of capital to India's private sector, especially for the purchase of badly needed steel imports.[97] Vance Brand, Director of the DLF, could proudly report to Congress in March 1960, that 32 percent of all the bank's loans had gone to private sector activities in the various recipient nations.[98]

Providing direct assistance to private enterprise in India was only one aspect of the campaign to nurture capitalistic development. One provision of the legislation that created the DLF encouraged recipient nations to issue investment guarantees against currency inconvertibility and nationalization of foreign firms. Under financial pressure as a result of its foreign exchange crisis in 1957, the government of India readily agreed to guarantee foreign investors the right to unlimited repatriation of profits in dollars, and two years later promised to compensate foreign companies in the event of nationalization.[99] In addition to these measures, American officials negotiated a double tax treaty with India in 1959 whereby the United States agreed to refrain from taxing benefits derived by American companies due to Indian tax breaks. A series of Indian tax incentives for foreign investors—including exemptions for returns of up to 6 percent during the first five years of operation, depreciation allowances 25 percent greater than normal for the first eight years, and exemptions from India's "supertax" on dividends—accompanied the double tax agreement. Secretary of State Christian Herter proclaimed in late 1959 that the revised tax codes raised the possibility that "the vitality of free enterprise will increasingly emerge in India's economic development."[100]

At the same time, the Indian government also loosened restrictions on foreign investment. Since 1948, Indian law had stipulated that foreign companies participating in joint stock ventures with Indian businessmen would not be allowed to own more that 49 percent of any given operation. In 1957, however, the government granted permission to Parke-Davis Corporation to own 83.3 percent of the stock in its new, Indian pharmaceutical subsidiary; allowed Godfrey L. Cabot Company 50 percent control over a planned, carbon plant; and permitted Merke, Sharpe, and Dohme Company—another pharmaceutical firm—60 percent ownership in a joint venture.[101] In 1959, the Indian government reversed an earlier policy in regard to foreign oil companies by granting full refinery concessions to Stanvac and Caltex corporations.[102] "India may now be willing to give foreign private enterprise the opportunity we have been hoping for," one Council on Foreign Economic Policy report noted.[103] Even the conservative editors of *Business Week* ran a story on Indian investment policies in late 1959 that heaped praise on the Nehru government.[104] Although United States private investment in India came to only $200 million by the end of the Eisenhower era, that amount was double what total investment had been before the launching of an enlarged aid program in 1957. And in 1959 the United States replaced the United Kingdom as the principal source of new foreign capital in India.[105]

Finally, American policymakers worked to enhance Indo-American trade. The United States sponsored a series of trade fairs in New Delhi, Bombay, and other major Indian cities during the late 1950s that featured an array of American agricultural and industrial goods.[106] Between 1958 and 1960 four official trade missions visited India to scout markets. One trade mission report, completed for the Department of Commerce in 1958, stressed vast opportunities in India. "Standards of living," it noted, "are gradually being raised for some four hundred million people. This ensures an unprecedented expanded market for a variety of essential products."[107] Whereas United States exports to India had totaled only $212 million in 1950, they had reached a value of nearly $500 million by 1961. Indian exports to the United States, on the other hand, climbed to a value of only $255 million. Although the Indian trade accounted for only a small portion of the United States' $20.6 billion in total exports, it was growing rapidly and possessed enormous potential for the future.[108]

In essence, United States policymakers had determined to export liberal welfare state capitalism to India. Mutually beneficial, capitalistic growth was the goal, but along the way it was recognized that the government would play a central role in economic management. They envisioned Tennessee Valley Authorities for India's river valleys, an Indian version of the Reconstruction Finance Corporation, and perhaps an American-backed, public sector steel mill. Behind the effort lay a self-confident belief in the exportability of American modes of economic organization. As C. D. Jackson told Dulles: "The economic phase of the world struggle has reached a fateful crossroad. . . . The true magic of our system and its potency in a universal as well as an American context must be made manifest in new and imaginative terms."[109]

Ironically, the overall attitude usually meshed with the goals and aims of the Indian government. Differences arose, of course, over the degree of public and private sector activity to be encouraged, but Nehru's advocacy of a mixed economy, and his emphasis on increasing production rather than effecting a redistribution of wealth, demonstrated an eclectic planning formula. Nehru welcomed the welfare state as a comfortable niche between socialism and capitalism. "In a sense," he wrote in the *All India Congress Committee Economic Review* in 1958, "every country, whether it is capitalist, socialist, or communist, accepts the ideal of the welfare state."[110] More than anything else, the prime minister continued to stress that India's primary need was rapid industrialization and an increase in productivity. "It has to be remembered," he explained to a group of Indian businessmen, "that it is not by some adoption of socialist or capitalist methods that poverty leads to riches. The only way is through hard work and increasing the productivity of the nation." During that same talk, Nehru even invoked the Rostow thesis: "We are struggling to get out of the morass of poverty, and to reach the stage of what is called the take-off into sustained growth."[111]

The crucial question was whether or not the Western-style welfare state fit the Indian setting. Rostow's theory, after all, assumed that because Western Europe and the United States modernized in a particular way this pattern must be the inevitable path for the Third World to follow. Yet India had a very different historical experience from that of the West, and it confronted numerous unique internal and external restrictions to growth. Under colonialism the United States had not gone through the systematic deindustrialization of its economy as had been the case for India. And while American society had always been marked by inequalities, it had never maintained the all-pervasive caste structure that characterized Indian society. Finally, when the United States began to industrialize in the nineteenth century the international economic order had not been overwhelmingly dominated by a group of already developed nations. India, on the other hand, faced a twentieth-century world order in which economically and technologically advanced Western nations held tremendous advantages, and where opportunities for growth were more limited than they had been a century before.

Perhaps the most serious flaw of the Indo-American development scheme was the lack of emphasis placed on India's agricultural sector—which employed the vast majority of the nation's workers and attempted to feed its rapidly expanding population. Driven by dreams of rapid industrialization, Indian planners cut funding for agricultural projects to a bare minimum during the second planning period. American interest in Indian food production also waned during the late 1950s as policymakers adopted the Rostow thesis of development, and as they sought to counteract Soviet support for industrial undertakings. In 1958, for instance, the United States allocated only $14 million of its enlarged, India program for the rural-oriented Community Development Program.[112] Consequently, as India met or surpassed targets set in the industrial sector—by 1961 output of steel had more than doubled since 1950, production of chemicals had nearly tripled, and machinery production had increased five-fold—output of foodgrains lagged behind. In 1961, Indian government statistics showed that food production had only increased from 65 million tons to 76 million tons during the second plan, four tons short of the projected goal. Indeed, the increase in the food supply had not kept up with the rate of population growth.[113]

Aggregate figures on production alone do not adequately depict the problem. In 1961, after a decade and one-half of political independence, the Planning Commission reported that 50 to 60 percent of the population, or about 211 million people, lived below minimum levels of consumption. The minimum level was defined primarily in terms of caloric intake necessary to avoid malnutrition. In other words, two five-year plans had not diminished Indian poverty—much of which was concentrated in rural areas. Here rested the nub of the matter. Eager to accelerate the rate of industrialization, many Indian and American officials had assumed that the introduction of improved technology and agricultural advisers, through the Community Development Program, had already solved the food problem. Yet India's complex rural setting limited the potential success of the technocratic method. Whereas the nation's largely undeveloped industrial sector responded to government initiatives, the agricultural sector contained entrenched interest groups and social traditions that inhibited growth. Large landholders often showed more enthusiasm for raising tenant's rents and fees than for raising productivity. The benefits of the increased production that did come about, moreover, usually accrued to the wealthier classes. One government study of the Community Development Program, published in 1957, reported that in two closely examined villages in northern India nearly 70 percent of government-distributed inputs—seeds, tools, fertilizer, and irrigation works—had gone to the locality's most affluent farmers.[114]

Underlying these developments was the fact that the Indian government never took effective steps toward rural reform. As early as 1952, Nehru and the Planning Commission recommended the implementation of legal ceilings on land holdings and the confiscation of land not personally cultivated by the proprietor.[115] Yet a government study of land reform observed in 1957 that the distribution of land had changed little, if any, since independence.[116] State governments, to which the Indian constitution gave ultimate responsibility for land reform legislation, dutifully passed laws in accordance with the Planning Commission's guidelines. They usually limited the maximum size of holdings to three times the acreage of a single family unit, or about forty-five acres. But legislative bodies, frequently dominated by powerful rural elites, purposely wrote loopholes into the laws. They commonly provided exemptions for cultivators who adopted efficient methods of production. Provisions requiring "personal cultivation" defined the term so loosely as to include land worked by hired labor and tenants. Large farmers who still faced the possibility of confiscation often simply transferred legal title to extended family members, friends, or even trusted servants.[117] Daniel Thorner, a respected American commentator on Indian society, toured the state of Kashmir shortly after passage of the country's most progressive reform bill that established a 22.75-acre limit on land ownership. Recalling a conversation with a village revenue official, Thorner wrote: "Some of the well-off families in his village, when they got wind of the impending land reforms, had gone through the legal forms of breaking up their joint families. Thus they were entitled to 22 and three-quarter acres per adult male. He gave us the names of three or four families which had adopted this procedure, although all members of the family still lived under a common roof and took their meals together."[118]

The onus for land reform failure cannot be placed on the state governments alone. The central government remained ever aware that state and local Congress party machines, largely controlled by landed interests, served as vote banks in nationwide elections. Nehru consequently never directly challenged state-sponsored reforms. After sending two delegations to China in 1956 to study the formation of agricultural cooperatives, the prime minister had issued a call for the creation of service and credit cooperatives and joint farming in India. But, as previously noted, membership in cooperatives was voluntary. Thus, very few experiments in communal cultivation were ever launched. Service and credit cooperatives, supported by government grants and loans, did begin to multiply after 1957, but in 1959 a government report observed that in case after case, cooperatives had fallen under the control of influential local politicians, money lenders, and landed interests.[119] From December 1958 to May 1959, Thorner conducted a survey of cooperatives sponsored by the independent Indian Cooperative Union. After visiting 117 cooperatives scattered throughout the country and conducting extensive interviews, Thorner concluded that many of the people whom he had met were "anxious to impress upon me the importance of the heads of their cooperatives." "They took pride," Thorner observed, "in telling me that these cooperators were big men in trade, in Government contracts, in rice milling, in landholding, and in local politics. In general, I found that the heads of the cooperatives were the big people of the villages and that they had their hands in many other pies as well as cooperation."[120]

In spite of the increasingly obvious shortcomings, Indian and American officials pressed ahead with a developmental strategy that overlooked the need for structural reform. As Indian planners worked out the details of their Third Five-Year Plan in 1959 and 1960, they kept in close touch with the MIT Center for International Studies. India's finance minister Moraji Desai and ambassador-at-large B. K. Nehru each paid visits to MIT in 1959, and the Charles River economists advised that India should continue the drive toward industrial take-off by making the third plan even more ambitious than the second. Assurances were given that the United States and other Western donors would donate up to $1 billion annually from 1961 to 1966.[121] Policymakers in Washington encouraged these consultations. As a March 1959, NSC report on South Asia noted: "U.S. agencies are attempting to keep as well informed as possible on current [Indian] planning. . . . The ability of the U.S. to affect these decisions is limited and any discussions with Indian officials have to be undertaken informally and with utmost discretion. U.S. officials keep in close contact with officials of IBRD, Ford Foundation, and the MIT economists, who are often in a position to influence more directly Indian planning officials."[122]

The United States did make use of one private group, the Ford Foundation, to attempt to convince the Indian government to complement the emphasis on industrialization with accelerated activities in the agricultural sector. The most significant statement of the American position came in April 1959, with the publication of the Ford Foundation's *Report of India's Food Crisis and Steps to Meet It.* The report, commissioned by India's Food and Agriculture Ministry, warned that India would have to increase substantially food production during the third planning period to meet the needs of a growing population. But the Ford Foundation study team also proposed that the best method for bringing about the increase would be through intensified efforts to make available modern agricultural technology to Indian farmers, especially improved seed and fertilizer. The report patently opposed measures to redistribute land or promote other institutional reforms. "Assurance of stability of tenure," it argued, "can contribute substantially to food production. The team's recommendation is that land ceilings and other land reforms should be settled as quickly as possible, and stay settled for the duration of the Third Plan."[123] Later that year, the American embassy in New Delhi endorsed these proposals and began formulating plans to employ United States–owned Indian rupees, generated through PL 480 sales, to help cultivators finance the cost of seed, fertilizer, and other technical inputs.[124]

The *Draft Outline* of the third plan, published in June 1960, continued the effort to achieve "self-sustained growth." Overall outlays came to $21 billion—about 45 percent greater than total second plan expenditures. The plan designated 57 percent of its budget for the expansion of power facilities, improved transportation and communications, and development of manufactures. Heavy industries such as metallurgy, chemicals, tool making, electrical, and mining took the bulk of the plan's foreign exchange component—with the fourth government-owned steel mill being the most celebrated, proposed project. In contrast, outlays for agriculture, community development, and irrigation comprised only 23 percent of plan expenditures. While the absolute amount of spending for these headings rose 70 percent over the previous plan, Indian officials expected the output of foodgrains to grow from 75 million tons to 100 to 105 million tons, or 33 percent to 40 percent—as opposed to the second plan increase of only 16 percent. The Planning Commission, therefore, proposed that foodgrain production would more than double with only a 70 percent rise in expenditures.[125]

Nor did Indian planners address the crucial question of land reform. The *Draft Outline* called for the implementation of ceilings on ownership and the establishment of cooperatives but did not recommend specific timetables or compulsory legislation. Instead, the Planning Commission followed the advice of the Ford Foundation and placed emphasis on increasing food production through the distribution of improved seeds, farm tools, fertilizer, and irrigation facilities.[126] Although the formula would bring about an increase in production, that increase would not be large enough to keep up with population growth and consumer demand. The Indian government admitted as much in May 1960, when it negotiated the purchase of 16 million tons of wheat and 1 million tons of rice under the PL 480 program for the upcoming four-year period. The magnitude of the transaction is demonstrated by computing that India would receive, on average, a shipload of American wheat each day for four years.[127] While the productive effort, along with PL 480 supplies, would meet India's immediate food needs, the strategy perpetuated a way of development whereby large, landed cultivators prospered most. The vast population of landless and marginal farmers, the largest single segment in Indian society, would see little immediate improvement in their lot.

The Indo-American approach to development had its positive aspects. Through rapid industrialization India enhanced its national strength and laid a crucial foundation for modernization. No plan for India's future would have been complete without a special emphasis on industrialization. Nevertheless, industrialization alone could not solve the problem of widespread poverty. The unalterable fact remained that 80 percent of India's population, and the overwhelming majority of India's poor, lived in rural villages that were far removed from industrial centers in terms of geography and life styles. The growth of factories offered, moreover, little respite to India's masses. While the *Draft Outline* of the third plan predicted that India's labor force would expand by 17 million people by 1966, it estimated that only 10.5 million new jobs would be created over the same period. Unable to keep up even with the growth of the labor force, new undertakings certainly did not provide opportunities for alternative employment for many of India's rural poor.[128] Without a major restructuring of rural institutions, it seems, little hope existed for a reduction of poverty over the short term.

By 1961, the Eisenhower administration had modified the Indian aid program to the point that a small-scale operation involving only limited funds became a major policy initiative. In the process, Dwight D. Eisenhower and Secretary of State John Foster Dulles clearly demonstrated a new willingness to be flexible in dealing with India. Moral absolutes gave way to greater tolerance for the nonaligned perspective. Antagonism toward Nehru gave way to friendly, personal diplomacy. The drive to accommodate India culminated in an enlarged economic aid program. At the end of the Eisenhower era, Indo-American relations were probably friendlier than they had ever been.

While these initiatives in some ways signaled a constructive readjustment of United States policy toward India, they did not mark a fundamental reorientation. In the last analysis, the new approach to India was still a product of Cold War thinking. Absent the Soviet economic offensive, the specter of Afro-Asian revolution, and the shadow of China, it is doubtful that the Eisenhower administration would have attached an intrinsic value to assisting India's development. Indeed, as the level of assistance to India rose, American policymakers seemed to expect more of their aid dollars. Administration officials came to believe that grants and loans to India might not only contribute to political stability in that nation but also that they would counter Soviet diplomatic gains and bolster India as a model for non-Communist development in the Third World. Eisenhower's personal hope that economic aid could be used to help solve the intractable Kashmir dispute and link India and Pakistan in a collective security arrangement best illustrates the administration's Cold War myopia. Guided by global, strategic considerations, the White House badly misread South Asian regional realities.

Although the administration devised an enlarged, Indian economic program primarily to serve Cold War ends, in doing so it became intimately involved in the shaping of India's economic future. A misreading of the Indian scene characterized this aspect of American activity as well. The diffusionist model conveniently merged the goals of containing communism and promoting liberal capitalism, but it underestimated the difficulties inherent to economic development in India. Politically influential social scientists and government officials placed tremendous faith in the ameliorative effects of modern science, technology, and trade. Guided by a can-do American spirit, they downplayed the importance of India's colonial legacy and the obstacles posed by rural social and economic institutions. They believed that armed with a few hundred million dollars each year and adequate technical expertise, the United States would help propel India out of the take-off stage and into self-sustained economic growth. By 1961, the dogged persistence of unacceptable rates of poverty and human suffering should have called some of these assumptions into question.

Seven

JFK and India's Development Decade, 1961–1963

By the time John F. Kennedy became president in January 1961, most American officials agreed that policy toward India and the rest of the Third World needed further modification. Although the Eisenhower administration had begun to make a number of important policy adjustments, the political factors that had stimulated the change remained in force during the early 1960s. Decolonization spawned political unrest in Africa, civil wars raged on in Southeast Asia, and revolutionary impulses swept across Latin America following Fidel Castro's rise to power in Cuba. More than ever, the strategy of cultivating Third World military allies to meet the threat of direct Soviet aggression, a legacy of the Korean War era, seemed obsolete. Washington increasingly showed concern over the Kremlin's alleged "indirect aggression" in emerging areas, especially its support for certain insurgencies and its economic aid to established governments. No one seemed more cognizant of the changing international realities than the youthful, new president. "Today's struggle does not lie here," Kennedy told Paul Henri Spaack of Belgium in early 1963, "but rather in Asia, Latin America, and Africa."[1]

In certain ways Kennedy worked to reshape United States policy to meet the needs of the new era. A long-time critic of Eisenhower's emphasis on military aid, the new president showed greater determination to pursue American interests through economic measures. Proclaiming the 1960s to be the "development decade," he raised the level of United States economic commitments abroad, launched a multibillion dollar "Alliance for Progress" in Latin America, and sent idealistic Peace Corps volunteers to distant Third World villages. The president also demonstrated his interest in the Third World by appointing well-known liberals such as Adlai Stevenson, Chester Bowles, and Michigan Governor G. Mennen Williams to high-ranking posts in the administration. Sensitive to Third World nationalism, Kennedy made a special effort to reach out to nonaligned nations such as India, Egypt, and Ghana. "We cannot permit all those who call themselves neutral to join the Communist bloc," he lectured the NSC on one occasion.[2]

Yet in many respects, the policies of the development decade resembled those of the past. More flexible in his choice of tactics than his predecessors, John F. Kennedy still largely viewed non-Western regions through a Cold War prism. To meet the Communist challenge he not only adopted new diplomatic and economic strategies, he also fell back upon tried and tested formulas. The Kennedy administration, for example, resorted to covert activities in Cuba and military escalation in Vietnam to roll back Communist advances. Cold War considerations, moreover, still loomed large in economic aid policy. At a January 1963 meeting of the NSC, Kennedy echoed Eisenhower's frequent lament that some members of Congress failed to see the irresistible logic of foreign aid expenditures: "We would not like to see four or five countries to suddenly turn communist just because we did not give a certain amount of aid. . . . We must look this over very carefully and put aid on the basis it will best serve our interests."[3]

The administration's policy toward India reflected both its willingness to experiment with new tactics and its adherence to traditional Cold War goals. A strong advocate of increased economic assistance to India while in the Senate, Kennedy appointed a special preinaugural task force on Indian aid that recommended that $500 million over and above PL 480 food aid be allocated annually to make India the administration's number one economic aid recipient.[4] Even more than Eisenhower, Kennedy viewed a strong and rapidly developing India as a counterbalance to the influence of the People's Republic of China. The Kennedy White House also hoped that friendly relations with India—bordering on, but falling just short of outright alliance—would demonstrate Washington's sympathy for Third World nationalism. For these reasons, Arthur M. Schlesinger, Jr., White House adviser and historian, has written: "Of all the neutral countries, Kennedy was most interested in India, which he regarded as the 'key area' in Asia."[5]

The administration's Cold War orthodoxy, however, limited the prospects for Indo-American friendship. In spite of the increased economic commitment, Washington and New Delhi remained sharply at odds on a wide variety of international issues such as nuclear arms, Berlin, and Vietnam. Equally important, the American military alliance with Pakistan continued to undermine relations with New Delhi. Thus, India never quite measured up to Kennedy's expectations—even in the aftermath of India's 1962 border war with China when New Delhi turned desperately to Washington for military as well as economic aid. During the Kennedy years, United States relations with India underwent one more transformation. While economic aid reached its highest levels, the momentum for improved relations began to diminish, and the future did not auger well for America's continued participation in India's development.

Numerous journalists, political scientists, and historians have commented upon the "can do" spirit of the New Frontiersman and the almost boundless optimism of the Kennedy years.[6] The president himself captured the mood in his inaugural address when he issued his famous clarion call to action and national service. Symbolic of a new generation having come of age, an elite corps of bright, young administrators marched to Washington—including Secretary of Defense Robert McNamara, the youthful president of Ford Motor Company; McGeorge Bundy, the former Harvard dean and now special assistant for National Security Affairs; Bundy's ambitious young assistant Walt W. Rostow of MIT; and forty-three-year-old Harvard historian Arthur Schlesinger, Jr. Proud of their managerial skills and their pragmatic approach to problem solving, the Kennedyites were soon at work on the nation's foreign policy. They called for increases in defense spending, which Eisenhower had long resisted, and devised new strategies such as "flexible response" and "counterinsurgency," designed to bring about Cold War victories. Schlesinger did not exaggerate when he concluded: "Euphoria reigned; we thought for a moment that the world was plastic and the future unlimited."[7]

The administration's approach to Third World economic development reflected this upbeat attitude. Like his Republican predecessor, Kennedy drew upon the well-known diffusionist ideas of social scientists Rostow and Millikan. Unlike Ike, the new president brought the two grand theorists directly into his administration, along with other Charles River economists such as John Kenneth Galbraith, David Bell, Edward S. Mason, and Lincoln Gordon. The White House embraced the global Keynesianism of these thinkers and immediately began to lay plans for an expansion in United States economic assistance for emerging nations. The key concept was "modernization," the process whereby developing nations would be guided through the supposedly universal stages of economic growth. The underlying assumption was that gradualistic change would establish a foundation for political stability and help contain the Communist threat.[8]

Of course, the ideas were not new, but the Kennedy team confronted development issues with a new sense of confidence and with nearly total disregard for the many economic, cultural, and political factors that impeded Third World development. Shortly after Kennedy assumed office, Rostow sent a memorandum to the president that dealt exclusively with foreign aid and bespoke of the administration's gargantuan goals. The MIT professor outlined for Kennedy a "new idea" of declaring the 1960s to be the "development decade." Rostow calculated that during the next ten years the United States faced "the peak historical requirement for special external aid." With mathematical certainty, he predicted that during the ensuing ten years a good many countries in the developing world—including Argentina, Brazil, Colombia, Venezuela, India, the Philippines, Taiwan, Turkey, and Greece; and possibly Egypt, Pakistan, Iran, and Iraq—would move from the take-off stage of development into a condition of self-sustained growth. What was needed was one last surge of aid to boost the process along. Rostow confidently asserted that after 1970 these key nations, which together received most of America's aid dollars, would no longer be in need of assistance—a factor that would help persuade the American people and Congress that we were "not entering into an endless job." Rostow closed by adding that the development decade concept would also appeal to Third World opinion: "As I look over the Congo, Cuba, Laos, Vietnam, Indonesia, Iran, etc.—we shall need some such big new objective in the underdeveloped areas to keep them off our backs as we try to clear up the spots of bad trouble."[9]

As Rostow worked out the administration's theoretical framework, a White House task force led by Under Secretary of State George Ball, but including both Rostow and Max Millikan, made specific policy recommendations. In keeping with Kennedy's record in the United States Senate, their report found fault with the Eisenhower administration's emphasis on military aid and called for a reorientation of priorities toward economic development assistance. They nonetheless drew many of their recommendations from the Eisenhower agenda. Economic aid to developing nations, they concluded, would be more effective if it were placed on a long-term basis and if Congress authorized multiyear funding. To improve planning and reduce the strain on the U.S. Treasury, the financial burden should be shared with the industrialized nations of Western Europe, Canada, and Japan, as had already been done for India and Pakistan under World Bank consortiums. To demonstrate the administration's fiscal responsibility and its hard-headedness on aid matters, interest rates on DLF loans should be raised. Finally, the foreign aid program, which currently required coordination between a myriad of agencies such as the International Cooperation Agency, the DLF, the Export-Import Bank, and Food for Peace, should be placed under unified administration and operation.[10]

Armed with these recommendations, the new administration presented its first foreign aid program to Congress in spring 1961. Kennedy led the way with his foreign aid message, which heralded the beginning of the development decade. "The fundamental task of our foreign aid program in the 1960s," he declared, "is not negatively to fight Communism: its task is to make an historical demonstration that in the twentieth century, as in the nineteenth—in the southern half of the globe as in the north—economic growth and political democracy go hand in hand."[11] Before congressional committees, administration officials presented their specific request for a $4.75 billion aid package for fiscal year 1962. The most innovative aspect of the administration's program was its request for a five-year lending authority of $8.8 billion: $900 million already included in the fiscal year 1962 budget, and $1.6 billion for each succeeding year, solely for development loans. In arguing for this departure in authorization procedures, policymakers repeatedly drew attention to the need for long-term planning to combat the Soviet economic offensive in the Third World.[12]

Although setbacks occurred, the administration did make significant progress toward reaching its foreign aid goals. As had happened to Eisenhower's 1959 proposal, Congress rejected Kennedy's plea for multiyear funding. In addition, of the $4.75 billion slated for fiscal year 1962, only $4.1 billion was ultimately appropriated, nearly one-half consisting of military assistance.[13] Still, the White House took solace in the relatively large economic aid appropriations, and most administration officials eventually concluded that multiyear authorization would not be essential to their long-range plans.[14] In the following months, Kennedy also succeeded in reorganizing the aid bureaucracy under the Agency for International Development (AID), headed by New York lawyer Fowler Hamilton.

One final victory for the Kennedy administration came in 1961 with the creation of the president's innovative Peace Corps program. The idea of a "Youth Peace Corps" had first been suggested by Senator Hubert Humphrey, Representative Harry Reuss of Wisconsin, and others during the 1950s, but had been picked up by Kennedy during the 1960 presidential campaign. When it seemed to catch on with his audiences, the Kennedy people gave it more importance. Established by executive order in 1961 and headed by the president's brother-in-law, Sargent Shriver, the Peace Corps initially sent 5,000 young volunteers abroad. It symbolized both the idealism and the Cold War orientation of the Kennedy foreign aid program. On the one hand, Peace Corps volunteers were required to undergo intensive language training, were taught to respect the cultural integrity of their host countries, and were skilled in areas such as engineering, health care, and education. At the same time, most of the enlistees lacked real experience in development work, all were screened for leftist political activity and required to take loyalty oaths, and in some cases basic training included seminars in Marxist political thought.[15] The president himself openly acknowledged the linkage between humanitarian and political goals: "I want to demonstrate to Mr. Khrushchev and others," he declared on one occasion, "that a new generation of Americans has taken over the country—young Americans [who will] serve the cause of freedom as servants of peace around the world."[16]

As the Kennedy administration laid the foundation for the development decade, it also made a special effort to reach out to India. The president signaled his intention to pursue close relations with that nonaligned nation in his inaugural address when he referred to Prime Minister Jawaharlal Nehru's "soaring idealism."[17] More important, in choosing a new ambassador for the New Delhi post, Kennedy tapped the well-known Harvard economist John Kenneth Galbraith. Galbraith had acquired government experience in the Office of Price Administration during World War II, and during the 1950s he had emerged as a leading, intellectual figure in the liberal wing of the Democratic party. Although he lacked diplomatic experience, he had written and taught extensively on economic development at Harvard, and in 1956 he had served as a consultant to the governments of India, Pakistan, and Ceylon.[18] He brought to the job of ambassadorship a deep commitment to the internationalist goals of the development decade, and a warm, personal relationship with the president, whom he had assisted as an adviser and speechwriter during the 1960 campaign. Charming, urbane, witty, and openly disdainful of State Department protocol, Galbraith made a fitting representative for the New Frontier in India.

Galbraith's unabashed liberalism, and his willingness to question certain Cold War assumptions, did make his status in Washington seem somewhat insecure at times. Following his appointment, some of his friends speculated that Kennedy had decided to send the left-leaning economist to India in order to isolate him from domestic policy-making. Galbraith, however, dispelled such rumors. "The terrible truth is that I always wanted to go to

India," he confided to one such friend, ". . . and I am quite persuaded that I have neither the temperament nor the patience to be a good Washington bureaucrat."[19] More significantly, the ambassador-designate faced tough questioning during his confirmation hearing before the Senate Foreign Relations Committee, particularly when he spoke out in favor of diplomatic recognition for the People's Republic of China.[20] Galbraith weathered the storm and won unanimous approval, but during his nearly two years in New Delhi doubts about his suitability for diplomatic service lingered.

The ambassador also frequently found himself at odds with the State Department's cautious hierarchy, especially Secretary of State Dean Rusk. Rusk was not considered to be part of the New Frontier's inner circle of dynamic, young advisers. Rather, at age fifty-one he had served as president of the Rockefeller Foundation, and in Dean Acheson's State Department during the late 1940s and early 1950s where he had developed a reputation as a quiet bureaucrat and a staunch Cold Warrior.[21] While the president often circumvented Rusk's authority by relying on McGeorge Bundy at the NSC, Galbraith had little choice but to engage in "guerilla warfare" with the secretary. Indeed, the ambassador constantly irritated Rusk by defending India's nonalignment, questioning the wisdom of the Pakistan alliance, and pushing for ever-larger economic aid appropriations.[22] In spite of these difficulties, Galbraith embraced the Kennedy administration's basic Cold War goals, and his stature as a renowned economist proved to be an asset in India. One United States Information Service bulletin aptly summed up the public relations value of Galbraith's appointment: "*The Affluent Society* is to democracy what *Das Kapital* is to Communism."[23]

The most significant component of United States diplomacy toward India continued to be the economic aid program. In keeping with the recommendations of Kennedy's preinaugural task force on Indian aid, the White House intended to make India its number one aid priority. The administration allocated $500 million of its fiscal year 1962 developmental budget of $900 million for India alone.[24] Although Congress cut back on the administration's overall lending authority, India still received $465.5 million in United States loans. In June 1961, the World Bank-sponsored India Consortium met in Washington, D.C. to devise a multilateral program of support for India's $24 billion Third Five-Year Plan (1961–66). Working from Indian estimates that placed the plan's external assistance requirement at $5.5 billion, the consortium delegates decided to provide about $2 billion for the first two years of the plan period.[25] After vigorous negotiations the United States pledged $1 billion in loans with the stipulation that the other consortium members match that amount. In the end, West Germany, France, the United Kingdom, and Canada contributed a combined total of $780 million, and the World Bank pledged an additional $400 million.[26]

As had been the case during the last few years of the Eisenhower administration, the United States aid program concentrated on India's industrial development. The majority of loan dollars for fiscal year 1962 went to assist in the construction of large-scale dams for hydroelectric power and irrigation facilities in the Indus Waters region. In addition, large sums went toward the purchase of steel, machinery parts, and other expensive commodities needed to spur rapid industrialization in India.[27] Termed "nonproject" aid, the United States government did not tie these dollars to any particular development project. Instead, the money was simply transferred to the government of India, which in turn used it to import goods that might otherwise have strapped the nation's meager foreign exchange reserves. This gave the Indians maximum flexibility in carrying out their Third Five-Year Plan.

While nonproject aid promoted liberal, diffusionist development in India, some officials within the administration worried that "untied" aid diminished the potential political impact of United States assistance. Ambassador Galbraith, in particular, wanted to devote a larger proportion of American aid to specific projects that carried what he called "high-visibility."[28] To this end, Galbraith resurrected the idea of giving American backing to India's plans for the construction of a fourth government-owned steel mill. Although the Eisenhower administration had begun to consider such a project in 1959, the matter had laid dormant for nearly two years due to internal debate in Washington over the desirability of providing aid to a large public-sector enterprise. In early 1961, the Indian government approached the United States embassy in New Delhi seeking support for a four-million ton capacity steel plant at Bokaro in the state of Orissa. According to Indian plans, the Bokaro plant would take fifteen years to construct at a total cost of $1.5 billion. The foreign exchange requirements, which the United States was being asked to provide, would come to $900 million, making it the largest single public sector project in the history of American foreign aid.[29]

Although Galbraith had been given no instructions from the State Department, he quickly seized the initiative. Speaking off the cuff at a New Delhi press conference in April 1961, the ambassador put the Bokaro plant "within the range" of United States aid. And within a short period he had managed to enlist President Kennedy's support.[30] Yet the proposal fueled controversy. Congressional conservatives remained skeptical of providing American aid for nationalized industries abroad, and the project garnered less than enthusiastic support from the State Department and AID bureaucracies that questioned both the technical feasibility of the plant and the political wisdom of supporting the project.[31] Sensing that the American envoy had failed to gauge the level of opposition, the Indian government removed the Bokaro plant from its priority list of assisted projects later in the year.[32] The issue of United States aid for large, public-sector enterprise in India, however, was only temporarily shelved.

As the Kennedy administration searched for innovative ways to spur India's industrial development, it also continued the Eisenhower policy of downplaying the once highly regarded Community Development Program in rural India.[33] Galbraith constantly lamented the nearly impossible task of reaching India's 500,000 villages with effective agricultural technology, health care, and community planning. On the Indian side, he suspected that Community Development resources all too often fell into the hands of local elites and provided a tempting alternative to "more fundamental social reforms."[34] Regarding American activities, the ambassador complained of overstaffing and the tendency to concentrate too many development "experts" in New Delhi. Quite a few experts came for short tours of duty, Galbraith noted in a letter to the president, and afflicted the mission with the "divine revelations" of every newcomer to India. "It may be debated in the matter of religion," he remarked, "but no one seems to question the doctrine of immaculate conception where ideas on economic development are involved."[35]

In place of the ambitious, multifaceted CDP, Galbraith suggested that United States assistance for rural India be concentrated mainly on increasing food production, and that the effort be limited to certain geographic areas where quick, positive results seemed most promising. This orientation conformed to the recommendations advanced in the Ford Foundation's 1959 report on India's food crisis. To carry out these measures, Galbraith redirected American assistance toward forty Indian colleges of agricultural and veterinarian sciences with established, outreach programs to nearby villages. These programs focused on a limited number of technical matters, such as soil conservation, pest control, irrigation, and development of high-yielding varieties of seed. "No more home economists or communications specialists, whatever in hell communication specialists are," the ambassador resolved in his diary.[36]

Galbraith also stepped up efforts, first initiated in the mid-1950s, to establish contacts between the Indian agricultural college system and a number of American land-grant universities. By the end of the Kennedy years five such universities—the Universities of Illinois, Missouri, and Tennessee, Ohio State University, and Kansas State College—had contracted with the United States government and the Ford Foundation to provide staff training and American advisers and consultants to their Indian counterparts.[37] The newly established Indian agricultural universities offered an integrated program in agricultural education, research, and extension work. The United States government assisted the effort by providing funds for the exchange of professors, the supply of laboratory equipment, and university operating expenses.

The community development philosophy did find limited expression through Kennedy's famous Peace Corps program. The Peace Corps enabled young volunteers to work in educational and social areas of village uplift that had once fallen under the domain of the CDP. Sensitive to India's national pride and the possibility that New Delhi might prove hesitant to engage large numbers of inexperienced Americans in rural development, Galbraith approached the matter cautiously. In early May 1961, when Sargent Shriver visited India, the ambassador arranged for a meeting with Nehru to discuss the program. Much to their surprise, the prime minister responded enthusiastically and even suggested a larger initial undertaking than either Galbraith or Shriver had envisioned.[38] Twenty-six Peace Corps volunteers arrived in India in December and soon took up a wide range of projects, mainly in the northern state of Punjab. Most of their work centered upon efforts to increase food production, such as drilling tube wells for irrigation, introducing improved seed, and teaching new farming methods to local villagers. Only a few of the volunteers held college degrees in agriculture, and most spoke only broken Punjabi, but their work did complement the efforts of India's agricultural colleges and fit well into the Ford Foundation agenda for agricultural modernization. The presence of the Peace Corps in India also initially served a public relations plus for the United States.[39]

Although the amount of aid sent to India more than doubled, American development strategies during the Kennedy years largely grew out of the policies laid down by the Eisenhower administration. American officials continued to place the same emphasis on industrialization and agricultural production and practiced the same neglect of basic, rural reform. Work relating to food crops showed real promise in some areas of the country, but the discovery of high-yielding varieties of seed needed for a "green revolution" was still nearly a decade away. Most important, policymakers in Washington still primarily viewed development assistance to India as a tool of diplomacy. And as the American investment in Indian development deepened, the New Frontiersmen expected larger political returns.

During the first few months of 1961, the outlook for improved Indo-American political relations seemed bright. In May, Prime Minister Nehru wrote to Kennedy to express his gratitude for the increased levels of economic aid that had been made available to his country. "Our task great as it is," Nehru remarked, "has been made light by the good will and generous assistance that has come from the United States."[40] At the same time, the Indian government made a particularly concerted effort to work closely with the Kennedy administration to help mediate civil wars in the Congo and Laos. In the case of the recently decolonized Congo, India sent a contingent of 5,000 troops to participate in a United Nations peace-keeping force that sought to extinguish a secessionist movement in Katanga province.[41] In Laos, Nehru interceded with Premier Khrushchev to win Soviet support for a cessation of hostilities between Communist and non-Communist forces and the strengthening of the neutralist government of Prince Souvana Phouma.[42] The implication seemed to be that Washington's respect for the nonaligned perspective, and its willingness to extend large levels of aid to India, could persuade New Delhi to play a constructive mediator's role in certain Third World conflicts.

The hope for extensive diplomatic collaboration proved to be short lived, however. In spite of the success of the Congo and Laos negotiations, Indo-American relations continued to fall subject to many of the same Cold War tensions that had plagued them in the past. The New Frontiersmen prided themselves on their pragmatic acceptance of Third World neutralism, and in a few cases, such as Laos, they even proved willing to encourage nonalignment as an alternative to communism. Yet the Kennedy White House still encountered numerous obstacles as it tried to nurture constructive relations with most nonaligned nations, including India. The president at times expressed frustration when neutralist states refused to line up with the United States on Cold War issues, and he was often taken aback by the harsh tone of Third World rhetoric. This certainly proved to be the case in regard to the Belgrade Conference of nonaligned nations. The Belgrade Conference convened in early September 1961 just as the United States and the Soviet Union faced off over Berlin, and at a time when the issue of nuclear testing dominated international headlines. On each question the Afro-Asian nations counseled compromise and held the East and the West equally accountable for the state of tension.[43] As far as Kennedy was concerned, neutralist criticisms of United States policy seemed naive, unfair, and dangerously forgiving of Soviet aggression. When Nehru publicly questioned the president's call for a $3.2 billion emergency defense appropriation at the height of the Berlin Crisis, Kennedy complained to Galbraith: "Why [does] a small U.S. arms build-up get more attention than a big Soviet one?"[44]

India and the United States also clashed on a variety of issues in Asia. The Kennedy administration's failed efforts to draw the Nehru government into the maelstrom of South Vietnamese politics best illustrates the limits to Indo-American diplomatic cooperation. Buoyed perhaps by India's helpfulness in the Congo and Laos, the Kennedy team set out in early 1961 to enlist India's support for the struggling anti-Communist regime of Ngo Dinh Diem in Saigon. The president entrusted Vice-President Lyndon Johnson, who undertook a tour of South Asia in May 1961, to meet with Nehru in New Delhi and encourage a stronger Indian stand against "Communist aggression" in South Vietnam. The personable and energetic LBJ made a favorable impression on Nehru and the Indian people. But when the vice-president raised the Vietnam matter with Nehru during private conversations and asked the Indian leader to speak out "in stirring and ringing tones" against Communist tactics in South Vietnam, the latter remained noncommittal.[45] While India continued to take a deep interest in regional affairs, Nehru told Galbraith, it sought "to avoid disfavor from telling other neighboring and perhaps jealous countries what they should do."[46] At the close of the vice-president's visit, the Indo-American joint communiqué made reference to the importance of India's advice and leadership in Southeast Asia but omitted specific mention of South Vietnam.[47]

The United States military alliance with Pakistan continued to be the most disruptive issue in Indo-American relations. Although Kennedy had emerged in the late 1950s as a critic of the 1954 alliance, as president he showed no inclination to sever military ties with Pakistan. By that time, Pakistan had become highly valued not only in terms of its potential role in Middle East defense but also for its air base at Peshawar, which served as a point of departure for American U-2 intelligence flights over the Soviet Union. Thus, while the Kennedy administration sought improved economic and political relations with India, it also hoped to maintain its strategic alliance with Pakistan. One State Department paper underscored the point: "United States efforts to improve understanding with neutral nations does not represent any lessening of our conviction that collective defense is an essential safeguard of any free world security."[48]

Predictably, the United States–Pakistani relationship became strained as Indo-American relations showed signs of improvement. Pakistan's President Ayub Khan especially took issue with Washington's enlarged economic aid program for India, which he feared would allow India to divert its own financial resources toward a military buildup.[49] When the World Bank Consortium in early 1961 allocated only $350 million for Pakistan for the upcoming two-year period, in contrast to its $2 billion program for India, the Pakistani leader made his concerns public. "Can it be," Ayub declared at one press interview, "the United States is abandoning its good friends for the people who may not prove such good friends?"[50] To signal its displeasure with Washington, the Pakistani government went so far as to initiate talks with the Soviet Union on economic aid and to engage the People's Republic of China in talks on Sino-Pakistani border issues.

To reassure the Pakistanis, Kennedy welcomed Ayub Khan's state visit to Washington in July 1961, well in advance of a Nehru visit in November. During Ayub's stay in the United States, Kennedy publicly praised Pakistan's alliance with the United States through the Central Treaty Organization (CENTO) and SEATO.[51] In private, the president promised also to expedite the delivery of twelve F-104 supersonic aircraft that had been pledged to Pakistan by the Eisenhower administration. While Kennedy refused to accede to Ayub's demand that the United States make continued economic aid to India contingent on a Kashmir settlement, he did agree to discuss Kashmir with Nehru during the latter's upcoming visit.[52] Ayub Khan left Washington still suspicious of American intentions, but the United States–Pakistan alliance remained intact.

The continued flow of arms to Pakistan, however, continued to upset United States relations with India. In an effort to minimize difficulties with New Delhi, the United States attempted to keep the delivery of the twelve F-104's to Karachi a secret. In almost comic fashion, the planes arrived in Karachi on an American aircraft carrier in early August, and were shuttled to a nearby airport in the dark of the night. The delivery of the large aircraft did not elude the attention of either Pakistani or Indian news reporters. The supersonic jets, Galbraith later told Kennedy, "were unloaded in all the secrecy that would attend mass sodomy on the BMT at rush hour."[53] When Indian press estimates of the number of F-104's rose from thirty to seventy-five, the State Department finally gave Galbraith permission to announce the shipment of the twelve planes. But the damage had already been done. Shortly following the fiasco, the government of India initiated negotiations with the Soviet Union for the purchase of Russian-made MIG fighters.[54] The whole episode illustrated Kennedy's difficulty in merging new and old approaches to fighting the Cold War. No less than the previous administration, the Kennedy team found itself locked into Cold War strategies—economic in India and military in Pakistan—that worked at cross purposes on the subcontinent.

In spite of the vast differences with India, the Kennedy administration still held high hopes for a successful state visit by Jawaharlal Nehru in November 1961. Most Washington officials fully expected that Kennedy and Nehru, each known for his idealism, wit, and aristocratic demeanor, would certainly strike up a cordial, personal relationship.[55] Their initial meeting seemed promising. After Nehru's arrival in the United States on 5 November, the two leaders were whisked away for a day of talks in the relaxing atmosphere of first lady Jacqueline Kennedy's family home in Newport, Rhode Island. Cruising across Newport bay on the presidential yacht *Honey Fitz*, Nehru seemed delighted as the president pointed to the mansion-studded coast, and interjected: "I want you to see how the average American lives." To which Nehru replied that he had already learned all about the "affluent society" from the American ambassador.[56]

As Kennedy and Nehru moved on to a discussion of issues, however, the ambience quickly vanished. The president pressed Nehru for suggestions on what could be done to put down the "Communist terror" in South Vietnam, but Nehru could only recommend that the United States refrain from additional military escalation. When Kennedy steered the conversation to the topics of Berlin and disarmament, Nehru simply lectured the young president on Eisenhower's warning about the growing power of the military-industrial complex. Keeping his promise to Ayub Khan, Kennedy raised the Kashmir issue, but the Indian leader showed little desire to undertake serious negotiations with Pakistan. Instead, Nehru criticized the administration's decision to provide Pakistan with advanced weaponry such as the F-104, emphasizing the threat that such arrangements posed to India's security.[57]

Kennedy later spoke of the meeting as "a disaster . . . the worst head-of-state visit I have had." Talking to Nehru, he complained, was "like trying to grab something in your hand, only to have it turn out to be just fog."[58] The New Frontiersmen attributed the "disaster" to Nehru's advance in years.

Schlesinger later recalled: "I had the impression of an old man, his energies depleted, who heard things at a great distance and answered most questions with indifference."[59] On the Indian side, Nehru viewed Kennedy as a somewhat brash and inexperienced world leader caught up in the emotion of Cold War politics. In the end, the Nehru visit further diminished hopes for Indo-American diplomatic collaboration.

Before the first year of the New Frontier came to a close, United States relations with India suffered one more setback. Five weeks following his departure from the United States, Nehru ordered the Indian army to occupy the Portuguese colony of Goa. When United States Ambassador Adlai Stevenson condemned Indian aggression in the U.N. and ridiculed India for its advocacy of world peace, the issue rocked Indo-American relations. Although the Kennedy White House sympathized with India's anticolonial nationalism, it would not countenance the use of force in Goa and resented the fact that Nehru had not discussed the possibility of using military force during his talks with the president. In addition, the State Department had hoped that a peaceful resolution to the problem could be found that would not disrupt American relations with its NATO ally Portugal.[60] The Indians viewed the continued colonization of Goa as an affront to their national dignity and had been disheartened by over two years of fruitless negotiation with Portugal. Responding to Stevenson's criticisms, Nehru wrote an eight-page letter to Kennedy that expressed misgivings on the use of force, but also drew attention to the importance of Goa as an emotional, symbolic issue in India. "Why is it," he queried, "that something that thrills our people should be condemned in the strongest language in the United States?"[61] The Goa incident marked the end of a year in Indo-American relations that had started off in an atmosphere of mutual optimism, only to be followed by frustration and mutual recrimination.

By early 1962 the Kennedy administration had largely abandoned its exaggerated hopes for making India a bulwark for United States policy in the non-Western world. Yet the Kennedy team did not intend to reverse its policy of extending large economic aid to India and seeking constructive relations with the nonaligned giant. Discouraged by Nehru's unwillingness to line up with the United States on issues such as Vietnam, Berlin, and disarmament, American policymakers still considered India and other nonaligned nations too important in Cold War terms to be relegated to secondary status. Thus, during the course of 1962 the New Frontiersmen

After an unfriendly meeting between President John F. Kennedy and Prime Minister Jawaharlal Nehru in Newport, a somber welcoming ceremony is held for the prime minister at Andrews Air Force Base, 6 November 1961. U.S. ambassador John Kenneth Galbraith, Indian ambassador B. K. Nehru, Secretary of State Dean Rusk, and Vice-President Lyndon B. Johnson stand (left to right) behind Nehru and President John F. Kennedy. (Courtesy John F. Kennedy Library)

continued to search for the elusive means by which to accommodate India's sensitivities and interests to America's global, Cold War objectives.

In January 1962, a special NSC Steering Group completed a report on United States military assistance programs that carried significant ramifications for the Third World as a whole and the Indian subcontinent in particular. The guiding assumption of the NSC report was that the major threat to United States interests in non-Western areas during the 1960s derived from indirect Soviet aggression rather than the possible direct use of Soviet military power. The NSC group particularly highlighted Soviet assistance for revolutionary insurgents and the Soviet economic offensive. As an antidote, the study emphasized the need to increase levels of economic aid to Third World nations and proposed modest cuts in military aid.[62] Noting that six countries—South Korea, the Republic of China, Pakistan, Iran, Greece, and Turkey—accounted for 50 percent of American military aid appropriations, the NSC recommended that the Department of Defense defer $80.88 million in aid for fiscal year 1962 by "stretching out" deliveries and "resisting requests" for additional, sophisticated equipment. Looking to the future, the NSC group also recommended a ceiling of $3.9 billion in appropriations for fiscal years 1962 through 1967, about $1 billion less than the 1955–61 level.[63]

The Steering Group's recommendations faced stiff opposition from the Joint Chiefs of Staff. The JCS agreed that economic aid should play an important role in United States security policy and that levels of economic assistance should be raised, but they also advised that military assistance programs should be maintained at current levels.[64] In the end, the JCS lost the debate. At a meeting of the NSC on 18 January, President Kennedy directly addressed the matter of United States policy toward the Third World. Citing Nikita Khrushchev's 1961 speech that voiced support for wars of national liberation in emerging areas as "possibly one of the most important speeches of the decade," Kennedy once again underscored the need for an effective economic strategy. Economic aid to nonaligned nations in particular would be sustained at high levels. India must have been on the president's mind when he remarked: "The independence of countries sometimes cause problems. . . . Our relations to such countries could never be like those of the Soviet Union to its satellites. We should simply have to live with those difficulties."[65]

Although the new policy reflected a genuine shift in emphasis, it still involved only an incremental retreat from Washington's reliance on Third World military allies. In fact, the administration's projected cuts in military aid for the five leading allies during the 1962–67 period amounted to only $200 million per year. As devoted as Kennedy was to forging constructive ties with India and other nonaligned states, Cold War considerations simply did not permit a more substantial reordering of strategic priorities.

Given the constraints the Kennedy White House continued to experience difficulties in its dealings with India. The most profound problem that arose in Indo-American relations during the first half of 1962 came about precisely as a result of the administration's efforts to juggle economic and military strategies on the subcontinent. While large sums of American economic aid flowed to each country, both New Delhi and Rawalpindi spent increasingly large portions of their national budgets on armaments.[66] As long as Kashmir and other issues generated tension between India and Pakistan, the possibility of stable United States relations with either nation seemed remote, and peace on the subcontinent remained fragile.

The need for resolute action intensified when the Pakistanis announced in January 1962 that they intended to raise the Kashmir issue before the United Nations, as they had done on numerous previous occasions. Convinced that confrontational politics in the international forum would only make matters worse, the Kennedy team responded with a major diplomatic initiative. At a White House meeting on 11 January, the president decided to propose to both India and Pakistan that a highly respected American, such as World Bank President Eugene Black, be appointed to serve as mediator for talks on the Kashmir dispute. Stressing his own concern over the future of the economic aid program, Kennedy noted that he "wanted it emphasized to both India and Pakistan that their arms race was ruining our economic aid program by diverting their assets from economic development."[67]

The president followed up with personal letters to Nehru and Ayub offering the services of Eugene Black as mediator.[68] But as had been the case with previous efforts at mediation, the initiative had little chance of succeeding. Ayub showed a willingness to explore the option, but Nehru predictably vetoed any possibility of a change in the status quo. Reiterating India's long-held policy, the prime minister simply declared that direct negotiations between India and Pakistan provided the only possible avenue to rapprochement.[69] Disappointed by Nehru's intransigence, Galbraith admitted: "This effort has clearly been a bust and leaves matters worse than before. However well-intentioned, it was based on a clear miscalculation of what we could get the Indians to do."[70]

Complications deepened in May 1962 when India announced the purchase of two squadrons of Soviet-made MIG 21 aircraft. Irritated by the United States' military support for Pakistan and seeking to maintain a strategic balance with its neighbors' forces, India accepted a Russian offer to purchase the aircraft at subsidized prices. The arms deal left the Kennedy White House in a quandary. Administration officials hoped that the United States might use diplomatic pressure to block the sale, primarily by urging India to purchase either subsidized American-made or British-made aircraft in place of the Soviet equipment.[71] Yet it seemed clear that such a transaction would "raise hob with (the) Paks." After careful deliberation, Kennedy decided to protest the Soviet arms sale "for effect," but to eventually acquiesce in the Indian purchase.[72] National Security adviser Robert Komer summed up the matter for McGeorge Bundy in July: "At this point further frenetic efforts on our part will merely depreciate our currency further and create bad blood."[73]

Not everyone in Washington adopted the administration's pragmatic perspective. In May, the White House went to Capitol Hill to request $4.9 billion in foreign assistance for fiscal year 1963, approximately $700 million more than had been appropriated for fiscal year 1962. Out of this total, the administration slated about $450 million for India.[74] Congressional opponents of foreign aid criticized the enlarged program as a whole, but India provided an especially easy target. Led by Democratic Senator Stuart Symington of Missouri, these critics drew attention to India's obstinacy in Goa and Kashmir, its purchase of military hardware from the Soviet Union, and the negative impact of increased aid for India on the delicate military alliance with Pakistan.[75] Symington, a widely respected authority on defense matters, complained to the president that "the policies of no other non-Communist nation have been more critical of, and therefore more embarrassing to, the United States than the policies consistently espoused by India."[76]

While the administration shared in some of Symington's frustration, it defended its Indian aid program. Appearing on the ABC television program *Issues and Answers*, Secretary of State Rusk explained that "two great countries in opposite parts of the world with different positions, different problems, are bound to have particular points of disagreement. . . . But we also have great common commitments that are important and it would be a great mistake, I think, if we did not take an active, even if only a small, part in the Indian development program."[77] In the end, the White House succeeded in shielding India from large Congressional cuts. Whereas legislators trimmed the overall foreign aid budget to $3.9 billion and reduced development lending authority by 20 percent, grant and loan commitments for India remained relatively stable at nearly $400 million.[78]

Passage of Indian aid in 1962 represented, in many ways, a Pyrrhic victory. The Kennedy administration clung to the policies of the development decade, but conflicting economic and military strategies in South Asia produced a series of intractable problems for the New Frontier. After two years of heavy foreign aid expenditures, India seemed no friendlier to the United States than had been the case before Kennedy took office, and the Pakistan alliance showed growing signs of stress and strain. While the United States stood by its commitment to assist India's development, the sense of hopefulness and enthusiasm that had characterized the first months of the Kennedy era had been lost.

Indo-American relations remained in an uncomfortable state of flux through the summer of 1962, but events began to unfold during the fall that momentarily revived the Kennedy administration's hopes for making India central to its foreign policy plans. The turning point came in October, when India's troublesome border dispute with the People's Republic of China suddenly escalated into armed conflict. For several preceding months each nation had carried out provocative troop movements near the contested territories, but on 20 October Chinese forces launched major attacks on Indian outposts at opposite ends of the Himalayas—along India's northwest border in Aksai Chin in the Ladakh area of Kashmir and in the northeast along the Indian-Tibetan border between Burma and Bhutan.[79] Inadequately prepared for the attack and hampered by the rugged, mountainous terrain in each area, Indian troops reeled back in retreat. A shaken and emotionally drained Nehru addressed his proud nation and despaired of India's lack of preparedness: "We were getting out of touch with reality in the modern world, and we were living in an artificial atmosphere of our own creation. We have been shocked out of it, all of us, whether it is the government or the people."[80] Resolving to defend India's territorial claims, the Nehru government immediately began to sound out Washington on the prospect for obtaining emergency military assistance.[81]

The Kennedy White House at the time was caught up in the drama of the Cuban missile crisis, but administration officials did not minimize the importance of the Sino-Indian conflict. Long convinced that an aggressive and militant China posed a threat to all of Asia, the Kennedy team drew dire conclusions about Chinese ambitions on the subcontinent. While no one contended that Beijing planned to undertake the conquest of India, a consensus emerged that the Chinese sought to consolidate their control over Tibet and perhaps expand southward to eventually detach Nepal, Sikkim, and Bhutan from Indian influence. Galbraith commented: "We regard this as far more than a mere border squabble. . . . By the Chinese action, the subcontinent has become a new area of major confrontation between the free world and the Communists. We must take this into our account in our global policy."[82] The NSC's South Asian specialist Robert Komer concluded that the conflict constituted "potentially one of the most crucial events of the decade."[83]

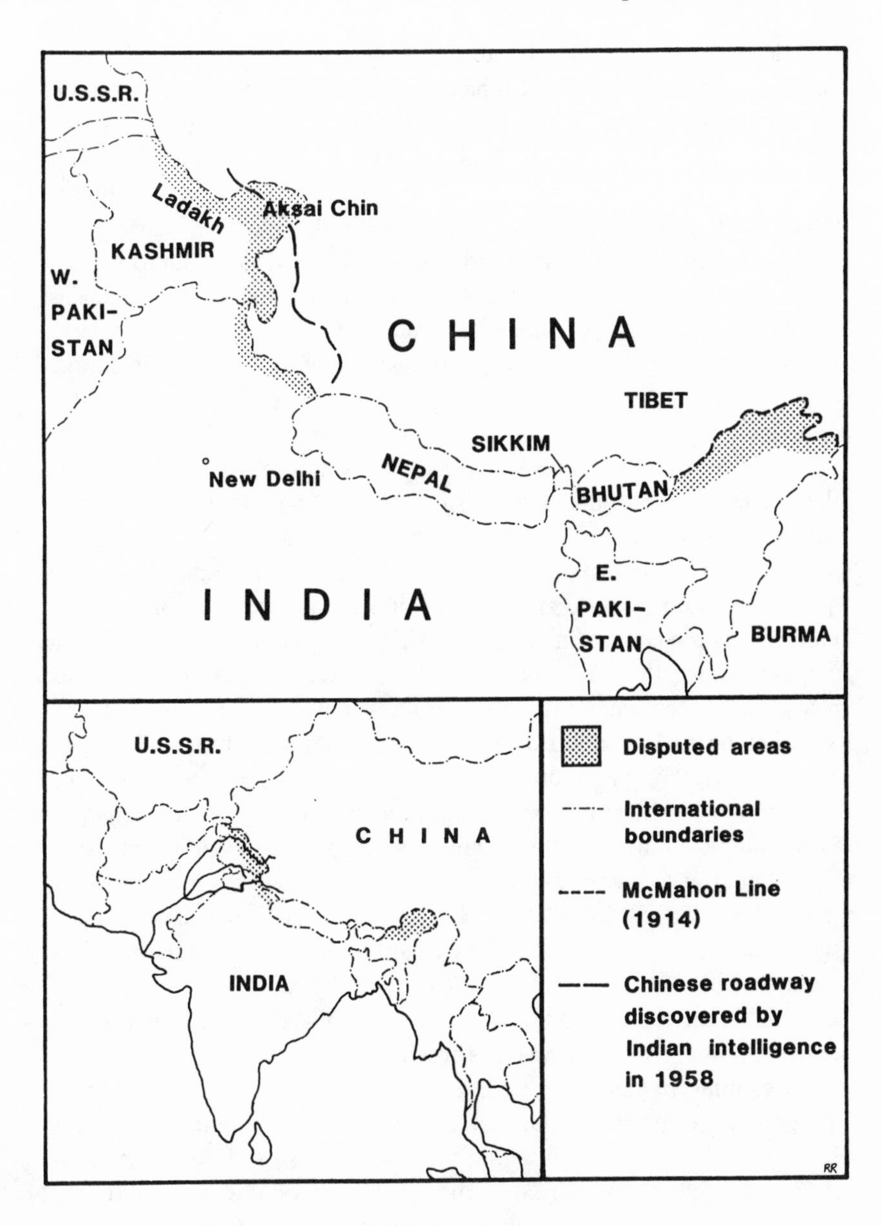

Map. 2. *Sino-Indian Border Conflict*

Policymakers in Washington also quickly deduced that the outbreak of hostilities between India and China presented a series of new opportunities for the advancement of United States security interests in South Asia. As early as 1959, the Eisenhower administration had observed that Sino-Indian tensions seemed likely to force Nehru to reevaluate his nonaligned foreign policy. India's poor performance in the October fighting and Nehru's urgent plea for military aid deeply reinforced this assumption. On 24 October, Komer wrote to Assistant Secretary of State for the Near East and South Asia Phillips Talbot, to make the case for a timely, positive response to Nehru's request. Komer reasoned that the Sino-Indian conflict might contribute to at least three major United States objectives. First, it provided a chance to bring India out of the neutral camp and into a much closer relationship with the West, perhaps even a military alliance. "The sheer magnitude of India's reversals on the Chicom border," the NSC aide wrote, "may at long last awaken Delhi to the weakness of its position." Second, if properly exploited by the United States, the Sino-Indian confrontation could provide an impetus for Indo-Pakistani negotiations on Kashmir and collaboration between the two regional rivals on South Asian defense. Third, the outbreak of fighting between China and India had placed the Soviet Union in an awkward position due to its formal alliance with Beijing and its desire to nurture close ties with India. The whole episode, therefore, might quicken the pace of a growing Sino-Soviet split. With these considerations in mind, Komer concluded that the United States should immediately offer military aid to India, even at the risk of unsettling relations with Pakistan or appearing to be too eager to align India to the West. "The Sino-Indian conflict," he concluded "may have entered a stage where the long-term implications are fully comparable to those arising from Cuba."[84]

In short, the Kennedy administration suddenly confronted the prospect of overcoming nearly two years of frustrations and successfully engineering a genuine reorientation in India's foreign policy. President Kennedy grasped the opportunity. On 28 October he sent a personal letter to Jawaharlal Nehru in which he told the prime minister: "I want to give you support as well as sympathy." Nehru quickly took up the offer, and United States emergency assistance, in the form of light weapons, mortars, and ammunition, soon began to flow to Indian troops stationed along the Himalayan frontier.[85]

As the administration moved swiftly to assist India, it also had to obtain Pakistan's cooperation. When news of United States military aid to India reached Rawalpindi, the Pakistani press launched heated attacks on Washington's policy, and violent anti-American demonstrations broke out across the nation. Accordingly, on 28 October Kennedy wrote to President Ayub Khan to inform him of the administration's intent to help the Indian's meet "their immediate needs." Expressing regret over the recent unrest, Kennedy reassured Ayub of America's continued support and asked the Pakistani leader to send a "friendly signal" to Nehru. "You could tell him that he can count on Pakistan's taking no action on the frontiers to alarm India," Kennedy suggested.[86] At the same time, Secretary of State Rusk instructed Galbraith to inform Nehru that a personal letter to Ayub "would strengthen the President's hand on persuading Ayub to act in [a] helpful way in [the] subcontinent's hour of crisis."[87]

Ayub Khan remained skeptical. In his response to Kennedy he downplayed the importance of the Sino-Indian border clash and warned that India had exaggerated the incident as a pretext for obtaining American military equipment. Parroting the traditional Indian argument against military aid for Pakistan, Ayub further predicted that arms shipped to New Delhi would eventually be deployed against Pakistan. "Is it in conformity with human nature," he asked rhetorically, "that we should cease to take steps that are necessary for our survival?"[88] Somewhat exasperated by the Pakistani position, but still hoping for a diplomatic breakthrough on the subcontinent, Kennedy decided to send a special mission, headed by W. Averell Harriman, assistant secretary for Far Eastern Affairs, to both India and Pakistan. Harriman would be accompanied by Great Britain's secretary of state for Commonwealth Affairs, Duncan Sandys. British cooperation, the president believed, would reduce Indian and Pakistani suspicions of United States motives and involve a sharing of the cost of any long-term military assistance to India. The president charged the Harriman mission with the task of assessing India's military needs and persuading both Nehru and Ayub to put their differences aside.[89]

By the time the Harriman mission arrived in New Delhi on 22 November, Beijing had declared a cease-fire along the Indian border, and the mood of impending disaster had subsided. Still, American officials believed that the border dispute, and India's need for continued assistance, would provide the levers needed to bring New Delhi closer to the West and pave the way for Indo-Pakistani negotiations.[90] Surprisingly, the Harriman mission achieved a degree of success. After shuttling between New Delhi and Rawalpindi, Harriman won each government's approval for beginning talks on Kashmir and other related issues. Although Ayub warned that his nation's cooperation hinged on real progress toward a Kashmir settlement, he did acknowledge that limited United States military aid to India seemed warranted. Encouraged by the outcome of these meetings, Harriman recommended that the United States and Great Britain begin to ship additional military equipment to India and to undertake planning for an Anglo-American air-defense system for New Delhi and other major Indian cities.[91]

Heeding Harriman's advice and the recommendations of a special NSC subcommittee on South Asia, President Kennedy on 10 December authorized $60 million in emergency military aid for India, a figure that was to be matched by the British. The president also approved a proposal to begin planning for a joint Anglo-American air-defense system in India, which included the supply of radar and related communications equipment.[92] On the diplomatic front, Kennedy followed up on Harriman's efforts to encourage an Indo-Pakistani rapprochement by sending another pair of letters to Ayub and Nehru. Writing to the troublesome Ayub, the president praised the Pakistani leader's "statesmanship" and his willingness to negotiate with India. In his letter to Nehru, Kennedy referred to the prime minister's "bravery" in the face of Communist aggression and welcomed his efforts to move forward toward a solution of "the difficult Kashmir question."[93]

In spite of these substantial efforts, the administration failed to achieve a diplomatic breakthrough. On 26 December, just days before the first round of ministerial-level talks between India and Pakistan began, the Pakistanis stunned both Washington and New Delhi by announcing that they had reached an agreement in principle with the People's Republic of China on the demarcation of their borders. Ayub obviously believed that the move would strengthen his bargaining position with both India and the United States. Since the agreement pertained to certain territories in Kashmir, it also had the effect of scuttling any hope, however remote, of an Indo-Pakistani accord. Talks between the two states went ahead, but India refused to consider any significant modification in the status quo in Kashmir. For its part, Pakistan refused to soften its traditional demand for a Kashmiri plebiscite.[94]

The White House continued to try to broker a compromise between the two antagonists during the first half of 1963. The president kept up his correspondence with Nehru and Ayub and even went so far as to suggest a possible partition of Kashmir.[95] These efforts proved to be of no avail. In April, Robert Komer and Walt Rostow, now head of the State Department's Policy Planning Staff, visited the subcontinent to make one last attempt at mediation. Upon their return to Washington, they reported that the Indo-Pakistani talks had simply reached an impasse, and that no hope of success existed.[96]

As Indo-Pakistani negotiations floundered, the Kennedy team grappled with the difficult question of meeting India's requests for additional military aid. During the preceding months, the Indian government had assembled a request for a five-year, $1.3 billion military assistance program.[97] While no one in Washington gave serious consideration to such a large expenditure, some administration officials, especially Ambassador Galbraith and NSC aide Robert Komer, did press for a five-year commitment in the range of $500 million.[98] Other policymakers, led by Secretary of State Rusk and Secretary of Defense McNamara, took issue with these proposals. Noting India's hard line on Kashmir negotiations and the detrimental effect of Indian military aid on United States relations with Pakistan, the Rusk-McNamara camp counseled restraint.[99]

After months of delay, President Kennedy decided in November, just several days before his assassination, that India warranted assistance, but that the level of aid should be kept in the range of $50 million per year.[100] The Pakistan military alliance, of which Kennedy had once been a leading critic, was simply too valuable to forfeit. In New Delhi, a disappointed Nehru government still hoped to maintain friendly political relations with Washington. But it also accelerated its search for defense support elsewhere—primarily the Soviet Union.[101] The opportunity for a major realignment of Indian foreign policy in favor of the West evaporated.

After having come so near to securing a close military relationship with India, only to have the arrangement derailed by its continued commitment to Pakistan, the Kennedy administration began to lose enthusiasm for India. While the New Frontier by no means withdrew its support for Indian economic development, the momentum for a growing aid relationship abated. Small reductions in the level of economic assistance resulted largely from growing congressional opposition to large expenditures for troublesome, neutral India. But the available evidence suggests that by the middle of 1963 the White House had also begun to pull back from its plans for making India a primary beneficiary of the "development decade."

The administration's disillusionment with India coincided with Ambassador Galbraith's departure from New Delhi. The Harvard economist had planned from the outset to serve only a two-year period in India, but his stepping down in early 1963 left India without a strong advocate in Kennedy's inner circle of foreign policy advisers. To fill the New Delhi post, the president turned to former ambassador Chester Bowles: a strong advocate of the development decade philosophy whose support for Indian aid during the Truman years had helped to make him immensely popular in New Delhi. "Chet" Bowles's appointment turned out to be a public relation's success in India, and during his second tour of duty Bowles attacked the assignment with his characteristic enthusiasm, energy, and persistence. Yet, as had been the case during the Truman era, Bowles never succeeded in winning Washington's full support for his initiatives.

Bowles's association with the New Frontier went back to the early stages of the 1960 presidential campaign, when the Connecticut Democrat became one of the first nationally known liberals to endorse Kennedy's candidacy. Kennedy, in turn, made Bowles a top foreign policy adviser and strongly hinted at the latter's future appointment as secretary of state.[102] Although Bowles openly expressed disappointment when the president instead chose Dean Rusk for the top foreign policy job, he eagerly embraced the responsibilities of being under secretary, the position which Kennedy ultimately offered.

Bowles's brief tenure in the State Department proved to be an unhappy one. While he managed to push through a number of innovative ambassadorial appointments, he never maneuvered his way into a position of real authority. The under secretary's criticism of the failed Bay of Pigs invasion in early 1961 and his questioning of Vietnam policy won him few admirers in the administration. Most important, his liberal idealism and overt sympathy for the Third World irritated the pragmatic, action-oriented president. "Chet is a fine fellow," Kennedy confided to Arthur Schlesinger, "but he's just not doing his job. He was perfect as Ambassador to India. A job like that could use all his good qualities—his intelligence, his sympathy, his willingness to listen to problems. But he is not precise enough or decisive enough to get things done."[103]

Kennedy eased Bowles out of Washington in the fall of 1961 by creating a new foreign policy slot bearing the title "Special Representative and Adviser to the President for African, Asian, and Latin American Affairs."[104] Still, Bowles sensed that he carried little influence, and in December 1962 he drafted a letter of resignation. It was at this point that Kennedy offered him the soon-to-be vacant ambassadorship to India. A reluctant Bowles accepted the new assignment only after receiving the president's personal assurances that India still ranked as a foreign policy priority.[105]

A long-time proponent of close Indo-American relations, the new ambassador immediately replaced Galbraith as the administration's foremost advocate of large military aid for India. In a series of memoranda written prior to his departure for New Delhi, Bowles raised the old points that the Sino-Indian conflict offered a unique opportunity to bring India into a "defacto alliance" and to exploit the growing Sino-Soviet rift. He even went so far as to suggest that if Pakistan should object too strenuously, the United States should jettison its alliance with that nation. A friendly India, he argued, would serve as a lynchpin of stability in Asia and assist the United States in seeking peaceful, mediated solutions to conflicts in the region, especially in Indochina.[106] After discussing his points with Kennedy, Bowles left for India in the summer, confident that he would play a leading role in bringing about a fundamental shift in American foreign policy.[107]

The irony of all of this, of course, was that by the time Bowles arrived in New Delhi in July, the administration had already moved away from any serious consideration of a "defacto alliance" with India. Bowles continued to lobby for a large Indian military program, but his power in Washington had long since waned.[108] While the Kennedy White House patiently endured Bowles's entreaties, it never seriously considered implementing his recommendations. The ambassador returned to Washington in November 1963 to press for a five-year, $500 million military aid package, but the president had already decided in favor of a much smaller program. Even Robert Komer, who had originally led the pro-India lobby, felt exasperated with Bowles. "We've explained to Chet that it isn't our policy but circumstances that have changed," Komer advised Kennedy, "while giving Bowles a friendly hearing, I'd urge holding off on any responses yet 'till we can talk further with him. . . . The important thing to do with Bowles is to reassure him that we intend to go forward with India, while getting him to set his sights a little lower and more realistically."[109]

As the Kennedy White House sought to contain Chester Bowles's enthusiasm, it also set its sights lower regarding the highly trumpeted goals of the development decade in India. In 1962, the Indian economic program had weathered vociferous attacks in Congress, but skepticism over the efficacy of expensive development assistance continued to grow in the wake of the Sino-Indian conflict and the unsuccessful mediation of Indian-Pakistani tensions. Added to this, a group of ideologically oriented Congressmen led by Republican Representative Burton Hickenlooper of Indiana voiced opposition to aid for Third World nations, such as India, that promoted publicly owned industries. During the previous year Congress had approved, despite administration objections, the Hickenlooper Amendment, which mandated the suspension of aid to nations that expropriated American business holdings without prompt and adequate compensation.

Kennedy attempted to ameliorate congressional doubts about aid by appointing a special, blue-ribbon commission to examine the foreign assistance program.[110] Overriding Bowles and Galbraith, who suggested that World Bank president Eugene Black head the study group, the president recruited the more conservative General Lucius Clay, who had previously served as Kennedy's personal representative in West Berlin.[111] The president's reliance on General Clay indicated that the administration had conceded the inevitability of foreign aid cuts. When Kennedy first met with Clay in November 1962, the general warned that his committee would criticize certain aspects of the program and might very well call for budget reductions. Kennedy offered little resistance, apparently believing that a conservative endorsement of aid, at least in principle, would strengthen rather than undermine his already weak position.[112]

It turned out to be a disastrous strategy. When the Clay Committee issued its report in March 1963, it did back the administration's basic argument that foreign assistance remained indispensable to United States national security. The committee, however, recommended a tightening up of foreign aid objectives and a reduction in the costs of the program. "There has been a feeling," the committee observed, "that we are trying to do too much for too many too soon, that we are over-extended in resources and under compensated in results, and that no end of foreign aid is either in sight or in mind."[113] Although the published report did not go into budget specifics, Clay weakened the administration's posture when he subsequently told a press conference that Kennedy's request of $4.9 billion for fiscal year 1964 could easily be cut back by $500 million.[114]

Hoping to forestall more drastic budget cuts, Kennedy agreed to reduce his overall request to $4.5 billion, but the Clay report had already seriously undermined the administration's credibility.[115] The urge to trim budgets seemed infectious as the federal deficit grew slightly in 1963, and the White House simultaneously talked of substantial tax cuts to boost the domestic economy. Fueled by the Clay Commission's recommendations and his own disdain for expensive foreign aid projects, the chairman of the House Appropriations Committee, Democratic Representative Otto Passman of Louisiana, vowed to slice a hefty $2.4 billion from the president's program.[116] Soon a coalition of Republicans and southern Democrats lined up behind the powerful committee chairman. General Clay only added to Kennedy's problems when he testified before the House Foreign Affairs Committee in April that even the president's revised foreign aid budget could absorb additional cuts of up to another $500 million.[117]

The White House countered that the president's $4.5 billion budget constituted the minimum needed to protect United States security interests. Before the Senate Foreign Relations Committee, Secretary Rusk sounded the old Cold War theme that "there is nothing the Communists want more than for us to withdraw our support from other independent countries."[118] Still, funding for the Foreign Assistance Act of 1963 slowly diminished as it moved through the Congress. The bill suffered its most serious reversal in the House when Passman's committee appropriated only $2.8 billion. Finally, in late December, more than a month following President Kennedy's death, a congressional conference agreed to appropriate only $3 billion of the administration's original $4.9 billion request—enacting the largest foreign aid cut in history.[119]

The foreign aid controversy of 1963 naturally resulted in reductions in the size of the India program. Planned allocations for India plummeted from approximately $400 million in fiscal year 1963 to less than $350 million for the upcoming, fiscal year 1964. The Kennedy team, with the exception of Bowles and Galbraith, showed no inclination to fight the budget cut or to seek special funding for India. Indeed, by 1963 aid to India seemed at best an unfortunate necessity, and at worst a liability to the foreign aid program as a whole. The costly defeat in Congress, moreover, constituted only the last of many setbacks to Indo-American relations. From Kashmir, to Goa, to Belgrade; India had continuously frustrated the White House. Writing to Ambassador Galbraith in May, as the aid battle raged on Capitol Hill, Secretary Rusk signaled the growing mood of disenchantment and despair when he warned: "It would be folly to assume that aid levels to India will increase in years ahead." A troubled Galbraith fired back an angry rebuttal and urged the administration to take a more combative posture toward Congress. "Does this mean," the ambassador queried, "the New Frontier is relapsing into defeat on what, without doubt, is the strongest and most successful part of our policy in this area of the world?"[120] In fact, the New Frontier had lost its momentum in India and South Asia, and by the time Congress acted on the foreign aid bill, Galbraith had long since departed from the Indian scene.

Although support for India had begun to erode in Washington, the aid process went forward in India. Under the enthusiastic leadership of Ambassadors Galbraith and Bowles, the American embassy in New Delhi continued to implement a wide array of development projects, and most of those associated with the program in India probably did not detect any lessening of America's commitment. Yet even in the area of project choice and implementation, evidence exists that the momentum for a growing aid relationship had begun to diminish.

The MIT Center for International Studies continued to provide the intellectual foundation for the aid program. Working out of the center's office in New Delhi, a host of MIT and Harvard economists established important contacts with the Indian Ministry of Finance and the Planning Commission. The center, working closely with the Ford Foundation, also nurtured collaborative relationships with India's leading economic research institutes—including the Indian Statistical Institute in New Delhi, the National Council of Applied Economic Research in New Delhi, the Institute of Economic Growth at Delhi University, and the Gokhale Institute of Politics and Economics in Pune. In early 1964, the book *Invisible Government* by David Wise and Thomas B. Ross revealed that the United States Central Intelligence Agency had helped to finance the establishment of CENIS in the early 1950s, and that Max Millikan had left a job at the agency in 1952 to become director of the MIT center. After Millikan and MIT admitted to the CIA link, CENIS's effectiveness in India quickly declined.[121] But with a large presence in New Delhi and many friends in high positions in the Kennedy administration in Washington, the center's influence in 1962 and 1963 was at its peak.

The primary focus of United States aid programs continued to be the promotion of rapid industrial take-off. Nonproject loans for "maintenance imports," or the importation of industrial raw materials and equipment, constituted one of the largest areas of expenditure. The first such loan agreement was signed on 26 October 1961 under the Development Loan Fund to finance the purchase of $20 million worth of imported nonferrous metals. Two additional loans in 1962 and 1963, totaling over $400 million, helped to pay for imported steel, automobile parts, and machine tools.[122]

Promotion of electric power, an essential element of industrial infrastructure, also emerged as an American priority. The Kennedy administration made available nearly $250 million in United States aid from 1961 through 1963 to assist the construction of numerous hydroelectric and thermal power projects.[123] By 1968, thirty United States–assisted power projects accounted for one-third of India's total generated electricity.[124] One of the most impressive undertakings was the the Sharavathi power development scheme, which harnessed the Sharavathi River in India's southern state of Mysore. Through a series of dams and large-scale generators, the completed plant carried a generating capacity of 890,000 kilowatts, making it one of the largest hydroelectric complexes in South Asia.[125] In addition to hydroelectric and thermal power, the Kennedy administration also helped to propel India into the nuclear age by providing $72 million in 1963 for the construction of the Tarapur Nuclear Power Station located outside of Bombay. In later years, the project generated a great deal of controversy when India siphoned off fissionable materials to its atomic weapons program. But in the early 1960s, the project bespoke of the optimism of development planners in both the United States and India regarding the prospects for peaceful nuclear power.[126]

As had been the case during the late Eisenhower years, American development planners made India's agricultural sector a secondary concern. Work went forward with the process of making modern inputs—fertilizer, improved seed, and irrigation equipment—available to Indian farmers. Although Ambassadors Galbraith and Bowles each spoke out on the importance of economic reform, neither the United States embassy nor the Indian government made substantive proposals for land reform. Meanwhile, India's food production, American technical assistance notwithstanding, failed to keep pace with population growth. After rising from a level of 50 million to 76 million tons between 1950 and 1960, Indian foodgrain production leveled off at about 80 million tons in the early 1960s. New hybrid seeds that could provide a key to increased production did not become available until later in the decade. Prices for crops, moreover, remained so low—in part, due to the availability of American PL 480 imports—that cultivators hesitated to invest in fertilizers and pesticides.[127]

Faced with the prospect of spiraling food deficits, India's food minister, S. K. Patil, traveled to Washington in June 1963 and secured an extension of the 1960 PL 480 agreement and a tentative understanding for an additional 2 million tons of rice.[128] Yet India's increased dependence on PL 480 also carried a price. American food assistance provided a cushion that permitted Indian officials to avoid hard policy choices, such as the implementation of land reform or the adoption of market-oriented price incentives, that might have spurred production. Large-scale imports, moreover, made the Indian economy increasingly vulnerable to political and economic pressure from Washington. Indeed, by 1967, one-quarter of the

American wheat crop made its way to Indian ports in the form of PL 480 assistance.[129]

Yet India's precarious food supply did not preoccupy the American embassy in 1963. Instead, Congress's rejection of a revised administration proposal to assist the building of the highly publicized, 4-million-ton capacity, Bokaro steel plant ranked as the most hotly debated aid issue of the Kennedy period. And it was in regard to this matter that Washington took another step away from its commitment to the India program. The central significance of the plant, in terms of American aid, arose from the fact that it would be government-owned, like several previously constructed steel mills in India, and would symbolize the Kennedy administration's willingness to accommodate itself to nationalistic development strategies in the Third World.

The Kennedy White House, of course, strongly supported established programs to use aid to promote private enterprise abroad, such as Cooley loans through the PL 480 program and direct AID loans to privately owned industries and investment corporations. Indeed, by the early 1960s United States aid had successfully laid a foundation for substantial United States trade and investment in India. In 1963, United States direct investment in India approached a value of $300 million, and Indo-American trade had climbed to nearly $1.1 billion—$800 million of which consisted of United States exports to India. These figures represented significant increases from 1950s levels. Still, Galbraith and Bowles, in particular, hoped that the New Frontier could distinguish itself from its predecessors by supporting government-owned industries. Partly to appease critics, and in part out of conviction, they emphasized that American support for India's Bokaro plant would, in the long run, benefit that nation's private sector by increasing the supply of steel for commercial use. Galbraith took the initiative before leaving New Delhi by persuading the Indian government to resurrect the $1.5 billion project and to seek United States assistance.[130]

The proposal immediately sparked congressional opposition. First, critics decried its $900 million foreign aid price tag, which made it the most expensive proposed project for fiscal year 1964. Second, opponents questioned the political wisdom of singling out neutral India for so generous an undertaking. Third, the project faced challenges from those in Congress who denounced United States aid for "socialist" development overseas.[131] "It will be putting the government of India and the United States into business in direct contravention of the fiscal policies which have placed this nation and some of those reconstructed after World War II far ahead of the other economic and industrial powers," one senator protested.[132] These arguments were reinforced by the Clay Committee report, which while not addressing the Bokaro issue in particular, included strong recommendations against assistance for public sector projects in principle.[133]

The Kennedy administration attempted to answer the critics. AID director Bell testified before the Senate Foreign Relations Committee that public construction and ownership of the plant made sense in India where private investors "do not have that much capital, and there is no foreign capital available that would be sizable enough to do this sort of thing." Secretary of State Rusk noted that the owners of India's two private steel plants and even the Indian Chamber of Commerce backed the Bokaro project.[134] In May 1963, President Kennedy even entered the fray. "The Congress may have other views," the president declared during a news conference, "but I think it would be a great mistake not to build it. India needs the steel."[135]

Yet opposition to the Bokaro project mounted during the summer months, and the Kennedy administration once again faced the prospect of a major foreign aid defeat. Fearing that the Bokaro proposal might endanger passage of the foreign aid program as a whole, the White House gradually softened its commitment to the project. In early September, Kennedy wrote to Prime Minister Nehru expressing regret over the stalemate and asked that the Indian government quietly withdraw the Bokaro project. Nehru acceded to the request.[136] As had been the case with the previous year's rejection of Indian military aid, Washington's rejection opened new opportunities for the Kremlin. Over the ensuing months India successfully negotiated Soviet assistance for building the prestigious Bokaro plant.[137]

Following the Bokaro debacle, the American embassy in New Delhi tried to put the best face possible on the development program. The level of aid, of course, remained substantial and the failure to move ahead with support for India's public sector seemed to many to be only a minor setback. In December 1963, Ambassador Bowles addressed an audience of visiting Americans in New Delhi and highlighted the impressive economic gains of the past decade. Contrasting contemporary India with the nation he had first encountered in the early 1950s, he ticked off the statistical evidence: a 42 percent rise in national income, a 10 percent annual rate of industrial growth, the near eradication of malaria, and the extension of life expectancy from twenty-seven to forty-two years. All of this had occurred, moreover, within a democratic political context that ensured freedom of speech, freedom of religion, and freedom of the press. Bowles observed that India's success had "been in large measure due to its own efforts." But he also emphasized the importance of United States economic aid programs, which had provided nearly $3.9 billion in capital and commodity assistance over fifteen years. "Indians would be the first to admit," he declared, "that the outlook for success of Indian democracy would not be so bright today had it not been for the generous assistance from the U.S."[138]

Behind the scenes, however, Bowles entertained deep doubts by late 1963 concerning the future of United States development assistance. The Bokaro controversy seemed for the ambassador to mark a symbolic turning point in a steady retreat from the heady optimism of the early New Frontier. In one dark moment, immediately following news of Kennedy's reversal on the steel plant issue, Bowles wrote to Galbraith and poured out his troubles. Reviewing the administration's rejection of large military aid for India, its continued support for Pakistan, and its unwillingness to go to battle over foreign aid cuts, the ambassador expressed his view that the Kennedy team seemed wedded to traditional Cold War policies. The "only reason" he had taken the job in New Delhi, Bowles complained, had been his conviction that the administration "fully understands our stake here." "After all my adventures within this administration," Bowles despaired, "I have no intention of ending up as a facade for policies that contradict everything that you and I have been advocating in this area for the last ten years."[139] Whether Bowles concluded that he had prejudged the administration, or simply decided to accept what New Frontier politics had to offer, he stayed on at the India post through the end of the 1960s. Yet it was clear by late 1963 that India's development decade was beginning to run out.

Numerous factors help to explain why the Kennedy administration failed to reorient United States policy toward India. Congress, of course, posed a formidable obstacle to the maintenance of a stable and enduring development assistance program. This turned out to be a special handicap for a Kennedy White House that was less adept at dealing with Congress on such matters than the preceding Eisenhower administration. Regional politics on the Indian subcontinent—especially the intractable Kashmir dispute—also ranked as a major stumbling block. Time and again, India and Pakistan each adopted intransigent positions on key issues that weakened the prospects for peaceful economic development in the region. In addition, India's intense nationalism and the unique diplomatic style of Jawaharlal Nehru contributed to Kennedy's problems. But the largest responsibility for the disappointing results must be traced to the administration itself. While the

New Frontier promised to abandon cherished Cold War verities and make peace with Third World nationalism, it constantly sparred with nonaligned India over a long list of global and regional issues. Whereas the Kennedy White House promised a bold redirection of American policy toward economic diplomacy, it also proved unwilling to forego the strategic benefits that accrued from certain military alliances. And while the Kennedy team took pride in its pragmatic approach to problem solving, its assumptions that economic aid could easily woo neutrals, solve intricate regional disputes, and propel developing societies quickly into the twentieth century, were nothing less than grandiose—and arguably unrealistic.

At bottom, it was probably the Kennedy administration's exaggerated sense of optimism that most seriously undermined the Indian economic aid program. The youthful president and his army of impressive advisers promised miracles both to Congress and to themselves. When India's expected drift into the Western camp failed to materialize, and when the economic and political obstacles inherent to development refused to melt away, the Kennedy team grew impatient and Congress became disillusioned. Of course, economic aid could contribute to gradual progress toward the goals of peace, development, and stability as the Kennedyites maintained. But development diplomacy required a willingness to experiment and fail; to come to terms with differences and compromise; and to always keep in mind the limitations that history imposes on any effort at social transformation. Guided by simplistic Cold War goals and a naive faith in America's own power of persuasion, the New Frontier never fulfilled its promise.

Eight

Conclusion

Previous chapters have explored the origins and implementation of United States economic assistance programs in India from 1947 to 1963. This conclusion summarizes the major themes of the study and reviews the chronology of events in the Indo-American aid relationship during those years. It also provides a brief glimpse into the course of Indo-American relations and the aid process after 1963, emphasizing trends and developments that largely grew out of the earlier period.

The Indo-American aid relationship began in July 1947, a month before India actually emerged as a free and independent state. The proud and nationalistic Jawaharlal Nehru spoke frankly to American Ambassador Henry Grady, spelling out his country's need for United States economic assistance. At that moment, India was caught up in the fervor of newly found independence and the hope of social and economic transformation. Nehru, and other Indian officials, looked to the affluent United States as a possible benefactor. In part, they viewed the United States as being exceptional among great powers, a country whose dynamic and expansive liberal capitalism would induce worldwide economic growth without initiating a new era of political imperialism. In part, they respected America's awesome economic power and sought to protect their weak nation from the possible disadvantages of dollar diplomacy. Either way, they had little choice but to invite the United States to participate in India's development effort.

The United States had an opportunity to respond to India's entreaties immediately following that nation's independence from colonial rule. At that point, the extension of economic aid to India might have laid the foundation for warm diplomatic relations between the two countries and helped to establish a partnership in liberal development. India seemed willing, in exchange for aid, to help the United States in a limited but constructive way to find peaceful solutions to the myriad of political problems that had accompanied decolonization in Asia. The Truman administration, however, chose instead to implement a more militant, anti-Communist strategy in the area in order to isolate the People's Republic of China and quell armed insurgencies in Southeast Asia. In so doing, it established a persistent pattern in American aid policy toward India and many other non-Western nations—Cold War containment assumed priority over liberal development.

By 1963, the United States had evolved and implemented a major economic aid program for India, but that policy was also wrapped in the garment of containment. The origins of the undertaking can be traced to the Truman years and the Cold War crisis in Korea. But it was the Eisenhower administration, acting in response to the French debacle at Dien Bien Phu, the spirit of Bandung, and the Soviet economic offensive, that initiated a dramatic expansion of the effort. Capital assistance to India rose from $44.3 million in fiscal year 1953, the last year of Truman's term, to $200.8 million in fiscal year 1961, when Eisenhower left the White House. In addition to large-scale financial assistance, between 1956 and 1961 India received nearly $1.5 billion in PL 480 commodity assistance. The India aid program reached its zenith during the Kennedy years when the words modernization and development became fully incorporated into the Cold War lexicon. Annual grant and loan commitments surpassed $400 million annually, supplemented by a nearly equal dollar value in PL 480 foodgrains, and India emerged as the Third World's leading recipient of United States economic aid.[1]

Although American policymakers hoped to eventually establish an open world that would nurture liberal capitalism, their immediate aims in India were usually political. Working in the emotional atmosphere of the Cold War, the Truman, Eisenhower, and Kennedy administrations sought, first and foremost, to prevent India's "fall" to communism and to diminish the possibility of increased Soviet influence there. At the same time, they hoped to lure nonaligned India into the Western camp, gain access to strategic raw materials, and make India a dependable military ally. Citing India as the world's largest democracy, United States officials ultimately worked to make India a model for non-Communist development in the Third World and an Asian counterweight to the People's Republic of China.

United States policy toward India abounded with contradictions. Wary of democratic India's neutral posture in the Cold War, American leaders initially gave preferential treatment to authoritarian regimes such as South Korea, Formosa, and South Vietnam in the dispersal of aid. In seeking to promote a stable world order, the United States gave military assistance to Pakistan, which helped intensify regional tensions in South Asia and encouraged both nations to divert precious resources from economic development to defense. And even as American policymakers proclaimed India to be a model nation, they often showed annoyance when Nehru steered too independent a course in foreign affairs. Indeed, from the time of the Korean War to the close of the Kennedy era, United States officials never abandoned hope that India might be persuaded to support American foreign policy initiatives, evolve a more market-oriented economy, and align militarily with the United States. These hegemonic ambitions often brought the United States into direct conflict with Indian nationalism.

The notion that the United States could employ its vast economic resources to gain a major political advantage in India proved a shibboleth. India's nationalist and regional perspectives never exactly coincided with America's global policy of anti-Communist containment. Although Prime Minister Nehru demonstrated a willingness to work with the United States in promoting political and economic stability in a volatile Asia, he was not willing to play too subservient of a role. Memories of a recent colonial past mitigated against India's close association with any great power. Equally important, whereas American Cold Warriors condemned radical political change and usually linked Asian revolution to Soviet intrigue, Indian officials defined the region's discontent as a legacy of the colonial era and economic imperialism. The most contentious point of disagreement arose over United States military aid to Pakistan, which Washington hoped would help to contain Soviet aggression, and which New Delhi feared would encourage Pakistani aggression.

A sense of self-righteousness and moral grandeur often colored both American and Indian perspectives, and larger-than-life personalities—such as Nehru, Menon, Acheson, and Dulles—frequently disrupted the conduct of diplomacy. The aid process, however, required the donor nation, whose relative wealth and power allowed for greater flexibility, to take the lead in fashioning compromise. United States foreign policymakers often failed to do so because of their exaggerated fear of communism, their tendency to underestimate the power of nationalism in India and other non-Western nations, and their serious misreading of regional politics. All too often American leaders lacked the historical perspective needed to gauge the vast political, economic, and ideological gaps that separated India and the United States.

Although the United States did not significantly influence Indian foreign policy, the aid process did ultimately affect India's economic development. The economic agenda usually proved secondary to diplomatic goals, and when policymakers did grapple with developmental issues, most demonstrated only limited comprehension of Indian social and economic needs. In the early 1950s, United States officials focused upon India's dire need for increased food production as a policy priority. But the level of financial assistance was not nearly adequate to implement Ambassador Chester Bowles's comprehensive Community Development Program. In the late 1950s, more substantial aid flowed to India. But by that time attention shifted to prestigious industrial projects that carried political impact, and were deemed necessary to promote economic take-off. India's crucial agricultural sector never received adequate American support during the period under consideration. Most important, whether they emphasized agriculture or industry, American policymakers consistently underestimated the enormity of India's dilemma. Downplaying that country's history, its unique customs, and its rigid socioeconomic hierarchy, they usually encouraged the adoption of American-style capitalism in India. The American strategy failed to address some of India's most pressing needs—particularly the desirability of substantial land reform.

Yet American policymakers did not single-handedly chart India's economic future. Prime Minister Nehru demonstrated great skill in denouncing the evils of superpower diplomacy, but he proved far less willing to confront powerful interests within his own Congress party on the issue of social change. Land reform legislation often looked impressive on paper but rarely led to any significant redistribution of wealth in the Indian countryside. Agricultural cooperatives preached the doctrine of community development and grassroots democracy but usually fell under the domination of elite interests. And the Indian government's emphasis on rapid industrialization led to an ill-placed sense of complacency regarding agriculture. Finally, Indian planners can be faulted for their overreliance on Western developmental models that were not wholly applicable to the nation's social and economic needs.

The Indo-American aid relationship survived beyond the Kennedy years, but the level of bilateral assistance gradually fell as Cold War politics continued to define American attitudes toward India. Nehru's death in May 1964, and his replacement first by Lal Bahadur Shastri, and then in 1966 by Indira Gandhi, brought no major alteration of Indian foreign policy. Gandhi, Nehru's daughter, particularly won the wrath of President Lyndon

Johnson in 1966 when she publicly condemned United States bombing of North Vietnam. In his memoirs, Chester Bowles has written that following Gandhi's pronouncement, cables from Washington "burned with comments" about "those ungrateful Indians." The former ambassador further speculates that Johnson's decision to postpone PL 480 food shipments to India at that time, in the midst of an Indian drought and rising food shortages, came in part as a response to the Indian leader's outspokenness.[2]

America's military ties with Pakistan, moreover, continued to rankle Indo–United States relations. In the years immediately following the Sino-Indian border clash, tensions between India and Pakistan further escalated. In 1965 and 1966, the two nations each employed American weapons in a brief and indecisive border war.[3] Then in 1971, armed conflict subsumed the subcontinent once more. A brutal civil war between the predominantly Bengali population of East Pakistan and the West Pakistanis, two factions separated by over one thousand miles of Indian territory, provided the spark. As East Pakistan, soon to become Bangladesh, rebelled against the West Pakistani government, over 10 million Bengali refugees flooded into India. Seeing an opportunity to dismember its South Asian rival, India lent its support to the Bengali independence movement, and in December 1971, war once again broke out between India and Pakistan.[4]

The plight of the Bengali people won worldwide sympathy, but high-ranking officials in the administration of President Richard M. Nixon were not deeply moved. Not only was West Pakistan a longtime friend and ally of the United States, but that nation's president, Yayha Khan, had worked during the spring and summer of 1971 to help arrange national security adviser Henry Kissinger's secret July trip to the People's Republic of China. Ironically, Sino-American rapprochement, a goal which Jawaharlal Nehru had doggedly pursued throughout the 1950s, now served to undermine Indo-American relations altogether. In August 1971, perhaps in response to the growing evidence of a Sino-Pakistani entente, India's Prime Minister Gandhi signed a twenty-year treaty of friendship with the Soviet Union. This was not a military pact, and India continued to adhere to the substance of nonalignment, but each nation did agree to refrain from aiding a third party in the event of war.[5] Nixon and Kissinger, nevertheless, viewed the Indo-Pakistani war as a Soviet-inspired ploy to weaken an American ally and to possibly dominate the subcontinent. The United States "tilted" toward Pakistan in the war by continuing arms exports to that nation, dispatching a naval task force to the Bay of Bengal, and seeking a condemnation of India's actions in the United Nations.[6]

These events carried immense ramifications for the Indo-American aid relationship. United States economic assistance to India had begun to decline, of course, in the aftermath of the Sino-Indian border war in late 1962, when the Kennedy administration determined that the Nehru government showed little sign of significantly modifying its nonaligned posture and no intention of coming to terms with Pakistan over Kashmir. The process of decline, however, accelerated during the late 1960s. From 1967 to 1971 annual grant and loan commitments hovered between $160 million and $200 million—well below the $400 million mark that had been reached during the early days of the New Frontier.[7] In addition to the Indo-Pakistani conflict, American travails in Vietnam and mounting United States balance of trade difficulties diverted attention away from India's economic needs.[8] The final turning point came in December 1971, when in response to the Indo-Pakistani war the State Department announced the cancellation of $87.6 million in development loans to India, aid that was entirely economic in content and not military.[9] For the remainder of his term Nixon did not allocate any further economic aid for India, and neither did his successor Gerald Ford. In recent years, a small bilateral aid program has been reinstituted, but capital assistance to India has averaged $100 million to $150 million annually through the 1980s—a meager program compared to the heady days of the late 1950s and early 1960s, especially when the rate of inflation for the past two decades is factored into the equation.[10]

After 1971, large levels of economic assistance continued to make their way to India through international agencies such as the World Bank and the International Monetary Fund. But, for all intents and purposes, America's bilateral effort to combat poverty in the world's largest democracy had come to an end. It fell victim to political forces that were strikingly similar in character to those that gave rise to Indo-American economic cooperation in the first place. Underlying the configuration of Cold War alliances and loyalties that defined United States aid policies lay the basic premise that weaker nations such as India, China, and Pakistan had been destined to serve as junior partners to the great, world powers. This "arrogance of power," as former Senator J. William Fulbright termed it, all too often discounted the aspirations of the less-developed nations to determine their own future.[11] It explains, in large measure, the inability and the unwillingness of United States leaders to understand and respect India's nonaligned policies. It contributed to their misreading of regional realities in South Asia. It also helped United States officials and social scientists to believe that American modes of liberal development were nearly always appropriate for the Indian setting.

Over the course of two decades, from 1951 to 1971, the United States sent approximately $4 billion in bilateral capital assistance and an equal dollar value in PL 480 commodity assistance to India.[12] This influx of economic aid, combined with substantial technical assistance, certainly contributed to the growth of new industries. Indeed, India—perhaps through its independent policies—has avoided excessive economic dependence on external powers, and today ranks as the world's twelfth most industrialized country. Throughout the decade of the 1980s, India's gross national product has increased at an annual rate of 4.5 percent, which is well above the pace of previous decades. The value of India's annual foreign trade mushroomed in 1988 to over $30 billion, with Indo-American trade accounting for $5 billion, the balance of which favored India. The lion's share of Indian exports, moreover, consisted of nonagricultural items such as cotton apparel and fabrics, engineering goods, precious stones, handicrafts, and crude oil. And India's development has not been dominated by foreign investors. Although the United States ranked as the leading source of foreign private capital in India in 1987, total direct United States investment amounted to only $466 million—constituting only a tiny fraction of total American overseas investment.[13]

Significant advances have been made in agriculture as well, especially food production. During the late 1960s, ironically as India became less important to United States foreign policy goals, America's continued support for India's system of agricultural universities, irrigation facilities, and fertilizer imports helped build the foundation for a "green revolution." The introduction of high-yielding, hybrid wheat and rice seeds to India during the 1970s completed the process and by late in the decade output of food grains approached 150 million tons annually, enough to make India self-sufficient. During the past few years, agricultural production has continued to increase at an impressive annual rate of about 3 percent—outpacing India's 2 percent annual birthrate.[14]

Yet despite these achievements, one unalterable fact remains: the Indo-American aid effort did not bring about a significant reduction in poverty. Unfortunately, sweeping social and economic reforms—perhaps most importantly, land reform—did not accompany the gains in productivity. As a consequence, the diffusion of capital and technology from the United States, and a development strategy drawn largely from Western experiences, has hardly touched the lives of millions. In the late 1980s, 70 percent of India's work force is still engaged in agriculture, where the rhythm of life revolves around the daily struggle for subsistence. About one-third of India's agrarian population is either landless or owns fragments of less than 2.5 acres. Nearly one-half of the Indian people still live below the poverty level. Infant mortality stood at an estimated 90 per 1,000 in 1986—among the highest rates in the world. Life expectancy averages a mere 55.8 years.[15]

The mind-boggling incongruities of Indian development are readily apparent to perceptive visitors—rag-clad beggar children congregated outside fashionable Delhi shopping centers; affluent village homes, some even equipped with color televisions and video cam recorders, couched between mud huts; gleaming new factory buildings surrounded by colonies of makeshift, shanty dwellings. While United States aid policies alone by no means created these conditions, they all too often failed to ameliorate them. Once United States leaders lost the political will to participate in India's democratic development, they also surrendered the option of helping, in a significant way, to remedy its shortcomings.

Notes

Abbreviations

AWF	Ann Whitman File, Dwight D. Eisenhower Library
BP	Chester Bowles Papers, Sterling Library, Yale University, New Haven, Conn.
DDEL	Dwight D. Eisenhower Library, Abilene, Kans.
FR	U.S. Department of State, *Foreign Relations of the United States*, year and volume number
HSTL	Harry S. Truman Library, Independence, Mo.
JFKL	John F. Kennedy Library, Boston, Mass.
LBJL	Lyndon B. Johnson Library, Austin, Tex.
NSF	National Security File, John F. Kennedy Library and Lyndon B. Johnson Library
OSANSA	Office of the Special Assistant for National Security Affairs, Dwight D. Eisenhower Library
POF	President's Office File, John F. Kennedy Library
PRO	British Public Records Office, Kew Gardens
PSF	President's Secretary's File, Harry S. Truman Library
RG 16, DAR	Record Group 16, Department of Agriculture Records, National Archives, Washington, D.C.
RG 59, DSR	Record Group 59, Department of State Records, National Archives, Washington, D.C.
Speeches	India, Ministry of Information and Broadcasting, *Jawaharlal Nehru's Speeches*, volume number and date
USCFEP	United States Council on Foreign Economic Policy, Dwight D. Eisenhower Library
WHO	White House Office, Dwight D. Eisenhower Library

Preface

1. Special Message to Congress on the Mutual Security Program, 13 March 1959, *Public Papers of the Presidents of the United States: Dwight D. Eisenhower, 1959* (Washington, D.C., 1960), 258–72.

Chapter One

1. Senate Committee on Foreign Relations, *Hearings: Mutual Security Act of 1960*, 86th Cong., 2d sess., 1960, 155, 400; Robert C. Johansen, *The National Interest and the Human Interest* (Princeton, N.J., 1980), 180.

2. NSC 5909, "U.S. Policy toward South Asia," 22 July 1959, OSANSA, NSC Series, Box 68, WHO.

3. Similar questions are raised in Samuel Baily, *The United States and the Development of South America, 1945–1975* (New York, 1976), 8–9.

4. For in-depth analysis of liberal development ideology, see Emily Rosenberg, *Spreading the American Dream: American Economic and Cultural Expansion, 1890–1945* (New York, 1982); Robert A. Packenham, *Liberal America and the Third World: Political Development Ideas in Foreign Aid and Social Science* (Princeton, N.J., 1973).

5. Standard works that analyze the Open Door policy and the history of Sino-American relations include Warren Cohen, *America's Response to China* (New York, 1980); John King Fairbank, *The United States and China*, 4th ed. (Cambridge, Mass., 1979); Michael Hunt, *The Making of a Special Relationship: The United States and China to 1914* (New York, 1983); Akira Iriye, *Across the Pacific: An Inner History of American-East Asian Relations* (New York, 1967); Michael Schaller, *The United States and China in the Twentieth Century* (New York, 1979); James C. Thompson Jr., Peter W. Stanley, and John Curtis Perry, *Sentimental Imperialists: The American Experience in East Asia* (New York, 1981).

6. The literature on ideology and American foreign policy is voluminous, but several recent works which shed light on the matter include Michael Hunt, *Ideology and U.S. Foreign Policy* (New Haven, Conn., 1988); Frank Ninkovich, *The Diplomacy of Ideas: U.S. Foreign Policy and Cultural Relations, 1938–1950* (Cambridge, 1981) and "Ideology, the Open Door, and Foreign Policy," *Diplomatic History* 6 (Spring 1982): 185–208; Packenham, *Liberal America*; Rosenberg, *Spreading the American Dream*.

7. On the Philippines, see Gary R. Hess, *The United States' Emergence as a Southeast Asian Power, 1940–1950* (New York, 1987), 217–50; Stanley Karnow, *In Our Image: America's Empire in the Philippines* (New York, 1989); Stuart C. Miller, *'Benevolent Assimilation': The American Conquest of the Philippines, 1899–1903* (Cambridge, Mass., 1974); Peter W. Stanley, *A Nation in the Making: The Philippines and the United States, 1899–1921* (Cambridge, Mass., 1974); Thompson et al., *Sentimental Imperialists*, 106–20.

8. Standard works on inter-American relations include Bruce J. Calder, *The Impact of Intervention: The Dominican Republic during the U.S. Occupation of 1916–1924* (Austin, Tex., 1984); Walter LaFeber, *Inevitable Revolutions: The United States in Central America* (New York, 1984); Lester Langley, *The Banana Wars: An Inner History of the American Empire, 1900–1974* (Lexington, Ky., 1983); Dana Munro, *Intervention and Dollar Diplomacy in the Caribbean, 1900–1921* (Princeton, N.J., 1964); Stephen G. Rabe, *The Road to OPEC: United States Relations with Venezuela, 1919–1976* (Austin, Tex., 1982); Gordon Connel Smith, *The United States and Latin America* (New York, 1974).

9. In addition to the works listed in the preceding note, see Baily, *The United States and the Development of South America.*

10. On the Good Neighbor policy, see Irwin Gelman, *Good Neighbor Diplomacy: United States Policies in Latin America, 1933–1945* (Baltimore, 1979); David Green, *The Containment of Latin America* (Chicago, 1971); Bryce Wood, *The Making of the Good Neighbor Policy* (New York, 1961).

11. George Rosen, *Western Economists and Eastern Societies: Agents of Change in South Asia, 1950–1970* (Baltimore, 1985), 19–24.

12. Ibid., 25–26.

13. On postwar economic diplomacy, see Alfred Eckes, *A Search for Solvency: Bretton Woods and the International Monetary System from World War II to the Present* (Austin, Tex., 1977); Richard N. Gardner, *Sterling-Dollar Diplomacy: The Origins of Our International Monetary System* (New York, 1969); Michael Hogan, *The Marshall Plan: America, Britain, and the Reconstruction of Western Europe, 1947–1952* (Cambridge, 1987); Thomas G. Paterson, *Soviet-American Confrontation: Postwar Reconstruction and the Origins of the Cold War* (Baltimore, 1973); Robert A. Pollard, *Economic Security and the Origins of the Cold War, 1945–1950* (New York, 1985).

14. Gary R. Hess, *America Encounters India, 1941–1947* (Baltimore, 1971), 3–6, 16–17; L. Natarajan, *American Shadow Over India* (Delhi, 1956), 3–5, 9.

15. Norman Brown, *The United States and India, Pakistan, and Bangladesh*, 3d ed. (Cambridge, Mass., 1974), 392–93.

16. Introductory surveys of Indian society, culture, and history include N. Brown, *The United States and India*; Judith Brown, *Modern India: The Origins of an Asian Democracy* (Delhi, 1984); Lloyd I. Rudolphe and Susanne Hoeber Rudolphe, *The Modernity of Tradition: Political Development in India* (Chicago, 1967); Percival Spear, *A History of India*, vol. 2 (Middlesex, 1970); Stanley Wolpert, *A New History of India* (New York, 1982).

17. In addition to the works in the preceding note, the following provide an introduction to Indian economic history: Amiya Kumar Bagchi, *The Political Economy of Underdevelopment* (Cambridge, 1982); Francine Frankel, *India's Political Economy* (Delhi, 1978); D. R. Gadgil, *The Industrial Evolution of India in Recent Times, 1860–1939* (Delhi, 1979); Dharma Kumar, ed., *The Cambridge Economic History of India*, 2 vols. (Delhi, 1984); Gunnar Myrdal, *Asian Drama: An Inquiry into the Poverty of Nations*, 3 vols. (New York, 1968); Sumit Sarkar, *Modern India, 1885–1947* (Delhi, 1983); Daniel Thorner, *The Shaping of Modern India* (New Delhi, 1980).

18. Kumar, *Economic History of India*, 2:947–48.

19. Sarvepalli Gopal, *Jawaharlal Nehru: A Biography*, 3 vols. (Delhi, 1975–84), 2:34.

20. Gopal, *Jawaharlal Nehru*, 2:34; Frankel, *India's Political Economy*, 24–25; Myrdal, *Asian Drama*, 1:260–61.

21. Broadcast speech from New Delhi, 7 September 1946, printed in A. Appadorai, ed., *Select Documents on India's Foreign Policy and Relations, 1947–1972* (Delhi, 1982), 1:3.

22. On India's nonalignment, see Michael Brecher, *Nehru: A Political Biography* (Lon-

don, 1959), 555–64; B. R. Nanda, *Indian Foreign Policy: The Nehru Years* (Honolulu, 1976).

23. Speech inaugurating Asian Relations Conference, 23 March 1947, in *Speeches*, 1:302–3.

24. Gopal, *Jawaharlal Nehru*, 1:28.

25. Kenton J. Clymer, "Jawaharlal Nehru and the United States: The Pre-Independence Years," *Diplomatic History* 14 (Spring 1990): 143–62. Hess, *America Encounters India*, 8; Jawaharlal Nehru, *An Autobiography* (London, 1936; reprint, New Delhi, 1982), 161–65.

26. Gopal, *Jawaharlal Nehru*, 2:62.

27. Ibid., 2:290. On the United States and India's independence see Kenton J. Clymer, "Franklin D. Roosevelt, Louis Johnson, India, and Anti-colonialism: Another Look," *Pacific Historical Review* 57 (August 1988): 261–84 and "The Education of William Phillips: Self-Determination and American Policy toward India, 1942–1945," *Diplomatic History* 8 (Winter 1984): 13–36; Hess, *America Encounters India*; M. S. Venkataramani and B. K. Shrivastava, *Quit India: The American Response to the 1942 Struggle* (New Delhi, 1979) and *Roosevelt, Churchill, and Gandhi* (New Delhi, 1983); Betty Unterberger, "American Views of Mohammad Ali Jinnah and the Pakistan Liberation Movement," *Diplomatic History* 5 (Fall 1981): 313–36.

28. Jawaharlal Nehru, *The Discovery of India* (London, 1946; reprint, Delhi, 1981), 286–87.

29. Speech to the Constituent Assembly, 14 August 1947, in *Speeches*, 1:6.

30. Grady to Secretary of State, 9 July 1947, *FR, 1947*, 3:160–61.

31. *Department of State Bulletin*, 17 (9 March 1947): 50.

32. President Truman to Governor General Louis Mountbatten and Interim Prime Minister Jawaharlal Nehru, 14 August 1947, printed in *Department of State Bulletin*, 17 (24 August 1947): 396.

Chapter Two

1. Thomas G. Paterson, *Soviet-American Confrontation: Postwar Reconstruction and the Origins of the Cold War* (Baltimore, 1973), 1–29.

2. Thomas G. Paterson, *On Every Front: The Making of the Cold War* (New York, 1979), 79.

3. Paterson, *Soviet-American Confrontation*, 6.

4. "Report of the Special Adhoc Committee of the State-War-Navy Coordination Council," 21 April 1947, *FR, 1947*, 3:204–19.

5. Special Message to Congress on Greece and Turkey: The Truman Doctrine, 12 March 1947, *Public Papers of the Presidents of the United States: Harry S. Truman* (Washington, D.C., 1961–66), 176–80.

6. On aid to Greece and Turkey, see John O. Iatrides, *Ambassador McVeagh Reports:*

Greece, 1933–1947 (Princeton, N.J., 1980); Bruce R. Kuniholm, *The Origins of the Cold War in the Near East: Great Power Conflict and Diplomacy in Iran, Turkey, and Greece* (Princeton, N.J., 1980); Lawrence S. Wittner, *American Intervention in Greece, 1943–1949* (New York, 1982).

7. The standard account of the Marshall Plan is Michael Hogan, *The Marshall Plan: America, Britain, and the Reconstruction of Western Europe, 1947–1952* (Cambridge, 1987).

8. On the United States and decolonization, see Gary R. Hess, *The United States' Emergence as a Southeast Asian Power, 1940–1950* (New York, 1987); W. Roger Louis, *Imperialism at Bay: The United States and the Decolonization of the British Empire* (New York, 1978); Robert J. McMahon, *Colonialism and Cold War: The United States and the Struggle for Indonesian Independence, 1945–1949* (Ithaca, N.Y., 1981); Andrew J. Rotter, *The Path to Vietnam: Origins of the American Commitment to Southeast Asia* (Ithaca, N.Y., 1987); Christopher Thorne, *Allies of a Kind: The United States, Britain, and the War against Japan* (New York, 1978).

9. On the Truman administration and China, see Robert Blum, *Drawing the Line: The Origin of the American Containment Policy in South Asia* (New York, 1982); Dorothy Borg and Waldo Heinrichs, eds., *Uncertain Years: Chinese-American Relations, 1947–1950* (New York, 1980); Warren Cohen, *America's Response to China* (New York, 1980); Akira Iriye, *The Cold War in Asia* (Englewood Cliffs, N.J., 1974); William Stueck, *The Road to Confrontation: American Policy toward China and Korea, 1947–1950* (Chapel Hill, N.C., 1981); Nancy Tucker, *Patterns in the Dust: Chinese-American Relations and the Recognition Controversy, 1949–1950* (New York, 1983).

10. Dennis Merrill, "Indo-American Relations, 1947–1950: A Missed Opportunity in Asia," *Diplomatic History* 11 (Summer 1987): 203–26.

11. CIA Report, SR-21, "India-Pakistan," 16 September 1948, Box 180, PSF; Report by the State-Army-Navy-Air Force Coordinating Committee for the Near and Middle East, SANACC 360/14, "Appraisal of U.S. National Interests in South Asia," 19 April 1949, *FR, 1949*, 11:8.

12. Alfred Eckes, *The United States and the Global Struggle for Minerals* (Austin, Tex., 1979), 154.

13. On Joint Chiefs of Staff, see Melvyn P. Leffler, "The American Concept of National Security at the Beginning of the Cold War, 1945–1948," *American Historical Review* 89 (April 1984): 352–53.

14. See n. 12.

15. M. S. Venkataramani, *The American Role in Pakistan* (New Delhi, 1982), 21.

16. Sarvepalli Gopal, *Jawaharlal Nehru: A Biography*, 3 vols. (Delhi, 1975–84), 2:34; Francine Frankel, *India's Political Economy* (Delhi, 1978), 24–25; Gunnar Myrdal, *Asian Drama: An Inquiry into the Poverty of Nations*, 3 vols. (New York, 1968), 1:260–61.

17. Lawrence Rossinger, *India and the U.S.: Political and Economic Relations* (New York, 1950), 102–3.

18. Marshall to Embassy, New Delhi, 22 January 1947, *FR, 1947*, 3:139–40.

19. Grady to Truman, 19 July 1947, Subject File, Box 180, PSF.

20. Truman to Grady, 8 August 1947, ibid.

21. Gopal, *Jawaharlal Nehru*, 2:19–20.

22. Memorandum of Conversation between British and American officials in Washington, 10 January 1948, *FR, 1948*, 5:276–78.

23. U.S. note to India and Pakistan, 31 December 1947, *FR, 1947*, 3:192–93; Secretary of State (Marshall) to U.S. Representative at the U.N. (Warren Austin), 6 January 1948, *FR, 1948*, 5:272–73; Marshall to Austin, 5 May 1948, *FR, 1948*, 5:338–39; Venkataramani, *American Role in Pakistan*, 32–60.

24. Draft Report, State-War-Navy Coordinating Committee, "India: Economic Considerations," 16 June 1947, 845.50/6-1647, RG 59, DSR; U.S. Department of Commerce, *Survey of Current Business, August 1963,* (Washington, D.C., 1963); United Nations, *Yearbook of International Trade Statistics, 1950* (New York, 1951), 167.

25. Unpublished Grady autobiography, Box 10, Grady Papers, HSTL.

26. Rossinger, *India and the U.S.*, 50–51.

27. M. S. Sundaran (Education Attaché to Agent General in U.S.) to Frank S. Coan (War Manpower Commission), 6 February 1946, XR 845. 64a, RG 59, DSR.

28. India, Planning Commission, *First Five Year Plan: A Draft Outline* (New Delhi, 1951), 122–23; India, Planning Commission, *First Five Year Plan* (New Delhi, 1953), 335.

29. Grady to Secretary of State, 3 September 1947, 845.01/9-347, RG 59, DSR; Grady autobiography, chapter 10, Box 10, Grady Papers, HSTL; Grady to Brayton Wilbur, 7 October 1947, sent with Grady to Bechtel, 16 October 1947, Box 1, Grady Papers, HSTL.

30. Grady to Bechtel, 16 October 1947, Box 1, Grady Papers, HSTL.

31. Grady autobiography, chapter 10, Box 10, ibid; Bechtel to Grady, 21 October 1947, Box 1, ibid.; Bechtel to Grady, 27 October 1947, Box 1, ibid.; Bogden to Grady, 7 November 1947, ibid.

32. Grady to Bechtel, 13 November 1947, Box 1, Grady Papers, HSTL.

33. Department of State Memorandum of Conversation, 26 December 1947, 845./00/12-2647, RG 59, DSR.

34. Gopal, *Jawaharlal Nehru*, 2:45.

35. Moscow (Smith) to Secretary of State, 8 May 1948, 845.00B/5-848, RG 59, DSR.

36. Speech to Constituent Assembly, 8 March 1948, *Speeches*, 2:221–27.

37. Grady to Secretary of State, 18 March 1948, *FR, 1948*, 5:497–98; Grady to Secretary, 23 March 1948, ibid., 500–501.

38. Memorandum of Conversation by Acting Secretary of State James Lovett, 2 April 1948, ibid., 506–8; Memorandum of Conversation by Assistant Chief of the Division of South Asian Affairs, Elbert G. Matthews, ibid, 501–6.

39. Memorandum of Conversation by Acting Secretary of State James Lovett, 2 April 1948, *FR, 1948*, 5:506–8.

40. Venkataramani, *American Role in Pakistan*, 1–60.

41. Lovett to New Delhi, 31 March 1948, 845.00/3-2348, RG 59, DSR.

42. It seems that the Indian request for aid was handled only by lower-echelon officials. See Matthews to Sparks, 16 April 1948, 845.51/4-948, RG 59, DSR.

43. Memorandum of Conversation by Matthews, 2 April 1948, see n. 38.

44. Policy Planning Staff, PPS 51, "United States Policy toward Asia," 1 April 1949 Microfiche Lot 64, D 563, RG 59, DSR.

45. On United States policy toward Indonesia, see McMahon, *Colonialism and Cold War*; Hess, *The United States' Emergence*, 159–69, 184–93, 275–309.

46. Marshall is quoted in George C. Herring, *America's Longest War: The United States and Vietnam, 1950–1975* (New York, 1985), 8.

47. John King Fairbank, *The United States and China*, 4th ed. (Cambridge, Mass., 1979); Cohen, *America's Response to China*, 193–97.

48. Speech to the Constituent Assembly, 8 March 1949, *Speeches*, 1:226.

49. Nehru's views on Asia were presented to American policymakers over the course of several months from late 1948 to early 1950. Documentation for the assertions made in this paragraph appear in subsequent paragraphs.

50. Secretary of State to the Acting Secretary of State, 16 October 1948, *FR, 1948*, 5:516–19.

51. Henderson to Secretary of State, 22 December 1948, 845.00/12-2248, RG 59, DSR; Henderson to Secretary of State, 3 January 1949, 890.00/1-349, RG 59, DSR.

52. Henderson to Secretary of State, 3 January 1949, 890.00/1-349, RG 59, DSR.

53. McMahon, *Colonialism and Cold War*, 251–303; Hess, *The United States' Emergence*, 159–216, 275–310.

54. Henderson to Secretary of State, 3 January 1949, 890.00/1-349, RG 59, DSR.

55. Lovett to Henderson with enclosed Kennan to Henderson, 5 January 1949, 890.00/1-549, RG 59, DSR.

56. Henderson to Secretary of State, 8 January 1949, 890.00/1-849, RG 59, DSR.

57. For a summary of the proceedings, see Acheson to Bangkok (Southeast Asian Fortnightly Summary), 26 January 1949, 890.00/1-2649, RG 59, DSR; *The Hindu*, 24 January 1949; Gopal, *Jawaharlal Nehru*, 2:55.

58. Henderson to Secretary of State, 29 January 1949, 890.00/1-2949, RG 59, DSR.

59. Acheson to Bangkok, 26 January 1949, see n. 57.

60. Cohen, *America's Response to China*, 197–98.

61. Thomas G. Paterson, "Foreign Aid under Wraps: The Point Four Program," *Wisconsin Magazine of History* 56 (Winter 1972–73): 119–26. On Acheson's news conference, see *The Hindu*, 28 January 1949.

62. Venkataramani, *American Role*, 90–91.

63. Ibid. See also PPS 51, 1 April 1949, see n. 44.

64. *New York Herald Tribune*, 10 January 1949.

65. *Life*, 29 January 1949; *Time*, 30 January 1949; *U.S. News and World Report*, 3 December 1949.

66. Hubert Humphrey to Blair Moody, 26 April 1949, Box 627, Hubert H. Hum-

phrey Papers, Minnesota State Historical Society.

67. Gopal, *Jawaharlal Nehru*, 2:59.

68. India, Ministry of Food and Agriculture, *Report of the Foodgrains Enquiry Committee* (New Delhi, 1957), 6; India, Planning Commission, *First Five Year Plan*, 117.

69. Donovan (New Delhi) to Secretary of State, re: conversation with S. T. Raja (Under Secretary of Agriculture), 26 April 1949, 845. 61/4-2649, RG 59, DSR; Memorandum of Conversation between Henderson and Madame Pandit, 28 April 1949, 845.00(W)/4-2949, RG 59, DSR; Memorandum of Conversation between C. C. Taylor (U.S. Agricultural Attaché, New Delhi) and K. T. Punjabi (Secretary, Ministry of Agriculture), 23 June 1949, 845. 50/6-2349, RG 59, DSR; Whitman to Jessup, "Economic Aspects of U.S. Policy With Respect to South and East Asia," 22 August 1949, 890.00/8-2249, RG 59, DSR; Donovan to Secretary of State, re: talks with R. L. Gupta (Ministry of Food), 24 August 1949, 845.613/8-2449, RG 59, DSR; India, Ministry of Food and Agriculture, *Report of the Foodgrains Enquiry Committee*, 20.

70. Henderson to Secretary of State, 2 February 1949, 845.002/2-249, RG 59, DSR; Henderson to Secretary of State, 14 April 1949, 845.002/4-1449, RG 59, DSR.

71. On the Commonwealth question, see Gopal, *Jawaharlal Nehru*, 2:45–55.

72. M. E. Dening (Head, Far Eastern Division, British Foreign Office) to Sir Cecil Syers (Commonwealth Relations Office), 18 March 1949, FO 371, File 1023, 76023, PRO.

73. Dening to Secretary of State Ernest Bevin, 23 March 1949, ibid.; Report of the Permanent Under Secretary's Committee, PUSC 53, "Regional Cooperation in Southeast Asia," 20 August 1949, FO 371, File 1055, 76030, PRO. See also Report of the Permanent Under Secretary's Committee, PUSC 32, 28 July 1949, FO 371, File 1055, 76030, PRO.

74. PUSC 32, 28 July 1949, see n. 73.

75. PUSC 53, 20 August 1949, see n. 73.

76. Bevin to Gordon Walker (Commonwealth Relations Office), 4 January 1949, FO 371, File 1071, 76146, PRO; I. N. R. Maclinma (Commonwealth Relations Office) to Dening, 21 March 1949, FO 371, File 1023, 76023, PRO.

77. Vijaya Lakshmi Pandit, *The Scope of Happiness: A Personal Memoir* (London, 1979), 250.

78. Memorandum of Conversation with British Foreign Secretary Bevin by Secretary of State Acheson, 4 April 1949, *FR, 1949*, 5:50–54.

79. Sir Oliver Franks to Foreign Office, 10 May 1949, FO 371, File 18, 75566, PRO.

80. To see how the British planned to coordinate the lobbying effort, see Record of Meeting in the Foreign Relations Office between Sir Oliver Franks (Ambassador to the United States), Sir Archibald Nye (High Commissioner to India), and Dening, 20 July 1949, FO 371, File 1122, 76100, PRO.

81. Douglas to Secretary of State, 29 July 1949, 898.00/7-2949, RG 59, DSR.

82. Henderson to Secretary of State, 12 September 1949, 845.51/9-1249, RG 59, DSR.

83. Memorandum of Conversation by the Director of the Office of Far Eastern Affairs (W. W. Butterworth), 12 September 1949, *FR, 1949*, 7:1197–1203.

84. Ibid.

85. Henderson to Secretary of State, 12 September 1949, 845.51/9-1249, RG 59, DSR.

86. Acheson to Truman, 18 August 1949, 845.002/8-1849, RG 59, DSR.

87. Johnson to Acheson, 9 September 1949, 845.002/9-949, RG 59, DSR.

88. Webb to Johnson, 8 October 1949, 845.002/9-949, RG 59, DSR.

89. Matthews to McGhee, 6 September 1949, 845.002/9-649, RG 59, DSR. Also, see "Background Memoranda to President on Visit to the United States of Pandit Jawaharlal Nehru," 3 October 1949, Subject File, Box 180, PSF.

90. As directed by Secretary of State Acheson, Jessup organized the consultants' committee in July 1949. Consultants included businessman Raymond Fosdick and the president of Colgate University, Everett Case, as well as Jessup. The major aim of the committee was to examine United States policy in Asia with an eye toward promoting administration policy with Congress and the public. See Rusk to Secretary, 18 July 1949, 890.00/7-1849, RG 59, DSR; Jessup Memorandum of Conversation with Acheson, 20 July 1949, 890.00/11-1847, RG 59, DSR; Memorandum by Jessup, Fosdick, and Case to Secretary of State, 2 September 1949, 711.90/9-249, RG 59, DSR.

91. Henderson to Webb, 3 October 1949, 845.50/10-349, RG 59, DSR.

92. McGhee to Webb and Acheson, 7 October 1949, 845.002/10-749, RG 59, DSR; Wilds to Jessup, 11 October 1949, 845.00/10-1499, RG 59, DSR. Also, on Jessup recommendations for expanded talks with Nehru, see Jessup to Acheson, 29 September 1949, 845.002/9-2949, RG 59, DSR.

93. "Background Memoranda to President on Visit to the United States of Pandit Jawaharlal Nehru," 3 October 1949 (includes Nehru's itinerary), see n. 89; Rossinger, *India and the U.S.*, 132–36; Gopal, *Jawaharlal Nehru*, 2:60.

94. Nye to Foreign Relations Office enclosing Memorandum of Conversation with Henderson, 9 December 1949, FO 371, File 10345, 76097, PRO.

95. Dean Acheson, *Present at the Creation* (New York, 1969), 334.

96. Memorandum of Conversation by Acheson, 12 October 1949, Subject File, Box 180, PSF.

97. Memorandum of Conversation between Nehru, Madame Pandit, Bajpai, Acheson, Kennan, Jessup, Thorpe, McGhee, Battle, and Matthews, 13 October 1949, Box 64, Acheson Papers, HSTL.

98. Memorandum of Conversation between Truman, Acheson, Nehru, and Bajpai, 13 October 1949, Subject File, Box, 180, PSF.

99. C. D. Deshmukh, *The Course of My Life* (Delhi, 1974), 161–62. See also Memorandum of Conversation between Truman, Acheson, Nehru, and Bajpai, 13 October 1949, see n. 98.

100. Acheson, *Present at the Creation*, 336.

101. Gopal, *Jawaharlal Nehru*, 2:60–61.

102. Acheson to Henderson, 21 November 1949, 845.61311/10-2749, RG 59, DSR.

103. Eckes, *Global Struggle for Minerals*, 156, 171.

104. Department of State Memorandum of Conversation, 18 October 1949, 845. 61311/10-1849, RG 59, DSR.

105. Department of State Memorandum of Conversation between Kennedy and Deshmukh, 16 November 1949, 845.5034/11-1649, RG 59, DSR; McGhee to Acheson, 17 November 1949, 845.50/11-1749, RG 59, DSR; Acheson to Henderson, 17 November 1949, 845.61311/11-1749, RG 59, DSR; Department of State Memorandum of Conversation, 18 November 1949, 845.61311/11-1849, RG 59, DSR; B. K. Nehru (Finance Counselor, Indian Embassy, Washington) to Kennedy, 28 December 1949, 845.61311/12-2849, RG 59, DSR.

106. A Report to the NSC by the Executive Secretary on "The Position of the United States With Respect to Asia," NSC 48/1 Draft, 23 December 1949, Subject File, Box 211, PSF; NSC 48/1 was discussed and approved at a meeting of the NSC on 29 December 1949. After minor amendments it was approved by the president on 30 December 1949.

107. Ibid.

108. Ibid.

109. Memorandum by Secretary of State (Acheson) to President, 9 March 1950, *FR, 1950*, 7:40–44.

110. Venkataramani, *American Role in Pakistan*, 110–13. See also Herring, *America's Longest War*, 12.

Chapter Three

1. A Report to the NSC by the Executive Secretary, Draft, NSC 48/1, "The Position of the United States with Respect to Asia," 23 December 1949, Subject File, Box 211, PSF.

2. NSC 68, "United States Objectives and Programs for National Security," 14 April 1950, *FR, 1950*, 1:237–42.

3. Thomas G. Paterson, *On Every Front: The Making of the Cold War* (New York, 1979), 169–70.

4. *New York Times*, 26 June 1950. Standard works on the Korean War include Burton I. Kaufman, *The Korean War: Challenge in Crisis, Credibility, and Command* (New York, 1986); Bruce Cummings, ed., *Child of Conflict: The Korean-American Relationship, 1943–1953* (Seattle, 1983); Peter Lowe, *The Origins of the Korean War* (London, 1986); James I. Matray, *The Reluctant Crusade: American Foreign Policy in Korea, 1941–1950* (Honolulu, 1985); William Stueck, *The Road to Confrontation: American Policy toward China and Korea, 1947–1950* (Chapel Hill, N.C., 1981).

5. Beverly Smith, "The White House Story: Why We Went to War in Korea," *Saturday Evening Post*, 10 November 1951, 80.

6. Kaufman, *The Korean War*, 45–47, 61–67.

7. Notes of Foreign Secretary Ernest Bevin of Proceedings at Colombo Conference, 10 January 1950, FO 371, File 10345, 84818, PRO. Also, see Memorandum of Conversation between Secretary of State Acheson and Indian Ambassador Madame Pandit, 6 December 1949, Box 64, Acheson Papers, HSTL; Sarvepalli Gopal, *Jawaharlal Nehru: A Biography*, 3 vols. (Delhi, 1975–84), 2:63–65.

8. Gopal, *Jawaharlal Nehru*, 2:62. For the United States position, see Acheson to Warren Austin (U.S. Delegate at the UN), 3 January 1950, *FR, 1950*, 5:1367; Prime Minister Nehru to Acheson, 14 January 1950, *FR, 1950*, 5:1369–70.

9. On the United States and Pakistan from 1947 to early 1950, see Robert J. McMahon, "United States Cold War Strategy in South Asia: Making a Military Commitment to Pakistan, 1947–1954," *Journal of American History* 75 (December 1988): 815–22.

10. Gopal, *Jawaharlal Nehru*, 2:63.

11. Henderson to Secretary of State, 6 February 1950, 611.91/2-650, RG 59, DSR.

12. Telegram from U.S. Ambassador in India (Henderson) to Secretary of State (Acheson), 12 April 1950, *FR, 1950*, 5:1461–63; Acheson to U.S. Embassy in India, 21 April 1950, *FR, 1950*, 5:1465–66.

13. Robert C. Johansen, *The National Interest and the Human Interest* (Princeton, N.J., 1980), 128–29; Thomas G. Paterson, "Foreign Aid under Wraps: The Point Four Program," *Wisconsin Magazine of History* 56 (Winter 1972–73): 122.

14. Memorandum by the Assistant Secretary of State for Near Eastern, South Asian, and African Affairs (McGhee) to the Secretary of State, 7 June 1950, *FR, 1950*, 5:169–70. For background on the proposal, see paper prepared in the Bureau of Near Eastern, South Asian, and African Affairs, 6 March 1950, *FR, 1950*, 5:239–44. For McGhee biography, see George McGhee, *Envoy to the Middle World: Adventures in Diplomacy* (New York, 1983), xvi–xviii; M. S. Venkataramani, *The American Role in Pakistan* (New Delhi, 1982), 150–51, 440. McGhee is described as a "brilliant young man" by an unnamed State Department source in *New York Times*, 4 April 1951.

15. McGhee to Secretary, 7 June 1950, see n. 14.

16. Oral history interview with Loy Henderson, conducted in Washington, D.C., June 1975, HSTL, 184–86; Gopal, *Jawaharlal Nehru*, 2:100–103.

17. Gopal, *Jawaharlal Nehru*, 2:100.

18. Ibid., 2:103.

19. Testimony of Secretary of State Dean Acheson, 24 July 1950, Senate, *Executive Sessions of the Senate Foreign Relations Committee*, 2, pt. 1:333. See also Dean Acheson, *Present at the Creation* (New York, 1969), 419–20.

20. *Department of State Bulletin*, 23 (31 July 1950): 170–71.

21. Memorandum of a Meeting with the President, 31 July 1950, Box 65, Acheson Papers, HSTL; McGhee quoted in Venkataramani, *American Role in Pakistan*, 131.

22. Memorandum of Conversation with the President by the Secretary of State, 28 August 1950, *FR, 1950*, 5:180–81; Memorandum by Assistant Secretary of State for Near Eastern, South Asian, and African Affairs (McGhee) to the President, 28 August 1950, *FR, 1950*, 5:178–80.

23. Memorandum of Conversation with the President by Acheson, 28 August 1950, Box 65, Acheson Papers, HSTL.

24. McGhee, *Envoy to the Middle World*, 213–20.

25. Venkataramani, *American Role in Pakistan*, 132.

26. Record of Informal United States–United Kingdom Discussions, London, 18 September 1950, *FR, 1950*, 5:196–206.

27. Policy statement prepared in the Office of South Asian Affairs, 9 October 1950, ibid., 245–54.

28. Ibid.

29. Gopal, *Jawaharlal Nehru*, 2:104–5.

30. Charles Heimsath and Surjit Mansingh, *A Diplomatic History of Modern India* (New Delhi, 1971), 69.

31. McGhee to Acheson, 3 November 1950, transmitting "Nehru's Attitude toward the United States," by Elbert Matthew (Office of South Asian Affairs), 611.91/11-350, RG 59, DSR.

32. High Commissioner in United States to Foreign Office, 5 August 1950, FO 371, 83014, PRO. See also High Commissioner in India to Foreign Office, 27 October 1950, FO 371, 84203, PRO; High Commissioner in India to Commonwealth Relation Office, 31 October 1950, FO 371, 84204, PRO.

33. Memorandum of Conversation on Far East by M. E. Dening, 22 July 1950, FO 371, 83014, PRO.

34. McGhee to Acheson, 3 November 1950, see n. 31.

35. Ibid.

36. Memorandum of Conversation with Madame Pandit by McGhee, 6 September 1950, 611.91/9-650, RG 59, DSR; Memorandum of Conversation with Madame Pandit by McGhee, 26 October 1950, 611.9/10-2650, RG 59, DSR; Memorandum of Conversation with Madame Pandit by McGhee, 6 November 1950, 611.91/11-650, RG 59, DSR.

37. Henderson to Secretary of State, 29 September 1950, 611.91/9-2950, RG 59, DSR.

38. Henderson to Secretary of State, 3 November 1950, 611.91/11-350, RG 59, DSR.

39. Acheson to New Delhi, 27 October 1950, 611.91/10-2750, RG 59, DSR; Gopal, *Jawaharlal Nehru*, 2:107–8.

40. Walter LaFeber, *America, Russia, and the Cold War, 1945–1984* (New York, 1985), 119.

41. A Report to the NSC by the Executive Secretary (Lay), NSC 98/1, Draft "The Position of the United States with Respect to South Asia," 5 January 1951, Subject File, Box 211, PSF; NSC 98/1, Final Draft "The Position of the United States with Respect to South Asia," 25 January 1951, Subject File, Box 211, PSF.

42. A Report to the NSC by the Executive Secretary (Lay), NSC 98/1, Final Draft "The Position of the United States with Respect to South Asia," 25 January 1951, Subject File, Box 211, PSF.

43. Ibid.

44. Ibid.

45. Streeper (Consul General Madras) to Secretary of State, 18 January 1950, Box 214, RG 16, DAR; Derry (Calcutta) to Department of State, 24 July 1950, 891.03/7-2450, RG 59, DSR; Taylor (Agricultural Attaché, New Delhi) to Department of State, 7 November 1950, 893.03/10-2250, RG 59, DSR; Henderson to Secretary of State, 13 November 1950, Box 207, RG 16, DAR; *Economic Weekly* (Bombay), 5 August 1950, 756.

46. Speech delivered at the twenty-second annual meeting of the Federation of Indian Chambers of Commerce and Industry, 4 March 1949, *Speeches*, 1:145.

47. Gopal, *Jawaharlal Nehru*, 2:158.

48. Acheson to Truman, 9 September 1950, 891.231/9-950, RG 59, DSR; McGhee, *Envoy to the Middle World*, 297–98.

49. India, Ministry of Food and Agriculture, *Report of the Foodgrains Enquiry Committee* (New Delhi, 1957), 184; Devki Nandan Prasad, *Food for Peace: The Story of U.S. Food Assistance to India* (New Delhi, 1979), 5.

50. Henderson to Secretary of State, 6 November 1950, 891.231/11-650, RG 59, DSR.

51. Memorandum of Conversation with Madame Pandit, 16 December 1950, Box 65, Acheson Papers, HSTL.

52. Steere to Department of State, enclosed "Glimpses of Malnutrition in Certain Villages in Madras State," by Evelyn Hersey, 3 November 1950, 891.03/10-2250, RG 59, DSR.

53. Taylor to Department of State, 7 November 1950, 893.03/10-2250, RG 59, DSR; Senate, *Executive Sessions of the Senate Foreign Relations Committee*, 82d Cong., 1st sess., 1951, 3, pt. 1:27–51.

54. Taylor to Department of State, 7 November 1950, 893.03/10-2250, RG 59, DSR; Senate, *Executive Sessions of the Senate Foreign Relations Committee*, 1951, 3, pt. 1:27–51.

55. McMahon, "Food as a Diplomatic Weapon: The India Wheat Loan of 1951," *Pacific Historical Review* 56 (August 1987): 358.

56. Ibid., 361.

57. Ibid., 358.

58. Memorandum of Conversation between Secretary of State Acheson, George McGhee, and the Indian Ambassador by Weil (Office of South Asian Affairs), 29 December 1950, Box 65, Acheson Papers, HSTL.

59. Memorandum of Conversation with Madame Pandit by George McGhee, 29 December 1950, 611.91/12-2950, RG 59, DSR.

60. Ibid.

61. Ibid.

62. Ibid.

63. Memorandum of Conversation between Secretary of State Acheson, George McGhee, and the Indian Ambassador, 29 December 1950, see n. 58.

64. Gopal, *Jawaharlal Nehru*, 2:113, 134–36.

65. Radio broadcast, 24 January 1951, *Speeches*, 2:138.

66. McGhee to Secretary of State, 25 January 1951, 611.91/1-2551, RG 59, DSR.

67. State Department Memorandum of Conversation between Acheson, McGhee, Matthews, Weil, and Madame Pandit, 27 January 1951, Box 66, Acheson Papers, HSTL.

68. Department of State Report, "India's Request for Foodgrains: Political Considerations," transmitted by McGhee to Acheson, 24 January 1951, *FR, 1951*, 6(2):2085–86.

69. Senate, *Executive Sessions of the Senate Foreign Relations Committee*, 1951, 3, pt. 1:25–45.

70. McMahon, "Food as a Diplomatic Weapon," 362.

71. Ibid., 363; Memorandum of Conversation with the President by Acheson, 1 February 1951, Box 66, Acheson Papers, HSTL.

72. Meeting between President and Congressional Representatives, 6 February 1951, Box 4, David Lloyd File, HSTL.

73. McMahon, "Food as a Diplomatic Weapon," 364.

74. *Department of State Bulletin* 24 (26 February 1951): 359–61.

75. *Congressional Record*, 82d Cong., 1st sess., June 1951, 97, pt. 5:6339–46; McMahon, "Food as a Diplomatic Weapon," 364.

76. *Washington Post*, 21 April 1951; *The Christian Science Monitor*, 9 April 1951; *New York Times*, 15 March 1951; poll conducted 26–31 March 1951, *The Gallup Poll: Public Opinion, 1935–1971*, 3 vols. (New York, 1972), 2:978–79.

77. Under Secretary of State Webb to President Truman, 29 March 1951, Box 1278, White House Central File, Official File, HSTL.

78. Prasad, *Food for Peace*, 34–35.

79. Ibid.

80. Henderson to Secretary of State, 24 March 1951, *FR, 1951*, 6(2):2130–31.

81. The President's News Conference of 29 March 1951, *Public Papers of the Presidents of the United States: Harry S. Truman* (Washington, D.C., 1961–66), 202.

82. Gopal, *Jawaharlal Nehru*, 2:137.

83. *Congressional Record*, 82d Cong., 1st sess., 1951, 97, pt. 4:4393.

84. Gopal, *Jawaharlal Nehru*, 2:137; McMahon, "Food as a Diplomatic Weapon," 371–72.

85. House Committee on Foreign Affairs, *Hearings: India Emergency Assistance Act of 1951*, 6, 9, 15, 17.

86. Prasad, *Food for Peace*, 30.

87. Senate, *Executive Sessions of the Senate Foreign Relations Committee*, 16 April 1951, 3, pt. 1:365. See also Memorandum of Discussions in the Department of State, 2 April 1951, *FR, 1951*, 6(2):2136–37.

88. *New York Times*, 3 May 1951; *New York Times*, 6 May 1951; Memorandum of Conversation between Matthews and B. K. Nehru, 2 May 1951, *FR, 1951*, 6(2):2153–55.

89. Acheson to Embassy in New Delhi, 2 May 1951, 891.03/5-251, RG 59, DSR.

90. Henderson to Secretary of State, 6 May 1951, *FR, 1951*, 6(2):2157–58; Prasad, *Food for Peace*, 31.

91. *Congressional Record*, 82d Cong., 1st sess., 1951, 97, pt. 5:6187, 6346; *Department of State Bulletin* 25 (2 July 1951): 37–39.

92. Robert A. Packenham, *Liberal America and the Third World: Political Development Ideas in Foreign Aid and Social Science* (Princeton, N.J., 1973), 50.

Chapter Four

1. Report to the NSC by the Executive Secretary, Draft, NSC 48/5, "United States Objectives, Policies, and Courses of Action in Asia," 17 May 1951, *FR, 1951*, 6(1):33–63.

2. Robert A. Packenham, *Liberal America and the Third World: Political Development Ideas in Foreign Aid and Social Science* (Princeton, N.J., 1973), 49.

3. Memorandum by Assistant Secretary of State for Near Eastern, South Asian, and African Affairs (McGhee) to the President, 28 August 1950, *FR, 1950*, 5:178–80.

4. Inaugural Address, 20 January 1949, *Public Papers of the Presidents of the United States, Harry S. Truman* (Washington, D.C., 1961–66), 112–16.

5. Schaetzel to Corbett, 11 August 1950, 890.00/8-1150, RG 59, DSR.

6. International Development Advisory Board, *Partners in Progress: A Report to the President by the International Development Advisory Board* (Washington, D.C., 1951); Gordon Gray, *Report to the President on Foreign Economic Policies* (Washington, D.C., 1950).

7. Record of Informal United States–United Kingdom Discussions, London, 18 September 1950, *FR, 1950*, 5:196–206; Record of Under Secretary of State's Meeting and Oral Report by George McGhee on Trip to London, Paris, and Tangier, 16 October 1950, *FR, 1950*, 5:215–16. On Colombo Plan, see also *Hindustan Times*, 28 November 1950; *Economic Weekly*, 23 December 1950.

8. A Report to the NSC by the Executive Secretary (Lay), NSC 68/3, "United States Objectives and Programs for National Security," 8 December 1950, *FR, 1950*, 1:432–61. On Colombo Plan, see Secretary of State (Acheson) to United States Embassy (London), 22 November 1950, *FR, 1950*, 5:160–61; Department of State Report, "Commonwealth Consultative Committee," 14 December 1950, 890.00/12-1450, RG 59, DSR.

9. The Secretary of State (Acheson) to United States Embassy (New Delhi), 22 May 1951, *FR, 1951*, 6(2):2162–63; Editorial Notes on the 1951 Mutual Security Program, *FR, 1950*, 1:317–18.

10. Editorial Notes on the 1951 Mutual Security Program, *FR, 1950*, 1:317–18; Charles C. Wolf, Jr., *Foreign Aid: Theory and Practice in South Asia* (Princeton, N.J., 1960), 132.

11. Memorandum of Discussion between the President and Budget Bureau, 1 March 1951, *FR, 1951*, 1:283–86; Packenham, *Liberal America*, 49–50.

12. Packenham, *Liberal America*, 43–50; Council on Foreign Relations, *Documents on American Foreign Relations, 1951* (New York, 1952), 13:118–21; Editorial Notes on 1951 Mutual Security Program, *FR, 1951*, 1:428–30.

13. NSC 114, "Status and Timing of Current U.S. Programs for National Security," 27 July 1951, Box 212, PSF; NSC 114/1, Annex no. 2, "Foreign Military and Economic Assistance," 8 August 1951, *FR, 1951*, 1:360–88; NSC 114/2 Annex no. 2, "Foreign Economic and Military Assistance Programs," 12 October 1951, *FR, 1951*, 1:412–24.

14. Chester Bowles, *Promises to Keep: My Years in Public Life, 1941–1969* (New York, 1971), 247. For biographical background, see 226–331. Bowles's background was also discussed during his confirmation hearings before the Senate Foreign Relations Committee, see Bowles Confirmation Hearings, 22 September 1951, Senate, *Executive Sessions of the Senate Foreign Relations Committee*, 82d Cong., 1st sess., 1951, 3, pt. 2:385–447.

15. Truman quoted in Bowles, *Promises to Keep*, 247. Benton appointment discussed on 226–31. Bowles appointment discussed on 245–47. See also Acheson Memorandum of Telephone Conversation with Benton, 21 November 1950, Box 65, Acheson Papers, HSTL; Acheson Memorandum of Telephone Conversation with Bowles, 16 January 1951, Box 65, Acheson Papers, HSTL; Acheson Memorandum of Conversation with Benton, 16 March 1951, Box 65, Acheson Papers, HSTL.

16. Bowles Confirmation Hearings, 22 September 1951, Senate, *Executive Sessions of the Senate Foreign Relations Committee*, 3, pt. 2:407; Bowles, *Promises to Keep*, 247–48.

17. *Times of India* (Bombay) 7 November 1951. For a lively, although incomplete, account of Bowles's ambassadorship, see Chester Bowles, *Ambassador's Report* (New York, 1954). Indian perspectives on Bowles are discussed in Escott Reid, *Envoy to Nehru* (New Delhi, 1981), 48. For Indian views of Bowles, see The Charge in India (Taylor) to the Department of State, 26 May 1952, *FR, 1952–1954*, 11(2):1645–46.

18. Address to the Annual Meeting of the Indian Chemical Manufacturing Association, 26 December 1950, *Speeches*, 2:15.

19. Francine Frankel, *India's Political Economy* (Delhi, 1978), 85. For a brief analysis of the conservative nature of the plan, see 80–89. See also Sarvepalli Gopal, *Jawaharlal Nehru: A Biography*, 3 vols. (Delhi, 1975–84), 2:96–99.

20. India, Planning Commission, *First Five Year Plan: A Draft Outline* (New Delhi, 1951), 37–39, 100, 152; Frankel, *India's Political Economy*, 80–89.

21. India, Planning Commission, *First Five Year Plan: A Draft Outline*, 100.

22. Gunnar Myrdal, *Asian Drama: An Inquiry into the Poverty of Nations*, 3 vols. (New York, 1968), 1:494.

23. Frankel, *India's Political Economy*, 88; Acharya J. B. Kripalani, *The Plan: A Gandhian Critique* (New Delhi, 1952); B. T. Randive, *The Indian Plan: A Critical Survey* (Bombay, 1954).

24. India, Ministry of Food and Agriculture, *Report of the Grow More Food Committee* (New Delhi, 1952), 112–14.

25. George Rosen, *Western Economists and Eastern Societies: Agents of Change in South Asia, 1950–1970* (Baltimore, 1985), 11.

26. Bowles, *Ambassador's Report*, 197–98.

27. Bowles to Sudhir Ghosh, 17 October 1951, File 9, Ghosh Papers, Nehru Library; Bowles to Ghosh, 14 April 1952, File 9, Ghosh Papers, Nehru Library; Ghosh to Bowles, 4 May 1952, File 9, Ghosh Papers, Nehru Library; Ghosh to Bowles, 12 May 1952, File 9, Ghosh Papers, Nehru Library; Ghosh to Bowles, 12 October 1952, File 9, Ghosh Papers, Nehru Library.

28. Bowles to McGhee, 18 November 1951, Box 96, BP.

29. "Tentative Proposal for Economic Aid and Development," November 1951, Box 109, ibid.

30. Bowles, *Ambassador's Report*, 200.

31. Indo-American Technical Cooperation Agreement, 5 January 1952, in *United States Treaties and Other International Agreements*, 1952, 3, pt. 2:2921–26; Rosen, *Western Economists*, 15.

32. Bowles to Assistant Secretary of State for Economic Affairs Willard Thorpe, 18 May 1952, Box 96, BP. See also Bowles to Director of Office of South Asian Affairs, Donald Kennedy, 13 October 1952, Box 95, BP; The Ambassador in India (Bowles) to the Secretary of State, 19 November 1952, *FR, 1952–1954*, 9(2):1679–81; Bowles to Director of the International Development Advisory Board Eric Johnston, 28 November 1952, Box 95, BP.

33. Bowles to Senator Brian McMahon (Connecticut), 3 January 1952, Box 81, BP.

34. Bowles to Kennedy, 13 October 1952, Box 95, BP.

35. Ibid.; Bowles to Johnston, 17 August 1952, Box 95, BP.

36. Bowles to Benton, 21 November 1951, Box 81, BP; Bowles to McMahon, 3 January 1952, Box 81, BP.

37. Bowles to Kennedy, 28 December 1951, Box 95, BP; Bowles to Benton, 9 April 1952, Box 81, BP; Bowles to Point Four Administrator, Jonathan Bingham, 18 April 1952, Box 94, BP; Bowles Memorandum of Conversation with Pandit Jawaharlal Nehru, 15 July 1952, Box 98, BP.

38. Bowles to Johnston, 28 November 1952, Box 95, BP.

39. Bowles to McGhee, 18 November 1951, Box 96, BP.

40. Bowles to Truman, 11 December 1951, Box 96, BP. See also The Ambassador in India (Bowles) to the Secretary of State, 6 December 1951, *FR, 1951*, 6(2):2885–86; Acheson to Bowles, 14 January 1952, 611.93/12-651, RG 59, DSR.

41. Bowles to McGhee, 18 November 1951, Box 96, BP.

42. Bowles to Phillip Coombs, 13 November 1951, Box 84, BP.

43. The Ambassador in India (Bowles) to the Secretary of State, 6 December 1951, *FR, 1951*, 6(2):2885–86.

44. Ibid.

45. Myrdal, *Asian Drama*, 1:22.

46. For a particularly insightful analysis of the shortcomings of Western conceptions of political and economic development in the Third World, see Myrdal, *Asian Drama*, 5–35.

47. Frankel, *India's Political Economy*, 92–93.

48. Bowles to Truman, 31 January 1952, Box 96, BP.

49. Testimony of Ambassador Chester Bowles, 16 January 1952, Senate, *Executive Sessions of the Senate Foreign Relations Committee*, 4, pt. 1:61–93; Memorandum of Conversation between Bowles and Senior NSC Staff Members, 17 January 1952, Box 7, Records of the Psychological Strategy Board, HSTL; Memorandum by Deputy Director of the Executive Secretariat (Barnes) to the Staff Assistant to the Assistant Secretary for Near Eastern, South Asian, and African Affairs (Hamba), 18 January 1952, *FR, 1952–1954*, 11(2):1633; Bowles to Truman, 31 January 1952, Box 96, BP; Bowles to Presidential Assistant Charles Murphy, 4 February 1952, enclosing "The Crucial Problem of India," a report sent to members of the Senate Foreign Relations Committee and the House Foreign Affairs Committee, Box 180, PSF; Bowles to Acheson, 11 February 1952, *FR, 1952–1954*, 11(2):1635; Bowles to Acheson, 21 February 1952, Subject File, Box 180, PSF.

50. Bowles to Edward Bernays, 15 November 1951, Box 82, BP; Bernays to Bowles, 15 December 1951, Box 82, BP; Bowles to McMahon, 31 January 1952, Box 84, BP; Bernays to Bowles, 7 March 1952, Box 82, BP.

51. Memorandum by the Acting Assistant Secretary of State for Near Eastern, South Asian, and African Affairs (Berry) to the Deputy Under Secretary of State (Matthews), 8 February 1952, *FR, 1952–1954*, 11(2):1634–35; Memorandum by the Deputy Director, Division of the Office of South Asian Affairs (Weil) to the Deputy Assistant Secretary of State for Near Eastern, South Asian, and African Affairs (Berry), 19 May 1952, *FR, 1952–1954*, 11(2):1641–43; Kennedy to Bowles, 29 February 1952, Box 95, BP; Coombs to Bowles, 12 February 1952, Box 84, BP.

52. Rani Dutta, "American Attitudes toward U.S. Technical and Economic Assistance to India, 1949–1953," *Indian Political Science Review* 3 (July–December, 1963): 171–73.

53. Memorandum by the Acting Assistant Secretary of State for Near Eastern, South Asian, and African Affairs (Berry) to the Deputy Under Secretary of State (Matthews), 8 February 1952, *FR, 1952–1954*, 11(2):1634–35; Memorandum by the Director of the Bureau of the Budget (Lawton) to the President, 30 June 1952, *FR, 1952–1954*, 11(2):1653–54; Memorandum by the Secretary of State and the Director of Mutual Security (Harriman) to the President, 5 June 1952, *FR, 1952–1954*, 11(2):1646–47; Coombs to Bowles, 12 February 1952, Box 84, BP; Kennedy to Bowles, 6 February 1952, Box 95, BP.

54. Coombs to Bowles, 26 February 1952, Box 84, BP. On administration actions, see Unsigned Memorandum for Lawton, 25 February 1952, Box 84, BP; Kennedy to Bowles, 29 February 1952, 12 February 1952, Box 84, BP; Memorandum by the Acting Assistant Secretary of State for Near Eastern, South Asian, and African Affairs (Berry) to the Deputy Under Secretary of State (Matthews), 8 February 1952, *FR, 1952–1954*, 11(2):1634–35; The Secretary of State to the Embassy in India, 3 March 1952, *FR, 1952–1954*, 11(2):1637–38.

55. Senate Committee on Foreign Relations, *Hearings: Mutual Security Act of 1952*, 82d Cong., 2d sess., 1952, 8; Wolf, *Foreign Aid*, 135–37.

56. Memorandum by the Secretary of State and the Director of Mutual Security (Harriman) to the President, 5 June 1952, *FR, 1952–54*, 11(2):1646–47.

57. Benton to Bowles, 13 May 1952, Box 81, BP.

58. *Congressional Record*, 82d Cong., 2d sess., 1952, 98, pt. 7:8491. Also, see Wolf, *Foreign Aid*, 146.

59. *Congressional Record*, 82d Cong., 2d sess., 1952, 98, pt. 7:8489.

60. Ibid., 8492.

61. Kennedy to Bowles, 10 July 1952, Box 95, BP.

62. Bowles to Truman, 22 May 1952, 791.5 MSP/5-2252, RG 59, DSR; Memorandum of Conversation by the Secretary of State, 9 June 1952, *FR, 1952–1954*, 11(2):1648–51; Memorandum of Conversation by Secretary of State, 12 June 1952, *FR, 1952–1954*, 11(2):1652; Bowles to Truman, 5 July 1952, *FR, 1952–1954*, 11(2):1655–57.

63. Memorandum by the Secretary of State and the Director for Mutual Security (Harriman) to the President, 5 June 1952, *FR, 1952–1954*, 11(2):1646–47; Bowles to Truman, 5 July 1952, *FR, 1952–1954*, 11(2):1653.

64. Memorandum of Conversation by Secretary of State, 12 June 1952, *FR, 1952–1954*, 11(2):1652; Memorandum by the Acting Secretary of State to the Executive Secretary of the NSC (Lay), Fourth Progress Report on NSC 98/1 "The Position of the United States with Respect to South Asia," 19 August 1952, *FR, 1952–1954*, 11(2): 1057–62.

65. Truman to Bowles, 1 July 1952, Subject File, Box 180, PSF.

66. The Ambassador in India (Bowles) to the Secretary of State, 28 October 1952, *FR, 1952–1954*, 11(2):1668–77.

67. Gopal, *Jawaharlal Nehru*, 2:199.

68. *Times of India* (Bombay), 3 October 1952.

69. India, Planning Commission, *First Five Year Plan* (New Delhi, 1953), 133–280.

70. Gopal, *Jawaharlal Nehru*, 2:144–48; Bowles, *Ambassador's Report*, 241–43.

71. For an excellent analysis of Menon, see Michael Brecher, *India and World Politics: Krishna Menon's View of the World* (London, 1968).

72. Barton Bernstein, "The Struggle over the Korean Armistice: Prisoners of Repatriation?" in *Child of Conflict: The Korean-American Relationship, 1943–1953*, edited by Bruce Cummings (Seattle, 1983), 261–307; Burton I. Kaufman, *The Korean War: Challenge in Crisis, Credibility, and Command* (New York, 1986), 296–300.

73. Acheson to Bowles, 8 January 1953, *FR, 1952–1954*, 11(2):1682–84.

74. NSC 141, "A Report to the NSC by the Secretaries of State, Defense, and the Director of Mutual Security on Re-examination of United States Programs for National Security," 19 January 1953, Averell Harriman Papers, from the files of Professor Richard D. McKinzie, University of Missouri, Kansas City. On United States strategic interests in the Middle East, see Bruce Kuniholm, *Origins of the Cold War in the Near East: Great Power Conflict and Diplomacy in Iran, Turkey, and Greece* (Princeton, N.J., 1980); Steven L. Spiegel, *The Other Arab-Israeli Conflict: Making America's Middle East Policy from*

Truman to Reagan (Chicago, 1985); Peter L. Hahn, "Containment and Egyptian Nationalism: The Unsuccessful Attempt to Establish the Middle East Command, 1950–1953," *Diplomatic History* 11 (Winter 1987): 23–40.

75. Robert J. McMahon, "United States Cold War Strategy in South Asia: Making a Military Commitment to Pakistan, 1947–1954," *Journal of American History* 75 (December 1988): 822–25; William Barnds, *India, Pakistan, and the Great Powers* (New York, 1972), 91–97.

76. CIA Report, SR-21 "India-Pakistan," 16 September 1948, Box 180, PSF.

77. McMahon, "United States Cold War Strategy," 818. See also "Report by State-Army-Navy-Airforce Coordinating Committee for the Near and Middle East," SANACC, 360/14, "Appraisal of U.S. National Interests in South Asia," 19 April 1949, *FR, 1949*, 11:8.

78. McMahon, "United States Cold War Strategy," 824.

79. Hahn, "Containment and Egyptian Nationalism," 31–38.

80. For British views, see files FO 371, 92875, 92876, 92878, PRO. An especially good summary is found in J. D. Murray, "Pakistan and Middle East Defense," 7 December 1951, FO 371, 92876, PRO.

81. Foreign Office to Embassy in Washington, 13 October 1951, FO 371, 92875, PRO.

82. Hahn, "Containment and Egyptian Nationalism," 38; McMahon, "United States Cold War Strategy," 828.

83. Bowles to Murphy, 11 December 1952, Box 81, BP; Bowles to Kennedy, 29 January 1953, Box 95, BP; Gopal, *Jawaharlal Nehru*, 2:183–84.

84. Memorandum of Conversation between Acheson and Mehta, 13 January 1953, Box 67, Acheson Papers, HSTL.

85. Stephen Ambrose, *Eisenhower: The President* (New York, 1984), 13–43.

86. Burton I. Kaufman, *Trade and Aid: Eisenhower's Foreign Economic Policy, 1953–1961* (Baltimore, 1982), 18–33.

87. Memorandum of Special Meeting of the National Security Council, 31 March 1953, *FR, 1952–1954*, 2(1):264–81.

88. Gopal, *Jawaharlal Nehru*, 2:137–38.

89. Bowles to Under Secretary of State Walter Bedell Smith, 15 January 1953, Box 96, BP; Bowles to Eisenhower, 5 February 1953, International Series, Box 26, AWF; Bowles to Dulles, 5 February 1953, Box 94, BP; Bowles to Smith, 6 February 1953, Box 96, BP; Bowles to Dulles, 25 February 1953, Box 94, BP; Bowles to Dulles, 20 March 1953, Box 94, BP.

90. Memorandum by Secretary of State to the Under Secretary (Smith), 4 March 1953, *FR, 1952–1954*, 11(2):1692. See also Eisenhower to Sherman Adams, 9 February 1953, International Series, Box 20, AWF; Memorandum by the Assistant Secretary of State for Near Eastern, South Asian, and African Affairs (Byroade) to Director of Policy Planning Staff (Nitze), 5 March 1953, *FR, 1952–1954*, 11(2):1693; Memorandum by Dulles to Eisenhower, 16 March 1953, White House Memoranda Series, Box 1, Dulles

Papers, DDEL; Eisenhower to Dulles, 17 March 1953, Dulles-Herter Series, Box 1, AWF.

91. Dulles to Ambassador Selection Committee, 26 January 1953, General Correspondence and Memoranda Series, Box 4, Dulles Papers, DDEL; Eisenhower Diary, 7 February 1953, DDE Diary Series, Box 9, AWF.

92. Senate Committee on Foreign Relations, *Hearings: Mutual Security Act of 1953*, 83d Cong., 1st sess., 1953, 374; Editorial Notes on 1953 Mutual Security Program, *FR, 1952–1954*, 11(2): 1694.

93. Senate Committee on Foreign Relations, *Hearings: Mutual Security Act of 1953*, 8.

94. The regional breakdown was as follows: Europe, $2.53 billion; Far East, $1 billion; Near East, $475 million; Latin America, $20 million, ibid., 11–14.

Chapter Five

1. Memorandum of Conversation by Secretary of State, 22 May 1953, *FR, 1952–1954*, 9(1):119–21. For Indian views, see Sarvepalli Gopal, *Jawaharlal Nehru: A Biography*, 3 vols. (Delhi, 1975–84), 2:148; Escott Reid, *Envoy to Nehru* (New Delhi, 1981), 45.

2. Minutes of the 147th Meeting of the NSC, 1 June 1953, *FR, 1952–1954*, 9(1):379–86.

3. Robert J. McMahon, "United States Cold War Strategy in South Asia: Making a Military Commitment to Pakistan, 1947–1954," *Journal of American History* 75 (December 1988): 832–33.

4. M. S. Venkataramani, *The American Role in Pakistan* (New Delhi, 1982), 225; McMahon, "United States Cold War Strategy," 834–36. See also W. H. Young to R. W. P. Fowler (Commonwealth Relations Office), 20 November 1953, FO 371, 106936, PRO.

5. "United States Military Aid to Pakistan," December 1953, FO 371, 106936, PRO; United Kingdom High Commissioner to India to Commonwealth Relations Office, 30 November 1953, FO 371, 106936, PRO; McMahon, "United States Cold War Strategy," 835–37.

6. Memorandum of Conversation by the Assistant Secretary of State for Near Eastern, South Asian, and African Affairs (Byroade), 14 January 1954, *FR, 1952–1954*, 9(1):453.

7. Memorandum of Conversation by Secretary of State, 5 January 1954, ibid., 443–44.

8. *New York Times*, 25 February 1954.

9. Memorandum of Conversation by Secretary of State, 22 May 1953, *FR, 1952–1954*, 9(1):119–21.

10. Gopal, *Jawaharlal Nehru*, 2:185.

11. The Ambassador in India (Allen) to the Department of State, 24 February 1954, *FR, 1952–1954*, 11(2):1737–39; Eisenhower to Dulles, 16 November 1953, DDE Diary Series, Box 3, AWF.

12. McMahon, "United States Cold War Strategy," 838–39; Gary R. Hess, "Global Expansionism and Regional Balances: The Emerging Scholarship on United States

Relations with India and Pakistan," *Pacific Historical Review* 61 (May 1987): 259–95; Venkataramani, *American Role in Pakistan*, 243–45.

13. Report to the NSC by the Executive Secretary, NSC 5409, "United States Policy toward South Asia," January 1954, *FR, 1952–1954*, 11(2):1096–1117.

14. Report to the NSC by the Executive Secretary, "United States Objectives and Courses of Action with Respect to Southeast Asia," 16 January 1954, *FR, 1952–1954*, 12(1):366–81.

15. Commission on Foreign Economic Policy, *Report to the President and the Congress* (Washington, D.C., 1954).

16. Burton I. Kaufman, *Trade and Aid: Eisenhower's Foreign Economic Policy, 1953–1961* (Baltimore, 1982), 34–46.

17. Senate Committee on Foreign Relations, *Hearings: Mutual Security Act of 1954*, 83d Cong., 2d sess., 1954, 54–56.

18. Ibid., 5–15.

19. Ibid.

20. Trudy Huskamp Peterson, *Agricultural Exports, Farm Income, and the Eisenhower Administration* (Lincoln, Nebr., 1979), 5, 25, 39, 129–30.

21. Ibid., 42.

22. Senate Committee on Foreign Relations, *Hearings: Mutual Security Act of 1954*, 5–15; Report to the NSC by the Executive Secretary, NSC 5409, "United States Policy toward Southeast Asia," January 1954, see n. 13.

23. R. K. Jain, ed., *U.S.-South Asian Relations, 1947–1981*, 2 vols. (New Delhi, 1983), 1:630.

24. Senate Committee on Foreign Relations, *Hearings: Mutual Security Act of 1954*, 12.

25. Kaufman, *Trade and Aid*, 49–51; Walt W. Rostow, *Eisenhower, Kennedy and Foreign Aid* (Austin, Tex., 1985), 95–108.

26. Jackson to Dulles, 27 December 1954, Box 56, Jackson Papers, DDEL.

27. Jackson to Dulles, 4 April 1954, Box 41, ibid.; Jackson Log, 11 August 1954, Box 54, ibid.; Jackson to Dulles, 19 August 1954, General Correspondence and Memoranda, Box 2, Dulles Papers, DDEL; Jackson to Hoover, 4 November 1954, Box 56, Jackson Papers; Jackson to Dodge, 18 December 1954, Box 38, Jackson Papers; Kaufman, *Trade and Aid*, 49–51; Rostow, *Foreign Aid*, 95–108.

28. Jackson to Eisenhower, 13 August 1954, Box 41, Jackson Papers, DDEL.

29. The debates are outlined in Jackson to Henry Luce (President, Time-Life Incorporated), 20 December 1954, Box 56, ibid. See also Kaufman, *Trade and Aid*, 49–51; Rostow, *Foreign Aid*, 95–108.

30. Eisenhower to Jackson, 16 August 1954, DDE Diary Series, Box 8, AWF.

31. Dulles to Jackson, 24 August 1954, General Correspondence and Memoranda, Box 2, Dulles Papers, DDEL.

32. Kaufman, *Trade and Aid*, 51–56.

33. Memorandum of Conversation between Stassen and Dulles, 9 August 1954, General Correspondence and Memoranda, Box 1, Dulles Papers, DDEL; Memorandum

of Conversation by the Secretary of State, 24 August 1954, *FR, 1952–1954*, 12(1):789–90; John W. Hanes Jr. (Special Assistant to the Secretary of State) to Assistant Secretary of State for Far Eastern Affairs Robertson, 9 August 1954, 890.00/8-954, RG 59, DSR. See also Memorandum by Director of Mutual Security (Stassen) to Richard Johnson and Norman Paul, 14 February 1953, *FR, 1952–1954*, 12(1):265–66.

34. Memorandum of Telephone Conversation between Eisenhower and Humphrey, 20 December 1954, DDE Diary Series, Box 7, AWF; Memorandum of Conversation between Stassen and Dulles, 5 October 1954, 890.00/10-854, RG 59, DSR; Memorandum of Discussion at the 216th Meeting of the NSC, 6 October 1954, *FR, 1952–1954*, 12(1):927–32; Memorandum by the Director of the Foreign Operations Administration to the Secretary of State, 11 October 1954, *FR, 1952–1954*, 12(1):947–49.

35. Kaufman, *Trade and Aid*, 53.

36. Report of the Asian Economic Working Group, 7 August 1954, Confidential File, Box 70, White House Central File, DDEL; Kaufman, *Trade and Aid*, 51–6; Rostow, *Foreign Aid*, 93–94.

37. Stassen to Eisenhower, 14 March 1955, Administrative Series, Box 38, AWF.

38. Legislative Leadership Meeting, 17 November 1954, Office of the Staff Secretary, Legislative Series, Box 2, WHO; Draft Position Paper Prepared in the Department of State, 30 December 1954, *FR, 1952–1954*, 12(1):1080–85.

39. Report of the NSC Ad Hoc Committee on Asian Economic Development, 24 January 1955, OSANSA, NSC Series, Policy Paper Subseries, Box 14, WHO. See also Memorandum by the Economic Coordinator in the Bureau of Far Eastern Affairs (Baldwin) to the Deputy Assistant Secretary of State for Far Eastern Affairs (Sebald), 2 November 1954, *FR, 1952–1954*, 12(1):959–60; Memorandum by Selma G. Freedman of the Bureau of Economic Affairs to the Deputy Assistant Secretary of State for Economic Affairs (Kalijarvi), *FR, 1952–1954*, 12(1):991–92; Draft Position Paper Prepared in the Department of State, 30 December 1954, *FR, 1952–1954*, 12(1):1080.

40. Jackson to Dulles, 3 August 1954, General Correspondence and Memoranda, Box 2, Dulles Papers, DDEL.

41. Report of the Asian Economic Working Group, 7 August 1954, see n. 36; McDiarmid (State Department Office of Far Eastern Affairs) to Stassen, 21 March 1955, Dodge Series, Subject Subseries, Box 5, USCFEP.

42. William Barnds, *India, Pakistan and the Great Powers* (New York, 1972), 136–41; Gopal, *Jawaharlal Nehru*, 2:226–33.

43. Barnds, *Great Powers*, 136–41; Gopal, *Jawaharlal Nehru*, 2:232–43.

44. Memorandum of Telephone Conversation between Eisenhower and Hoffman, 7 July 1954, DDE Diary Series, Box 7, AWF; Dulles to Eisenhower, 21 July 1954, White House Memoranda Series, Box 1, Dulles Papers, DDEL; Dulles to Hoffman, 23 July 1954, Dulles-Herter Series, Box 3, AWF; Eisenhower to Dulles, 27 July 1954, DDE Diary Series, Box 7, AWF; Memorandum of Conversation between Eisenhower and Hoffman, 10 August 1954, Box 3, AWF.

45. Memorandum of Telephone Conversation between Eisenhower and Hoffman, 7

July 1954, see n. 44; Memorandum of Conversation between Eisenhower and Dulles, 9 August 1954, DDE Diary Series, Box 7, AWF.

46. Eisenhower to Dulles, 6 December 1954, Dulles-Herter Series, Box 3, AWF. See also Memorandum of Conversation between Eisenhower and Dulles, 18 October 1954, White House Memoranda Series, Box 1, Dulles Papers, DDEL; Dulles to Eisenhower, General Correspondence and Memoranda, Box 2, Dulles Papers, DDEL; Eisenhower to Dulles, 28 December 1954, DDE Diary Series, Box 7, AWF; Interview with John Sherman Cooper, conducted by the author, Washington, D.C., 18 July 1983.

47. Memorandum of Conversation between Eisenhower and Muir, 25 May 1955, Ann Whitman Diary Series, Box 5, AWF.

48. On the Menon mediating effort, see Henry Cabot Lodge (United Nations) to Dulles, 9 June 1955, General Correspondence and Memorandum Series, Box 2, Dulles Papers, DDEL; Memorandum of Conversation between Eisenhower, Dulles, Menon, and Indian Ambassador to the United States G. L. Mehta, 14 June 1955, Box 3, Dulles Papers, DDEL (same conversation recorded in International Series, Box 26, AWF); Memorandum of Conversation between Dulles and Menon, 15 June 1955, General Correspondence and Memoranda, Box 1, Dulles Papers, DDEL; Dulles to Eisenhower, 15 June 1955, Dulles Papers, DDEL; Gopal, *Jawaharlal Nehru*, 2:243–44.

49. Eisenhower Diary entry, 14 July 1955, DDE Diary Series, Box 9, AWF.

50. Senate Committee on Foreign Relations, *Hearings: Mutual Security Act of 1955*, 84th Cong., 1st sess., 1955, 4–5; Report of the Asian Economic Working Group, 7 August 1954, see n. 36.

51. Supplementary Notes: Legislative Leadership Meeting, 28 June 1955, Legislative Meeting Series, Box 1, AWF.

52. Bipartisan Legislative Meeting Notes, 3 May 1955, ibid.

53. Supplementary Notes: Legislative Leadership Meeting, 28 June 1955, see n. 51.

54. Original Notes: Legislative Leadership Meeting, 28 June 1955, Office of the Staff Secretary, Legislative Series, Box 3, WHO.

55. Kaufman, *Trade and Aid*, 54–55.

56. Department of State Intelligence Report no. 81, "Communist Economic Diplomacy in Underdeveloped Areas," 2 April 1956, Randall Series, Agency Subseries, Box 4, USCFEP; A. Gorev and V. Zimyanin, *Jawaharlal Nehru* (Moscow, 1982), 298–309; Gopal, *Jawaharlal Nehru*, 2:243–50.

57. Gopal, *Jawaharlal Nehru*, 2:253. On the visit, see Department of State Intelligence Report no. 81, 2 April 1956, see n. 56; Barnds, *Great Powers*, 119; Gopal, *Jawaharlal Nehru*, 2:250–55.

58. Department of State Intelligence Report no. 81, 2 April 1956, see n. 56; Barnds, *Great Powers*, 118; Gopal, *Jawaharlal Nehru*, 2:250–55.

59. Telegram from the Embassy in India to the Department of State, 25 November 1955, *FR, 1955–1957*, 8:198–200.

60. Eisenhower to Dulles, 23 March 1955, ibid., 278.

61. Eisenhower to Nehru, 7 July 1955, International Series, Box 26, AWF; Eisen-

hower to Nehru, 12 July 1955, White House Memoranda, Box 1, Dulles Papers, DDEL; Eisenhower to Nehru, 1 August 1955, International Series, Box 26, AWF. On the exchange of visits, see Memorandum of Conversation between Eisenhower and Dulles, 19 July 1955, International Series, Box 26, AWF; Memorandum from the Assistant Secretary of State for Near Eastern, South Asian, and African Affairs (Allen) to the Secretary of State, 29 July 1955, *FR, 1955–1957*, 8:290–91; Eisenhower to Nehru, 1 August 1955, International Series, Box 26, AWF; Nehru to Eisenhower, 14 August 1955, International Series, Box 26, AWF.

62. Dulles to Cooper, 19 December 1955, General Correspondence and Memoranda, Box 2, Dulles Papers, DDEL. For background, see Robert G. Barnes (Department of State) to Andrew J. Goodpaster (Assistant to President), 13 December 1955, transmitting Cooper to Dulles, 11 December 1955, International Series, Box 26, AWF; Barnds, *Great Powers*, 121.

63. Jackson to Rockefeller, 10 November 1955, Administrative Series, Box 32, AWF.

64. Rockefeller to Eisenhower, 7 November 1955, Confidential File, Box 61, White House Central File, DDEL.

65. Hoover to Adams, 14 November 1955, enclosed Department of State Memorandum, 14 November 1955, ibid.

66. Hoover (State) and Burgess (Treasury) to Adams, 29 November 1955, transmitting Department of State/Department of Treasury Report, "Tata Negotiations with the Export-Import Bank," November 1955, ibid.

67. Rockefeller to Eisenhower, 29 October 1955, ibid.

68. Whitman Diary entry, 2 November 1955, Ann Whitman Diary Series, Box 7, AWF.

69. Department of State/Department of Treasury Report, "Tata Negotiations with the Export-Import Bank," November 1955, Confidential File, Box 61, White House Central File, DDEL.

70. Rockefeller to Dulles, 22 November 1955, Confidential File, Box 61, White House Central File, DDEL.

71. Memorandum of Conversation between Eisenhower and Adams, 15 November 1955, Ann Whitman Diary Series, Box 7, AWF.

72. Hoover (State) and Burgess (Treasury) to Adams, 29 November 1955, transmitting Department of State/Department of Treasury Report, see n. 69.

73. John P. Lewis, *Quiet Crisis in India* (Garden City, N.Y., 1964), 275.

74. Memorandum on Point Four Agreements, undated, Box 108, BP; U.S. Mission Correspondence, Memorandum on Community Development Program, undated, Box 108, BP; Wood to Bowles, November 1952, Box 39, BP; S. Chandrasekhar, *American Aid and India's Economic Development* (New York, 1965), 155.

75. Chandrasekhar, *American Aid*, 95–96, 128–30, 150; Lewis, *Quiet Crisis in India*, 276.

76. Rosen, *Western Economists and Eastern Societies: Agents of Change in South Asia, 1950–1970* (Baltimore, 1985), 13, 71–73; Bowles, *Ambassador's Report* (New York,

1954), 340; Interview with Douglas Ensminger conducted by the author, Columbia, Missouri, 12 December 1982; "Indo-American Technical Cooperation Program for Agriculture for Fiscal Year 1958," 3 March 1958, Series A-2, Box 464-D, Rockefeller Foundation Archives.

77. On investment and trade, see U.S. Department of Commerce, *Survey of Current Business, November 1954* (Washington, D.C., 1954) and United Nations, *Yearbook of International Trade Statistics, 1954* (New York, 1955), 543. On aid programs, see also Lewis, *Quiet Crisis in India*, 279.

78. CIA Economic Intelligence Report, EIC-R-14, "Sino-Soviet Bloc Post War Economic Activities in Underdeveloped Areas," 8 August 1956 (from the notes of Thomas Zoumaras, Northeast Missouri State University, Kirksville, Missouri).

79. Department of State Intelligence Report no. 81, 2 April 1956 see n. 56; CIA Intelligence Report, EIC-R-14, 8 August 1956, see n. 78; Study prepared by the Policy Planning Staff, "Soviet Economic Penetration," 4 April 1956, *FR, 1955–1957*, 9:13–18; Department of State Report, "The Nature and Problems of Soviet Economic Penetration in Underdeveloped Areas," [probably 1956], Dulles-Herter Series, Box 5, AWF; Department of State Report, "Soviet Economic Penetration," n.d., Box 10, Records of the U.S. President's Citizen Advisers on the Mutual Security Program, DDEL; Kaufman, *Trade and Aid*, 58–78; Blanche Cook, *The Declassified Eisenhower* (Garden City, N.Y., 1981), 293–346.

80. Eisenhower to Douglas, 20 January 1956, Dodge Series, Correspondence Subseries, Box 1, USCFEP.

81. CIA Economic Intelligence Report, EIC-R-14, 8 August 1956, see n. 78.

82. Department of State Report, "Soviet Economic Penetration," n.d., see n. 79.

83. Jackson to Luce, 16 April 1956, Box 56, Jackson Papers, DDEL.

84. Eisenhower to Dulles, 5 December 1955, *FR, 1955–1957*, 9:10–12.

85. Memorandum of Conversation between Eisenhower, Dulles, Humphrey, Dr. Snyder, and Wilson, 9 December 1955, White House Memoranda, Box 3, Dulles Papers, DDEL.

86. Ibid.

87. India, Planning Commission, *Second Five Year Plan* (New Delhi, 1956), 257–59.

88. Francine Frankel, *India's Political Economy* (Delhi, 1978), 117.

89. India, Planning Commission, *Second Five Year Plan: A Draft Outline* (New Delhi, 1956), 10. For an excellent discussion of the meaning of the term "socialism" in the Indian and South Asian context, see Gunnar Myrdal, *Asian Drama: An Inquiry into the Poverty of Nations*, 3 vols. (New York, 1968), 2:799–848.

90. Frankel, *India's Political Economy*, 117.

91. India, Planning Commission, *Second Five Year Plan*, 51–52; Frankel, *India's Political Economy*, 132–34.

92. India, Planning Commission, *Second Five Year Plan: A Draft Outline*, 91; Frankel, *India's Political Economy*, 136–37.

93. India, Ministry of Food and Agriculture, *Report of the Foodgrains Enquiry Committee* (New Delhi, 1957), 12; Frankel, *India's Political Economy*, 137–42.

94. Department of State Report, "A Feasible Program of U.S. Economic Assistance for India," 13 March 1956, *FR, 1955–1957*, 8:311–17.

95. Cooper's proposal is outlined in Goodpaster to Adams, 28 March 1956, Office of the Staff Secretary, Subject Series, Department of State Subseries, Box 1, WHO. See also Department of State Report, "A Feasible Program of U.S. Economic Assistance for India," 13 March 1956, see n. 94.

96. Thorsten Kalijarvi (Department of State) to Francis (Department of Agriculture), 4 May 1954, Box 8, Clarence Francis Records, DDEL; Stassen Asian Trip Report, 21 March 1955, Dodge Series, Subject Subseries, Box 5, USCFEP; Devki Nandan Prasad, *Food for Peace: The Story of U.S. Food Assistance to India* (New Delhi, 1979), 48.

97. Adams to Cooper, 2 April 1956, Confidential File, Box 71, White House Central File, DDEL.

98. Telegram from the Secretary of State to the Department of State, 12 March 1956, *FR, 1955–1957*, 8:308–11.

99. Gopal, *Jawaharlal Nehru*, 2:273–74.

100. Department of State, "A Feasible Program of U.S. Economic Assistance for India," 13 March 1956, see n. 94. On the State Department's consideration of the problem, see Fisher Howe (State Department) to Goodpaster, 24 March 1956, Confidential File, Box 71, White House Central File, DDEL; Dulles to Cooper, 30 April 1956, Office of the Staff Secretary, Subject Series, State Department Subseries, Box 1, WHO; Summary Minutes of a Meeting of the Ad Hoc Committee on Ambassador Cooper's India Aid Proposals, Department of State, 3 May 1956, *FR, 1955–1957*, 8:317–18.

101. Department of State, "A Feasible Program of U.S. Economic Assistance for India," 13 March 1956, see n. 94.

102. Senate Committee on Foreign Relations, *Hearings: Mutual Security Act of 1956*, 84th Cong., 2d sess., 1956, 173–76.

103. Kaufman, *Trade and Aid*, 68–71.

104. Address at the Annual Dinner of the American Society of Newspaper Editors, 21 April 1956, *Public Papers of the Presidents of the United States: Dwight D. Eisenhower* (Washington, D.C., 1958–61), 411–27.

105. For quotes and analysis of Congressional critics, see Kaufman, *Trade and Aid*, 68–71.

106. Ibid.

107. See table in chapter 1.

108. Earl Butz (Department of Agriculture) to Secretary of Agriculture Ezra Taft Benson, 1 June 1956, Commodities 5, RG 16, DAR; Gwynn Garnett (PL 480 Administrator) to Milan D. Smith (Executive Assistant to the Secretary of Agriculture), 16 August 1956, RG 16, DAR; "Surplus Agricultural Commodities Agreement with India," 29 August 1956, *United States Treaties and Other International Agreements, 1956* (Washington, D.C., 1957), 7(3):2803–28.

109. Senate Committee on Foreign Relations, *Hearings: Mutual Security Act of 1956*, 241.

110. Critics are quoted in Kaufman, *Trade and Aid*, 71–72.

111. Ibid.

112. Eisenhower to Gruenther, 2 July 1954, DDE Diary Series, Box 7, AWF.

113. Legislative Leadership Meeting Supplementary Notes, 5 June 1956, Legislative Meeting Series, Box 1, AWF.

114. Eisenhower to Edgar Eisenhower, 27 February 1956, DDE Diary Series, Box 13, AWF.

115. M. S. Rajan, *India in World Affairs* (Bombay, 1964), 259.

116. "Transcript of Secretary Dulles' News Conference, 23 July 1956," *Department of State Bulletin*, 35 (August 1956): 147–48.

117. Rajan, *India in World Affairs*, 260.

118. Telegram from the Secretary of State to the Department of State, 11 March 1956, see n. 98; Memorandum of Conversations between Secretary of State Dulles and Prime Minister Nehru, Prime Minister's Residence, New Delhi, 9 March 1956, 4 P.M. and 10 March 1956, 10:30 A.M., *FR, 1955–1957*, 8:306–8.

119. Eisenhower to Nehru, 24 August 1956, International Series, Box 26, AWF; Eisenhower to Nehru, 15 September 1956, Box 26, AWF.

120. Eisenhower to Nehru, 6 November 1956, Box 26, AWF; Eisenhower to Nehru, 11 November 1956, Box 26, AWF.

121. Memorandum of Conversation between Eisenhower, Nixon, Hoover, Phleger, and Hagerty, 5 November 1956, DDE Diary Series, Box 19, AWF. See also Minutes of the 303d Meeting of the NSC, 9 November 1956, NSC Series, Box 8, AWF; Eisenhower to Nehru, 6 November 1956, International Series, Box 26, AWF; Eisenhower to Nehru, 11 November 1956, International Series, Box 26, AWF; Gopal, *Jawaharlal Nehru*, 2:291–98.

122. Bipartisan Legislative Meeting, 22 March 1956, Legislative Meeting Series, Box 2, AWF; Whitman to Dulles, 30 August 1956, transmitting Cousins letters to the President, White House Memoranda, Box 3, Dulles Papers, DDEL; Telegram from the Embassy in India to the Department of State, 7 December 1956, *FR, 1955–1957*, 8:319–25 (on the scheduling of the visit, see footnotes on 319); Telegram from the Secretary of State to the Department of State, 12 December 1956, *FR, 1955–1957*, 8:326–27; Cooper to Eisenhower, 15 December 1956, International Series, Box 28, AWF; Cooper to Nehru, 12 December 1956, Box 28, AWF; State Department Briefing Paper on the Visit of Pandit Jawaharlal Nehru of India to the United States, December, 1956, Box 28, AWF.

123. Memorandum of Conversation between Eisenhower and Nehru, 17–18 December 1956, International Series, Box 28, AWF; Memorandum of Conversation between Eisenhower and Nehru, 19 December 1956, *FR, 1955–1957*, 8:331–40.

124. Memorandum of Telephone Conversation between Eisenhower and Hoover, 19 December 1956, DDE Diary Series, Box 20, AWF.

125. Memorandum of Conversation between Eisenhower and Nehru, 19 December 1956, see n. 123; Memorandum for the Record by Goodpaster, 17 December 1956, Office of the Staff Secretary, Subject Series, Department of State Subseries, Box 5, WHO.

Chapter Six

1. "Second Inaugural Address," 21 January 1957, *Public Papers of the Presidents of the United States: Dwight D. Eisenhower* (Washington, D.C., 1958–61), 60–72.

2. U.S. President's Citizen Advisers on the Mutual Security Program, *Report to the President by the President's Citizen Advisers on the Mutual Security Program*, 1 March 1957 (Washington, D.C., 1957); Senate Special Committee to Study the Foreign Aid Program, S. Rept. 52, 85th Cong., 1st sess., 1957; House Committee on Foreign Affairs, H. Rept. 551, 85th Cong., 1st sess., 1957, *Report on Foreign Policy and Mutual Security*; International Development Advisory Board, *A New Emphasis on Economic Development Abroad* (Washington, D.C., 1957); Burton I. Kaufman, *Trade and Aid: Eisenhower's Foreign Economic Policy, 1953–1961* (Baltimore, 1982), 96–99.

3. Department of State, Policy Planning Staff Report, "U.S. Foreign Economic Assistance Programs," 16 January 1957 (from the notes of Thomas Zoumaras, Northeast Missouri State University, Kirksville, Missouri).

4. Dulles to Eisenhower, 25 January 1957, Administrative Series, Box 29, AWF; Dulles to Eisenhower, 23 March 1957, Dulles-Herter Series, Box 6, AWF.

5. "Special Message to the Congress on the Mutual Security Program," 21 May 1957, *Public Papers, Eisenhower, 1957*, 372–85; Kaufman, *Trade and Aid*, 96–112.

6. Department of State, Policy Planning Staff Report, "U.S. Foreign Economic Assistance Programs", 16 January 1957, see n. 3.

7. *New York Times*, 6 December 1960.

8. NSC 5701, "U.S. Policy toward South Asia," 10 January 1957, *FR, 1955–1957*, 8:29–43.

9. Ibid.

10. For a discussion of the China factor, see Walt W. Rostow, *Eisenhower, Kennedy, and Foreign Aid* (Austin, Tex., 1985), 22–33.

11. NSC 5701, "U.S. Policy toward South Asia," 10 January 1957, see n. 8.

12. Minutes of the 310th Meeting of the NSC, 24 January 1957, NSC Series, Box 8, AWF.

13. Ibid.

14. "Summary of the Report of the Interdepartmental Working Group on India," 2 May 1957, Randall Series, Subject Subseries, Box 6, USCFEP; *New York Times*, 7 January 1958. See also Francine Frankel, *India's Political Economy* (Delhi, 1978), 147–49.

15. Frankel, *India's Political Economy*, 147–49.

16. India, Planning Commission, *Second Five Year Plan* (New Delhi, 1956), 268.

17. Frankel, *India's Political Economy*, 142.

18. India, Ministry of Food and Agriculture, *Report of the Indian Delegation to China on Agricultural Planning and Techniques* (New Delhi, 1956); India, Planning Commission, *Report of the Indian Delegation to China on Agrarian Cooperatives* (New Delhi, 1957). See also Frankel, *India's Political Economy*, 139, 141.

19. India, Planning Commission, *Second Five Year Plan*, 201–33; India, Planning

Commission, Evaluation Report, *Study Team for Community Development and National Extension Service on Plan Projects* (New Delhi, 1957), 86–88.

20. India, Planning Commission, *Third Five Year Plan: A Draft Outline* (New Delhi, 1960), 145.

21. Randall to Adams, 9 April 1957, Randall Series, Correspondence Subseries, Box 1, USCFEP; Memorandum of Conversation, Department of State, 13 May 1957, *FR, 1955–1957*, 8:341–44; Memorandum of Conversation, Department of State, 31 May 1957, ibid., 344–48.

22. *New York Times*, 6 September 1957.

23. Letter from the Ambassador in India (Bunker) to Frederic P. Bartlett, at London, 27 June 1957, *FR, 1955–1957*, 8:348–52; Randall to Adams, 11 September 1957, Randall Series, Subject Subseries, Box 6, USCFEP; Dulles to Eisenhower, 7 October 1957, International Series, Box 26, AWF; Memorandum of Conversation between Dulles, Bartlett, and Indian Ambassador G. L. Mehta, 24 December 1957, Confidential File, Box 75, White House Central File, DDEL.

24. "Summary of the Report of the Interdepartmental Working Group on India," 2 May 1957, see n. 14; Memorandum from Elbert G. Mathews of the Policy Planning Staff to the Deputy Under Secretary of State for Economic Affairs (Dillon), 11 September 1957, *FR, 1955–1957*, 8:367–68.

25. Letter from the Deputy Under Secretary of State for Economic Affairs (Dillon) to the Chairman of the Council on Foreign Economic Policy (Randall), 15 July 1957, *FR, 1955–1957*, 8:359–61; Letter from Ambassador in India (Bunker) to Frederic P. Bartlett, at London, 27 June 1957, see n. 23.

26. Memorandum from the Director of the Office of South Asian Affairs (Bartlett) to Assistant Secretary of State for Near Eastern, South Asian, and African Affairs (Rountree), 30 September 1957, *FR, 1955–1957*, 8:377–82.

27. Memorandum from the Secretary of State to the President, 4 November 1957, ibid., 393–95.

28. Memorandum of a Conference with the President, 16 November 1957, ibid., 404–6.

29. Memorandum of Conversation between Dulles and Mehta, 17 January 1958, Confidential File, Box 75, White House Central File, DDEL; *Department of State Bulletin*, 51 (March 1958): 464–66.

30. See table in chapter 1.

31. Rostow, *Foreign Aid*, 154. For background, see 152–54.

32. "Surplus Agricultural Commodities Agreement with India," 4 May 1960, *United States Treaties and Other International Agreements* (Washington, D.C., 1960), 8(2):1544–58.

33. Kaufman, *Trade and Aid*, 135, 152–206.

34. Legislative Leadership Meeting, 1 July 1958, Legislative Meeting Series, Box 2, AWF.

35. Senate Committee on Foreign Relations, *Hearings: Mutual Security Act of 1957*, 85th Cong., 1st sess., 1957, 4.

36. A Report by the Assistant Secretary of State for Economic Affairs Douglas Dillon to the Draper Committee, "Moderating the African-Asian Revolution," 22 December 1958, Box 9, Records of the U.S. President's Committee on Military Assistance Programs, DDEL.

37. Supplementary Notes: Legislative Leadership Meeting, 16 February 1960, Office of the Staff Secretary, Legislative Series, Box 6, WHO.

38. A collection of Bowles's writings and speeches can be found in Boxes 115–16, BP.

39. *New York Times*, 18 October 1957; *Newsweek*, 14 December 1959, 66; *Business Week*, 15 November 1958, 102–6.

40. Rostow, *Foreign Aid*, 6–8.

41. Ibid., 11.

42. Rostow to Millikan, 22 February 1959, Box 559, Pre-Presidential File, JFKL; Memorandum of Conversation between P. N. Rosenstein-Rodan and Indian Ambassador-at-large B. K. Nehru, 4 March 1959, Box 559, Pre-Presidential File, JFKL.

43. Proceedings of the conference are in Selig S. Harrison, ed., *India and the United States* (New York, 1961).

44. Ibid., 144–46.

45. Memorandum of Conversation between Eisenhower, Dillon, Bell, Staats, Brand, Riddleberger, Irwin, Palmer, Persons, Morgan, and Merriam, 4 February 1960, DDE Diary Series, Box 47, AWF; Senate Committee on Foreign Relations, *Hearings: Mutual Security Act of 1960*, 86th Cong., 2d sess., 1960, 155, 400. See also Kaufman, *Trade and Aid*, 199.

46. Memorandum of Conversation between Fred Bartlett (South Asian Affairs), Robert W. Adams (South Asian Affairs), Benjamin Fleck (India Desk), and W. Spielman (Economic Affairs), 16 March 1959, Box 20, Records of the U.S. President's Committee to Study the Military Assistance Program, DDEL.

47. *New York Times*, 4 February 1960.

48. NSC, Operations Coordinating Board Progress Report on NSC 5409, "U.S. Policy toward South Asia," 24 August 1955, NSC Series, Policy Paper Subseries, OSANSA, Box 15, WHO; NSC, Operations Coordinating Board Progress Report on NSC 5409, "U.S. Policy toward South Asia," 30 March 1956, *FR, 1955–1957*, 8:1–10.

49. Memorandum of a Conference with the President, 12 November 1957, *FR, 1955–1957*, 8:404–6.

50. Memorandum from the Deputy Under Secretaries of State for Political Affairs (Murphy) and Economic Affairs (Dillon) and the Assistant Secretary of State for Near Eastern, South Asian, and African Affairs (Rountree) to the Secretary of State, 16 October 1957, *FR, 1955–1957*, 8:390–93; Eisenhower to Dulles, 7 April 1958, Office of the Staff Secretary, Box 2, WHO; Eisenhower to Dulles, 21 April 1958, Dulles-Herter Series, Box 7, AWF.

51. William Barnds, *India, Pakistan, and the Great Powers* (New York, 1972), 141–62; Sarvepalli Gopal, *Jawaharlal Nehru: A Biography*, 3 vols. (Delhi, 1975–84), 3:75–105.

52. Gopal, *Jawaharlal Nehru*, 3:75–105.

53. Memorandum for the Record, 5 December 1959, DDE Diary Series, Box 45, AWF.

54. "U.S. Policy toward South Asia," n.d., OSANSA, NSC Series, Briefing Notes Subseries, Box 16, WHO. See also R. W. Komer (CIA) to Colonel Lincoln (Draper Committee), 24 March 1959, Box 20, Records of the U.S. President's Committee to Study the Military Assistance Program, DDEL; CIA Report, "The Practicality of a Package Settlement between India and Pakistan," 24 March 1959, Box 16, Records of the U.S. President's Committee to Study the Military Assistance Program, DDEL; William Draper to General N. F. Twining (JCS), 9 April 1959, Box 16, Records of the U.S. President's Committee to Study the Military Assistance Program, DDEL; NSC Draft Discussion Paper, "U.S. Policy toward South Asia," 27 May 1959, OSANSA, NSC Series, Briefing Notes Subseries, Box 16, WHO; Memorandum on Admiral Felt's View on Policy in South and Southeast Asia, 23 November 1959, OSANSA, NSC Series, Briefing Notes Subseries, Box 16, WHO.

55. NSC 5909, "U.S. Policy toward South Asia," 22 July 1959, OSANSA, NSC Series, Policy Paper Subseries, Box 27, WHO.

56. NSC, Operations Coordinating Board Progress Report on NSC 5909, "U.S. Policy toward South Asia," 9 November 1960, ibid.

57. Memorandum for the Record, 5 December 1959, ibid.

58. Stephen Ambrose, *Eisenhower: The President* (New York, 1984), 552–53.

59. Memorandum of Conference between Eisenhower, McCone, and Lord Plowden, n.d. [1959], DDE Diary Series, Box 45, AWF.

60. Bunker to Herter, 22 December 1959, International Series, Box 26, AWF.

61. Memorandum of Conversation between Eisenhower, Ambassador Richard Murphy, Ambassador Ellsworth Bunker, Nehru, M. R. Pillai (Secretary General Ministry of External Affairs), and S. Dutt (Foreign Secretary), 10 December 1959, sent from New Delhi to Department of State, 14 December 1959, Office of the Staff Secretary, International Trips and Meetings Series, Box 9, WHO; Memorandum of Conversation between Eisenhower and Nehru, 13 December 1959, sent from New Delhi to Department of State, 14 December 1959, Office of the Staff Secretary, International Trips and Meetings Series, Box 9, WHO.

62. Memorandum of Conversation between Eisenhower and Nehru, 13 December 1959, see n. 61.

63. Eisenhower to Herter, 15 December 1959, Dulles-Herter Series, Box 10, AWF.

64. "Annual Message to Congress on the State of the Union," 7 January 1960, *Public Papers, Eisenhower, 1960–1961*, 3–17.

65. "Special Message to Congress on the Mutual Security Program," 16 February 1960, ibid., 177–87.

66. Gopal, *Jawaharlal Nehru*, 3:142–44.

67. NSC, Operations Coordinating Board Progress Report on NSC 5909, "U.S. Policy toward South Asia," 9 November 1960, see n. 56.

68. Memorandum of conversation between Eisenhower, Dillon, Bell, Staats, Palmer, Persons, Morgan, and Merriam, 4 February 1960, see n. 45.

69. Jackson to Dulles, 9 April 1954, Box 41, Jackson Papers, DDEL; Jackson to

Hoover, 4 November 1954, Box 56, Jackson Papers, DDEL; Jackson to Dodge, 24 November 1954, Dodge Series, Subject Subseries, Box 2, USCFEP; Colonel Paul D. Carroll to Eisenhower, n.d., Administrative Series, Box 24, USCFEP; Walt W. Rostow and Max Millikan, Draft, "Proposal for a New United States Foreign Economic Policy," 1954, Box 26, Jackson Papers, DDEL; Rostow and Millikan, Draft, "Notes on Foreign Economic Policy," 1954, Box 68, Jackson Papers, DDEL; Rostow and Millikan, Draft, "The Crisis of 1954," 1954, Box 69, Jackson Papers, DDEL. See also Rostow, *Foreign Aid*, 84–108.

70. For a good summary of the Rostow thesis, see Samuel Baily, *The United States and the Development of South America, 1945–1975* (New York, 1976), 9–10.

71. Walt W. Rostow, *Stages of Economic Growth: A Non-Communist Manifesto* (London, 1959); Rostow and Millikan, Draft, "Proposal for a New United States Foreign Economic Policy," Box 26, Jackson Papers, DDEL.

72. "The Stages of Economic Growth and the Problems of Peaceful Coexistence," address by Walt W. Rostow before the Institute of World Economy and International Relations, Moscow, 25 May 1959, Box 75, Jackson Papers, DDEL.

73. Gerald Meier, ed., *Leading Issues in Economic Development* (New York, 1964), 601.

74. U.S. Congress, Senate, Committee on Foreign Relations, *Hearings: Mutual Security Act of 1957*, 7.

75. Jackson to Eisenhower, 1 July 1959, Box 41, Jackson Papers, DDEL; Eisenhower to Jackson, 6 July 1959, Box 41, Jackson Papers, DDEL.

76. Wilfred Malenbaum, *East and West in India's Economic Development* (Washington, D.C., 1959). See especially "Introduction" by Max Millikan.

77. Rostow, *Foreign Aid*, 3–35, 152–69.

78. Rostow to Jackson, 29 February 1956, Box 56, Jackson Papers, DDEL.

79. Arthur Smithies to Draper Committee Members, 25 February 1959, enclosing Millikan, "India," 20 February 1959, Box 2, Records of U.S. President's Committee to Study the Military Assistance Program, DDEL.

80. Malenbaum, *East and West*, v.

81. Millikan, "India", 20 February 1959, see n. 79.

82. Rostow to Vorys, 28 May 1958, Box 573, Pre-Presidential File, JFKL.

83. An excellent series of aid disbursement charts drawn from the Government of India's Ministry of Finance appears in the appendix of R. K. Jain, ed., *U.S.-South Asian Relations, 1947–1981*, 2 vols. (New Delhi, 1983), 1:632–47.

84. Memorandum of Conversation between Eisenhower and Dulles, 7 February 1955, White House Memoranda Series, Box 3, Dulles Papers, DDEL.

85. Whitman to O'Connor, 10 February 1955, with Eisenhower to Goodpaster enclosed, Dulles-Herter Series, Box 3, AWF.

86. Memorandum of Conversation between Eisenhower and Menon, 15 March 1955, Ann Whitman Diary Series, Box 3, AWF.

87. Humphrey to Hoffman, 26 March 1957, Administrative Series, Box 23, AWF.

88. Ibid.

89. Ibid.

90. Brown (New Delhi) to Secretary of State, 21 June 1959, Randall Series, Subject Subseries, Box 6, USCFEP.

91. Randall to Dillon, 1 July 1959, Randall Series, Subject Subseries, Box 6, USCFEP; Randall to Dillon, 20 July 1959, Randall Series, Subject Subseries, Box 6, USCFEP; Dillon to Randall, 29 July 1959, Randall Series, Agency Subseries, Box 3, USCFEP; Randall to Dillon, 1 August 1959, Chronological File, Box 1, USCFEP; Randall to Dillon, 18 September 1959, Randall Series, Subject Subseries, Box 6, USCFEP.

92. Randall to Kearns, 8 June 1959, Randall Series, Subject Subseries, Box 6, USCFEP.

93. Minutes of Interagency Meeting on Indian Steel Problems, 12 January 1960, Randall Series, Subject Subseries, Box 6, USCFEP.

94. Randall Report on Visit to India, December 1959, Randall Series, Trip Subseries, Box 4, USCFEP.

95. Kaufman, *Trade and Aid*, 148.

96. United States Technical Cooperation Mission (New Delhi) to Department of State, 1 April 1957, Policy Paper Series, Box 3, USCFEP; Galbraith to Randall, 8 July 1958, Chronological File, Box 2, USCFEP.

97. R. K. Jain, *U.S.-South Asian Relations*, 1:632–34.

98. Senate Committee on Foreign Relations, *Hearings: Mutual Security Act of 1960*, 391.

99. *New York Times*, 20 September 1957, 12 November 1959.

100. Ibid., 11 November 1959.

101. *Business Week*, 11 May 1957, 127–31.

102. Ibid., 12 December 1959, 74–76.

103. NSC, Operations Coordinating Board Progress Report on NSC 5707, "U.S. Policy toward South Asia," 16 July 1958, OSANSA, NSC Series, Policy Paper Subseries, Box 19, WHO.

104. *Business Week*, 12 December 1959, 74–76.

105. NSC 5909, "U.S. Policy toward South Asia," 22 July 1959, see n. 55; Randall Report on Visit to India, December 1959, see n. 94; U.S. Department of Commerce, *Survey of Current Business, August 1963* (Washington, 1963); *Business Week*, 11 May 1957, 127–31; *Business Week*, 12 December 1959, 74–76. For a comparison of British and American investment, see Elliot K. Baker to Colonel Paul Cullen, 5 December 1959, Randall Series, Subject Subseries, Box 6, USCFEP.

106. NSC, Report on Trade Fair Program, 5 October 1960, OSANSA, OCB Series, Subject Subseries, Box 2, WHO.

107. Report of the 1958 United States Trade Mission to Northern India, n.d. [1958], Box 7, Joseph Rand Papers, DDEL. See also *New York Times*, 7 January 1960.

108. United Nations, *Yearbook of International Trade Statistics, 1964* (New York, 1965), 795.

109. Jackson to Dulles, 27 December 1956, Box 40, Jackson Papers, DDEL.

110. "The Basic Approach," a note published in the *All India Congress Economic Review*, 15 August 1958, in *Speeches*, 4:119.

111. "Progress through Planning," speech delivered at the Golden Jubilee of the Indian Merchants Chamber, 3 February 1958, *Speeches*, 4:111.

112. Senate Committee on Foreign Relations, *Hearings: Mutual Security Act of 1958*, 85th Cong., 2d sess., 1958, 284.

113. India, Planning Commission, *Third Five Year Plan* (New Delhi, 1961), 37, 39.

114. India, Planning Commission, *Study Team for Community Development and National Extension Service on Plan Projects* (New Delhi, 1957), 1:44. See also Myrdal, *Asian Drama: An Inquiry into the Poverty of Nations*, 3 vols. (New York, 1968), 1:134 and 2:888; Frankel, *India's Political Economy*, 4; René Dumont and Bernard Rosier, *The Hungry Future* (London, 1969), 193–95.

115. India, Planning Commission, *First Five Year Plan* (New Delhi, 1953), 192.

116. India, Planning Commission, *Report of the Committee of the Panel on Land Reforms* (New Delhi, 1958), 37.

117. For a discussion of land reform failure, see Frankel, *India's Political Economy*, 190–95; Myrdal, *Asian Drama*, 1:292–93 and 3:1326–32; Manilal Nanavati and J. J. Anjaria, *The Indian Rural Problem* (Bombay, 1970), 251–53; Daniel Thorner, *The Shaping of Modern India* (New Delhi, 1980), 154–56.

118. Thorner, *Shaping of Modern India*, 155.

119. India, Planning Commission, *The Sixth Evaluation Report on Working of Community Development and N.E.S. Blocks* (New Delhi, 1959), 122–24; Myrdal, *Asian Drama*, 1:290.

120. Thorner, *Shaping of Modern India*, 169.

121. Rostow to Millikan, 22 February 1959, Box 559, Pre-Presidential File, JFKL; Memorandum of Conversation between P. N. Rosenstein-Rodan and Ambassador-At-Large B. K. Nehru, 4 March 1959, ibid.; B. K. Nehru to CENIS, 30 June 1959, Box 573, Pre-Presidential File, JFKL.

122. NSC, OCB Progress Report on NSC 5701, "U.S. Policy toward South Asia," 18 March 1959, OSANSA, NSC Series, Policy Paper Subseries, Box 19, WHO.

123. India, Ministry of Food and Agriculture and Ministry of Community Development and Cooperation, *Report of India's Food Crisis and Steps to Meet It* (New Delhi, 1959), 3–6.

124. Bunker to Secretary of State, 14 October 1959, Box 13, Don Paarlberg Papers, DDEL.

125. India, Planning Commission, *Third Five Year Plan: A Draft Outline* (New Delhi, 1960), 27–28, 35, 204–25, 210; Gopal, *Jawaharlal Nehru*, 3:118; Frankel, *India's Political Economy*, 181.

126. India, Planning Commission, *Third Five Year Plan: A Draft Outline*, 145–67.

127. Draft Press Release by Press Secretary James G. Hagerty, 4 May 1960, DDE Diary Series, Box 10, AWF.

128. Frankel, *India's Political Economy*, 186.

Chapter Seven

1. Richard J. Barnet, *Intervention and Revolution: The United States in the Third World* (New York, 1968), 27.

2. Minutes of the 508th Meeting of the NSC, 22 January 1963, Meeting and Memoranda Series, Box 314, NSF, JFKL.

3. Ibid.

4. "Report of the Task Force on U.S. Policy with Respect to India," 27 December 1960, Box 1074, Pre-Presidential File, JFKL.

5. Arthur Schlesinger, Jr., *A Thousand Days: John F. Kennedy in the White House* (Boston, 1965), 522.

6. For example, see James Barber, *The Presidential Character* (Englewood Cliffs, N.J., 1972); David Burner and Thomas West, eds., *The Torch is Passed: The Kennedy Brothers and American Liberalism* (New York, 1984); Henry Fairlie, *The Kennedy Promise: The Politics of Expectation* (Garden City, N.Y., 1973); David Halberstam, *The Best and the Brightest* (New York, 1983); Jim F. Heath, *Decade of Disillusionment: The Kennedy-Johnson Years* (Bloomington, Ind., 1975); Bruce Miroff, *Pragmatic Illusions* (New York, 1976); Thomas G. Paterson, ed., *Kennedy's Quest for Victory: American Foreign Policy, 1961–1963* (New York, 1988); Richard J. Walton, *Cold War and Counter Revolution: The Foreign Policy of John F. Kennedy* (Baltimore, 1973); Garry Wills, *The Kennedy Imprisonment: A Meditation on Power* (New York, 1983).

7. Thomas G. Paterson, *Meeting the Communist Threat: Truman to Reagan* (New York, 1988), 202.

8. For a thoughtful analysis of the modernization concept, see Michael Hunt, *Ideology and U.S. Foreign Policy* (New Haven, Conn., 1988), 159–70; Robert A. Packenham, *Liberal America and the Third World: Political Development Ideas in Foreign Aid and Social Science* (Princeton, N.J., 1973), 59–110.

9. Rostow to Kennedy, 2 March 1961, Staff Memoranda Series, Box 64a, POF.

10. Senate Committee on Foreign Relations, *Hearings: Foreign Assistance Act of 1961*, 87th Cong., 1st sess., 1961, 34–35. See also Schlesinger, *Thousand Days*, 594–600.

11. Special Message to Congress on Foreign Aid, 22 March 1961, *Public Papers of the Presidents of the United States: John F. Kennedy* (Washington, D.C., 1961–63), 205.

12. Testimony of Secretary of State Rusk, 16 June 1961, Senate, *Executive Sessions of the Senate Foreign Relations Committee*, 87th Cong., 1st sess., 1961, 13, pt. 2:184; Senate Committee on Foreign Relations, *Hearings: Foreign Assistance Act of 1961*, 34–35.

13. Senate Committee on Foreign Relations, *Hearings: Foreign Assistance Act of 1962*, 87th Cong., 2d sess., 1962, 595.

14. Schlesinger, *Thousand Days*, 594–600.

15. Gerard T. Rice, *The Bold Experiment: JFK's Peace Corps* (South Bend, Ind., 1986); Gary May, "Passing the Torch and Lighting Fires: The Peace Corps," in Paterson, ed., *Kennedy's Quest*, 284–316; S. Chandrasekhar, *American Aid and India's Economic Development* (New York, 1965), 159; Heath, *Decade of Disillusionment*, 76–79.

16. Schlesinger, *Thousand Days*, 606.

17. Inaugural Address, 20 January 1961, *Public Papers, Kennedy, 1961*, 1–3.

18. White House Press Release, 15 March 1961, Box 78, Galbraith Papers, JFKL.

19. Galbraith to Elmo Roper, 24 March 1961, ibid.; Galbraith to Lloyd Reynolds, 2 February 1961, Box 52, ibid.

20. Senate Committee on Foreign Relations, *Hearings: Ambassadorial Nominations, 1961*, 87th Cong., 1st sess., 1961, 34–48.

21. Walter LaFeber, *The American Age: United States Foreign Policy at Home and Abroad since 1750* (New York, 1989), 554.

22. John Kenneth Galbraith, *Ambassador's Journal* (Boston, 1965), 6, 172, 178, 212, 215. See also Schlesinger, *Thousand Days*, 523.

23. Galbraith, *Ambassador's Journal*, 40. For Nehru's favorable response, see Nehru to Kennedy, 15 April 1961, Countries File, Box 111, NSF, JFKL.

24. "Report of the Task Force on U.S. Policy with Respect to India," 27 December 1960, see n. 4; Senate Committee on Foreign Relations, *Hearings: Foreign Assistance Act of 1961*, 106; R. K. Jain, *U.S.-South Asian Relations, 1947–1981*, 2 vols. (New Delhi, 1983), 1:623; see table in chapter 1.

25. Congressional Briefing Book, 18 August 1961, Countries File, Box 118a, POF.

26. Ibid.; Kennedy to Rusk, 20 February 1961, Countries File, Box 118a, POF; Untitled Memorandum, May 1961, Box 118a, POF; NSC Action Memorandum, 16 December 1961, Meetings and Memoranda Series, Box 328, NSF, JFKL.

27. India, Ministry of Finance, Department of Economic Affairs, *External Assistance* (New Delhi, 1981), 192–95.

28. Galbraith to Secretary of State, 14 May 1963, Countries File, Box 118a, POF; Galbraith, *Ambassador's Journal*, 181, 187–88; Komer to Kennedy, 16 May 1963, Countries File, Box 118a, POF.

29. U.S. Congress, Senate, Committee on Foreign Relations, *Hearings: Foreign Assistance Act of 1963*, 88th Cong., 1st sess., 656–57.

30. Galbraith, *Ambassador's Journal*, 70.

31. Ibid.

32. Ibid., 167.

33. Mutual Security Program Annual Report, undated (probably late 1960 or early 1961), Name Series-Carl Kaysen, Box 373, NSF, JFKL; Senate Committee on Foreign Relations, *Hearings: Foreign Assistance Act of 1961*, 511.

34. Galbraith to Professor Paul Taylor (Institute for International Studies, University of California), 13 March 1961, Box 80, Galbraith Papers, JFKL; Galbraith, *Ambassador's Journal*, 94–95, 168, 182, 206–7.

35. Galbraith to Kennedy, 10 March 1961, quoted in Galbraith, *Ambassador's Journal*, 95.

36. Ibid., 182.

37. Dinesh Abroli, "American Involvement in Indian Agricultural Research," in Robert M. Crunden, Manoj Joshi, and R. V. R. Chandrasekhar, eds., *New Perspectives on America and South Asia* (New Delhi, 1984), 164.

38. Galbraith, *Ambassador's Journal*, 84.

39. Peace Corps, *Peace Corps Fact Book* (Washington, D.C., 1961); Peace Corps, *First Annual Report to Congress* (Washington, D.C., 1962); Peace Corps, *Peace Corps Handbook* (Washington, D.C., 1962); Chandrasekhar, *American Aid*, 159–60.

40. Nehru to Kennedy, 24 May 1961, Countries File, Box 111, NSF, JFKL.

41. Kennedy to Nehru, 18 February 1961, ibid.; Nehru to Kennedy, 20 February 1961, ibid.; Galbraith, *Ambassador's Journal*, 59; Sarvepalli Gopal, *Jawaharlal Nehru: A Biography*, 3 vols. (Delhi, 1975–84), 3:145–61.

42. Kennedy to Nehru, 23 March 1961, Countries File, Box 111, NSF, JFKL; Nehru to Kennedy, 16 April 1961, Countries File, Box 111, NSF, JFKL; Galbraith, *Ambassador's Journal*, 80; Gopal, *Jawaharlal Nehru*, 3:187–88.

43. "Prime Minister Nehru's Visit to Washington, D.C., 6–9 November 1961," Briefing Book, Countries File, Box 118a, POF; Secretary of State to Embassy in New Delhi, 24 August 1961, Countries File, Box 118a, POF; Gopal, *Jawaharlal Nehru*, 3:186.

44. Galbraith, *Ambassador's Journal*, 160; Schlesinger, *Thousand Days*, 520.

45. Johnson to Secretary of State, 22 May 1961, Box 1, Vice President's Security File, LBJL; Gopal, *Jawaharlal Nehru*, 3:188.

46. Galbraith to Secretary of State, 22 May 1961, Box 1, Vice President's Security File, LBJL.

47. Ibid.

48. "President Ayub's Visit to Washington, D.C., 11–13 July 1961," Briefing Book, Countries File, Box 123, POF.

49. Rountree to Secretary of State, 21 May 1961, Trips and Conferences Series, Box 242, NSF, JFKL; Memorandum of Conversation between Vice President Johnson and President Ayub Khan, 20 May 1961, Box 1, Vice President's Security File, LBJL.

50. *Washington Post*, 7 July 1961; Secretary of State to Embassy in Rawalpindi, 7 June 1961, Countries File, Box 123, POF; "President Ayub's Visit to Washington, D.C., 11–13 July 1961," see n. 48.

51. B. K. Jain, *India and the United States, 1961–1963* (New Delhi, 1987), 94.

52. Galbraith, *Ambassador's Journal*, 158; Rountree to Secretary of State, 21 May 1961, see n. 49; "President Ayub's Visit to Washington, D.C., 11–13 July 1961," see n. 48.

53. Galbraith to Kennedy, 15 August 1961, quoted in Galbraith, *Ambassador's Journal*, 163.

54. "Prime Minister Nehru's Visit to Washington, D.C., 6–9 November 1961," see n. 43.

55. Ibid.

56. Schlesinger, *Thousand Days*, 526.

57. Galbraith, *Ambassador's Journal*, 213–20; Gopal, *Jawaharlal Nehru*, 3:188–89.

58. Schlesinger, *Thousand Days*, 526.

59. Ibid., 525.

60. Ibid., 526; Galbraith, *Ambassador's Journal*, 237–47.

61. Nehru to Kennedy, 29 December 1961, Countries File, Box 118a, POF.

62. Komer to Kennedy, "Report on Long-Range MAP Guidelines," 13 January 1962, Meetings and Memoranda Series, Box 313, NSF, JFKL.

63. Ibid.; Jeffrey Kitchens to Secretary of Defense, 12 December 1961, ibid.; Bromley Smith to NSC, 22 January 1962, ibid.

64. "Appendix: Position of JCS on Draft Record of Action" in Komer to Kennedy, "Report on Long-Range MAP Guidelines," 13 January 1962, see n. 62.

65. "Summary of President's Remarks to NSC," 18 January 1962, Meetings and Memoranda Series, Box 313, NSF, JFKL.

66. CIA Report, "Deployment of Indian and Pakistani Armed Forces," 12 July 1961, Countries File, Box 123, POF; Congressional Briefing Book, undated, Countries File, Box 118a, POF; Senate Committee on Foreign Relations, *Hearings: Foreign Assistance Act of 1961*, 39.

67. Komer to Bundy, 12 January 1962, NSC History-South Asia, Box 24, NSF, LBJL.

68. Kennedy to Nehru, 15 January 1962, Countries File, Box 118a, POF.

69. Nehru to Kennedy, 30 January 1962, ibid.

70. Galbraith to Secretary of State, 27 January 1962, ibid.

71. Galbraith to Secretary of State, 30 June 1962, Countries File, Box 111, NSF, JFKL; Galbraith, *Ambassador's Journal*, 329; Gopal, *Jawaharlal Nehru*, 3:217–18.

72. Komer to Bundy, 9 May 1962, NSC History-South Asia, Box 24, NSF, LBJL; Komer to James Grant, 13 June 1962, NSC History-South Asia, Box 24, NSF, LBJL.

73. Komer to Bundy, 26 July 1962, ibid.

74. U.S. Congress, Senate, Committee on Foreign Relations, *Hearings: Foreign Assistance Act of 1962*, 87th Cong., 2d sess., 63, 187–88, 595.

75. Ibid., 40. See also Schlesinger, *Thousand Days*, 596.

76. Symington to Kennedy, 11 May 1962, Countries File, Box 118a, POF.

77. R. K. Jain, *U.S.-South Asian Relations*, 1:260–61.

78. On the overall foreign aid budget, see U.S. Congress, Senate, Committee on Foreign Relations, *Hearings: Foreign Assistance Act of 1963*, 88th Cong., 1st sess., 48. On the Indian allocation, see table in chapter 1.

79. Roger Hilsman, *To Move A Nation: The Politics of Foreign Policy in the Administration of John F. Kennedy* (New York, 1964), 320–21.

80. Gopal, *Jawaharlal Nehru*, 3:223.

81. Carl Kaysen to Kennedy, 26 October 1962, NSC History-South Asia, Box 24, NSF, LBJL.

82. Galbraith to Harriman, 25 November 1962, Countries File, Box 118a, POF; Hilsman to Rusk, 17 November 1962, "The Five-Fold Dilemma: The Implications of the Sino-Indian Conflict," Box 1, Hilsman Papers, JFKL.

83. Komer to Kaysen, 16 November 1962, NSC History-South Asia, Box 24, NSF, LBJL.

84. Komer to Phillips Talbot, 28 October 1962, ibid.

85. Kennedy to Nehru, 28 October 1962, Countries File, Box 118a, POF.

86. Kennedy to Ayub, 28 October 1962, ibid.

87. Secretary of State to Embassy in New Delhi, 28 October 1962, Countries File, Box 111, NSF, JFKL.

88. Robert J. McMahon, "Choosing Sides in South Asia," in Paterson, ed., *Kennedy's Quest*, 215.

89. Memorandum for the Record, Presidential Meeting on the Sino-Indian Conflict, 19 November 1962, NSC History-South Asia, Box 24, NSF, LBJL.

90. Thomas Hughes to Kennedy, undated, Box 1, Hilsman Papers, JFKL; Komer to Hilsman, 21 November 1962, Hilsman Papers, JFKL; "Report of the Harriman Mission," undated (probably November 1962), Box 10, Vice President's Security File, LBJL; Hilsman, *To Move A Nation*, 327–39.

91. "Report of the Harriman Mission," undated (probably November 1962), Box 10, Vice President's Security File, LBJL; Memorandum of Conversation between Harriman and Nehru, 22 November 1962, Box 1, Hilsman Papers, LBJL.

92. Komer to Kennedy, 6 December 1962, Meetings and Memoranda Series, Box 339, NSF, JFKL; Kennedy to Secretaries of State and Defense and AID Director, 10 December 1962, Meetings and Memoranda Series, Box 339, NSF, JFKL; Theodore C. Sorensen, *Kennedy* (New York, 1965), 663.

93. Kennedy to Ayub, 5 December 1962, Countries File, Box 118a, POF; Kennedy to Nehru, 6 December 1962, ibid.

94. Gopal, *Jawaharlal Nehru*, 3:256–57.

95. Galbraith to Secretary of State, 8 February 1963, Countries File, Box 111, NSF, JFKL; Kennedy to Nehru, 9 March 1963, Countries File, Box 118a, POF; Gopal, *Jawaharlal Nehru*, 3:257–58.

96. McMahon, "Choosing Sides in South Asia," 217–18; Galbraith, *Ambassador's Journal*, 457.

97. Komer to Kennedy, 17 May 1963, Countries File, Box 118a, POF.

98. Galbraith to Secretary of State, 13 May 1963, Countries File, Box 174, NSF, JFKL; Galbraith to Secretary, 16 May 1963, Countries File, Box 174, NSF, JFKL; Komer to Kennedy, 17 May 1963, see n. 97.

99. William Bundy to David Bell, 4 March 1963, Special Correspondence Series, Box 29, POF; Komer to Kennedy, 17 May 1963, see n. 97; McConaughy to Secretary, 22 June 1963, Countries File, Box 123, POF; Komer Memo, 8 July 1963, Countries File, Box 123, POF; CIA Report, SNIE 13-4-63, 31 July 1963, Meetings and Memoranda Series, Box 314, NSF, JFKL; Chester Bowles, *Promises to Keep: My Years in Public Service, 1941–1969* (New York, 1971), 439–40; Hilsman, *To Move A Nation*, 337.

100. Komer to Kennedy, 12 November 1963, Countries File, Box 118a, POF.

101. Gopal, *Jawaharlal Nehru*, 3:253; McMahon, "Choosing Sides in South Asia," 219; Bowles, *Promises to Keep*, 481–84.

102. Bowles, *Promises to Keep*, 294; Schlesinger, *Thousand Days*, 139.

103. Schlesinger, *Thousand Days*, 438. For a more in-depth discussion of Bowles's problems in the administration, see Schlesinger, *Thousand Days*, 437–42; Galbraith, *Ambassador's Journal*, 161–62; Sorensen, *Kennedy*, 288–90; Bowles, *Promises to Keep*, 299–420.

104. Schlesinger, *Thousand Days*, 439–42.

105. Bowles, *Promises to Keep*, 430–39.

106. Bowles to Kennedy, 18 May 1963, Countries File, Box 118a, POF; Bowles, *Promises to Keep*, 437–40.

107. Bowles, *Promises to Keep*, 437.

108. Bowles Memorandum, "Toward a Balance of Political and Military Forces in South Asia," 12 November 1963, Countries File, Box 118a, POF.

109. Komer to Kennedy, 12 November 1963, ibid.

110. Oral history interview with General Lucius Clay, conducted in New York, N.Y., 1 July 1964, JFKL, 17; Schlesinger, *Thousand Days*, 597; Heath, *Decade of Disillusionment*, 147; Hilsman, *To Move A Nation*, 394; Sorensen, *Kennedy*, 661–66.

111. Bowles to Kennedy, 16 November 1962, Special Correspondence Series, Box 28, POF.

112. Oral history interview with General Lucious Clay, 18–19, see n. 110.

113. U.S. Committee to Strengthen the Security of the Free World, *Report to the President of the United States by the Committee to Strengthen the Security of the Free World* (Washington, D.C., 1963), 1.

114. *New York Times*, 25 March 1963.

115. Special Message to the Congress on Free World Defense and Assistance Programs, 2 April 1963, *Public Papers, Kennedy, 1963*, 302.

116. *New York Times*, 21 March 1963.

117. U.S. Congress, Senate, Committee on Foreign Relations, *Hearings: Foreign Assistance Act of 1963*, 88th Cong., 1st sess., 315–16.

118. Ibid., 15.

119. *Congressional Record*, 88th Cong., 1st sess., 1963, 109, pt. 21:24632, 24720, D-67, D-648.

120. Galbraith to Secretary of State, 14 May 1963, Countries File, Box 118a, POF.

121. George Rosen, *Western Economists and Eastern Societies: Agents of Change in South Asia, 1950–1970* (Baltimore, 1985), 123–31.

122. India, Ministry of Finance, *External Assistance*, 192–211.

123. Ibid.

124. Vadilalal Dagli, ed., *Two Decades of Indo-American Relations* (Bombay, 1967), vi.

125. Chandrasekhar, *American Aid*, 115.

126. India, Ministry of Finance, *External Assistance*, 192–211; Galbraith, *Ambassador's Journal*, 328–29, 466–509.

127. India, Planning Commission, *Third Five Year Plan* (New Delhi, 1961), 39.

128. Chester Bowles, *A View from New Delhi* (New Haven, Conn., 1969), 74.

129. Francine Frankel, *India's Political Economy* (Delhi, 1978), 226–27.

130. United Nations, *Yearbook of International Trade Statistics, 1964* (New York, 1965), 795; Phiroze B. Medhara, "Trade and Aid: Approaches to the Fourth Plan," in Dagli, ed., *Two Decades*, 51; James A. Raj, "Cooperation in Private Enterprise," in Dagli, ed., *Two Decades*, 63–67.

131. U.S. Congress, Senate, Committee on Foreign Relations, *Hearings: Foreign Assis-*

tance Act of 1963, 88th Cong., 1st sess., 121–22, 324–27, 656–57; *Congressional Record*, 88th Cong., 1st sess. 1963, 109, pt. 7:9299, 9595, 15524.

132. *Congressional Record*, 88th Cong., 1st sess., 1963, 109, pt. 7:9299.

133. *Report to the President of the United States by the Committee to Strengthen the Free World*, 5–6, 12–13.

134. U.S. Congress, Senate, Committee on Foreign Relations, *Hearings: Foreign Assistance Act of 1963*, 88th Cong., 1st sess., 325, 38–39, 122.

135. Schlesinger, *Thousand Days*, 531.

136. Kennedy to Nehru, 4 September 1963, Countries File, Box 118a, POF; Gopal, *Jawaharlal Nehru*, 3:233.

137. Bowles to Secretary of State, 27 December 1963, Countries File, Box 128, NSF, LBJL; Bowles to Secretary, 1 May 1964, Countries File, Box 128, NSF, LBJL.

138. Bowles, *View from New Delhi*, 124–25.

139. Bowles to Galbraith, 10 September 1963, Box 330, BP.

Chapter Eight

1. See table in chapter 1; R. K. Jain, *U.S.-South Asian Relations, 1947–1981*, 2 vols. (New Delhi, 1983), 1:619–23.

2. Chester Bowles, *Promises to Keep: My Years in Public Service, 1941–1969* (New York, 1971), 526.

3. Ibid., 439; William Barnds, *India, Pakistan, and the Great Powers* (New York, 1972), 174–76.

4. Barnds, *Great Powers*, 183–236.

5. Ibid., 241–47; Norman Brown, *The United States and India, Pakistan, and Bangladesh* (Cambridge, Mass., 1974), 204–26; John G. Stoessinger, *Henry Kissinger: The Anguish of Power* (New York, 1976), 104–6, 225–26.

6. Barnds, *Great Powers*, 241–47; N. Brown, *The United States and India*, 204–26; Stoessinger, *Henry Kissinger*, 104–6, 225–26.

7. See table in chapter 1; R. K. Jain, *U.S.-South Asian Relations*, 1:619–23.

8. Walt W. Rostow, *Eisenhower, Kennedy, and Foreign Aid* (Austin, Tex., 1985), 170–95.

9. Barnds, *Great Powers*, 241–47; N. Brown, *The United States and India*, 204–6; Stoessinger, *Henry Kissinger*, 104–6, 225–26.

10. R. K. Jain, *U.S.-South Asian Relations*, 1:624–25.

11. J. William Fulbright, *The Arrogance of Power* (New York, 1966), 3.

12. See table in chapter 1; R. K. Jain, *U.S.-South Asian Relations*, 1:617–23.

13. Agency for International Development, *Development and the National Interest: U.S. Economic Assistance into the Twenty-First Century* (Washington, D.C., 1989); United States Department of State, "Background Notes, India, March 1989" (Washington, D.C., 1989).

14. United States Department of State, "Background Notes: India, June 1982" (Wash-

ington, D.C., 1982); Department of State, "Background Notes: India, March, 1989" (Washington, D.C., 1989); *Christian Science Monitor*, 30 July 1982.

15. Department of State, "Background Notes: India, June, 1982" (Washington, D.C., 1982); Department of State, "Background Notes: India, March, 1989"; *Christian Science Monitor*, 30 July 1982.

Selected Bibliography

Manuscript Collections

British Public Record Office, Kew Gardens
  Records of the Foreign and Commonwealth Relations Office, FO 371
Dwight D. Eisenhower Library, Abilene, Kans.
  John Foster Dulles Papers
  Dwight D. Eisenhower Papers
  C. D. Jackson Papers
  Don Paarlberg Papers
  Joseph Rand Papers
  Records of the U.S. President's Committee to Study the Military Assistance Program
  Records of the White House Office
  U.S. Council on Foreign Economic Policy, Records
  U.S. Council on Foreign Economic Policy, Office of the Chairman, Records
  U.S. President's Citizen Advisers on the Mutual Security Program, Records
  White House Central File
Lyndon B. Johnson Library, Austin, Tex.
  Lyndon B. Johnson Papers
John F. Kennedy Library, Boston, Mass.
  John Kenneth Galbraith Papers
  Roger Hilsman Papers
  John F. Kennedy Papers
Minnesota State Historical Society, St. Paul, Minn.
  Hubert H. Humphrey Papers
National Archives, Washington, D.C.
  Records of the Department of Agriculture, RG 16
  Records of the Department of State, RG 59
Jawaharlal Nehru Memorial Library, New Delhi
  Sudhir Ghosh Papers
Public Archives of Canada, Ottawa
  Escott Reid Papers
Rockefeller Foundation Archives, North Tarreytown, N.Y.
  Records of the Rockefeller Foundation
Sterling Library, Yale University, New Haven, Conn.
  Chester Bowles Papers
Harry S. Truman Library, Independence, Mo.
  Dean Acheson Papers
  Henry Grady Papers

Records of the Psychological Strategy Board
Harry S. Truman Papers
White House Central File

Interviews Conducted by the Author

Ellsworth Bunker, 1 August 1983, Putney, Vermont
John Sherman Cooper, 18 July 1983, Washington, D.C.
Moraji Desai, 9 January 1984, Bombay, India
S. K. Dey, 30 December 1983, New Delhi, India
Douglas Ensminger, 12 December 1982, Columbia, Missouri
Ashok Mitra, 16 July 1984, New Delhi
Walt W. Rostow, 19 October 1983, New Delhi
Tarlok Singh, 11 February 1984, New Delhi

Oral Histories

Dwight D. Eisenhower Library
Eugene Black Oral Interview
Milton S. Eisenhower Oral Interview
Dennis Fitzgerald Oral Interview
Jawaharlal Nehru Memorial Library
Chester Bowles Oral Interview
M. G. Desai Oral Interview
C. D. Deshmukh Oral Interview
A. P. Jain Oral Interview
T. T. Krishnimachari Oral Interview
G. L. Mehta Oral Interview
K. M. Munshi Oral Interview
Harry S. Truman Library
Stanley Andrews Oral Interview
W. Averell Harriman Oral Interview
Loy Henderson Oral Interview
George C. McGhee Oral Interview
Elbert G. Matthews Oral Interview
John W. Snyder Oral Interview
Willard L. Thorpe Oral Interview
C. Tyler Wood Oral Interview
John F. Kennedy Library
Chester Bowles Oral Interview

Lucius D. Clay Oral Interview
Walt W. Rostow Oral Interviews (2)

Published Documents

India

Ministry of Finance. Department of Economic Affairs. *External Assistance*. New Delhi, 1981.

Ministry of Food and Agriculture. *Report of the Grow More Food Committee*. New Delhi, 1952.

———. *Report of the Indian Delegation to China on Agricultural Planning and Techniques*. New Delhi, 1956.

———. Department of Agriculture. *Report of the Foodgrains Enquiry Committee*. New Delhi, 1957.

Ministry of Food and Agriculture and Ministry of Community Development and Co-operation. *Report of India's Food Crisis and Steps to Meet It*. New Delhi, 1959.

Ministry of Information and Broadcasting. *Jawaharlal Nehru's Speeches*. 4 vols. New Delhi, 1958–65.

Planning Commission. *First Five Year Plan*. New Delhi, 1953.

———. *First Five Year Plan, A Draft Outline*. New Delhi, 1951.

———. *Report of the Committee of the Panel on Land Reforms*. New Delhi, 1958.

———. *Report of the Indian Delegation to China on Agrarian Cooperatives*. New Delhi, 1957.

———. *Second Five Year Plan*. New Delhi, 1956.

———. *Second Five Year Plan, A Draft Outline*. New Delhi, 1956.

———. *Study Team for Community Development and National Extension Service on Plan Projects*. New Delhi, 1957.

———. *Third Five Year Plan*. New Delhi, 1961.

———. *Third Five Year Plan, A Draft Outline*. New Delhi, 1960.

———. Program Evaluation Organization. *Evaluation Report on First Year's Working of Community Projects*. New Delhi, 1954.

———. *Evaluation Report on Second Year's Working of Community Projects*. New Delhi, 1955.

———. *Evaluation Report on Working of Community Projects and N.E.S. Blocks*. New Delhi, 1956.

———. *Evaluation Report on Working of Community Projects and N.E.S. Blocks*. New Delhi, 1957.

———. *The Fifth Evaluation Report on Working of Community Development and N.E.S. Blocks*. New Delhi, 1958.

______. *The Sixth Evaluation Report on Working of Community Development and N.E.S. Blocks*. New Delhi, 1959.

United Nations

Yearbook of International Trade Statistics, 1950. New York, 1951.
Yearbook of International Trade Statistics, 1954. New York, 1955.
Yearbook of International Trade Statistics, 1964. New York, 1965.

United States

Agency for International Development. *Development and the National Interest: U.S. Economic Assistance into the Twenty-First Century*. Washington, D.C., 1989.
Commission on Foreign Economic Policy. *Report to the President and the Congress*. Washington, D.C., 1954.
Department of Commerce. *Survey of Current Business, November 1954*. Washington, D.C., 1954.
______. *Survey of Current Business, August 1963*. Washington, D.C., 1963.
Department of State. "Background Notes: India, June, 1982." Washington, D.C., 1982.
______. "Background Notes: India, March, 1989." Washington, D.C., 1989
______. *Department of State Bulletin*. Washington, D.C., 1947–63.
______. *Foreign Relations of the United States, 1947*. Vol. 3. Washington, D.C., 1972.
______. *Foreign Relations of the United States, 1948*. Vol. 5. Washington, D.C., 1976.
______. *Foreign Relations of the United States, 1949*. Vol. 6. Washington, D.C., 1977.
______. *Foreign Relations of the United States, 1949*. Vol. 7. Washington, D.C., 1977.
______. *Foreign Relations of the United States, 1949*. Vol. 11. Washington, D.C., 1977.
______. *Foreign Relations of the United States, 1950*. Vol. 1. Washington, D.C., 1977.
______. *Foreign Relations of the United States, 1950*. Vol. 5. Washington, D.C., 1978.
______. *Foreign Relations of the United States, 1950*. Vol. 7. Washington, D.C., 1976.
______. *Foreign Relations of the United States, 1951*. Vol. 6, pt. 2. Washington, D.C., 1977.
______. *Foreign Relations of the United States, 1952–1954*. Vol. 2, pt. 2. Washington, D.C., 1984.
______. *Foreign Relations of the United States, 1952–1954*. Vol. 11, pt. 2. Washington, D.C., 1983.
______. *Foreign Relations of the United States, 1952–1954*. Vol. 12, pt. 1. Washington, D.C., 1984.
______. *Foreign Relations of the United States, 1955–1957*. Vol. 8. Washington, D.C., 1988.
______. *United States Treaties and Other International Agreements, 1952*. Vol. 3, pt. 2. Washington D.C., 1953.

———. *United States Treaties and Other International Agreements, 1956*. Vol. 7, pt. 3. Washington, D.C., 1957.

———. *United States Treaties and Other International Agreements, 1960*. Vol. 7, pt. 2. Washington, D.C., 1961.

International Development Advisory Board. *A New Emphasis on Economic Development Abroad*. Washington, D.C., 1957.

———. *Partners in Progress: A Report to the President by the International Development Advisory Board* (Rockefeller Report). Washington, D.C., 1951.

Peace Corps. *First Annual Report to Congress*. Washington, D.C., 1962.

———. *Peace Corps Fact Book*. Washington, D.C., 1961.

———. *Peace Corps Handbook*. Washington, D.C., 1962.

Public Papers of the Presidents of the United States: Dwight D. Eisenhower. Washington, D.C., 1958–61.

Public Papers of the Presidents of the United States: John F. Kennedy. Washington, D.C., 1961–63.

Public Papers of the Presidents of the United States: Harry S. Truman. Washington, D.C., 1961–66.

Report to the President on Foreign Economic Policies (Gray report). Washington D.C., 1950.

U.S. Committee to Strengthen the Security of the Free World. *Report to the President of the United States by the Committee to Strengthen the Security of the Free World* (Clay report). Washington, D.C., 1963.

U.S. Congress. *Congressional Record*. 82d Cong., 1st sess., June 1951. Vol. 97.

U.S. Congress. House, Committee on Foreign Affairs. *Report on Foreign Policy and Mutual Security*. 85th Cong., 1st sess., 1957. H. Rept. 551.

U.S. Congress. Senate. *Executive Sessions of the Senate Foreign Relations Committee*. Vol. 3, pts. 1 and 2. 82d Cong., 1st sess., 1951. Historical Series. Washington, D.C., 1976.

———. *Executive Sessions of the Senate Foreign Relations Committee*. Vol. 4, pt. 1. 82d Cong., 2d sess., 1952. Historical Series. Washington, D.C., 1976.

———. *Executive Sessions of the Senate Foreign Relations Committee*. Vol. 13, pt. 2. 87th Cong., 1st sess., 1961. Historical Series. Washington, D.C., 1984.

———. Committee on Foreign Relations. *Hearings: Mutual Security Act of 1952*. 82d Cong., 2d sess., 1952.

———. *Hearings: Mutual Security Act of 1953*. 83d Cong., 1st sess., 1953.

———. *Hearings: Mutual Security Act of 1954*. 83d Cong., 2d sess., 1954.

———. *Hearings: Mutual Security Act of 1955*. 84th Cong., 1st sess., 1955.

———. *Hearings: Mutual Security Act of 1956*. 84th Cong., 2d sess., 1956.

———. *Hearings: Mutual Security Act of 1957*. 85th Cong., 1st sess., 1957.

———. *Hearings: Mutual Security Act of 1958*. 85th Cong., 2d sess., 1958.

———. *Hearings: Mutual Security Act of 1959*. 86th Cong., 1st sess., 1959.

———. *Hearings: Mutual Security Act of 1960*. 86th Cong., 2d sess., 1960.

———. *Hearings: Foreign Assistance Act of 1961*. 87th Cong., 1st sess., 1961.

———. *Hearings: Foreign Assistance Act of 1962*. 87th Cong., 2d sess., 1962.
———. *Hearings: Foreign Assistance Act of 1963*. 88th Cong., 1st sess., 1963.
———. Special Committee to Study the Foreign Aid Program. *Foreign Aid Program: Compilation of Studies and Surveys*. 85th Cong., 1st sess., 1957. S. Rept. 52.

Memoirs and Autobiographies

Acheson, Dean. *Present at the Creation*. New York, 1969.
Bowles, Chester. *Ambassadors' Report*. New York, 1954.
———. *Promises to Keep: My Years in Public Life, 1941–1969*. New York, 1971.
———. *A View from New Delhi*. New Haven, Conn., 1969.
Deshmukh, C. D. *The Course of My Life*. Delhi, 1974.
Dutt, S. *With Nehru in the Foreign Office*. Calcutta, 1977.
Eisenhower, Dwight D. *The White House Years: Mandate for Change, 1953–1956*. Garden City, N.Y., 1963.
———. *The White House Years: Waging Peace, 1956–1961*. Garden City, N.Y., 1965.
Galbraith, John Kenneth. *Ambassador's Journal*. Boston, 1965.
Gandhi, Mohandas K. *An Autobiography: The Story of My Experiments with the Truth*. London, 1927; reprint, Boston, 1957.
Ghosh, Sudhir. *Gandhi's Emissary*. Boston, 1967.
McGhee, George. *Envoy to the Middle World: Adventures in Diplomacy*. New York, 1983.
Nehru, Jawaharlal. *An Autobiography*. London, 1936; reprint, New Delhi, 1982.
———. *The Discovery of India*. London, 1946; reprint, New Delhi, 1981.
Pandit, Vijaya Lakshmi. *The Scope of Happiness: A Personal Memoir*. London, 1979.
Panikkar, K. M. *In Two Chinas*. London, 1955.
Reid, Escott. *Envoy to Nehru*. New Delhi, 1981.
Sorensen, Theodore C. *Kennedy*. New York, 1965.
Truman, Harry S. *Memoirs*. 2 vols. Garden City, N.Y., 1955–56.

Newspapers and Magazines

Business Week
Christian Science Monitor
Economic Weekly (Bombay)
Hindu (Madras)
Hindustan Times (New Delhi)
Life
New York Times

Newsweek
Saturday Evening Post
Time
Times of India (New Delhi)
U.S. News and World Report

Secondary Sources

Books

Alexander, Charles C. *Holding the Line: The Eisenhower Era, 1952–1961*. Bloomington, Ind., 1975.

Ambrose, Stephen. *Eisenhower: The President*. New York, 1984.

———. *Rise to Globalism: American Foreign Policy, 1938–1970*. 5th ed. Baltimore, 1988.

Appadorai, A., ed. *Select Documents on India's Foreign Policy and Relations, 1947–1972*. Vol 1. Delhi, 1982.

Bagchi, Amiya Kumar. *The Political Economy of Underdevelopment*. Cambridge, 1982.

Baily, Samuel. *The United States and the Development of South America, 1945–1975*. New York, 1976.

Barber, James. *The Presidential Character*. Englewood Cliffs, N.J., 1972.

Barnds, William. *India, Pakistan, and the Great Powers*. New York, 1972.

Barnet, Richard J. *Intervention and Revolution: The United States in the Third World*. New York, 1968.

Bauer, P. T. *U.S. Aid and Indian Economic Development*. Washington, D.C., 1959.

Bhagat, G. *Americans in India, 1784–1860*. New York, 1970.

Blum, Robert. *Drawing the Line: The Origin of American Containment Policy in South Asia*. New York, 1982.

Borg, Dorothy, and Heinrichs, Waldo, eds. *Uncertain Years: Chinese-American Relations, 1947–1950*. New York, 1980.

Brecher, Michael. *India and World Politics: Krishna Menon's View of the World*. London, 1968.

———. *Nehru: A Political Biography*. London, 1959.

Brown, Judith. *Gandhi and Civil Disobedience: The Mahatma in Indian Politics, 1928–1934*. Cambridge, 1977.

———. *Modern India: The Origins of an Asian Democracy*. Delhi, 1984.

Brown, Norman. *The United States and India, Pakistan, and Bangladesh*. 3d ed. Cambridge, Mass., 1974.

Burner, David, and West, Thomas, eds. *The Torch is Passed: The Kennedy Brothers and American Liberalism*. New York, 1984.

Calder, Bruce J. *The Impact of Intervention: The Dominican Republic during the U.S. Occupation of 1916–1924*. Austin, Tex., 1984.

Campbell, Charles. *From Revolution to Rapprochement: The United States and Great Britain, 1783–1900*. New York, 1974.

Chandrasekhar, S. *American Aid and India's Economic Development*. New York, 1965.

Cohen, Warren. *America's Response to China*. New York, 1980.

Cook, Blanche. *The Declassified Eisenhower*. Garden City, N.J., 1981.

Crunden, Robert; Joshi, Manoj; and Chandrasekhar, R. V. R., eds. *New Perspectives on America and South Asia*. New Delhi, 1984.

Cummings, Bruce, ed. *Child of Conflict: The Korean-American Relationship, 1943–1953*. Seattle, 1983.

Dagli, Vadilalal. *Two Decades of Indo-American Relations*. Bombay, 1967.

Dallek, Robert. *Franklin D. Roosevelt and American Foreign Policy, 1932–1945*. New York, 1979.

Dodwell, H. *Dupleix and Clive: The Beginning of Empire*. London, 1967.

Dumont, René, and Rosier, Bernard. *The Hungry Future*. London, 1969.

Dutte, R. Palme. *India Today*. London, 1940.

Eckes, Alfred. *A Search for Solvency: Bretton Woods and the International Monetary System from World War II to the Present*. Austin, Tex., 1977.

———. *The United States and the Global Struggle for Minerals*. Austin, Tex., 1979.

Eldridge, Philip. *The Politics of Foreign Aid in India*. New York, 1970.

Fairbank, John King. *The United States and China*. 4th ed. Cambridge, Mass., 1979.

Fairlie, Henry. *The Kennedy Promise: The Politics of Expectation*. Garden City, N.Y., 1973.

Ferrell, Robert H., ed. *The Diary of James C. Hagerty: Eisenhower at Mid-Course*. Bloomington, Ind., 1983.

Frankel, Francine. *India's Political Economy*. Delhi, 1978.

Gadgil, D. R. *The Industrial Evolution of India in Recent Times, 1860–1939*. Delhi, 1979.

Gardner, Richard N. *Sterling-Dollar Diplomacy: The Origins of Our International Monetary System*. New York, 1969.

Gelman, Irwin. *Good Neighbor Diplomacy: United States Policies in Latin America, 1933–1945*. Baltimore, 1979.

Gopal, Sarvepalli. *British Policy in India, 1858–1905*. Cambridge, 1965.

———. *Jawaharlal Nehru: A Biography*. 3 vols. Delhi, 1975–84.

Gorev, A., and Zimyanin, V. *Jawaharlal Nehru*. Moscow, 1982.

Green, David. *The Containment of Latin America*. Chicago, 1971.

Halberstam, David. *The Best and the Brightest*. New York, 1983.

Harrison, Selig S. *India and the United States*. New York, 1961.

Heath, Jim F. *Decade of Disillusionment: The Kennedy-Johnson Years*. Bloomington, Ind., 1965.

Heimsath, Charles, and Mansingh, Surjit. *A Diplomatic History of Modern India*. New Delhi, 1971.

Herring, George C. *America's Longest War: The United States and Vietnam, 1950–1975*. New York, 1985.

Hess, Gary R. *America Encounters India, 1941–1947*. Baltimore, 1971.

———. *Sam Higginbottom of Allahabad: Pioneer of Point Four*. Charlottesville, Va., 1967.

———. *The United States' Emergence as a Southeast Asian Power, 1940–1950*. New York, 1987.

Hilsman, Roger. *To Move a Nation: The Politics of Foreign Policy in the Administration of John F. Kennedy*. New York, 1964.

Hogan, Michael. *The Marshall Plan: America, Britain, and the Reconstruction of Western Europe, 1947–1952*. Cambridge, 1987.

Hoopes, Townsend. *The Devil and John Foster Dulles*. Boston, 1973.

Hope, Guy. *America and Swaraj: The U.S. Role in Indian Independence*. Washington, D.C., 1974.

Hunt, Michael. *Ideology and U.S. Foreign Policy*. New Haven, Conn., 1988.

———. *The Making of a Special Relationship: The United States and China to 1914*. New York, 1983.

Iriye, Akira. *Across the Pacific: An Inner History of American-East Asian Relations*. New York, 1967.

Jain, B. K. *India and the United States, 1961–1963*. New Delhi, 1987.

Jain, R. K., ed. *U.S.-South Asian Relations, 1947–1981*. 2 vols. New Delhi, 1983.

Johansen, Robert C. *The National Interest and the Human Interest*. Princeton, N.J., 1980.

Jones, M. Bence. *Clive of India*. London, 1974.

Karnow, Stanley. *In Our Image: America's Empire in the Philippines*. New York, 1989.

Kaufman, Burton I. *The Korean War: Challenge in Crisis, Credibility, and Command*. New York, 1986.

———. *Trade and Aid: Eisenhower's Foreign Economic Policy, 1953–1961*. Baltimore, 1982.

Kolko, Gabriel. *Confronting the Third World: United States Foreign Policy, 1945–1980*. New York, 1988.

Kumar, Dharma, ed. *The Cambridge Economic History of India*. Vol. 2. Delhi, 1984.

Kuniholm, Bruce. *Origins of the Cold War in the Near East: Great Power Conflict and Diplomacy in Iran, Turkey, and Greece*. Princeton, N.J., 1980.

LaFeber, Walter. *America, Russia, and the Cold War, 1945–1984*. 5th ed. New York, 1985.

———. *The American Age: United States Foreign Policy at Home and Abroad since 1750*. New York, 1989.

———. *Inevitable Revolutions: The United States in Central America*. New York, 1984.

Langley, Lester. *The Banana Wars: An Inner History of the American Empire, 1900–1974*. Lexington, Ky., 1983.

Lewis, John P. *Quiet Crisis in India*. Garden City, N.Y., 1964.

Lowe, Peter. *The Origins of the Korean War*. London, 1986.

McMahon, Robert J. *Colonialism and Cold War: The United States and the Struggle for*

Indonesian Independence, 1945–1949. Ithaca, N.Y., 1981.

Maddison, A. *Class Structure and Economic Growth: India and Pakistan since the Moghuls*. London, 1971.

Magdoff, Harry. *The Age of Imperialism: The Economics of U.S. Foreign Policy*. New York, 1969.

Malenbaum, Wilfred. *East and West in India's Economic Development*. Washington, D.C., 1959.

Marshall, P. J. *East Indian Fortunes: The British in Bengal in the Eighteenth Century*. Oxford, 1976.

———. *Problems of Empire: Britain and India, 1757–1813*. London, 1968.

Matray, James I. *The Reluctant Crusade: American Foreign Policy in Korea, 1941–1950*. Honolulu, 1985.

Meier, Gerald, ed. *Leading Issues in Economic Development*. New York, 1964.

Menon, V. P. *The Transfer of Power in India*. Princeton, N.J., 1957.

Miller, Stuart C. *'Benevolent Assimilation': The American Conquest of the Philippines, 1899–1903*. Cambridge, Mass., 1974.

Miroff, Bruce. *Pragmatic Illusions*. New York, 1976.

Munro, Dana G. *Intervention and Dollar Diplomacy in the Caribbean, 1900–1921*. Princeton, N.J., 1964.

Myrdal, Gunnar. *Asian Drama: An Inquiry into the Poverty of Nations*. 3 vols. New York, 1968.

Nanavati, Manilal B., and Anjaria, J. J. *The Indian Rural Problem*. Bombay, 1970.

Nanda, B. R. *Indian Foreign Policy: The Nehru Years*. Honolulu, 1976.

Natarajan, L. *American Shadow Over India*. Delhi, 1956.

Ninkovich, Frank. *The Diplomacy of Ideas: U.S. Foreign Policy and Cultural Relations, 1938–1950*. Cambridge, 1981.

Packenham, Robert A. *Liberal America and the Third World: Political Development Ideas in Foreign Aid and Social Science*. Princeton, N.J., 1973.

Palmer, Norman D. *South Asia and United States Policy*. Boston, 1966.

Paterson, Thomas G., *Kennedy's Quest for Victory: American Foreign Policy, 1961–1963*. New York, 1988.

———. *Meeting the Communist Threat: Truman to Reagan*. New York, 1988.

———. *On Every Front: The Making of the Cold War*. New York, 1979.

———. *Soviet-American Confrontation: Postwar Reconstruction and the Origins of the Cold War*. Baltimore, 1973.

Peterson, Trudy Huskamp. *Agricultural Exports, Farm Income, and the Eisenhower Administration*. Lincoln, Nebr., 1979.

Pollard, Robert A. *Economic Security and the Origins of the Cold War, 1945–1950*. New York, 1985.

Porter, Bernard. *The Lion's Share: A Short History of British Imperialism, 1850–1970*. London, 1975.

Prasad, Devki Nandan. *Food for Peace: The Story of U.S. Food Assistance to India*. New Delhi, 1979.

Rabe, Stephen G. *The Road to OPEC: United States Relations with Venezuela, 1919–1976*. Austin, Tex., 1982.

Rajan, M. S. *India in World Affairs*. Bombay, 1964.

Rice, Gerard T. *The Bold Experiment: JFK's Peace Corps*. South Bend, Ind., 1986.

Rosen, George. *Western Economists and Eastern Societies: Agents of Change in South Asia, 1950–1970*. Baltimore, 1985.

Rosenberg, Emily. *Spreading the American Dream: American Economic and Cultural Expansion, 1890–1945*. New York, 1982.

Rossinger, Lawrence. *India and the U.S.: Political and Economic Relations*. New York, 1950.

Rostow, Walt W. *Eisenhower, Kennedy, and Foreign Aid*. Austin, Tex., 1985.

———. *Stages of Economic Growth: A Non-Communist Manifesto*. London, 1959.

Rotter, Andrew J. *The Path to Vietnam: Origins of the American Commitment to Southeast Asia*. Ithaca, N.Y., 1987.

Rudolphe, Lloyd I., and Rudolphe, Susanne Hoeber. *The Modernity of Tradition: Political Development in India*. Chicago, 1967.

Sarkar, Sumit. *Modern India, 1885–1947*. Delhi, 1983.

Schaller, Michael. *The American Occupation of Japan: The Origins of the Cold War in Asia*. New York, 1985.

———. *The United States and China in the Twentieth Century*. New York, 1979.

Schlesinger, Arthur, Jr. *A Thousand Days: John F. Kennedy in the White House*. Boston, 1965.

Smith, Gordon Connel. *The United States and Latin America*. New York, 1974.

Spear, Percival. *A History of India*. Vol. 2. Middlesex, 1970.

Spiegel, Steven L. *The Other Arab-Israeli Conflict: Making America's Middle East Policy from Truman to Reagan*. Chicago, 1985.

Stanley, Peter W. *A Nation in the Making: The Philippines and the United States, 1899–1921*. Cambridge, Mass., 1974.

Stoessinger, John G. *Henry Kissinger: The Anguish of Power*. New York, 1976.

Stueck, William. *The Road to Confrontation: American Policy toward China and Korea, 1947–1950*. Chapel Hill, N.C., 1981.

Thompson, James C., Jr.; Stanley, Peter W.; and Perry, John Curtis. *Sentimental Imperialists: The American Experience in East Asia*. New York, 1981.

Thorne, Christopher. *Allies of a Kind: The United States, Britain, and the War against Japan*. New York, 1978.

Thorner, Daniel. *Investment in Empire: British Railway and Steamshipping in India, 1825–1849*. Philadelphia, 1950.

———. *The Shaping of Modern India*. New Delhi, 1980.

Tomlinson, B. R. *The Political Economy of the Raj, 1914–1947: The Economics of Decolonization in India*. London, 1979.

Tucker, Nancy. *Patterns in the Dust: Chinese-American Relations and the Recognition Controversy, 1949–1950*. New York, 1983.

Venkataramani, M. S. *The American Role in Pakistan*. New Delhi, 1982.

Venkataramani, M. S., and Shrivastava, B. K. *Quit India: The American Response to the 1942 Struggle*. New Delhi, 1979.

———. *Roosevelt, Churchill, and Gandhi*. New Delhi, 1983.

Walton, Richard J. *Cold War and Counter Revolution: The Foreign Policy of John F. Kennedy*. Baltimore, 1973.

Ward, Barbara. *The Rich Nations and the Poor Nations*. New York, 1962.

Wills, Gary. *The Kennedy Imprisonment: A Meditation on Power*. New York, 1983.

Wolf, Charles C., Jr. *Foreign Aid: Theory and Practice in South Asia*. Princeton, N.J., 1960.

Wolpert, Stanley. *A New History of India*. New York, 1982.

———. *Roots of Confrontation in South Asia: Afghanistan, Pakistan, India, and the Superpowers*. New York, 1982.

Wood, Bryce. *The Making of the Good Neighbor Policy*. New York, 1961.

Articles

Abroli, Dinesh. "American Involvement in Indian Agricultural Research." In *New Perspectives on America and South Asia*, edited by Robert Crunden et al., 155–69. New Delhi, 1984.

Bernstein, Barton. "The Struggle over the Korean Armistice: Prisoners of Repatriation?" in *Child of Conflict: The Korean-American Relationship, 1943–1953*, edited by Bruce Cummings, 261–307. Seattle, 1983.

Brodkin, E. I. "U.S. Aid to India and Pakistan: The Attitude of the Fifties." *International Affairs* 43 (Fall 1967): 664–77.

Chakravarti, P. C. "India, Nonalignment and U.S. Policy." *Current History* 44 (March 1963): 129–34.

Clymer, Kenton J. "The Education of William Phillips: Self-Determination and American Policy toward India, 1942–1945." *Diplomatic History* 8 (Winter 1984): 13–36.

———. "Franklin D. Roosevelt, Louis Johnson, India, and Anti-colonialism: Another Look." *Pacific Historical Review* 57 (August 1988): 261–84.

———. "Jawaharlal Nehru and the United States: The Pre-Independence Years." *Diplomatic History* 14 (Spring 1990): 143–62.

Cohen, Stephen P. "Security Issues in South Asia." *Asian Survey* 15 (March 1975): 203–15.

———. "U.S. Weapons and South Asia: A Policy Analysis." *Pacific Affairs* 49 (Spring 1976): 49–69.

Desai, Tripta. "Indo-American Wheat Negotiations of 1950–1951." *Indian Political Science Review* 9 (July 1975): 119–51.

Dutta, Rani. "American Attitudes toward U.S. Technical and Economic Assistance to India, 1949–1953." *Indian Political Science Review* 3 (July–December 1963): 157–84.

Franklin, Douglas A. "The Politician as Diplomat: Kentucky's John Sherman Cooper in India, 1955–1956." *Register of the Kentucky Historical Society* 82 (Winter 1984): 28–59.

Galbraith, John Kenneth. "A Positive Approach to Aid." *Foreign Affairs* 39 (April 1961): 444–57.

———. "Rival Economic Theories in India." *Foreign Affairs* 36 (July 1958): 587–96.

Griffith, Robert. "Dwight D. Eisenhower and the Corporate Commonwealth." *American Historical Review* 87 (February 1982): 87–122.

Hahn, Peter L. "Containment and Egyptian Nationalism: The Unsuccessful Attempt to Establish the Middle East Command, 1950–1953." *Diplomatic History* 11 (Winter 1987): 23–40.

Harrison, Selig S. "Fanning Flames in South Asia." *Foreign Policy* 45 (Winter 1981–82): 84–102.

Hess, Gary R. "Global Expansionism and Regional Balances: The Emerging Scholarship on United States Relations with India and Pakistan." *Pacific Historical Review* 61 (May 1987): 259–95.

Iriye, Akira. "Contemporary History as History: American Expansion into the Pacific Since 1941." *Pacific Historical Review* 53 (May 1984): 191–212.

Leffler, Melvyn P. "The American Concept of National Security at the Beginning of the Cold War, 1945–1948." *American Historical Review* 89 (April 1984): 331–62.

Loomba, Joanne F. "U.S. Aid to India, 1951–1967: A Study in Decision Making." *India Quarterly* 28 (October–December 1972): 304–31.

McMahon, Robert J. "Choosing Sides in South Asia." In *Kennedy's Quest for Victory: American Foreign Policy, 1961–1963*, edited by Thomas G. Paterson, 198–222. New York, 1988.

———. "The Cold War in Asia: Toward a New Synthesis?" *Diplomatic History* 12 (Summer 1988): 307–28.

———. "Eisenhower and Third World Nationalism: A Critique of the Revisionists." *Political Science Quarterly* 101 (Fall 1986): 453–73.

———. "Food as a Diplomatic Weapon: The India Wheat Loan of 1951." *Pacific Historical Review* 56 (August 1987): 349–77.

———. "United States Cold War Strategy in South Asia: Making a Military Commitment to Pakistan, 1947–1954." *Journal of American History* 75 (December 1988): 812–40.

Maheshwari, B. "Bokaro: The Politics of American Aid." *International Studies* 10 (July–October 1968): 163–80.

Maxwell, Nevil. "Jawaharlal Nehru: Of Pride and Principle." *Foreign Affairs* 52 (April 1974): 633–43.

Medhara, Phiroze B. "Trade and Aid: Approaches to the Fourth Plan." In *Two Decades of Indo-American Relations*, edited by Vadilalal Dagli, 45–52. Bombay, 1967.

Merrill, Dennis. "Indo-American Relations, 1947–1950: A Missed Opportunity in Asia." *Diplomatic History* 11 (Summer 1987): 203–26.

Nayar, Baldev Ray. "Treat India Seriously." *Foreign Policy* 18 (Spring 1975): 133–54.

Ninkovich, Frank. "Ideology, the Open Door, and Foreign Policy." *Diplomatic History* 6 (Spring 1982): 185–208.

Palmer, Norman D. "India and the U.S.: Maturing Relations." *Current History* 36 (March 1959): 129–34.

———. "Ups and Downs in Indo-American Relations." *Annals of the American Academy of Political and Social Sciences* 294 (July 1954): 113–23.

Paterson, Thomas G. "Foreign Aid under Wraps: The Point Four Program." *Wisconsin Magazine of History* 56 (Winter 1972–73): 119–26.

Raj, James A. "Cooperation in Private Enterprise." In *Two Decades of Indo-American Relations*, edited by Vadilalal Dagli, 63–67. Bombay 1967.

Shrivastava, B. K. "Indo-American Relations: Retrospect and Prospect." *International Studies* 14 (January–March 1974): 21–37.

Singh, Anita Inder. "Imperial Defence and the Transfer of Power in India, 1946–1947." *The International History Review* 4 (November 1982): 568–88.

Unterberger, Betty. "American Views of Mohammad Ali Jinnah and the Pakistan Liberation Movement." *Diplomatic History* 5 (Fall 1981): 313–36.

Index